OXFORD MONOGRAPHS IN INTERNATIONAL HUMANITARIAN AND CRIMINAL LAW

General Editor

THE LATE ANTONIO CASSESE

Rwanda's Gacaca Courts

OXFORD MONOGRAPHS IN INTERNATIONAL HUMANITARIAN AND CRIMINAL LAW

The aim of this series is to publish original and innovative books on fundamental, topical, or cutting-edge issues in international humanitarian law and international criminal justice. The primary purpose of the series is to publish books which, in addition to critically surveying existing law, also suggest new avenues for improving the law.

Special attention will be given to works by young scholars.

Rwanda's Gacaca Courts

Between Retribution and Reparation

PAUL CHRISTOPH BORNKAMM

OXFORD
UNIVERSITY PRESS

OXFORD
UNIVERSITY PRESS

Great Clarendon Street, Oxford, OX2 6DP,
United Kingdom

Oxford University Press is a department of the University of Oxford.
It furthers the University's objective of excellence in research, scholarship,
and education by publishing worldwide. Oxford is a registered trade mark of
Oxford University Press in the UK and in certain other countries

First published 2012

Published in the United States of America by Oxford University Press
198 Madison Avenue, New York, NY 10016, United States of America

British Library Cataloguing in Publication Data
Data available

ISBN 978-0-19-969447-1

Preface

Since the tragic events of the early 1990s, Rwanda has been struggling to come to terms with its violent past. Now the country is about to move on and declare this process complete: the neo-traditional Gacaca courts have prosecuted over one million people suspected of committing crimes during the genocide and are close to finishing their mandate. Gacaca is in line with recent trends that have sought to revive traditional grassroots mechanisms as a way of addressing past violence. The courts combine elements of both African dispute resolution and Western-style criminal tribunals. Having been devised as a holistic approach intended to address both prosecution and punishment as well as healing and repairing, they also reflect the increasing importance of victim participation in international criminal justice. The courts thus represent both a unique experiment and a fascinating exercise in transitional justice.

This volume is aimed at those working in the fields of transitional and international criminal justice and human rights whether at a practical or academic level. It examines the Gacaca courts' achievements as a mechanism of criminal justice and as a tool for healing, repairing, and bringing reconciliation to shattered communities. Drawing upon extensive observations of trial proceedings, this book provides an analysis of Gacaca legislation and its practical implementation, discussing the Gacaca courts within the framework of transitional and international criminal justice theory. In doing so, the book also contributes to the development and clarification of these principles.

This study was submitted as a doctoral thesis to the Law Faculty of the Humboldt University of Berlin in December 2009. I would like to thank Professor Gerhard Werle of the Humboldt University for supervising my work and for his support throughout the entire process. My thanks also go to Professor Lovell Fernandez of the University of the Western Cape for reviewing the thesis. I am deeply indebted to many friends in Rwanda and Germany without whose support this thesis would not have been possible. In particular, I would like to express my gratitude to Banamwana Richard and Ngoga Thierry for having welcomed me into their homes for long periods. Muhire Enock and Ruganda Cryspin provided invaluable support as interpreters, while Bikesha Denis of the National Service of Gacaca Courts was most welcoming and helpful throughout my stays in Rwanda. I am also very grateful to the staff of the NGOs in the field for their support, in particular Avocats Sans Frontières and Penal Reform International. Dieter Magsam provided me with a great deal of insider information as well as with numerous useful contacts. For their generous funding of my research stay in Rwanda, I would like to thank the German Academic Exchange Service (DAAD). I am also very grateful to Professor Antonio Cassese for his support during the publication process. For their linguistic support, I would like to thank James Lattimer, Joy Hawley, and Rebecca van Es. Finally,

I would like to thank my parents Nicola and Dr Joachim Bornkamm, as well as Norman Muschiol for the constant support they have given me for this project.

Paul Christoph Bornkamm

Contents

Table of Cases

All websites were last visited in June 2011.

International

African Commission on Human and Peoples' Rights

Committee against Torture

European Court of Human Rights

Human Rights Committee

Inter-American Commission on Human Rights

Inter-American Court of Human Rights

International Court of Justice

International Criminal Tribunal for Rwanda

Germany

Japan

Rwanda—ordinary courts

Rwanda—Gacaca courts[1]

[1] Most of the case minutes quoted herein are available at <http://www.asf.be/index.php?module=publicaties&lang=fr&id=53>.

United States of America

Uruguay

Table of Treaties and Other Relevant International Instruments

All websites were last visited in June 2011.

Table of Legislation and Other Relevant National Instruments

[1] Since 1997, laws have been published in English, in addition to Kinyarwanda and French; from then on, English versions are quoted. Some of the laws quoted are available online at <http://www.primature.gov.rw> or at <http://www.amategeko.net>, last visited in June 2011.

[2] Organic Law No 16/2004 of 19 June 2004 as modified by Organic Laws No 28/2006 of 27 June 2006, No 10/2007 of 1 March 2007, and No 13/2008 of 19 May 2008; see the coordinated version in the appendix.

Rwanda—Instructions of the Executive Secretary of Gacaca Courts[3]

[3] Originals in Kinyarwanda, translations by Muhire Enock and the author.

List of Abbreviations

ACHR	American Convention on Human Rights
AFDL	Alliance des Forces Démocratiques de la Libération
AfrComHPR	African Commission on Human and Peoples' Rights
AJIL	American Journal of International Law
ASF	Avocats Sans Frontières
ATCA	Alien Tort Claims Act
AustYBIL	Australian Year Book of International Law
BCIntl&CompLRev	Boston College International and Comparative Law Review
BGBl	Bundesgesetzblatt (German Federal Official Gazette)
BGHZ	Entscheidungen des Bundesgerichtshofs in Zivilsachen (Decisions by the German Federal Supreme Court on civil matters)
BJCrim	British Journal of Criminology
BTC	Belgian Technical Cooperation
BVerfGE	Entscheidungen des Bundesverfassungsgerichts (Decisions by the German Federal Constitutional Court)
BYBIL	British Yearbook of International Law
CalLR	California Law Review
CAT	Committee against Torture
CCOAIB	Conseil de Concertation des Organisations d'Appui aux Initiatives de Base
ch	chapter
CLADHO	Collectif des Ligues et Associations de Défence des Droits de l'Homme
ColHRLR	Columbia Human Rights Law Review
CrimLF	Criminal Law Forum
DenvJIntlL&Pol	Denver Journal of International Law and Policy
DR Congo	Democratic Republic of Congo
Duke JComp&IntlL	Duke Journal of Comparative & International Law
ECHR	European Convention for the Protection of Human Rights and Fundamental Freedoms
ECtHR	European Court of Human Rights
EHRR	European Human Rights Reports
EJIL	European Journal of International Law
FARDC	Forces Armées de la République Démocratique du Congo
FARG	Fonds d'assistance aux rescapés du génocide (assistance fund)
FDLR	Forces Démocratiques pour la Libération du Rwanda
FIDH	International Federation for Human Rights
FIND	Fonds d'indemnisation (compensation fund)
fn	footnote
Fordham IntlLJ	Fordham International Law Journal

FRw	Franc Rwandais
FSARG	Fund for the Support and Assistance to the Survivors of the Genocide
GTZ	Gesellschaft für technische Zusammenarbeit (German Technical Cooperation)
GYIL	German Yearbook of International Law
HarvHRJ	Harvard Human Rights Journal
HRC	Human Rights Committee
HRQ	Human Rights Quarterly
HRW	Human Rights Watch
IAComHR	Inter-American Commission on Human Rights
IACtHR	Inter-American Court of Human Rights
ibid	ibidem (at the same place)
ICC	International Criminal Court
ICCPR	International Covenant for Civil and Political Rights
ICG	International Crisis Group
ICJ	International Court of Justice
ICRC	International Committee of the Red Cross
ICTR	International Criminal Tribunal for Rwanda
ICTY	International Criminal Tribunal for the Former Yugoslavia
ILC	International Law Commission
ILM	International Legal Materials
ILR	International Law Reports
IRDP	Institut de Recherche et de Dialogue pour la Paix
IRIN	Integrated Regional Information Network
IsLR	Israel Law Review
ISS	Institute for Security Studies
JICJ	Journal of International Criminal Justice
LCP	Law and Contemporary Problems
LDF	Local Defence Force
LDGL	Ligue des Droits de la Personne dans la Région des Grands Lacs
LIPRODHOR	Ligue Rwandaise pour la Promotion et la Défence des Droits de l'Homme
LJIL	Leiden Journal of International Law
LRA	Lord's Resistance Army
MichJIntlL	Michigan Journal of International Law
MichLRev	Michigan Law Review
Minijust	Ministry of Justice
MRND	Mouvement Révolutionnaire Nationale pour le Développement
NGO	Non-Governmental Organization
NRA	National Resistance Army
NRM	National Resistance Movement
NURC	National Unity and Reconciliation Commission
NYUJIntlLaw&Pol	New York University Journal of International Law & Politics
NYULR	New York University Law Review

OAU	Organization of African Unity
OGRR	Official Gazette of the Republic of Rwanda
OHCHR	UN Office of the High Commissioner for Human Rights
Ohio NULRev	Ohio Northern University Law Review
OMCT	World Organisation against Torture
Ottawa LRev	Ottawa Law Review
PAPG	Projet d'Appui de la Société Civile au Processus Gacaca au Rwanda
PARMEHUTU	Parti du Mouvement d'Émancipation Hutu
PCIJ	Permanent Court of International Justice
PRI	Penal Reform International
RCN	Réseau des Citoyens Justice et Démocratie
RDF	Rwandan Defence Forces
Res	Resolution
RPA	Rwandan Patriotic Army
RPF	Rwandan Patriotic Front
RTLM	Radio-Télévision Libre des Mille Collines
TempLRev	Temple Law Review
TIG	Travaux d'Intérêt Général (community service)
TPI	Tribunal de Première Instance (Lower Instance Court)
TRC	Truth and Reconciliation Commission
UNAMIR	United Nations Assistance Mission for Rwanda
UNAR	Union Nationale Rwandaise
UNDP	United Nations Development Programme
UNHCR	United Nations High Commissioner for Refugees
UNTS	United Nations Treaty Series
USAID	United States Agency for International Development
USC	United States Codes
Yale JIntlL	Yale Journal of International Law
Yale LJ	Yale Law Journal
YBILC	Yearbook of the International Law Commission
ZStW	Zeitschrift für die gesamte Strafrechtswissenschaft

Introduction

In late May 2009 the Kigali-based, government-funded daily *The New Times* reported that many genocide survivors were frustrated with the work of the Gacaca courts. The survivors had voiced their dissatisfaction in connection with the conviction of a man whom they believed to be innocent. A survivor was quoted as saying that he or she felt 'intimidated because Gacaca judges here don't want to hear the truth. We are ready to tell the world'.[1] The reporter was, however, unable to research the background of the conviction and the reasons for the widespread frustration. This article still makes for interesting reading though, as it raises some critical issues at a time when many in Rwanda, particularly the government-friendly press, are asserting that the process of coming to terms with the past is now complete. The wish to declare this process closed is understandable. For the past 15 years, Rwandans have been struggling to find a way to confront their past, with their efforts to do so putting an enormous strain on both government resources and many ordinary citizens. As the Gacaca trials are now coming to a close, the ordinary courts are left only with a handful of pending cases, and the International Criminal Tribunal for Rwanda (ICTR) is approaching its completion deadline, it would seem like an appropriate time to make a provisional appraisal of the entire process. However, this does not mean an end to the need for further research. At the present time it is extremely difficult to assess the long-term repercussions of the Gacaca trials with regard to the future stability of Rwanda and the region. I hope that this study will aid future research efforts concerning the outcome of the Rwandan transition.

I. Gacaca: Transitional Justice in Rwanda

When the Gacaca courts became operational throughout Rwanda in 2006, judicial attempts to deal with the aftermath of the genocide had already been going on for a decade. Yet the classic approach of relying on criminal trials and civil damages claims had failed to provide an adequate solution to the enormous challenges the country was facing. Tens of thousands of suspects had been held in detention pending trial, often for several years at a time. While the government had raised victims' hopes of receiving justice, truth, and reparation, attempts to achieve these aims had failed. Creating the Gacaca courts was supposed to remedy this untenable situation.

[1] See 'Genocide Survivors in Kanombe Up in Arms over Gacaca Ruling', *The New Times*, 29 May 2009.

Gacaca was inspired by traditional African methods for resolving disputes and represents a form of grassroots justice. In 2001, a law was passed to provide for the creation of Gacaca courts in every community throughout the country. The courts were presided over by respected members of the community as elected by the community itself. With the help of the local population, these lay judges then investigated all the crimes relating to the genocide that had occurred in their community and subsequently put the suspects on trial. If a defendant confessed to having committed crimes, they would be treated with relative clemency, receiving a shorter prison term supplemented or even replaced by community service. Defendants who refused to confess, however, would be punished to the full extent of the law. Yet creating the Gacaca courts was not only aimed at prosecuting the perpetrators. Rwandan officials also argued that Gacaca would reveal what had happened in each community, allow victims to be heard, help reintegrate perpetrators into their communities, and form the basis for a reparation scheme.

Rwanda's quest for transitional justice[2] reflects the recent shift in focus within the debate on how societies should come to terms with their violent pasts in times of political transformation. At the start of this discourse, the challenges faced by societies in transition were commonly associated with dichotomies such as 'truth versus justice' or 'justice versus peace',[3] which characterize the debates and conflicts many Latin American countries went through in their transitions to democracy. The South African Truth and Reconciliation Commission created in 1995 provided an innovative synthesis of these conflicting concepts.

Breaking down transitional justice to a trade-off between truth, justice, and peace, however, turned out to be a simplistic view of the complex challenges transforming societies were facing. The 1990s brought about a number of new developments that would further enrich the debate on transitional justice. First, the establishment of international criminal tribunals has created a framework within which states are under pressure to prosecute grave human rights violations. Granting blanket amnesties, such as those implemented in several Latin American states in the 1980s, has become difficult if not impossible. In addition, developments in these countries have shown that trading justice for peace is not a sustainable option for societies in transition. In countries such as Argentina, Chile, or Uruguay, debates over past human rights abuses have resurfaced. Members of the former military dictatorships there are now facing justice.

The idea that transitions are potentially never-ending formed another new aspect of the discussion. Initial transitional justice case studies had involved clear-cut regime changes, whether from military rule to democracy or from authoritarian communist regimes to liberal rule. Yet the panoply of transitional justice measures developed

[2] For a definition of the term, see, eg, the report of the UN Secretary General, *The rule of law and transitional justice in conflict and post-conflict societies*, UN Doc S/2004/616 of 23 August 2004, para 8. See also N. Roht-Arriaza, 'The New Landscape of Transitional Justice' in N. Roht-Arriaza and J. Mariezcurrena (eds), *Transitional Justice in the Twenty-First Century* (2006) 1 *et seq*; R.G. Teitel, 'Transitional Justice Genealogy' 16 *HarvHRJ* (2003) 69.

[3] See E. Lutz, 'Transitional Justice' in N. Roht-Arriaza and J. Mariezcurrena (eds), *Transitional Justice in the Twenty-First Century* (2006) 327; R.G. Teitel, ibid, 78 *et seq*, 81 *et seq*.

could also be applied to more protracted processes of political transformation or even to situations where political transformation had hardly occurred. New regimes initiating transitional justice measures were often no more democratic or liberal than their predecessors. In some places, violent conflicts lingered on while transitional justice mechanisms were already underway. The work of the International Criminal Court (ICC) may also be seen as a catalyst for a broadening notion of transitional justice. Its investigations in countries such as the Democratic Republic of Congo or Uganda concern states where little political transformation has taken place and conflicts are still going on. Nevertheless, both countries regularly appear in the debate on appropriate transitional mechanisms. Transitional justice has become 'steady-state'.[4]

As situations of political transformation became ever more varied, it became obvious that tailor-made solutions were needed. In many post-colonial states in particular, where state institutions were weak and Western-style courts were not well established, grassroots mechanisms derived from local traditions were much more likely to reach the population than distant court room procedures or formalized truth commissions.[5] In recent years, this trend has materialized in many countries, including Mozambique, northern Uganda, Sierra Leone, Burundi, and East Timor in addition to Rwanda and its Gacaca courts.[6] While traditional institutions had long been regarded both as relics from primitive times and obstacles to development, it is acknowledged today that they are often much more reliable guarantors of social peace than a professional judiciary. They can be easily accessed by the local population, are in keeping with local culture, are more transparent than court proceedings, create a sense of ownership among the population, and are therefore more likely to be complied with voluntarily.[7] Given that such procedures are only amenable to official control and legal regulation to a limited extent, these processes are strongly influenced by civil society, churches, and often by international non-governmental organizations (NGOs). Even in Rwanda, where neo-traditional Gacaca courts are under close official control, NGOs and civil society organizations

[4] R.G. Teitel, ibid, 89, see also 85.

[5] See the report of UN Secretary General, *The rule of law and transitional justice in conflict and post-conflict societies*, UN Doc S/2004/616 of 23 August 2004, para 36, as well as E. Barkan, *The Guilt of Nations* (2000) 318 *et seq*; L. Huyse, 'Tradition-Based Approaches in Peacemaking, Transitional Justice and Reconciliation Policies' in L. Huyse and M. Salter (eds), *Traditional Justice and Reconciliation after Violent Conflict* (2008) 5 *et seq*; D.F. Orentlicher, '"Settling Accounts" Revisited' 1 *International Journal of Transitional Justice* (2007) 20 *et seq*; J. Widner, 'Courts and Democracy in Postconflict Transitions' 95 *AJIL* (2001) 65 *et seq*; I.W. Zartman, 'Introduction: African Traditional Conflict "Medicine"' in I.W. Zartman (ed), *Traditional Cures for Modern Conflict* (2000) 3 *et seq*.

[6] On traditional justice in Africa, see the contributions by B. Ingelaere, V. Igreja and B. Dias-Lambranca, J.O. Latigo, J.A.D. Alie, and A. Naniwe-Kaburahe in L. Huyse and M. Salter (eds), *Traditional Justice and Reconciliation after Violent Conflict* (2008). On East Timor, see the contribution by P. Burgess in N. Roht-Arriaza and J. Mariezcurrena (eds), *Transitional Justice in the Twenty-First Century* (2006) 176 *et seq*.

[7] See, eg, J.A.D. Alie, 'Reconciliation and Traditional Justice' in L. Huyse and M. Salter (eds), *Traditional Justice and Reconciliation after Violent Conflict* (2008) 143 *et seq*; T. Dexter and P. Ntahombaye, *The Role of Informal Justice Systems in Fostering the Rule of Law in Post-Conflict Situations* (2005) 17 *et seq*; J.O. Latigo, 'Tradition-Based Practices in the Acholi Region' in L. Huyse and M. Salter (eds), *Traditional Justice and Reconciliation after Violent Conflict* (2008) 112 *et seq*; A. Naniwe-Kaburahe, 'The Institution of Bashingantahe in Burundi' ibid, 163 *et seq*; L. Waldorf, 'Mass Justice for Mass Atrocities' 79 *TempLRev* (2006) 3 *et seq*; E. Wojkowska, *Doing Justice* (2006) 16 *et seq*.

have still managed to actively shape the process. Transitional justice has taken on a privatized form, thus mirroring the increasing privatization of violent conflict.[8]

II. Between Retribution and Reparation: An International Legal Framework for States in Transition

The increasing variety of different settings for transitional justice combined with the broad range of challenges specific to each situation does not however mean that there is no room for a set of values and rules common to all such situations. In fact, quite the opposite is true. There is an urgent need to clarify the rights and obligations of states and victims in situations of political transformation.[9] It would clearly be unrealistic to argue that states today have free discretion in dealing with crimes committed by a prior regime or during violent conflict. There is a rich body of jurisprudence, both national and international, that obliges transitional states to pay reparation to victims of serious human rights violations, or that declares national amnesty laws to be in breach of fundamental human rights.[10] These rulings evince a persistent uncertainty among politicians, academics, and human rights activists about the scope and the nature of rights and obligations in situations of political transformation.

Nevertheless, the ability to create a legal framework for transitional justice or even the essential desirability of such a framework is far from undisputed. The argument goes that promoting the rule of law in transitional and post-conflict societies usually involves standard measures based on Western ideas which do not take local specifics into consideration. Accordingly, legal mechanisms are inevitably imposed in top down fashion, with the state claiming the ownership of the conflict while tending to ignore or even quell grassroots initiatives aimed at bringing about transitional justice.[11] Some, more pessimistic arguments even assert that the prevalent human rights discourse may be employed by repressive regimes as a means of concealing their own human rights abuses.[12] Finally, it has been proposed that promoting the use of legal instruments in transitions is usually based on a retributive understanding of justice which does not pay due regard to the potentially destabilizing effects of prosecution in transition.[13]

It goes without saying that this criticism raises a number of important points. Lawyers working on transitional justice should not overlook these considerations

[8] See also K. McEvoy, 'Letting Go of Legalism' in K. McEvoy and L. McGregor (eds), *Transitional Justice from Below* (2008) 16 *et seq*; R.G. Teitel, 'Transitional Justice Genealogy' 16 *HarvHRJ* (2003) 88. On the privatization of violent conflict, see H. Münkler, *Die neuen Kriege* (2002).

[9] See also K. Ambos, 'The Legal Framework of Transitional Justice' in K. Ambos, J. Large and M. Wierda (eds), *Building a Future on Peace and Justice* (2009) 28.

[10] For details, see the discussion in ch 3, sections I and II below.

[11] R.E. Brooks, 'The New Imperialism' 101 *MichLRev* (2002/03) 2276 *et seq*, 2301; K. McEvoy, 'Letting Go of Legalism' in K. McEvoy and L. McGregor (eds), *Transitional Justice from Below* (2008) 19 *et seq*; S. Thomson and R. Nagy, 'Law, Power and Justice' 5 *International Journal of Transitional Justice* (2011) 12–13.

[12] S. Cohen, *States of Denial* (2001) 107 *et seq*.

[13] K. McEvoy, 'Letting Go of Legalism' in K. McEvoy and L. McGregor (eds), *Transitional Justice from Below* (2008) 24. See also M.J. Osiel, 'Why Prosecute?' 22 *HRQ* (2000) 137 *et seq*.

if they want to keep pace with the swiftly developing discourse on transitional justice. In particular, the criticism mentioned above demonstrates that combined approaches are needed. International criminal justice alone is unlikely to be able to provide a comprehensive solution to the problems of transitional societies. Instead, international efforts and local initiatives must work together to tackle the challenges a transitional or post-conflict society faces.[14] Lawyers must acknowledge that law is only one of the many facets of the modern transitional justice discourse.

Issues of law are particularly relevant to transitional justice whenever individual rights have been violated. Conflict between legal responses to violations and non-legal initiatives is most likely to occur following serious human rights abuses, with issues of prosecution and redress arising accordingly. It is precisely in such situations that legal frameworks are needed so as not to leave matters up to political discretion alone. If a society in transition leaves behind a legacy of grave human rights abuses, an official legal response to such abuses is required. Otherwise victims will always associate the institutions of the new government with having condoned past atrocities. Moreover, human rights would be of no use if they were unable to be invoked in the situations where they are most threatened.

These considerations are meant to illustrate the range of different issues a 'legal framework for transitional justice' should cover. The term used here is considerably narrower than seemingly similar notions, such as Teitel's 'transitional rule of law'.[15] Both share the idea there is a certain set of norms common to all transitions, thus providing some element of continuity in situations where normative and value systems are in flux. The framework relied on here, however, is only supposed to identify and define those binding international rules pertaining to the challenges commonly faced in transitions. While several other fields of law, such as the whole body of international criminal and human rights law, also inform transitional processes, these go far beyond the particular issues that arise in transitional contexts. The framework suggested here is limited to the question of how human rights abuses are to be addressed in transition. Transitional governments have relied on a number of different legal mechanisms to deal with past injustices, including prosecution, amnesty, truth commissions, or reparation.[16] These mechanisms are essentially governed by two sets of international norms.

The first of these is used to determine whether perpetrators of serious human rights violations are to be prosecuted and how this is to occur. The relevant norms here are the conventional and customary duties to prosecute crimes under international law as well as the human rights principles governing criminal procedures. The second set of norms pertains to the rights of victims of such abuses. This field is essentially covered by what is referred to as the right to reparation for serious

[14] This is also acknowledged by K. McEvoy, ibid, 44. See also M.A. Drumbl, *Atrocity, Punishment, and International Law* (2007) 181 *et seq*; D.L. Hafner and E.B.L. King, 'Beyond Traditional Notions of Transitional Justice' 30 *BCIntl&CompLRev* (2007) 91 *et seq*.

[15] See R.G. Teitel, 'Transitional Jurisprudence' 106 *Yale LJ* (1997) 2026 *et seq*; R.G. Teitel, *Transitional Justice* (2000) 18 *et seq*, 213 *et seq*; R.G. Teitel, 'Transitional Rule of Law' in A. Czarnota, M. Krygier and W. Sadurski (eds), *Rethinking the Rule of Law after Communism* (2005) 279 *et seq*.

[16] See G. Werle, *Principles of International Criminal Law*, 2nd edn (2009) paras 205 *et seq*; G. Werle and P. Bornkamm, 'Transitional Justice' in C. Weller (ed), *Transitional Justice und Zivile Konfliktbearbeitung* (2008) 79 *et seq*.

violations of human rights and humanitarian law.[17] It is the challenges common to all political transitions which allow these rules to be grouped under the heading of transitional justice: the need to find a balance between individual rights and collective interests or the difficulties arising from mass crimes involving great numbers of victims and perpetrators. Transitions are complex processes, in which the rights and duties of the different parties involved may not always be reconcilable. Rwanda is a typical example of such a predicament.

The legal framework for transitional justice discussed in this study is derived from customary international law and the various human rights conventions to which Rwanda is a party, namely the Genocide Convention,[18] the ICCPR,[19] the Banjul Charter,[20] and the Torture Convention.[21] In discussing the obligations of states in transition, I shall rely on jurisprudence by international human rights bodies, including the Inter-American and European Court of Human Rights. While their jurisprudence is very important in the interpretation of international human rights law, it goes without saying that it does not have a direct effect on Rwanda.

III. Scope of the Study

In recent years, a considerable quantity of academic writing has been published on Gacaca courts and the Rwandan transition in general. Most of these contributions are relatively short articles that provide an overview or try to shed light on a particular aspect of the process. In addition, NGOs have issued a number of very insightful reports. To the best of my knowledge, only one large monograph on the Gacaca process has been published in English until now.[22] The present study provides a detailed analysis of the Gacaca legislation and practice as well as a comprehensive

[17] See also K. Ambos, 'The Legal Framework of Transitional Justice' in K. Ambos, J. Large and M. Wierda (eds), *Building a Future on Peace and Justice* (2009) 19 *et seq*; G. Werle and P. Bornkamm, ibid, 85 *et seq*.

[18] *Convention on the Prevention and Punishment of the Crime of Genocide* of 9 December 1948, 78 UNTS 277. Rwanda ratified the Convention by *Décret-loi no 08/75 du 12 février 1975 approuvant et ratifiant diverses Conventions Internationales relatives aux droits de l'homme, au désarmement, à la prévention et à la répression de certains actes susceptibles de mettre en danger la paix entre les hommes et les nations*, Journal officiel de la République Rwandaise 1975, 230.

[19] *International Covenant on Civil and Political Rights* of 16 December 1966, 999 UNTS 171, to which Rwanda has been a party since 16 April 1975.

[20] *African Charter on Human and Peoples' Rights* of 27 June 1981, 1520 UNTS 217. Rwanda ratified the Charter on 15 July 1983.

[21] *Convention against Torture and Other Cruel, Inhuman or Degrading Treatment or Punishment* of 10 December 1984, 1465 UNTS 85. Rwanda ratified the Convention in 2008.

[22] P. Clark, *The Gacaca Courts, Post-Genocide Justice and Reconciliation in Rwanda: Justice Without Lawyers* (2010). Two such publications have appeared in German however: S. Friese, *Politik der gesellschaftlichen Versöhnung: Eine theologisch-ethische Untersuchung am Beispiel der Gacaca-Gerichte in Ruanda* (2010); S. Schilling, *Gegen das Vergessen: Justiz, Wahrheitsfindung und Versöhnung nach dem Genozid in Rwanda durch Mechanismen transitionaler Justiz: Gacaca Gerichte* (2005); there are also several short ones: P.E. Harrell, *Rwanda's Gamble: Gacaca and a New Model of Transitional Justice* (2003); A. Molenaar, *Gacaca: Grassroots Justice after Genocide* (2005); D. Rempfer, *Die Graswurzelgerichtsbarkeit gacaca: der ruandische Weg zur Aufarbeitung innerstaatlicher Gewalt* (2008); K. Weikl, *Gacaca im Spiegel der Menschenrechte: Rwandas schwieriger Weg zur Wahrheit* (2010).

appraisal of the system from the point of view of international law. In addition, it attempts to systematize the existing literature on the subject.

In the first chapter, Rwanda's recent history will be briefly outlined. Chapter two will provide a detailed commentary on, and analysis of, the legal foundations of Gacaca in light of the courts' practice as well as the external influences exerted by Rwandan institutions, civil society, and international NGOs. The third chapter will examine transitional justice in Rwanda by applying the analytical and legal framework set out above. First, the scope of Rwanda's duty to prosecute perpetrators of genocide and crimes against humanity will be discussed. Then the Gacaca system will be analysed against the backdrop of the fair trial principle and other relevant norms governing criminal procedure. Following this, the scope of the victims' right to reparation and Rwanda's practice in this field will then be examined. This covers both the forms of reparation provided within the framework of the Gacaca process and other criminal trials as well as the government's (unsuccessful) attempts to create a comprehensive reparation scheme. In the conclusion, I will discuss both the achievements and shortcomings of the approaches taken in the aftermath of the genocide.

The study is based on the premise that a transition following mass atrocities is not only governed to a considerable extent by universal legal rules, but also that each individual process of transition modifies these legal rules, namely if they are derived from soft law or (emerging) customary international law. Determining the impact of the Rwandan transition on the development of the law is one of the objectives of this study and forms the focus of the third and fourth chapters. Another premise of this study is that the degree of adherence to these legal rules is an important indicator for the credibility and the quality of the transition in question. In this way, certain legal rules may form part of the famous 'tool box' for transitions; while compliance with these rules may not always have exclusively positive effects, they nevertheless form a central and indispensable set of guidelines for any transition.

IV. Methodology

As stated above, this study analyses the Gacaca law and its use in practice. Given that there were over 10,000 Gacaca courts in the whole country, most of them sitting weekly, it was clear from the outset that my own first-hand experience of Gacaca trials would not be sufficient to provide a representative picture of such a huge scheme. My visits were therefore aimed instead at allowing me to form my own impression of the courts, to identify and describe the structural problems faced by the courts, and to gather material to illustrate my findings. I spent a total of six months in Rwanda during 2007 and 2008, attending 16 Gacaca sessions. The sites where I visited Gacaca were chosen in consultation with observers of the NGO Avocats Sans Frontières (ASF).

Since permits allowing foreigners to observe Gacaca court proceedings are only issued for specific regions, I decided to limit my observations to two areas, one being the city of Kigali, the other being the District of Nyanza in southern

Rwanda. One court I visited regularly was the Kimihurura Gacaca court of appeal in Kigali, a very dynamic court with highly capable judges. My focus here was on continuity. By visiting the court on a weekly basis over a period of six weeks, I was able to become familiar with the judges and how they approached the various different challenges arising from individual cases. Since the court proceedings are held in Kinyarwanda, I hired an interpreter who had worked previously with other researchers and had experience of Gacaca sessions.

My observations in the District of Nyanza allowed me to gain insight into how Gacaca proceedings are conducted in rural areas. I chose this region since it has always had a large Tutsi population, has a particularly high proportion of victims and perpetrators, and is the home to many survivors today.[23] It was for these reasons that ASF staff recommended I focus on this region, since they had found the courts there to be very dynamic.

In Nyanza District, I did not limit my observations to one court, visiting instead three different courts two or three times each. This enabled me to experience Gacaca proceedings in a range of different rural settings, including the small town of Nyanza, which is accessible by a full tarmac road, as well as the two very remote communities of Nyamiyaga and Mayaga, which can only be reached via dust roads. The sites I visited were selected in consultation with my interpreter there, a lawyer who was well informed about the activities of the courts and the cases they were hearing. Given the enormous differences between urban and rural Rwanda with regard to infrastructure, standards of living, and education, it was vital to visit a variety of different settings in order to be able to understand the whole spectrum of challenges faced by the Gacaca system.

In addition, I attempted to experience a wide range of different types of cases: trials involving large numbers of witnesses as well as cases based on a bare minimum of evidence, trials stretching over two or three sessions and trials completed within two hours, cases pertaining to high-level perpetrators as well as those concerned with mere accessories, cases involving wealthy and well-connected defendants as well as cases regarding less affluent ones, first instance cases, appeals cases, and review cases, trials involving female defendants and even cases where the defendant was a Tutsi.

It goes without saying that the cases I witnessed myself only represent a small part of the overall process. Nevertheless, I was still able to gain a detailed insight into Gacaca in different settings. Together with interviews conducted with other observers and stakeholders, as well as the analysis of a great number of NGO reports on Gacaca, my observations allowed me to identify a number of structural shortcomings of the system. Most of these are discussed in chapter three. Whenever my observations reflect a general trend, I use them to illustrate the points made in the discussion. I also draw upon the transcripts of Gacaca trials published by ASF. The organization runs a large monitoring programme and has made transcripts of several hundred trials available. I rely on the *Recueil de jurisprudence* edited by the Rwandan Supreme Court and ASF with regard to the jurisprudence of ordinary Rwandan courts.

23 National Service of Gacaca Courts, *Number of Survivors of Genocide* (2006); National Service of Gacaca Courts, *Summary of Persons Prosecuted* (2006).

1

A Short History of the Rwandan Genocide and its Aftermath

To understand the massive challenges faced by the Gacaca process in the aftermath of the Rwandan genocide, a brief overview of Rwandan history up to the present day is necessary. The following chapter will outline the critical developments in the internal and regional politics of Rwanda in order to demonstrate what is at stake in the reconciliation process.

I. The Origins of the Hutu–Tutsi Antagonism

The Hutu and the Tutsi live all over the Central African Great Lakes region. Along with the Twa, they make up the population of Rwanda, Burundi, and parts of the eastern Congolese Kivu provinces.[1] Writing about Hutu–Tutsi relations certainly raises the question of their origins. This issue is somewhat more complicated than the relations between different groups in other countries in the region. The distinction between Hutu and Tutsi is not a typically ethnic one. It can, in fact, be better understood as a class or caste distinction: the Tutsi were traditionally cattle herders and were strongly represented in political functions. The Hutu, in contrast, were agriculturalists. Both speak the same language, share a common cultural heritage, and have always lived side by side in the same communities. For the present study, it is not of primary importance where the Hutu–Tutsi distinction originally comes from. It is sufficient to state that, when the first Europeans came to Rwanda in the 1890s, the distinction was not perceived as an ethnic one.[2] This does not mean that the two groups lived together in perfect harmony. Rwandan society was a highly organized one, structured hierarchically according to a three-class system: the aristocratic Tutsi, who were pastoralists, the agriculturist Hutu, and the Twa, who were hunter-gatherers and often worked as servants. The king or *mwami* was

[1] In Rwanda, the Hutu make up approximately 85% of the population, the Tutsi 14%, with the third group, the Twa, representing only about 1%, K. Ellicott (ed), *Countries of the World*, vol 2 (2006) 1562. These ratios are approximately the same both before and after the genocide due to the massive return of Tutsi refugees from neighbouring countries.

[2] J. Vansina, *Le Rwanda ancien* (2001) 178.

Tutsi and considered divine.[3] In the second half of the nineteenth century, social tensions increased as land shortages forced many Hutu peasants into patron-client relations. Under the reign of *mwami* Kigeri Rwabugiri (1860–95), the exploitation of the lower classes became increasingly institutionalized, triggering several Hutu rebellions.[4]

When the whole African continent was divided among the colonial powers, the kingdoms of Rwanda (Ruanda) and Burundi (Urundi) became part of German East Africa. As the kingdom was far away from the coast and poor in natural resources, the Germans chose to rely on the institutions of the Tutsi monarchy. The feudal and strongly centralized organization of the kingdom by the Tutsi elite was unique in Africa and can be compared to absolutism in Europe a hundred years before. Against the backdrop of the emergent idea of Social Darwinism and supported by colonial anthropology, the colonizers concluded that the Tutsi must be a superior race, more closely related to Europeans.[5] In this way, the idea of the Tutsi and the Hutu being different races was born. The colonizers were aware that propagating Tutsi supremacy would win them the loyalty of the ruling class. Racial education thus became an important element of the colonizers' strategy.[6]

Following the defeat of the German Reich in World War I, Ruanda-Urundi was put under a League of Nations mandate administered by Belgium.[7] Like the Germans, the Belgians believed that the territory could only be controlled in an effective way with the support of the ruling Tutsi monarchy. Under Belgian administration, however, the colonizers' grasp on power tightened. A rigid regime of compulsory labour was imposed on the Hutu population, which was enforced by local chiefs.[8] This required the authorities to classify every individual as either Tutsi, Hutu, or Twa. In 1933, an official census was organized in order to determine the 'race' of every Rwandan. Anyone with 10 cows or more was declared Tutsi.[9] Along with the census, every Rwandan was given an identity card showing which group he or she belonged to. This was later to prove lethal for thousands of Tutsi.

II. The First and Second Republic

The situation in Rwanda changed once again in the wake of the new world order brought about by the end of World War II. Within just a few years, the subdued Hutu majority shook off the yoke of forced labour, toppled the monarchy, and

[3] P.J. Magnarella, 'The Background and Causes of the Genocide in Rwanda' 3 *JICJ* (2005) 803; J. Vansina, *Le Rwanda ancien* (2001) 54.

[4] J. Vansina, *Le Rwanda ancien* (2001) 175.

[5] Missionary Father François Ménard wrote in 1917 that the Tutsi 'is a European concealed under a black skin', quoted in J.-P. Chrétien, 'Hutu et Tutsi au Rwanda et au Burundi' in J.-L. Amselle and E. M'Bokolo (eds), *Au cœur de l'ethnie* (1985) 137.

[6] M. Mamdani, *When Victims Become Killers* (2001) 89.

[7] A. Kagame, *Un abrégé de l'histoire du Rwanda de 1853 à 1972*, vol 2 (1975) 174.

[8] P. Gourevitch, *We Wish To Inform You That Tomorrow We Will Be Killed With Our Families* (1998) 57.

[9] M. Mamdani, *When Victims Become Killers* (2001) 98.

formed the first government of the newly independent Republic of Rwanda. The reasons for this development were manifold. By the 1950s, the loyalty of the Tutsi aristocracy towards the colonial administration had been eroded. Inspired by the movements in the neighbouring countries, the Tutsi elite no longer sought to avoid confrontation and began to openly demand independence.[10] At the same time, Belgian rule in the Congo was in danger. The Belgians realized that they would lose their influence in Central Africa unless they found new allies in the region. In 1946, Rwanda had become a trusteeship territory under the new UN system. The UN Trusteeship Council had the right to send missions to those territories and made extensive use of that power in the case of Rwanda. Several reports denounced Hutu discrimination and called for political representation of the Hutu majority. Finally, it was the Catholic Church that played another crucial role in the rise of the Hutu. The relations between the church and the monarchy had always been tense, since the *mwami* and most chiefs had long been reluctant to convert to Christianity.[11] The Hutu, however, proved much more receptive to the Gospel spread by the missionaries. Many of these missionaries were sympathetic towards the Hutu's endeavours for emancipation and advocated their political representation. In 1957, supported by a Belgian priest, several members of the small Hutu elite, among them future President Grégoire Kayibanda, published the Hutu Manifesto. The document branded the Tutsi as a different race that had invaded Hutu land, demanded independence from both the Belgian and the Tutsi oligarchy, and favoured legal distinctions between the 'races' in order to implement egalitarian representation of the Hutu in political functions.[12]

In the late 1950s political parties were founded which were essentially divided along ethnic fault lines. Kayibanda's PARMEHUTU (Parti du Mouvement d'Émancipation Hutu) adopted the demands of the Hutu Manifesto. The UNAR (Union Nationale Rwandaise) was Tutsi-dominated, but stood for the unity of all Rwandans, and called for independence under the reign of the Tutsi monarchy.[13] Tensions between the two camps increased when the incumbent *mwami* mysteriously died in July 1959. The Tutsi elite suspected the Belgians and the Hutu of having assassinated the king. In November 1959, anti-Tutsi violence openly broke out when UNAR activists attacked a leading PARMEHUTU politician. In the following weeks the colonial authorities began to replace Tutsi chiefs with Hutu and proclaimed an end to Tutsi dominance. This, however, only served to spur on outbreaks of violence against the Tutsi, which led to more than 100,000 of them seeking refuge in neighbouring countries. The 'social revolution' had begun.

In the wake of the 1959 turmoil, the king had also left for Uganda. The monarchy was formally abolished in 1961. Communal and national elections initiated by the UN were held in a climate of intimidation, with both resulting in an overwhelming PARMEHUTU majority.[14] Violent reprisals against the Tutsi

[10] G. Prunier, *The Rwanda Crisis 1959–1994* (1995) 47 *et seq.*

[11] Ibid, 44.

[12] C. Newbury, *The Cohesion of Oppression* (1988) 191.

[13] See M. Mamdani, *When Victims Become Killers* (2001) 120 *et seq.*

[14] L. Melvern, *A People Betrayed* (2000) 14 *et seq*; C. Newbury, *The Cohesion of Oppression* (1988) 198 *et seq.*

remained frequent. When Rwanda gained independence on 1 July 1962, Grégoire Kayibanda became the first president. He initially appeased international observers with a seemingly moderate leadership, forming a coalition government with the UNAR and another party.[15] Despite the unresolved refugee crisis, the situation seemed to improve. In late 1963, however, militant Tutsi exiles invaded the country from Burundi in an unsuccessful bid to reverse the current situation and bring the Tutsi back to power. The invasion was followed by reprisals against the ordinary Tutsi population and Kayibanda's political opponents. These raids reached unprecedented proportions, leading to an international outcry of horror.[16] In just over three years, the 'social revolution' had left more than 10,000 dead and another 130,000 in exile.[17]

Despite Kayibanda's racist ideology, his government was criticized for not effectively promoting Hutu dominance in the country. Although the Tutsi had been eliminated from political functions, they still held dominant positions in other fields.[18] In addition to this, Rwanda's economic situation had not improved since independence. Rising discontentment within the Hutu middle class was further fuelled when chaos broke out in neighbouring Burundi. Rwanda's 'twin country' has a largely identical population structure. Until independence, development in both countries took place in an essentially parallel manner. From then on, however, the situations in Rwanda and Burundi can be described as being located at 'two opposite ends of a political seesaw'.[19] In Burundi, a military junta had come to power which had actually further consolidated Tutsi dominance over the country. In 1972, Hutu rebels staged an unsuccessful coup against the regime. An estimated 200,000 Hutu were then killed in response to it.[20] There was then a massive influx of refugees into Rwanda; the Rwandan Tutsi also came under attack in order that the Burundian Hutu could be avenged. In 1973, Rwandan army chief Major General Juvénal Habyarimana took advantage of this volatile situation, ousted Kayibanda, and declared himself president of the Second Republic.

Habyarimana was a Hutu from northern Rwanda. His seizure of power must be understood in the context of regional tensions. Habyarimana's presidency put an end to the southern-dominated reign of the PARMEHUTU and paved the way for northern clans to take up the reins of power. In the early 1990s, these elites would become the masterminds of the genocidal ideology that was to prove so effective. The political change of 1973 nourished hopes that tensions would ease, and that the refugees could finally return. Although Habyarimana's presidency did indeed usher in over 15 years of relatively peaceful relations between the Hutu and Tutsi, anti-Tutsi violence was replaced by brutal reprisals against political

[15] M. Mamdani, *When Victims Become Killers* (2001) 128.

[16] British philosopher Bertrand Russell called the killings the most horrible and systematic extermination of a people since the Holocaust, 'Trois mille Tutsis réfugiés au Congo-Léopoldville lanceraient une "attaque-suicide" contre le Ruanda', *Le Monde*, 6 February 1964.

[17] P.J. Magnarella, 'The Background and Causes of the Genocide in Rwanda' 3 *JICJ* (2005) 809, 810.

[18] M. Mamdani, *When Victims Become Killers* (2001) 136.

[19] G. Prunier, *The Rwanda Crisis 1959–1994* (1995) 198.

[20] R. Lemarchand and D. Martin, *Selective Genocide in Burundi* (1974); M. Mamdani, *When Victims Become Killers* (2001) 137.

opponents. The situation of the Tutsi did not improve, however. The exiles' hopes for return remained frustrated. Those who had stayed in the country were subject to unchanged discrimination and continued to be marginalized in public life.[21]

Habyarimana's reign was totalitarian. Every Rwandan became a member of his party, the Mouvement Révolutionnaire National pour le Développement (MRND).[22] Under the Second Republic, ties with France also became closer; Habyarimana was said to have personal friends in the Elysée palace, one of them being François Mitterrand. In the eyes of international public opinion, the development in Rwanda was promising. Habyarimana's regime brought stability to the region and was perceived as the democratic rule of the majority.[23] The country's economic development appeared equally promising thanks to high coffee prices on the world market.

In the mid-1980s, Habyarimana's strong hold on power in Rwanda started to crumble. Although the collapse in coffee prices already represented the beginning of the end for Habyarimana, the main reason for his political demise was his failure to resolve the refugee crisis. Uganda was one of the largest host countries for Rwandan refugees at the time. In the early 1980s, thousands of them had joined the upcoming Ugandan opposition party, the National Resistance Movement (NRM) and its army (NRA).[24] The NRM promised Ugandan citizenship to all refugees who had resided there for at least 10 years. In 1986, following a five-year guerrilla war, the NRM seized power, and Yoweri Museveni became Uganda's new president. However, the NRM's promise of citizenship caused severe protests from local farmers and, following a major political crisis, Museveni gave in.[25] The refugees' hopes for acceptance there were shattered. At the same time, Habyarimana's regime grew more and more unstable, with the President increasingly trapped between the interests of his own extremist clan and those of international donors, who were urging him to allow multi-party elections.

On 1 October 1990, while both Museveni and Habyarimana were attending a UN summit in New York, NRA soldiers of Rwandan origin invaded the country under the name of the new Rwandan Patriotic Army (RPA). The RPA was the military arm of the Rwandan Patriotic Front (RPF), an organization founded in Uganda in the mid-1980s. The Western world, which was at this stage still largely sympathetic towards Habyarimana, was outraged. In French military circles, the invasion was perceived as a British-Ugandan conspiracy against *la francophonie*.[26] France did not hesitate in sending troops. With their support, the Rwandan army

[21] See L. Melvern, *A People Betrayed* (2000) 25.

[22] G. Prunier, *The Rwanda Crisis 1959–1994* (1995) 76 *et seq*.

[23] In 1978, 1983, and 1988, Habyarimana was re-elected as the only candidate who stood for election, L. Melvern, *A People Betrayed* (2000) 25.

[24] W.C. Reed, 'Exile, Reform, and the Rise of the Rwandan Patriotic Front' 34 *The Journal of Modern African Studies* (1996) 484, 485.

[25] M. Mamdani, *When Victims Become Killers* (2001) 176 *et seq*; M. Mamdani, 'African States, Citizenship and War' 78 *International Affairs* (2002) 497.

[26] The motivations of France's interventions in Africa were described by a French author in a both colourful and polemic way in G. Prunier, *The Rwanda Crisis 1959–1994* (1995) 103 *et seq*. See also R. Lemarchand, 'The Rationality of Genocide' 23 *Issue* (1995) no 2, 8.

was able to repel the invasion at least partially. The exiles still, however, posed a threat to the regime. The RPA soldiers were highly experienced in guerrilla warfare. Under the command of Major Paul Kagame, their frequent incursions destabilized the north and resulted in an overwhelming number of people becoming internally displaced.[27] The war against the RPA could not be won. Under pressure from the Organization of African Unity (OAU), Belgium, and the US, the regime agreed to enter into negotiations with the RPF. In August 1993, after more than a year of talks, the Arusha Accords were signed, an overly ambitious peace agreement stipulating far-reaching political and military reforms. A transitional government representing all factions was to be formed, with the UN to deploy a peacekeeping force to ensure the smooth running of the process.[28]

III. Genocide 1990–94

It has been mentioned above that Habyarimana's rule prepared the ground for extremist clans from northern Rwanda to gain influence. Habyarimana's wife, first lady Agathe Kanziga, was a central figure among these elites. She came from a powerful family that had already played a crucial role in the *coup d'état* of 1973. She was surrounded by the notorious *akazu*, a group of extremist politicians and businessmen,[29] who formed the core of the Hutu Power movement. According to their radical ideology, it was the Hutu alone who constituted the Rwandan nation; the Tutsi were deemed an alien race that had invaded Rwanda from Ethiopia. According to this extremist ideology, the Tutsi's only objective was to reinstate the monarchy, and to subdue and exploit the Hutu. When the RPA invaded, the *akazu* realized that this was the ideal opportunity to spread their ideology.[30] With the support of northern communal politicians close to the *akazu*, a chain of anti-Tutsi massacres was organized—the first after almost 20 years of relatively peaceful Hutu–Tutsi relations.[31] In November 1990, the extremist *akazu*-sponsored newspaper *Kangura* printed the 'Hutu Ten Commandments',[32] calling upon all Hutu to refrain from any relations with Tutsi. At the same time, pressured by international donors, the regime eased its totalitarian grip on state affairs, leading to the legalization of political parties in 1991. In a climate of rising ethnic tensions, however, this move ended up fostering extremist tendencies rather than bringing about a shift towards a pluralistic society. In

[27] See M. Mamdani, *When Victims Become Killers* (2001) 186–9.

[28] UNAMIR, established by UN Security Council Resolution 872 (1993) of 5 October 1993.

[29] *Akazu* means 'little house' and traditionally referred to the circle of courtiers around the *mwami*, G. Prunier, *The Rwanda Crisis 1959–1994* (1995) 85. This group included some of the masterminds of the genocide such as Théoneste Bagosora, Ferdinand Nahimana, and Tharcisse Renzaho, all of whom were indicted before the ICTR.

[30] See G. Prunier, *The Rwanda Crisis 1959–1994* (1995) 166 *et seq*.

[31] The massacre of Kibilira in the north-western Prefecture of Gisenyi on 11 October 1990 is often referred to as the beginning of the genocide, ibid, 84. See also A. Des Forges, *Leave None to Tell the Story* (1999) 87; R. Lemarchand, 'The Rationality of Genocide' 23 *Issue* (1995) no 2, 9; M. Mamdani, *When Victims Become Killers* (2001) 192.

[32] The 'Hutu Ten Commandments' are reprinted in J.-P. Chrétien, '"Presse libre" et propagande raciste au Rwanda' 42 *Politique Africaine* (1992) 119 *et seq*.

the wake of the 'liberalization', the Hutu Power movement swiftly began to develop its own institutions: a radio and television station, Radio-Télévision Libre des Mille Collines (RTLM), and its own militias, including the notorious *Interahamwe*.[33]

Despite all these developments, there still seemed to be a light at the end of the tunnel for Rwanda in mid-1993. The Arusha Accords had finally been signed, and neighbouring Burundi provided an example of peaceful Hutu–Tutsi co-existence. In June, free and fair elections had been held there. The winner of the election, Melchior Ndadaye, became the first democratically elected president of his country and the first Hutu to hold this position. A political moderate, Ndadaye went on to form a broad-based government, with the transition taking place peacefully.[34] However, in October that year, Ndadaye fell victim to a plot by Tutsi military staff and was killed. This event seemed to confirm all the propaganda spread by Hutu Power. The turmoil in Burundi following Ndadaye's assassination resulted in tens of thousands of casualties and a flood of refugees into Rwanda.[35] At the same time, Hutu Power was furious with Habyarimana for having become involved with the RPF and signing the Arusha Accords. With the prospect of a coalition government looming, the *akazu* realized that their days were numbered, and pressed for a 'final solution'. It was the RTLM in particular that became an increasingly powerful and outspoken advocate of genocide.[36]

On 6 April 1994, Juvénal Habyarimana was on his way back to Kigali from Dar es Salaam on his private plane together with Burundian President Cyprien Ntaryamira. As they approached Kigali airport, the plane was hit by a missile, killing both presidents and the entire crew.[37] The news was broadcast on RTLM half an hour later. The very same night, raids began against Tutsi all over the country. With the President's death, Prime Minister Agathe Uwilingiyimana had become the nominal head of state. She was a moderate Hutu and had played a leading role in the peace negotiations with the RPF. On 7 April, just as she was about to address

[33] See M. Mamdani, *When Victims Become Killers* (2001) 209.

[34] G. Prunier, *The Rwanda Crisis 1959–1994* (1995) 199.

[35] R. Lemarchand, 'The Rationality of Genocide' 23 *Issue* (1995) no 2, 10; G. Prunier, ibid.

[36] F. Chalk, 'Hate Radio in Rwanda' in H. Adelman and A. Suhrke (eds), *The Path of Genocide* (1999) 93 *et seq*; J.-P. Chrétien, *Les médias du génocide* (1995) 63 *et seq*. See also *Prosecutor v Nahimana, Barayagwiza and Ngeze*, ICTR, Trial Chamber, Judgment of 3 December 2003 (ICTR-99-52-T) paras 342–463.

[37] The circumstances surrounding the attack have never been cleared up. However, there are strong indications that Hutu Power launched the missile, see G. Prunier, *The Rwanda Crisis 1959–1994* (1995) 213 *et seq*, 223; see also the Mutsinzi-Report commissioned by the Rwandan Government, *Report of the Investigation into the Causes and Circumstances of and Responsibility for the Attack of 6 April 1994 against the Falcon 50 Rwandan Presidential Aeroplane, Registration Number 9XR-NN* (2010). In November 2006, French judge Jean-Louis Bruguière issued arrest warrants against nine senior RPF officials for downing Habyarimana's plane. After the arrest of President Kagame's head of protocol Rose Kabuye in Frankfurt in November 2008 however, the principal witness for the prosecution, former RPF colonel Abdul Ruzibiza withdrew his testimony, claiming that he had lied, 'Ruzibiza, le témoin rwandais de Bruguière se rétracte', *Libération*, 14 November 2008. The arrest warrants were dropped in December 2010 after documents made public by Wikileaks revealed that Bruguière had consulted President Jacques Chirac before issuing the warrants, 'French Judges Lift Arrest Warrants against Rwandan Military Officials', *The East African*, 20 December 2010.

the nation on Radio Rwanda in order to appeal for calm, she and the 10 Belgian peacekeepers intended to protect her were killed by the Presidential Guard.[38]

During the next few weeks, unprecedented levels of anti-Tutsi violence broke out, spreading quickly throughout the whole country, constantly fuelled by RTLM's hate propaganda. UNAMIR was left with nothing to do but stand aside and watch the genocide unfold. Not only did they lack sufficient supplies and manpower, their mandate also did not permit intervention. UNAMIR was further weakened following the Belgian government's decision to withdraw its contingent in reaction to the murder of 10 of its peacekeepers. On 21 April, the Security Council decided to reduce the mission's strength from over 2,500 to 270 following a proposal by the Secretary General.[39] By mid-July 1994, an estimated 800,000 to one million Tutsi and moderate Hutu had been brutally murdered.[40]

Two days after Habyarimana's death, the RPA resumed their military operations and crossed the border in the north. They advanced quickly through the north-east of the country, often finding deserted villages as most Tutsi had been killed and the Hutu had taken flight, fearing reprisals by the RPA. The rebels entered Kigali on 11 April 1994, reuniting with a small RPA battalion there, which had been stationed at the Parliament building under the Arusha Accords. The battle for the capital, however, was to last until early July.[41] On 18 July 1994, the last Hutu Power stronghold in the country fell.

There can be no doubt that it was the RPA alone that finally ended the killings in Rwanda. Nevertheless, their role in the conflict is highly disputed. Human Rights Watch estimates that at least 25,000 to 30,000 people were killed by the RPA—combatants, *génocidaires*, but also unarmed civilians.[42] Violent reprisals by RPA troops continued throughout 1996.[43] Yet there is very little confirmed information about these massacres, as human rights workers and journalists were unable to move freely in the RPA-controlled zone.[44] The RPF government admitted that there were instances of war crimes committed by RPA forces, but refused to conduct a comprehensive and transparent investigation.[45] The RPA offensive triggered a major flood of Hutu refugees into the neighbouring countries. In mid-1994, when the world's attention had finally turned to Rwanda, the refugee crisis was perceived as the real humanitarian catastrophe.

Although thousands of people were being killed every day in Rwanda, the Security Council failed to react in an appropriate manner. The US in particular was strictly opposed to any extension of UNAMIR and its mandate as they feared a repetition of the fiasco in Somalia in 1993. It was only in mid-June of 1994 that France put forward a proposal to send its troops to Rwanda in order to stop the killings. The press had increasingly focused on France's unfortunate involvement

[38] A. Des Forges, *Leave None to Tell the Story* (1999) 187 *et seq*; L. Melvern, *A People Betrayed* (2000) 116 *et seq.*

[39] UN Security Council Resolution 912 (1994) of 21 April 1994, para 8.

[40] For a detailed account of the genocide, see A. Des Forges, *Leave None to Tell the Story* (1999).

[41] G. Prunier, *The Rwanda Crisis 1959–1994* (1995) 268.

[42] A. Des Forges, *Leave None to Tell the Story* (1999) 734.

[43] See the new chapter in the second edition of G. Prunier's book, *The Rwanda Crisis* (1997) 360 *et seq.*

[44] N. Eltringham, *Accounting for Horror* (2004) 101.

[45] Amnesty International, *Reports of Killings and Abductions by the Rwandese Patriotic Army* (1994) 10.

in the civil war and the genocide, which prompted Mitterrand to intervene in the 'name of humanity'.[46] The Security Council received the offer with relief and vested the so-called *Opération Turquoise* with a powerful Chapter VII mandate.[47] The operation was limited to the *Zone Turquoise*, a territory in the south-west of the country. The intervention turned out to be a disaster. The *Zone Turquoise* became a safe haven for the killers and provided shelter from the RPA, with the massacres continuing widely unnoticed by the French troops. Many *génocidaires* managed to escape into Zaire through the refugee corridor provided by the operation and were later involved in further massacres in Zairian refugee camps.[48]

At this point it is necessary to return briefly to the origins of the genocide in order to better understand the various challenges to the future stability of Rwanda. There is no doubt that the extent and intensity of the killings, and the massive participation of the ordinary population in them are unprecedented. Yet they also recall the massacres of 1963 in that ordinary people suddenly attacked and killed their Tutsi neighbours. Lemarchand points out that the 1963 massacres revealed an extreme, pathological sense of inferiority among the Hutu.[49] The humiliations of forced labour and racial inferiority were still a vivid memory for many of them. In 1994, the killings showed a similar pattern of extreme violence and mass participation as in the 1963 massacres.[50] Yet most Hutu in 1994 had not personally experienced the oppression of colonial times. The Hutu's trauma had been constantly nurtured by aggressive propaganda that alleged that the Tutsi were about to reinstate a regime of forced labour, which could only be avoided by the Hutu taking up arms and exterminating every last one of them. The long tradition of 'systematic, centralised and unconditional obedience to authority'[51] also explains why Hutu Power propaganda proved so effective. The reverse political situation in Burundi and the anti-Hutu pogroms there appeared to support the ideas propagated by Hutu Power.

IV. The Refugee Crisis and the War in Zaire/Congo

The events of mid-1994 had a devastating effect on security in the whole region. The floods of refugees fleeing from the advancing RPA troops provoked a massive humanitarian crisis in Tanzania, Burundi, and especially in Zaire, where over a million people had set up camps in Goma and Bukavu just across the border from Rwanda. In the early 1990s, the Mobutu regime had lost control over eastern Zaire. Overpopulation, ethnic divisions, and conflicts over the access to natural resources had increased tensions in the region. The Kivu province bordering Rwanda had

[46] France was, inter alia, accused of having trained the Presidential Guard that was involved in the killings, G. Prunier, 'Opération Turquoise' in H. Adelman and A. Suhrke (eds), *The Path of Genocide* (1999) 283.

[47] UN Security Council Resolution 929 (1994) of 22 June 1994.

[48] G. Prunier, 'Opération Turquoise' in H. Adelman and A. Suhrke (eds), *The Path of Genocide* (1999) 297.

[49] R. Lemarchand, *Rwanda and Burundi* (1970) 44.

[50] See the account of the massacres in 1963 by R. Lemarchand, ibid, 223 *et seq.*

[51] G. Prunier, *The Rwanda Crisis 1959–1994* (1995) 141.

long been home to a strong Banyarwanda minority composed of both Hutu and Tutsi. Under Zairian law, most of them were considered foreigners. Many 'indigenous Zairians' in the region wanted these 'foreigners' off their lands. The massive influx of Hutu from Rwanda in mid-1994—tens of thousands of them heavily armed—further complicated the situation, and pitted Zairian and Rwandan Hutu against Zairian Tutsi and the other ethnic groups in the region.[52] When the Mobutu regime tried to expel the Banyarwanda from eastern Zaire in 1996, Rwanda intervened. The RPA attacked the Hutu militias in the refugee camps, and massacred thousands of Hutu.[53]

For some time already, Zaire's East African neighbours, led by former Tanzanian President Julius Nyerere, had nurtured the idea of ridding the continent of Mobutu's corrupt regime. In the wake of the turmoil following the Rwandan genocide, they had pushed for former guerrilla Laurent Désiré Kabila to act as the figurehead of a 'democratic opposition'. With Rwanda invading the Kivus and the fatally ill Mobutu losing control over his own security apparatus, the situation for Kabila's opposition movement was favourable. Within only a few months, his Alliance des Forces Démocratiques de la Libération (AFDL), supported by Rwanda, Uganda, and Angola, took Kinshasa and obtained control over much of the country's territory. In May 1997, Kabila became president of the renamed Democratic Republic of Congo.[54]

Relations between Kabila and his Rwandan and Ugandan allies deteriorated however, as the situation in eastern Congo remained insecure. In 1997, Hutu militias staged an insurgency in the north-western Rwandan provinces of Gisenyi and Ruhengeri, both of which border the Congo, attacking the Tutsi once again. As support for the insurgency increased among the Hutu population, the RPA responded with brutal reprisals that resulted in the killing of hundreds of unarmed civilians. The Rwandan government was convinced that the militias in the north-west were operating from bases in the Congo with the collusion of the Kabila regime. With the Hutu militias still intact in the eastern Congo, the Tutsi living there feared becoming the target of a new genocide. In the face of Kabila's passive stance towards these threats, Rwanda and Uganda decided to intervene again.[55] Yet their motivation to reinvade the Congo was also fuelled by the prospect of gaining increased control over the Kivus as well as access to the Congo's resources. Their exploitation of coltan, gold, and diamond mines ended up allowing their armies to carry out sustained operations far inside DRC territory.[56] When Rwanda withdrew its troops in 2002, the Hutu militias had been considerably weakened yet

[52] N. Eltringham, *Accounting for Horror* (2004) 121 *et seq*; M. Mamdani, 'African States, Citizenship and War' 78 *International Affairs* (2002) 501 *et seq*.

[53] See G. Nzongola-Ntalaja, *The Congo from Leopold to Kabila* (2002) 225 *et seq*; OHCHR, *Democratic Republic of the Congo, 1993–2003* (2010) paras 191 *et seq*.

[54] C. Braeckman, *L'enjeu congolais* (1999) 47 *et seq*; L. Ndikumana and K.F. Emizet, 'The Economics of Civil War' in P. Collier and N. Sambanis (eds), *Understanding Civil War* (2005) 76; G. Prunier, *Africa's World War* (2009) 67 *et seq*, 115 *et seq*.

[55] T. Longman, 'The Complex Reasons for Rwanda's Engagement in Congo' in J.F. Clark (ed), *The African Stakes of the Congo War* (2002) 129 *et seq*.

[56] G. Prunier, *Africa's World War* (2009) 218 *et seq*.

not entirely dismantled. Since late 2008, the Rwandan Defence Forces (RDF) and the Congolese army (FARDC) have been carrying out joint operations against the Forces Démocratiques pour la Libération du Rwanda (FDLR), which unites former Hutu militias.[57] The situation in eastern Congo remains extremely volatile.

V. Rwanda Today

After the fall of the last Hutu Power stronghold in the north-west in mid-July 1994, the RPF established a new government under President Pasteur Bizimungu. All of the existing parties except for the MRND were represented in the government. The President and most of the ministers were Hutu, with the most important cabinet posts being held by Tutsi.[58] Former RPA-commander Paul Kagame became vice president and minister of defence. The new administration confirmed its adherence to the Arusha Accords and called for democratic elections after a transition period of five years, which was later extended to nine years. In May 1995, a new Fundamental Law amending the Constitution came into force.[59] The RPF victory encouraged nearly 800,000 Rwandan exiles to return.[60] The new regime has managed to restore peace and stability to the country within only a few years, attracted considerable foreign investment, and achieved solid economic growth.

When I first came to Rwanda and visited the Gisozi Genocide Memorial in Kigali, I was initially very impressed with the open reckoning with recent history and the total rejection of any sort of independence myth—an indispensable unifying force in other African countries. Compared to my home country in particular, it appeared that Rwandans had learned quickly how to confront their past. Very soon, however, I realized that Rwanda and Germany were hardly comparable in that regard. From the very outset, the new Rwandan elite that had risen from the ruins in 1994 had had its foundations in the victory over a genocidal dictatorship, a virtually inexhaustible source of legitimacy for the new regime. The genocide had become the central reference point and, as it were, the 'founding myth' of the new Rwanda. To this day, the genocide and its aftermath are dominant topics in public debate. The discourse on the genocide and its origins is characterized by a dominant official narrative which is taught in schools and propagated by government newspapers, politicians, and local leaders.[61]

Despite initial steps towards multi-party democracy, the government has ended up pursuing a fairly authoritarian policy in the name of national unity.[62]

[57] ICG, *Une stratégie globale pour désarmer les FDLR* (2009) 3.

[58] M.A. Drumbl, 'Rule of Law amid Lawlessness' 29 *ColHRLR* (1998) 564.

[59] According to its art 1, the Fundamental Law (*Loi fondamentale de la République rwandaise du 25 mai 1995*, Journal officiel de la République Rwandaise No 11 du 1 juin 1995) comprised, inter alia, the 1991 Constitution and the Arusha Peace Agreement. For the texts, see W.A. Schabas and M. Imbleau, *Introduction to Rwandan Law* (1997) 229 *et seq.*

[60] C. André, 'Terre rwandaise, accès, politique et réformes foncières' in F. Reyntjens and S. Marysse (eds), *L'Afrique des Grands Lacs 1997/1998* (1998) 160 *et seq.*

[61] For details, see J. Pottier, *Re-Imagining Rwanda* (2002) 110 *et seq.*

[62] See G. Hankel, 'An der Realität vorbei' 43 *Der Überblick* (2007) nos 1/2, 78 *et seq.*

The RPF leadership is guided by the idea that Rwandans can only exercise full democratic rights once all ethnic divisions have been eradicated. Stringent and far-reaching criminal legislation has been enacted to prohibit any form of divisionism, sectarianism,[63] or genocide ideology.[64] The activities of opposition parties are severely restricted, a great number of opposition members have left the country, and instances of politically motivated killings have been reported.[65]

Since 1994, the RPF has consolidated its rule: the majority of important posts in government and regional administration are held by RPF loyalists, many of them Tutsi. The RPF's authoritarian rule has forced parts of the opposition into exile and led to political radicalization.[66] In March 2000, President Bizimungu resigned over disputes concerning a government shakeup. RPF-leader Paul Kagame was elected as the new president. Shortly afterward, Bizimungu announced the foundation of a new opposition party. The party was banned immediately despite the lack of any legal basis for such an act.[67] Bizimungu was arrested and sentenced to 15 years in prison for inciting rebellion, creating a criminal association, and embezzlement of public funds. In April 2007, after spending five years in prison, he was pardoned by President Kagame.[68]

In 2003, presidential elections were held, resulting in a clear victory for Kagame, who won over 95 per cent of the vote. In the same year, a new Constitution[69] replacing the Fundamental Law was adopted in a referendum. The Constitution set up a presidential republic, and contains a commitment to national unity, human rights, multi-party democracy, and non-discriminatory representation of women in politics. The president can be re-elected once, and serves for a term of seven years (article 101). The Constitution incorporated the creation of the National Commission for Human Rights (article 177),[70] the National Unity and Reconciliation Commission (NURC, article 178),[71] and the post of an Ombudsman (article 182).[72] These bodies can release reports on the human rights situation, instances of discrimination or xenophobia, and corruption.

Nevertheless, Rwanda's record in human rights and democratization remains poor. Government control over the press has grown tighter in the last few years.

[63] *Law No 47/2001 of 18 December 2001 instituting punishment for offences of discrimination and sectarianism*, OGRR no 4 of 15 February 2002.

[64] *Law No 18/2008 of 23 July 2008 relating to the punishment of the crime of genocide ideology*, OGRR no 19 of 1 October 2008. On that, see Amnesty International, *Safer to Stay Silent* (2010); L. Waldorf, 'Censorship and Propaganda in Post-Genocide Rwanda' in A. Thompson (ed), *The Media and the Rwanda Genocide* (2007) 404 *et seq.*

[65] HRW, *World Report 2002* (2002) 77.

[66] ICG, *Rwanda at the End of the Transition* (2002) 1 *et seq.* See also F. Reyntjens, 'Rwanda, Ten Years On' 103 *African Affairs* (2004) 187 *et seq*, 191 *et seq.*

[67] ICG, *Rwanda at the End of the Transition* (2002) 30.

[68] L. Waldorf, 'A Justice "Trickle-Down"' in E.L. Lutz and C. Reiger (eds), *Prosecuting Heads of State* (2009) 161 *et seq.*

[69] *Constitution of the Republic of Rwanda of 4 June 2003*, OGRR no special of 4 June 2003.

[70] As amended by art 54 of *Amendment No 4 of 17 June 2010 of the Constitution of the Republic of Rwanda of 4 June 2003*, OGRR no special of 17 June 2010.

[71] As amended by art 55 of Amendment No 4. On the NURC, see B. Oomen, 'Justice Mechanisms and the Question of Legitimacy' in K. Ambos, J. Large and M. Wierda (eds), *Building a Future on Peace and Justice* (2009) 190 *et seq.*

[72] As amended by art 59 of Amendment No 4.

Independent journalists are subject to harassment[73] and most independent newspapers are no longer active. The new media law enacted in August 2009 gives the Media High Council sweeping powers to suspend newspapers and have them closed down.[74] The Council made use of this in April 2010 by suspending the two leading independent newspapers *Umuseso* and *Umuvugizi*.[75] The run-up to the presidential elections in August 2010 was characterized by reprisals against those regarded as political opponents. In April 2010, three senior officials of the influential victim organization *Ibuka*, including Executive Secretary Benoit Kaboyi, and presidential candidate Victoire Ingabire Umuhoza were arrested within only a few days of one another, the latter being charged with supporting terrorist organizations in the DRC, propagating ethnic division and genocide denial.[76]

In the wake of the 2003 Constitution, a comprehensive administrative reform aimed at decentralization and democratization at a local level was undertaken. Rwanda is now divided up into provinces, districts, sectors, cells, and villages (so-called *imidugudu*).[77] The number of entities at each administrative level has been substantially reduced.[78] The 30 districts form the most important local entities. They have legal personality, financial autonomy,[79] and are in charge of local infrastructure and services.[80] An essential innovation is that the authorities at the district, sector, and cell levels are no longer appointed by the central government, but rather elected by the local population.[81] These important steps towards democratization are, however, to some extent being countered by the so-called *imidugudu* or 'villagization' programme. This policy started in the mid-1990s with the aim of regrouping the rural population in villages (*imidugudu*) in order to provide housing and land for returning refugees, facilitate access to basic services, and to ensure the security of the population. Besides the coercive nature of this programme, it has often been criticized as a means for the government to increase their control over the population.[82]

[73] LIPRODHOR, *Situation des droits de la personne au Rwanda en 2006* (2007) 102 *et seq.*

[74] Arts 83–4 of *Law No 22/2009 of 12 August 2009 on media*, OGRR no 33 of 17 August 2009. Among the grounds for suspension and shutdown are 'publication of those publications which endanger public law and order or public decency'.

[75] Media High Council, Press Release of 14 April 2010; Committee to Protect Journalists, *Rwanda Shuts Critical Papers in Run-Up to Presidential Vote*, 13 April 2010.

[76] 'IBUKA Officials Jailed over Survivors' Fund', *The New Times*, 24 April 2010; 'Kagame Rival Arrested in Rwanda', *BBC*, 21 April 2010.

[77] Art 3(1) of the Rwandan Constitution as amended by art 1 of *Amendment No 2 of 8 December 2005 of the Constitution of the Republic of Rwanda of 4 June 2003*, OGRR no special of 8 December 2005; *Organic Law No 29/2005 of 31 December 2005 determining the administrative entities of the Republic of Rwanda*, OGRR no special of 31 December 2005, as modified by *Organic Law No 04/2010/OL of 12 August 2010 modifying and completing Organic Law No 29/2005 of 31 December 2005*, OGRR no special of 2 September 2010.

[78] See the table in UNDP, *Turning Vision 2020 to Reality* (2007) 66.

[79] Art 2(1) of *Law No 08/2006 of 24 February 2006 determining the organisation and functioning of the District*, OGRR no special of 24 February 2006.

[80] Arts 5–8 of Law No 08/2006.

[81] Strategies 2000, *Rwanda Decentralization Assessment* (2002) 17.

[82] M. van Leeuwen, 'Rwanda's Imidugudu Programme' 39 *Journal of Modern African Studies* (2001) 632; on the villagization programme and its possible bearings on Gacaca, see also E. Daly, 'Between Punitive and Reconstructive Justice' 34 *NYUJIntlLaw&Pol* (2002) 378 *et seq.*

VI. Dealing with the Events between 1990 and 1994

A. The 1993 Truth Commission

The first investigation into ethnically motivated human rights violations had already been carried out before tensions came to a head in April 1994. As provided for in the Arusha Accords, which were signed into effect later that year, an independent International Commission of Investigation on Human Rights Violations in Rwanda since 1 October 1990, which had been set up by and received funding from several Rwandan and international NGOs, was dispatched to Rwanda in January 1993. The Commission was made up of 10 individuals, mostly lawyers and human rights activists. Its mandate was to investigate human rights violations committed by the government side during the civil war. Although it was officially welcomed by President Habyarimana, the government did everything it could to obstruct the Commission's work. In the days before its arrival, a handful of potential witnesses were attacked and killed. Despite these difficulties and the fact that the Commission had only two weeks to complete their work, its report on human rights violations by government forces[83] had an enormous impact. Massacres against Tutsi stopped for a few months after its publication.[84] The report also caused Belgium to reconsider its attitude towards the Habyarimana government. France began withdrawing its troops from Rwanda shortly after the report was released. In the weeks after the Commission had left the country, the government launched a campaign focusing on the crimes committed by the RPF. Following a request by the RPF, the Commission planned a second visit in order to clear up these charges. Before it could do so, however, the events of April 1994 unfolded.[85]

B. Rebuilding the justice apparatus

Shortly after its formation on 19 July 1994, the new transitional government announced that it was willing to criminally prosecute every single perpetrator involved in the genocide. Many alleged *génocidaires* had already been incarcerated during the RPA offensive between April and July 1994. Even though a sustainable solution to deal with the caseload had not yet been found, the prison population increased massively during 1998. That year, the International Committee of the Red Cross (ICRC) registered a record number of over 124,000 detainees,[86] who were held in regular prisons or in communal lock-ups (*cachots*). Usually arrests had been made based on vague denunciations, often linked to the settling of personal

[83] *Rapport de la Commission internationale d'enquête sur les violations des droits de l'homme au Rwanda depuis le 1er Octobre 1990* (1993).

[84] A. Des Forges, *Leave None to Tell the Story* (1999) 94.

[85] For details on the Commission, see P.B. Hayner, 'Fifteen Truth Commission' 16 *HRQ* (1994) 629 *et seq*; J. Sarkin, 'The Necessity and Challenges of Establishing a Truth and Reconciliation Commission in Rwanda' 21 *HRQ* (1999) 777 *et seq*.

[86] Rwanda: Annual Report 1998, 1 June 1999.

scores,[87] and had been effected by personnel not appropriately trained in police work. Often no case files were prepared and no evidence gathered.[88] It must be assumed that a high percentage of the detainees were innocent. The mass of detainees put a massive strain on Rwanda's prison capacities and on the judiciary. After the genocide, the judicial infrastructure was almost entirely destroyed. Public buildings had been wrecked and looted. The Ministry of Justice was housed in a building without telephones and window panes; there was no paper and no typewriters. In addition to this, the judiciary lacked trained personnel. Only 16 educated lawyers had survived the genocide.[89]

With the massive support of foreign donors, the basic infrastructures were re-established by 1996. Personnel were trained, court buildings were renovated and refurnished, and the prison capacity was tripled.[90] In late 1995, the Rwandan government convened an international conference on 'Genocide, Impunity and Accountability'. The conference underlined the need for perpetrators of genocide to be criminally prosecuted, emphasized the importance of fairness in their trials, and put forward suggestions as to how to deal with the caseload. Some favoured a special court for genocide cases with special procedural provisions tailored to large-scale crimes, for example a reversal of the burden of proof for members of militias. Others advocated setting up special chambers in ordinary courts. Besides ordinary criminal prosecutions, the conference proposed 'alternative forms of justice' that would not primarily focus on punishment.[91] South African scholars and politicians in particular supported the idea of an amnesty process modelled upon the Truth and Reconciliation Commission in their country.[92] The RPF government, however, rejected any kind of amnesty.

C. Genocide trials under Organic Law No 08/96

On the basis of the proposals made by the conference, Organic Law No 08/96[93] provided the framework for prosecuting the perpetrators of the Rwandan genocide. The

[87] L. Waldorf, 'Mass Justice for Mass Atrocities' 79 *TempLRev* (2006) 41. See also M. Rettig, 'Gacaca' 51 *African Studies Review* (2008) no 3, 39.

[88] HRW, *Playing the 'Communal Card'* (1995) 13; M.H. Morris, 'The Trials of Concurrent Jurisdiction' 7 *DukeJComp&IntlL* (1997) 352.

[89] M. Cousineau, 'L'établissement de l'Etat de droit au Rwanda' 28 *Ottawa LRev* (1997) 176; C.J. Ferstman, 'Domestic Trials for Genocide and Crimes against Humanity' 9 *African Journal of International and Comparative Law* (1997) 859 *et seq.*

[90] S. Vandeginste, 'Poursuite des présumés responsables du génocide et des massacres politiques devant les juridictions rwandaises' in S. Marysse and F. Reyntjens (eds), *L'Afrique des Grands Lacs 1996/1997* (1997) 107 *et seq.*

[91] *Recommendations of the Conference Held in Kigali from November 1st to November 5th, 1995*, 16–24.

[92] J. Sarkin, 'The Necessity and Challenges of Establishing a Truth and Reconciliation Commission in Rwanda' 21 *HRQ* (1999) 767 *et seq*; J. Sarkin, 'Promoting Justice, Truth and Reconciliation in Transitional Societies' 2 *International Law Forum* (2000) 117; J. Sarkin, 'The Tension Between Justice and Reconciliation in Rwanda' 45 *Journal of African Law* (2001) 167 *et seq.* See also D. Tutu, *No Future without Forgiveness* (1999) 257 *et seq.*

[93] *Loi organique No 08/96 du 30 août 1996 sur l'organisation des poursuites des infractions constitutives du crime de génocide ou de crimes contre l'humanité, commises à partir du 1er octobre 1990*, Journal officiel de la République Rwandaise No 17 du 1er septembre 1996. For details, see D. De Beer, *Loi*

law rejected the idea of a special court being set up to deal with charges in connection with the genocide. Instead, it established specialized chambers in the ordinary and military courts (article 19). The chambers were competent to try cases of genocide, crimes against humanity, and crimes in relation with these (article 1). The temporal jurisdiction of the chambers extended from the beginning of the civil war in October 1990 to the end of 1994. Each chamber was composed of three magistrates (article 21), most of whom had received only six months of legal training.[94] The law contained two central elements that were maintained in the Gacaca Laws: the confession procedure (articles 4 *et seq*); and the categorization of suspects according to the gravity of their crimes (article 2), which is crucial in determining penalties.[95] Perpetrators of the first category incurred the death penalty (article 14(a)). Unless otherwise provided for, the body of criminal law remained applicable under Organic Law No 08/96 (article 39). When the law was drafted, it was decided not to incorporate substantive criminal provisions, but rather to rely on the criminal law that was applicable at the time of the genocide. As the Rwandan Penal Code[96] did not contain the crime of genocide, perpetrators could only be sentenced for murder.[97] The chambers were able to impose the death penalty. However, due to international protests following the public execution of over 20 convicted prisoners in 1998, the government suspended the execution of the death penalty.[98] It was finally abolished in 2007.[99]

The response to the trials in the human rights community was anything but uniform. In a report published in 1997, Amnesty International harshly denounced the lack of legal counsel in most cases as well as inadequate legal knowledge and bias among judges.[100] In 1997, Canadian-Irish law professor William A. Schabas attended the trial of Froduald Karamira, a leading figure in the genocide and probably the 'biggest fish' ever tried for genocide in Rwanda. He reported that the proceedings were fair, and that the accused and his counsel were given opportunity to rebut all charges.[101] In fact, it appears that the quality of the trials had improved over the years. Michel Moussalli, Special Representative for the UN Commission

rwandaise du 30 août 1996, 2nd edn (1999); V. Thalmann, 'Rwandan Genocide Cases' in A. Cassese (ed), *The Oxford Companion to International Criminal Justice* (2009) 498 *et seq*.

94 UN Commission on Human Rights, *Report on the Situation of Human Rights in Rwanda* (1999) para 39.

95 For further details, see ch 2, section V C below.

96 *Décret-Loi no 21/77 du 18 août 1977 instituant le Code pénal au Rwanda*, Journal officiel de la République Rwandaise, no 13*bis* du 1 juillet 1978.

97 U.P. Behrendt, *Die Verfolgung des Völkermordes in Ruanda durch internationale und nationale Gerichte* (2005) 166, 167; M.A. Drumbl, 'Rule of Law amid Lawlessness' 29 *ColHRLR* (1998) 576.

98 B. Oomen, 'Donor-Driven Justice and its Discontents' 36 *Development and Change* (2005) 897; B. Oomen, 'Rwanda's *Gacaca*' in R. Haveman and O. Olusanya (eds), *Sentencing and Sanctioning in Supranational Criminal Law* (2006) 167.

99 Art 2 of *Organic Law No 31/2007 of 25 July 2007 relating to the abolition of the death penalty*, OGRR no special of 25 July 2007.

100 Amnesty International, *Justice Denied* (1997) 14; for a similarly critical view on the early trials, M. Cousineau, 'L'établissement de l'Etat de droit au Rwanda' 28 *Ottawa LRev* (1997) 190.

101 W.A. Schabas, 'Genocide Trials and *Gacaca* Courts' 3 *JICJ* (2005) 887; W.A. Schabas, 'Post-Genocide Justice in Rwanda' in P. Clark and Z.D. Kaufman (eds), *After Genocide* (2008) 217. See also TPI Kigali, *Affaire Froduald Karamira*, Judgment of 14 February 1997, in *Recueil de jurisprudence I*, 70 *et seq*.

on Human Rights, observed in 1999 that most defendants had counsel.[102] In 2000, he merely found that the trials 'conform[ed] with international standards'.[103]

D. The evolution of the new Gacaca

Despite a remarkable number of trials being held in the specialized chambers,[104] the courts were still faced with a daunting number of prison inmates who had never even been informed of the charges against them. It was obvious that the system implemented by Organic Law No 08/96 would never in a lifetime be able to complete the prosecutions. The quest for solutions therefore continued. During the 'Saturday talks' in 1998, a series of informal meetings of leading figures held at Village Urugwiro, the presidential residence near Kigali, it was proposed that the traditional Gacaca system could be redesigned and adapted to the requirements of criminal proceedings.[105] In October 1998, a commission was created and given the mandate to study whether Gacaca could be adapted to the requirements of criminal trials.[106] The idea of resorting to traditional forms of justice was not entirely new. The comprehensive reintroduction of Gacaca as an organ for settling disputes had already been suggested in a paper presented by the Ministry of Justice in August 1994.[107] In September 1995, Professor Joseph Jyoni wa Karega, Dean of the Faculty of Arts of the National University of Rwanda, had proposed employing Gacaca for the prosecution of perpetrators.[108] The international genocide conference in Kigali in 1995 had regarded Gacaca as a means of dealing with minor offences during the genocide.[109] In 1996, the UN Office of the High Commissioner for Human Rights issued a report written by a group of Rwandan academics that discusses Gacaca's potential in rebuilding the country.[110] However, it remained disputed whether neo-traditional Gacaca courts were an appropriate forum for genocide trials. Even an amnesty appeared possible at the time.[111]

[102] UN Commission on Human Rights, *Report on the Situation of Human Rights in Rwanda* (1999) para 35.

[103] UN Commission on Human Rights, *Report on the Situation of Human Rights in Rwanda* (2000) para 137.

[104] Almost 7,200 trials between 1997 and 2002, see W.A. Schabas, 'Genocide Trials and *Gacaca* Courts' 3 *JICJ* (2005) 888. For a statistical overview of the trials held between 2000 and 2003, see N.A. Jones, *The Courts of Genocide* (2010) 88.

[105] U.A. Karekezi, 'Juridictions gacaca' in E. Ntaganda (ed), *Cahiers du Centre de Gestion des Conflits no 3* (2001) 30; U.A. Karekezi, A. Nshimiyimana and B. Mutamba, 'Localizing Justice' in E. Stover and H.M. Weinstein (eds), *My Neighbor, My Enemy* (2004) 71.

[106] Amnesty International, *Gacaca* (2002) 20; W.A. Schabas, 'Genocide Trials and *Gacaca* Courts' 3 *JICJ* (2005) 891.

[107] C. Ntampaka, 'Le gacaca rwandais, une justice répressive participative' 6 *Actualité du droit international humanitaire* (2001) 213.

[108] Speech reprinted in Annex 3 to OHCHR, *Gacaca: Le droit coutumier au Rwanda: Rapport final de la première phase d'enquête sur le terrain* (1996).

[109] *Recommendations of the Conference Held in Kigali from November 1st to November 5th, 1995*, 23.

[110] OHCHR, *Gacaca: Le droit coutumier au Rwanda: Rapport final de la première phase d'enquête sur le terrain* (1996), and *Rapport final de la deuxième phase d'enquête sur le terrain* (1996).

[111] The most eminent critic of Gacaca as a forum for genocide trials was then-Prosecutor General Gerald Gahima, see L. Waldorf, 'Mass Justice for Mass Atrocities' 79 *TempLRev* (2006) 49 *et seq.*

In January 2001, after lengthy debates, the Transitional National Assembly adopted Organic Law No 40/2000,[112] which provided for the establishment of approximately 11,000 Gacaca tribunals at four administrative levels. The courts consist of a bench of lay judges and a general assembly that represents the population. The new system provides for a double-tracked approach: the Gacaca courts hear the major part of genocide cases, whereas only the top of the command chain remains within the competence of the regular courts. In 2002, a pilot phase was launched, which envisaged 751 courts taking up their work. The experiences gained in these tribunals led to a further simplification of the Gacaca system. In June 2004, the Gacaca Law was replaced by Organic Law No 16/2004.[113] Minimal, essentially editorial, changes were made in 2006.[114] In March 2007 and May 2008 the law was amended again, introducing several changes in the system in order to accelerate the process.[115] Under the new system, a total of over 12,000 Gacaca courts operate on two administrative levels, the cell and the sector. Gacaca courts are competent to prosecute crimes in connection with genocide and crimes against humanity committed between October 1990 and December 1994 (article 1 of the Gacaca Law). Since 2006 the tribunals have been fully operational throughout the whole country.[116]

The introduction of Gacaca courts coincides with and reflects a paradigm shift among the Rwandan political elite. In the years immediately after the genocide, justice and accountability were the paramount goals of the government's policy and an aim in itself, whereas truth and reconciliation were not much of an issue. Paul Kagame, for instance, is reported to have said: 'I don't understand what reconciliation would mean unless some of those responsible were brought to justice'.[117] Towards the end of the 1990s, the attitude among Rwandan officials regarding the importance of reconciliation and truth changed. The prosecutions carried out until that point had not produced satisfying results. They had drained the judiciary's resources and had hardly relieved the overpopulated prisons. In the context

See also U.A. Karekezi, 'Juridictions gacaca' in E. Ntaganda (ed), *Cahiers du Centre de Gestion des Conflits no 3* (2001) 57.

[112] *Organic Law No 40/2000 of 26 January 2001 setting up 'Gacaca Jurisdictions' and organizing prosecutions for offences constituting the crime of genocide or crimes against humanity committed between October 1, 1990 and December 31, 1994*, OGRR no 6 of 15 March 2001. The law was slightly amended shortly afterwards by *Organic Law No 33/2001 of 22 June 2001 modifying and completing Organic Law No 40/2000 of 26 January 2001*, OGRR no 14 of 15 July 2001.

[113] *Organic Law No 16/2004 of 19 June 2004 establishing the organisation, competence and functioning of Gacaca Courts charged with prosecuting and trying the perpetrators of the crime of genocide and other crimes against humanity, committed between October 1, 1990 and December 31, 1994*, OGRR no special of 19 June 2004.

[114] *Organic Law No 28/2006 of 27 June 2006 modifying and complementing Organic Law No 16/2004 of 19 June 2004*, OGRR no special of 12 July 2006.

[115] *Organic Law No 10/2007 of 1 March 2007 modifying and complementing Organic Law No 16/2004 of 19 June 2004*, OGRR no 5 of 1 March 2007 and *Organic Law No 13/2008 of 19 May 2008 modifying and complementing Organic Law No 16/2004 of 19 June 2004*, OGRR no 11 of 1 June 2008. A coordinated version is reprinted in the appendix. This version is referred to as the Gacaca Law. For details, see the appendix.

[116] 'General Opening of the Semi-Traditional Tribunals', *Hirondelle*, 3 January 2007.

[117] Quoted in P.E. Harrell, *Rwanda's Gamble* (2003) 37.

of the debates about the introduction of modernized Gacaca, the issues of truth and reconciliation appeared on the agenda. While reconciliation had been equated with imposed forgiveness and amnesia in the immediate aftermath of the genocide, it now became an objective of national policy.[118]

International reactions to the Gacaca proposals were mixed. Human rights organizations and scholars warned of mob justice, summary convictions, and potentially destabilizing effects.[119] The donors were more pragmatic and saw Gacaca as a solution likely to bring about swift results. In addition, Gacaca's traditional, participatory, and reconciliatory elements had a special appeal.[120] Considerable financial support for Gacaca comes from the Belgian Technical Cooperation, USAID, the Swiss, the Dutch, the British, the Swedish, and the German governments.[121]

The approach of donors and the NGOs in the field was to cooperate with the Rwandan government and to exert influence on the implementation of the Gacaca system so as to make it conform as far as possible with international standards. A number of scholars, in contrast, called for more substantial modifications. They proposed a much stronger focus on Gacaca's restorative roots. Erin Daly, an American scholar, suggested that Gacaca courts be given amnesty powers, and that the conditions for such an amnesty could be determined by each community itself—a model akin to the community reconciliation processes in East Timor.[122] She mentioned a full disclosure of the relevant facts, sincere remorse, efforts to reconcile with the victim or to provide the victim with reparation, or efforts to rebuild the community as possible conditions for amnesty.[123] Another American scholar, Mark A. Drumbl, had found out in a series of interviews conducted in the late 1990s that the vast majority of persons detained for genocide were completely unwilling to accept responsibility. Most detainees were of the opinion that they had fought a war, that their conduct did not represent a deviation from the

[118] H. Rombouts and S. Vandeginste, 'Reparation for Victims in Rwanda' in K. De Feyter et al. (eds), *Out of the Ashes* (2005) 312 *et seq*; UN Commission on Human Rights, *Report on the Situation of Human Rights in Rwanda* (2000) para 180.

[119] Particularly, Amnesty International, *The Troubled Course of Justice* (2000) 31 *et seq*. On that, see also R. Nagy, 'Traditional Justice and Legal Pluralism in Transitional Context' in J.R. Quinn (ed), *Reconciliation(s)* (2009) 97.

[120] B. Oomen, 'Donor-Driven Justice and its Discontents' 36 *Development and Change* (2005) 903. See also S. Buckley-Zistel, 'Frieden entwickeln?' 25 *Sicherheit und Frieden* (2007) 80; T. Longman, 'Justice at the Grassroots?' in N. Roht-Arriaza and J. Mariezcurrena (eds), *Transitional Justice in the Twenty-First Century* (2006) 212; P. Uvin, 'Difficult Choices in the New Post-Conflict Agenda' 22 *Third World Quarterly* (2001) 181 *et seq*.

[121] B. Oomen, ibid; P. Uvin and C. Mironko, 'Western and Local Approaches to Justice in Rwanda' 9 *Global Governance* (2003) 228; L. Waldorf, 'Remnants and Remains' in R.A. Wilson and R.D. Brown (eds), *Humanitarianism and Suffering* (2009) 300 *et seq*.

[122] See P. Burgess, 'A New Approach to Restorative Justice' in N. Roht-Arriaza and J. Mariezcurrena (eds), *Transitional Justice in the Twenty-First Century* (2006) 176; N.J. Kritz, 'Progress and Humility' in M.C. Bassiouni (ed), *Post-Conflict Justice* (2002) 79 *et seq*.

[123] E. Daly, 'Between Punitive and Reconstructive Justice' 34 *NYUJIntlLaw&Pol* (2002) 388 *et seq*. See also E. Daly, 'Transformative Justice' 12 *International Legal Perspective* (2001/2002) 180. See also the works of J. Sarkin, who proposed conditional amnesty modelled upon the South African truth and reconciliation process, especially: 'The Necessity and Challenges of Establishing a Truth and Reconciliation Commission in Rwanda' 21 *HRQ* (1999) 767 *et seq*.

norm, and that they were simply unlucky to end up on the losing side.[124] Against this backdrop, Drumbl argued that criminal trials could generate the dangerous misconception of collective innocence among all those whose participation in or sympathy for the genocide did not surpass the threshold of criminal responsibility: by declaring certain persons individually guilty, criminal trials absolve bystanders of their moral responsibility.[125] He therefore questioned the rejection of collective guilt that underlies enlightened criminal law theory,[126] and propagated traditional sanctions and shaming as more appropriate.[127] Others proposed to limit punitive sanctions to perpetrators of killings or attempted killings.[128]

E. Criminal prosecution before the ICTR

Although the actual number of trials conducted in Arusha has been negligible, they have played a major part in shedding light on the anatomy of the genocide.[129] When taken as a whole, the judgments of the ICTR provide the most comprehensive account of the machinery of genocide. The ICTR was established by the Security Council in November 1994.[130] Rwanda, a member of the Council at the time, initially advocated establishing an international tribunal to bring the leading figures in the genocide to justice. However, there was disagreement between Rwanda and the other Council members over several provisions in the Statute, and the Rwandan ambassador was the only one to vote against the proposal. He argued that the tribunal was ill-equipped, which was, in fact, an accurate prognosis of the

[124] M.A. Drumbl, 'Punishment, Postgenocide' 75 *NYULR* (2000) 1290 *et seq*; M.A. Drumbl, 'Sclerosis' 2 *Punishment & Society* (2000) 289 *et seq*; M.A. Drumbl, *Atrocity, Punishment, and International Law* (2007) 97 *et seq*. See also C. Honeyman et al., 'Establishing Collective Norms' 10 *Peace and Conflict* (2004) 4.

[125] M.A. Drumbl, 'Law and Atrocity' 31 *Ohio NULRev* (2005) 67 *et seq*. See also H. Cobban, 'The Legacies of Collective Violence' 27 *Boston Review* (2002) no 2, who points out the impossibility of individual assignment of responsibility; and the rebuttal by K. Roth and A. Des Forges, 'Justice or Therapy?' 27 *Boston Review* (2002) nos 3–4.

[126] M.A. Drumbl, 'Law and Atrocity' 31 *Ohio NULRev* (2005) 68.

[127] M.A. Drumbl, 'Punishment, Postgenocide' 75 *NYULR* (2000) 1253 *et seq*; M.A. Drumbl, 'The (Al)lure of the Genocide Trial' in D. Barnhizer (ed), *Effective Strategies for Protecting Human Rights* (2001) 226; M.A. Drumbl, *Atrocity, Punishment, and International Law* (2007) 93.

[128] M. Goldstein Bolocan, 'Rwandan Gacaca' *Journal of Dispute Resolution* (2004) 397 *et seq*.

[129] As of June 2011, 46 cases had been completed (including one conviction for false testimony), 29 trials were still underway, two persons were awaiting trial, <http://www.unictr.org>, last visited June 2011. A small number of *génocidaires* were tried in third countries, such as Belgium, Canada, and Switzerland, see U.P. Behrendt, *Die Verfolgung des Völkermordes in Ruanda durch internationale und nationale Gerichte* (2005) 234 *et seq*; U.P. Behrendt, 'The Prosecution of the Rwandan Genocide' in G. Werle (ed), *Justice in Transition* (2006) 233 *et seq*; A. Des Forges and T. Longman, 'Legal Responses to Genocide in Rwanda' in E. Stover and H.M. Weinstein (eds), *My Neighbor, My Enemy* (2004) 57 *et seq*; W.A. Schabas, 'Justice, Democracy, and Impunity in Post-Genocide Rwanda' 7 *CLF* (1996) 555 *et seq*.

[130] UN Security Council Resolution 955 (1994) of 8 November 1994. For details, see M.C. Bassiouni, *Introduction to International Criminal Law* (2003) 431 *et seq*; V. Morris and M.P. Scharf, *The International Criminal Tribunal for Rwanda*, vol 1 (1998); S. Werle, *Principles of International Criminal Law*, 2nd edn (2009) paras 54 *et seq*.

tribunal's initial lack of capacity.[131] He also opposed the tribunal being established outside Rwanda, the exclusion of the death penalty in the Statute[132] (article 23(1)), and criticized the limitation of its jurisdiction *ratione temporis* to acts committed in 1994. On the one hand, the Rwandan government argued that the tribunal should be given jurisdiction over the period since the beginning of the civil war in 1990, which would have allowed prosecution for planning the genocide and for massacres during that period. On the other hand, the government was anxious to prevent prosecution of acts committed by the RPA after the end of the genocide and therefore favoured limiting the tribunal's jurisdiction to acts committed up until July 1994.[133] In the end, the tribunal was set up in the northern Tanzanian city of Arusha and given jurisdiction over acts committed throughout the whole year of 1994. Despite the dispute concerning its Statute, Rwanda pledged to support the tribunal and to cooperate fully.[134]

Yet the relations between the tribunal and the Rwandan government remain tense. The government has always criticized the slow pace of the proceedings. In 1999, these tensions came to a head when the government suspended its cooperation with the tribunal and refused to issue an entry visa for Chief Prosecutor Carla del Ponte. The government was outraged by a decision handed down by the appeals chamber in the *Barayagwiza* case. The chamber had found that the rights of Jean-Bosco Barayagwiza had been severely violated during pre-trial proceedings. It had therefore dismissed the indictment, and had ordered the defendant's release.[135] This decision was reversed shortly after, and Rwanda resumed its cooperation with the tribunal.[136] When del Ponte began investigations into the crimes committed by the RPA during its offensive in 1994, this put a new strain on relations between the government and the tribunal, despite the fact that indictments were never issued in these cases.[137] Since the ICTR is under pressure to complete

[131] See V. Peskin, *International Justice in Rwanda and the Balkans* (2008) 164–5. The original version of the Statute provided for only two trial chambers with three judges in each. In 1998 the Statute was amended, adding a third trial chamber, UN Security Council Resolution 1166 (1998) of 13 May 1998.

[132] *Statute of the International Tribunal for Rwanda* (ICTR Statute), Annex to UN Security Council Resolution 955 (1994) of 8 November 1994, as amended to date, see the tribunal's website, <http://www.unictr.org>, last visited June 2011.

[133] V. Peskin, *International Justice in Rwanda and the Balkans* (2008) 161–2. See also the transcripts of the Security Council meeting, UN Doc S/PV.3453 (1994) 14–16.

[134] M.H. Morris, 'The Trials of Concurrent Jurisdiction' 7 *Duke JComp&IntlL* (1997) 357.

[135] *Barayagwiza v Prosecutor*, ICTR, Appeals Chamber, Decision of 3 November 1999 (ICTR-97–19-AR72).

[136] *Barayagwiza v Prosecutor*, ICTR, Appeals Chamber, Decision of 31 March 2000 (ICTR-97–19-AR72). On the *Barayagwiza* affair see V. Peskin, *International Justice in Rwanda and the Balkans* (2008) 177–84.

[137] It is widely believed that del Ponte was replaced because of her eagerness to bring indictments against RPF personnel, G. Hankel, 'Justice in Transition—The Case of Rwanda' in G. Werle (ed), *Justice in Transition* (2006) 178; V. Peskin, *International Justice in Rwanda and the Balkans* (2008) 221–2. The new prosecutor, however, has also declared his willingness to investigate RPA crimes, see Statement by Justice Hassan B. Jallow, Prosecutor of the ICTR, to the UN Security Council, 15 December 2006, <http://www.unictr.org/tabid/155/Default.aspx?id=1054>; Statement by Justice Hassan B. Jallow, Prosecutor of the ICTR, to the UN Security Council, 10 December 2007, <http://www.unictr.org/tabid/155/Default.aspx?id=980>, both last visited June 2011. For more

its mandate,[138] it is highly unlikely that RPA personnel will still be tried before the ICTR.

Among ordinary Rwandans, the ICTR has never been seen in a very positive light either. Most of them believe that the form of justice that the tribunal represents has nothing to do with them and is simply incapable of helping to solve their problems.[139] Often the ICTR is just associated with scandals, such as the genocide charges against persons on the tribunal's payroll.[140] In fact, it actually appears that most Rwandans are largely unaware of the ICTR's work. Media coverage in Rwanda on proceedings before the ICTR is poor.[141] This has changed to a certain extent with *The Arusha Tapes*, a film produced by the US News Agency Internews in order to raise awareness of the ICTR proceedings. The film has been screened all over the country and has been received with a great deal of interest by the population.[142] As part of its outreach programme, the tribunal has, inter alia, initiated a schools programme to sensitize pupils to the work of the tribunal. It has also opened up information centres all over Rwanda intended to provide lawyers, researchers, and ordinary citizens with books and documents on the genocide and international criminal justice.[143]

details, see ICG, *International Criminal Tribunal for Rwanda* (2001) 8 *et seq*; ICG, *Tribunal Pénal International pour le Rwanda* (2002) 14 *et seq*; ICG, *Tribunal Pénal International pour le Rwanda* (2003) 7 *et seq*.

[138] On the completion strategy for the ad hoc tribunals, see UN Security Council Resolution 1503 (2003) of 28 August 2003 and J.-P. Fomété, 'Countdown to 2010' in E. Decaux, A. Dieng and M. Sow (eds), *From Human Rights to International Criminal Law* (2007) 345 *et seq*.

[139] See A. Akilimali, 'Le TPIR comme un élément du retour à la réconciliation nationale' *Revue juridique du Rwanda* (2006) no 1, 164 *et seq*; J. Strain and E. Keyes, 'Accountability in the Aftermath of Rwanda's Genocide' in J.E. Stromseth (ed), *Accountability for Atrocities* (2003) 109.

[140] See ICG, *Tribunal pénal international pour le Rwanda* (2002) 10 *et seq*; 'UN Tribunal Investigates 12 on Its Payroll', *IRIN*, 29 June 2006.

[141] J.M. Kamatali, 'The Challenge of Linking International Criminal Justice and National Reconciliation' 16 *LJIL* (2003) 120.

[142] E. Harpster, 'Rwanda and the Problem of Peace' 2 *The American Undergraduate Journal of Politics & Government* (2002) no 1, 51. See also A.E. Tiemessen, 'After Arusha' 8 *African Studies Quarterly* (2004) 62, 63.

[143] See ICTR Newsletters of June 2009, July/August 2009, and March 2010, available at <http://www.unictr.org/News/ICTRNewsletter/tabid/66/Default.aspx>, last visited June 2011.

2

The Implementation of Modern Gacaca

When Rwanda decided to entrust community-based tribunals with the prosecution of the genocide, the country embarked on a completely unprecedented experiment in transitional justice. Gacaca courts have their roots in traditional dispute resolution, they are a form of participatory justice, and they are strictly non-professional. While Gacaca's extensive powers to prosecute and convict make it a unique phenomenon so far, it is in line with a general trend, especially in Africa, of an increased reliance on traditional mechanisms when it comes to rebuilding communities that have suffered mass atrocities.[1] The following chapter will analyse the implementation of the Gacaca system and how it operates. To fully understand Gacaca and its place in Rwandan society, we shall first examine its predecessor, the traditional dispute resolution mechanism.

I. Traditional Gacaca

Rwandan politicians have often invoked the Gacaca system's traditional roots in order to justify its implementation.[2] Yet little is known about traditional Gacaca, even among Rwandans, and when the new Gacaca was implemented, many had never heard of it.[3] In fact, *inkiko gacaca*, the Kinyarwanda term for the new Gacaca,[4] shares only some superficial features with its predecessor: both are grassroots institutions located at the very site of the events in question; and both rely on the judgment of laymen and on popular participation. However, the new system's predominantly retributive character deviates fundamentally from the idea upon which traditional Gacaca is based.

[1] On the Ugandan institution of *mato oput*, eg, see T. Allen, 'The International Criminal Court and the Invention of Traditional Justice in Northern Uganda' 107 *Politique Africaine* (2007) 147 *et seq*; T. Murithi, 'African Approaches to Building Peace and Social Solidarity' 6 *African Journal on Conflict Resolution* (2006) no 2, 24 *et seq*; on other forms of traditional mechanisms in the aftermath of violent conflicts, see the contributions in L. Huyse and M. Salter (eds), *Traditional Justice and Reconciliation after Violent Conflict* (2008) and L. Waldorf, 'Mass Justice for Mass Atrocities' 79 *TempLRev* (2006) 16 *et seq*.

[2] See, eg, the speech given by President Paul Kagame at the University of Connecticut, 19 September 2005, <http://www.gov.rw/government/president/speeches/2005/19_09_05_connect.html>, last visited July 2009.

[3] PRI, *Report III* (2002) 9, fn 16; E.H. Thelle, 'The Gacaca Jurisdictions' 13 *Human Rights in Development* (2001) 83 *et seq*.

[4] *Inkiko gacaca* simply means Gacaca courts.

It is presumed that Gacaca has existed since the thirteenth century.[5] With its informal, restorative, and participative character, it demonstrates all the typical features commonly ascribed to traditional African justice systems.[6] Sessions were held spontaneously somewhere on a green patch in the village.[7] Gacaca was not able to rely on any public institutions to generate respect for its decisions. Instead, it derived its authority from its general acceptance as a reconciliatory mechanism, from the traditional rites practised to confirm the settlement of a dispute, and from the social pressure exerted by the community.[8] Gacaca sessions did not follow a pre-determined procedure, nor could a clear distinction be made between the quarrelling parties, witnesses, and the audience.[9] The sessions were convened and presided over by clan elders whenever a dispute in the community arose. A Gacaca process was not only of concern to the individual complainant and respondent, but also to their clans or families. Legal responsibility lay collectively with the entire clan or family.[10] A conflict in the community would, however, not merely involve two groups. Any disruption of the social order was considered to be a concern for the community as a whole. The entire male population therefore actively took part in Gacaca meetings. Women would not participate, unless a woman was involved in the dispute.[11] Although Gacaca usually dealt with matters concerning disputes over land, inheritance rights, damage to property, marital disputes, or disputes concerning contractual obligations,[12] it could also deal with graver offences.

In general, Gacaca focused on a redress of damages, with sanctions being aimed at reintegration and reconciliation.[13] Theft and intentional destruction of property, however, were considered such serious violations of communal solidarity that they would often be punished by death.[14] In cases of murder, the victim's family would seek retribution. An act of vengeance could then be directed against every male member of the perpetrator's family. Even such cases as these, however, could also be

[5] I. Plumat, 'Les juridictions *gacaca*' in *RCN Bulletin no spécial* (2004) 6.

[6] A. Molenaar, *Gacaca* (2005) 13. On the features of traditional African justice systems, see PRI, *Access to Justice in Sub-Saharan Africa* (2000) 22; J. Vanderlinden, *Les systèmes juridiques africains* (1983) 8 *et seq*, 19 *et seq*. For a colourful description of the rituals accompanying traditional dispute settlement among East African tribes, see A. Kitereza, *Mr. Myombekere and His Wife Bugonoka* (2002) 47 *et seq*.

[7] 'Agacaca' is the Kinyarwanda word for 'lawn' or 'grass'.

[8] C. Ntampaka, 'Le retour à la tradition dans le jugement du génocide rwandais' 48 *Bulletin des Séances Académie royale des Sciences d'Outre-mer* (2002) 433 *et seq*; S. Schilling, *Gegen das Vergessen* (2005) 207.

[9] S. Vandeginste, 'Dealing with Genocide' in N. Biggar (ed), *Burying the Past* (2001) 239.

[10] M. Capellà i Roig, 'Jurisdicciones *gacaca*' 56 *Revista Española de Derecho Internacional* (2004) 771; U.A. Karekezi, 'Juridictions gacaca' in E. Ntaganda (ed), *Cahiers du Centre de Gestion des Conflits no 3* (2001) 32; C. Ntampaka, 'Le gacaca' in C. de Lespinay and E. Mworoka (eds), *Construire l'Etat de droit* (2000) 222. See also T.O. Elias, *The Nature of African Customary Law* (1956) 87 *et seq*.

[11] P. Clark, 'Hybridity, Holism, and "Traditional" Justice' 39 *The George Washington International Law Review* (2007) 778; A. Molenaar, *Gacaca* (2005) 12.

[12] OHCHR, *Gacaca: Le droit coutumier au Rwanda: Rapport final de la première phase d'enquête sur le terrain* (1996) 10 *et seq*; J. Sarkin, 'The Tension Between Justice and Reconciliation in Rwanda' 45 *Journal of African Law* (2001) 160.

[13] M. Goldstein Bolocan, 'Rwandan Gacaca' *Journal of Dispute Resolution* (2004) 377; S. Schilling, *Gegen das Vergessen* (2005) 206.

[14] OHCHR, *Gacaca: Le droit coutumier au Rwanda: Rapport final de la première phase d'enquête sur le terrain* (1996) 17 *et seq*.

settled peacefully, for example by marriage. A man from the victim's family would marry a woman from the other family, with the woman giving birth to children as a form of 'compensation' for the deceased.[15] Usually, however, it was the *mwami* or a local chief whose role it was to deal with the perpetrators of serious crimes.[16]

The solutions to a dispute were not necessarily based on customary law or the idea of equity. The principal objective of dispute settlement was not to render justice. Customary legal rules were only a starting point for the discussion. The primary objective was always to restore peaceful relations within the community, which could even justify an unfair result.[17] While the damage caused would certainly have to be compensated to some extent, the wrongdoer also had to be fully reintegrated in the community.[18] In fact, many traditional African societies perceived formal justice according to pre-established rules as working contrary to reconciliation. It was believed that a final judgment would only further exacerbate a conflict rather than settle it.[19]

With the onset of colonialism, traditional Gacaca initially remained largely untouched, and was still being employed extensively up until the 1920s. The German Reich only had a handful of officers in Ruanda-Urundi and did not make any efforts to establish a formal justice system.[20] The territory was subsequently occupied by Belgian troops in 1916 and was officially put under Belgian administration in 1919. The legislation passed by the occupying power in 1917[21] largely respected traditional laws and customs, and left litigation to indigenous jurisdictions, although these were subject to supervision by the Belgian Resident. The traditional jurisdictions, however, were stripped of their competence to hear cases under colonial criminal law. These cases were assigned to newly created tribunals.[22] Under their League of Nations mandate, the Belgian administration

[15] F. Digneffe and J. Fierens (eds), *Justice et gacaca* (2003) 15; C. Ntampaka, 'Le retour à la tradition dans le jugement du génocide rwandais' 48 *Bulletin des Séances Académie royale des Sciences d'Outre-mer* (2002) 426.

[16] C. Ntampaka, 'Le retour à la tradition dans le jugement du génocide rwandais' 48 *Bulletin des Séances Académie royale des Sciences d'Outre-mer* (2002) 425; OHCHR, *Gacaca: Le droit coutumier au Rwanda: Rapport final de la première phase d'enquête sur le terrain* (1996) 10.

[17] C. Ntampaka, 'Le retour à la tradition dans le jugement du génocide rwandais' 48 *Bulletin des Séances Académie royale des Sciences d'Outre-mer* (2002) 426, 434.

[18] See A.N. Allott, 'African Law' in J.D.M Derrett (ed), *An Introduction to Legal Systems* (1968) 144 *et seq*; C. Ntampaka, ibid, 434.

[19] M. Alliot, 'Les résistance traditionnelles au droit moderne dans les Etats d'Afrique francophones et à Madagascar' in J. Poirier (ed), *Etudes de droit africain et de droit malgache* (1965) 245; C. Ntampaka, 'Le gacaca rwandais, une justice répressive participative' 6 *Actualité du droit international humanitaire* (2001) 215; C. Ntampaka, 'Le retour à la tradition dans le jugement du génocide rwandais' 48 *Bulletin des Séances Académie royale des Sciences d'Outre-mer* (2002) 424.

[20] S. Makoroka, 'La justice de droit écrit' in C. de Lespinay and E. Mworoka (eds), *Construire l'Etat de droit* (2000) 97.

[21] *Ordonnance-loi no 2/5 du 6 avril 1917*, Bulletin officiel du Ruanda-Urundi 1924, no 14 suppl., 4 *et seq* and *Ordonnance-loi no 10 du 28 avril 1917* (unpublished). For details, see J. Gakwaya, 'Utilisation erronée de l'institution du Gacaca dans la recherche d'une solution au génocide rwandais' 4 *Revue de Droit Africain* (2000) 226 *et seq*.

[22] *Ordonnance-loi no 45 du 30 août 1924*, Bulletin officiel du Ruanda-Urundi 1924, no 4 suppl., 47 *et seq*; on that, see U.A. Karekezi, 'Juridictions gacaca' in E. Ntaganda (ed), *Cahiers du Centre de Gestion des Conflits no 3* (2001) 32; F. Reyntjens, *Pouvoir et droit au Rwanda* (1985) 35 *et seq*, 149 *et seq*.

went on to strengthen formal tribunals, and established the primacy of written law over custom.[23] Although the measures taken never interfered directly with Gacaca, they did undermine the authority of traditional organs and confined them to rural areas.[24] The new political elite that emerged in the wake of independence had a similar attitude to that of the Belgian administration, believing that such traditional organs were relics of primitive times. The 1962 Constitution renounced the idea of legal dualism and emphasized the importance of a uniform body of written law.[25] Gacaca continued to exist, but in the ever more totalitarian climate, local elders were gradually replaced with representatives of local authorities.[26] In a study carried out in 1986–87, Belgian law professor Filip Reyntjens came to the conclusion that Gacaca was still the most important institution for solving petty conflicts, especially in rural areas.[27]

Since 1994, Gacaca or similar institutions inspired by tradition have been in use for resolving disputes in addition to their use for genocide cases. In the immediate aftermath of the genocide, many communities had to contend with land disputes between residents and repatriates. In 1996, the authorities in the eastern province of Kibungo encouraged the population to revive traditional Gacaca in order to be able to deal with these disputes.[28] In some parishes, a religious Gacaca, *gacaca nkristu*, is practised, which consists of confessing everyday sins to the group.[29] However, the most prominent descendant of traditional Gacaca is the institution of *Abunzi*. The *Abunzi* are community-based mediation committees presided over by lay judges. They were created in 2004 in accordance with article 159 of the 2003 Constitution.[30] Every community has its own mediation committee, which is made up of 12 volunteer mediators called *inyangamugayo* in Kinyarwanda—an

[23] This was enacted by *Ordonnance législative no 348/A.I.M.O du 5 octobre 1943*, Bulletin officiel du Ruanda-Urundi 1943, ann., 626 *et seq.* See J. Gakwaya, 'Utilisation erronée de l'institution du Gacaca dans la recherche d'une solution au génocide rwandais' 4 *Revue de Droit Africain* (2000) 227; F. Reyntjens, *Pouvoir et droit au Rwanda* (1985) 153 *et seq.*

[24] See J. van Houtte, 'Litiges et besoin juridiques au Rwanda' 5 *Revue juridique du Rwanda* (1981) 195.

[25] Art 109 of the *Constitution de la République Rwandaise du 24 novembre 1962*, Journal officiel de la République Rwandaise 1962, 439, reads: 'Une loi organique détermine la procédure selon laquelle les coutumes-lois sont codifiés et mises en harmonie avec les principes fondamentaux de la présente Constitution.' See also J.W. Salacuse, *An Introduction to Law in French-Speaking Africa*, vol 1 (1969) 534.

[26] A. Molenaar, *Gacaca* (2005) 20; C. Ntampaka, 'Le gacaca rwandais, une justice répressive participative' 6 *Actualité du droit international humanitaire* (2001) 216 *et seq.*

[27] See F. Reyntjens, 'Le *gacaca* ou la justice du gazon au Rwanda' 40 *Politique africaine* (1990) 38. Similarly N.A. Jones, *The Courts of Genocide* (2010) 54 *et seq.*

[28] U.A. Karekezi, 'Juridictions gacaca' in E. Ntaganda (ed), *Cahiers du Centre de Gestion des Conflits no 3* (2001) 33.

[29] P. Clark, 'Hybridity, Holism, and "Traditional" Justice' 39 *The George Washington International Law Review* (2007) 785; P. Clark, 'The Rules (and Politics) of Engagement' in P. Clark and Z.D. Kaufman (eds), *After Genocide* (2008) 307; U.A. Karakezi, ibid, 34.

[30] Art 159 was amended by art 17 of Amendment No 2. The *Abunzi* were introduced by *Organic Law No 17/2004 of 20 June 2004 on organization, powers and functioning of the Mediation Committee*, OGRR no special of 8 July 2004; this law has been replaced with *Organic Law No 31/2006 of 14 August 2006 on organisation, jurisdiction, competence and functioning of the Mediation Committee*, OGRR no special of 16 August 2006, which has, in turn, been replaced by *Organic Law No 02/2010/OL of 9 June 2010 on organisation, jurisdiction, competence and functioning of the Mediation Committee*, OGRR no 24*bis* of 14 June 2010.

obvious reference to traditional Gacaca and to *inkiko gacaca*.[31] The *Abunzi* have obligatory jurisdiction over certain civil disputes and minor criminal offences.[32] Decisions made by mediation committees at the cell level are subject to appeal before a committee at the sector level. Only then can a case be brought before a regular court.[33] The *Abunzi* are supposed to reduce the workload of the regular courts by mediating agreements between quarrelling parties. If their decisions are not complied with voluntarily, they can be enforced by way of a court order.[34]

II. The Introduction of *Inkiko Gacaca*

A. Preparation and implementation (1998–2011)

On 26 January 2001, the Transitional National Assembly enacted Organic Law No 40/2000 as the legal basis for the modernized Gacaca system, shortly after the Supreme Court had declared the draft law constitutional.[35] The implementation of the new system was accompanied by various preparatory measures. From 1998 onwards, 'prison Gacacas' had been held in several prisons throughout the country. The detainees were encouraged by the authorities to organize their own Gacaca sessions. A commission composed of prisoners heard confessions from other inmates. These meetings proved very effective in that they provided a platform for the detainees to express themselves more freely. In some prisons, the Gacaca commissions compiled detailed lists in writing of the events that took place during the genocide and the people involved. Given the lack of independence of these commissions, their records certainly have to be read with caution. Yet they do point to the tendency that a great number of the detainees were innocent or had at least not been directly involved in the killings.[36]

The information gathered during the prison Gacacas was used in what are known as the pre-Gacaca meetings, which were organized by the Prosecutor's Office with the support of the NGO Réseau des Citoyens Justice et Démocratie (RCN). These meetings began in 2001 in order to gather information about detainees without a

[31] Arts 2, 4 of Organic Law No 02/2010/OL.

[32] Arts 8–9 of Organic Law No 02/2010/OL.

[33] Arts 26–7 of Organic Law No 02/2010/OL.

[34] Art 24 of Organic Law No 02/2010/OL. On *Abunzi*, see also J. Busingye, *Reality and Challenges of Legal and Judicial Reconstruction in Rwanda* (2006) 21; S. Murerwa, M. Veldman and M. Lankhorst, 'An Insight into *Abunzi* Justice' *RCN Bulletin no 31* (2010) 9 *et seq*. On the similar institution of *ubushingantahe* in Burundi, see C. Deslaurier, 'Le "bushingantahe" peut-il réconcilier le Burundi?' 92 *Politique africaine* (2003) 76 *et seq*; V. Lohse, 'Bashingantahe' 36 *Verfassung und Recht in Übersee* (2003) 590 *et seq*; RCN, *La justice de proximité au Burundi* (2006) 33 *et seq*; S. Schilling, *Gegen das Vergessen* (2005) 209 *et seq*.

[35] Supreme Court, Judgment no 047/11.02/00 of 18 January 2001. At the time of research, neither the Supreme Court nor the Rwandan Parliament had a copy of the judgment in their archives. It appears that no more copies exist. On the judgment, see also S. Vandeginste, 'Réparation pour les victimes de génocide, de crimes contre l'humanité et de crimes de guerre au Rwanda' in S. Marysse and F. Reyntjens (eds), *L'Afrique des Grands Lacs 2000/2001* (2001) 106.

[36] PRI, *Report I* (2002) 29 *et seq*; PRI, *Report VII* (2005) 22. See also U.A. Karekezi, 'Juridictions gacaca' in E. Ntaganda (ed), *Cahiers du Centre de Gestion des Conflits no 3* (2001) 33 *et seq*.

case file or about those who had been declared innocent by prison Gacacas. A pre-Gacaca meeting involved transporting the detainees to the hills, where they were supposed to have committed their crimes. The local population was then assembled and was able to give testimony regarding what the suspects had or had not done.[37] By the end of 2002, 11,659 detainees had passed these pre-Gacacas, and over 23 per cent of them were released from prison pending trial.[38]

In the first half of 2003, pre-Gacaca activities were suspended and only recommenced in June, albeit at a much slower pace.[39] This can be put down to a Presidential Communiqué that ordered the provisional release of a considerable number of the prison population. The beneficiaries were detainees who had already confessed and risked spending more time in prison than their presumed sentence, those who had been minors at the time of their crimes, and those who were old or seriously ill.[40] Despite protests from victim organizations, 25,000 detainees were provisionally set free in January 2003 after the Communiqué was issued.[41] In order to reintegrate them into their communities, the detainees were required to spend two months in solidarity camps (*ingando*) organized by the National Unity and Reconciliation Commission (NURC).[42] Their reintegration went relatively peacefully.[43] In 2004, 2005, and 2007 new waves of releases followed, amounting to another almost 50,000 detainees.[44] Due to convictions of new suspects by Gacaca courts, the number of prison inmates remained high. In 2009, almost 39,000 from a total number of over 60,000 inmates were still in prison for crimes related to the genocide.[45]

The first step to institutionalize Gacaca was taken in early 2000 with the creation of the Department of Gacaca Jurisdictions (or 'Sixth Chamber of the Supreme Court').[46] Under Organic Law No 40/2000 this department was in charge of coordinating and supervising the activities of Gacaca courts (article 50). In 2004 it was

[37] Amnesty International, *Gacaca* (2002) 22; F. Digneffe and J. Fierens (eds), *Justice et gacaca* (2003) 106; LIPRODHOR, *Situation des droits de la personne au Rwanda en 2002* (2003) 57 *et seq*; PRI, *Report I* (2002) 20 *et seq*, 54 *et seq*; PRI, *Report VII* (2005) 13 *et seq*; RCN, *Rapport d'activités 2003* (2004) 16.

[38] PRI, *Report VII* (2005) 14.

[39] RCN, *Rapport d'activités 2003* (2004) 16.

[40] Presidential Communiqué of 1 January 2003, see Annex 2 to PRI, *Report IV* (2003) 20.

[41] Royaume de Belgique and Royaume des Pays-Bas, *Rapport de formulation* (2005) 28.

[42] PRI, *Report VI* (2004) 16; see also C. Mgbako, '*Ingando* Solidarity Camps' 18 *HarvHRJ* (2005) 221.

[43] An exception was the case of three murders in the former Gikongoro province, see PRI, *Report VI* (2004) 49 *et seq*. Throughout 2003, over 6,000 released detainees were re-arrested due to petty crime or new charges against them, see 'Government Re-Arrests 787 Genocide Suspects', *IRIN*, 14 May 2003; 'More Genocide Suspects Rearrested', *IRIN*, 11 June 2003.

[44] 'Rwanda Liberates over 9192 Prisoners', *Hirondelle*, 19 February 2007; ISS, *The Gacaca Process* (2005) 15; '4,500 Prisoners Released', *IRIN*, 23 March 2004; 'Release of Thousands of Prisoners Begins', *IRIN*, 1 August 2005.

[45] 'Over 38,000 in Jail over Genocide', *The New Times*, 23 October 2009; see also LIPRODHOR, *Rapport de monitoring des prisons au Rwanda* (2008) 14.

[46] 'Parliament Approves Gacaca Tribunals', *IRIN*, 16 February 2000. Before the judicial reform in 2004, the Supreme Court was made up of several chambers: the Department of Courts and Tribunals, the Court of Cassation, the Constitutional Court, the Council of State, and the Public Accounts Court, for details, see W.A. Schabas and M. Imbleau, *Introduction to Rwandan Law* (1997) 23.

replaced by the National Service of Gacaca Courts, which is no longer financially and organizationally dependent upon the Supreme Court.[47]

The implementation of Organic Law No 40/2000 started with the election of judges to the Gacaca courts. The procedure was governed by a Presidential Order issued a few months prior to the elections.[48] From 4 to 7 October 2001, Rwandans were called upon to cast their votes for candidates who would occupy the benches of the Gacaca courts in their particular cell. These in turn elected the benches for the sector courts from their own number.[49] The Gacaca judges, or *inyangamugayo* (persons of integrity), have to fulfil certain moral conditions, and may not carry out any political activities or hold any official function. Most importantly, they must not have participated in the genocide.[50] Despite the enormous sacrifices the judges have to make—some of them spending two days a week on Gacaca sessions and their preparation—they do not receive payment.[51]

The ballot to elect the judges was organized by the so-called *nyumbakumi*, leaders of a group of 10 households. They had to propose candidates as well as mobilize the population to take part in the election. Thanks to their commitment, but also due to the pressure exerted by security forces, election turnout amounted to almost 90 per cent. On the election days, the *nyumbakumi* presented the candidates to the population, and everyone had to line up behind the candidates of their choice.[52] Over 254,000 judges were elected according to this procedure for the 11,000 Gacaca courts that were to be set up under Organic Law No 40/2000.[53] Although female candidates were in the majority, a far greater number of men ended up being elected. This can be explained by the higher average level of education among men, an important criterion in the elections. It has also been pointed out that many Rwandans still consider men more appropriate for the task of being a judge.[54] However, after many of those initially elected had to be replaced due

[47] Art 152(3) of the Rwandan Constitution prior to its amendment by art 38 of Amendment No 4; *Law No 08/2004 of 28 April 2004 on the establishment, organization, duties and functioning of the National Service in charge of follow-up, supervision and coordination of the activities of Gacaca Jurisdictions*, OGRR no 9 of 1 May 2004. For details on the National Service of Gacaca Courts, see section X below.

[48] *Presidential Order No 12/01 of 26 June 2001 establishing modalities for organizing elections of members of 'Gacaca Jurisdictions' organs*, OGRR no 14 of 15 July 2001.

[49] See the diagram in Annex 5 to PRI, *Report I* (2002) 62. See also art 13(2) of Organic Law No 16/2004, its version after the amendment by art 2 of Organic Law No 10/2007, and art 13(3) of Organic Law No 40/2000.

[50] Arts 10–11 of Organic Law No 40/2000, arts 14–15 of the Gacaca Law as modified by art 3 of Organic Law No 10/2007 and art 4 of Organic Law No 28/2006.

[51] Judges were initially granted support for their children's school fees; see F. Digneffe and J. Fierens (eds), *Justice et gacaca* (2003) 111. Yet this put too great a strain on the government budget. Today, they merely receive a yearly sum of 5,000 FRw (about 10 US$) which goes towards public health care, see interview with Domitilla Mukantaganzwa, Executive Secretary of the National Service of Gacaca Courts, Kigali, 8 August 2007. On the situation of the judges in general, see African Rights, *Gacaca Justice* (2003) 16 *et seq.*

[52] Art 33 of Presidential Order No 12/01.

[53] '90 Percent of Electorate Vote for Traditional Judges', *IRIN*, 5 October 2001; PRI, *Report I* (2002) 32 *et seq*, 58 *et seq*; PRI, *Report VII* (2005) 15 *et seq.*

[54] PRI, *Report I* (2002) 36; PRI, *Report VII* (2005) 17. For details, see also S. Gasibirege, 'L'élection des juges inyangamugayo' in E. Ntaganda (ed), *Cahiers du Centre de Gestion des Conflits no 6* (2002) 93 *et seq.*

to genocide charges being brought against them, the number of female judges increased, since women had been involved in the crimes to a lesser extent. During the judgment phase, women were well represented among the judges and played a crucial role in the Gacaca process.[55]

In April and May of 2002 the Department of Gacaca Jurisdictions organized six weeks of training for the *inyangamugayo*. 781 instructors, mostly magistrates and law students in their final year who had themselves received training, were placed in charge of teaching groups of 70 to 90 judges, with each group receiving instruction for six days. The judges received special training on how the Gacaca system functions as well as on basic principles of law, group management, and conflict resolution.[56] After the amendments of the Gacaca Law in 2004, 2007, and 2008, the judges were then briefed about the new provisions.[57] In addition, the Department of Gacaca Jurisdictions, in collaboration with the NGO Avocats Sans Frontières (ASF), issued a manual in Kinyarwanda and French explaining in simple terms how to prepare and hold Gacaca sessions and pass judgments.[58]

One of the major points of criticism voiced during the Gacaca preparations was that no steps had been taken to implement the community service programme.[59] Under the Gacaca legislation, perpetrators of less serious crimes and those who give a full confession enjoy certain benefits, including the commutation of up to half of their prison term into community service, which can be served in their home region.[60] The community service programme is aimed at constructing and maintaining roads, schools, housing, hospitals, and public buildings, with various interest group committees and government authorities at different administrative levels proposing and organizing the respective projects.[61] In this way, the Rwandan government hopes to reduce the burden on the overcrowded prisons, to give the suspects an additional incentive to confess, and to reattach severed social ties within the communities.[62] In 2001 the organizational framework for the community service programme was set up by Presidential Order,[63] despite the fact that neither the required infrastructure nor the necessary funds were yet in existence.[64]

[55] B. Ingelaere, 'The Gacaca Courts in Rwanda' in L. Huyse and M. Salter (eds), *Traditional Justice and Reconciliation after Violent Conflict* (2008) 48 *et seq*, 52.

[56] Amnesty International, *Gacaca* (2002) 26. For a detailed account of the difficulties faced by trainers and trainees, see African Rights, *Gacaca Justice* (2003) 7 *et seq*.

[57] Interview with a representative of ASF Rwanda, Kigali, 20 March 2007; 'Gacaca Courts Will Start Trying Rape Cases Next Month', *Hirondelle*, 25 June 2008.

[58] Department of Gacaca Jurisdictions, *Manuel explicatif* (2001).

[59] PRI, *Report VII* (2005) 18.

[60] With the exception of perpetrators of the most serious crimes (category one crimes, see art 51 of Organic Law No 40/2000 and art 51 of the Gacaca Law as modified by art 11 of Organic Law No 10/2007). For the penalties, see arts 69–70 of Organic Law No 40/2000, art 73 of the Gacaca Law as modified by art 14 of Organic Law No 10/2007.

[61] S. Vandeginste, 'Victims of Genocide' in J. Torpey (ed), *Politics and the Past* (2003) 261.

[62] PRI, *Report I* (2002) 13; PRI, *Report VII* (2005) 49.

[63] *Presidential Order No 26/01 of 10 December 2001 relating to the substitution of the penalty of imprisonment for Community Service*, OGRR no 3 of 1 February 2002, replaced by *Presidential Order No 10/01 of 7 March 2005 determining the modalities of implementation of community service as alternative penalty to imprisonment*, OGRR no 6 of 15 March 2005, in turn modified by *Presidential Order No 50/01 of 16 October 2005*, OGRR no 24 of 15 December 2005.

[64] PRI, *Report III* (2002) 4; PRI, *Report VII* (2005) 18.

Another unsolved problem was the issue of compensation. The 1996 legislation on genocide trials had already stipulated the creation of a compensation fund for the victims (Fonds d'indemnisation, FIND), although it had not been specified how it was to function exactly.[65] Under Organic Law No 40/2000 the judgments by Gacaca courts were to allocate damages to the victims, and these damages were to be distributed by the FIND.[66] In 2001, a draft law on the creation of a compensation fund was debated in the National Assembly.[67] To the present day, however, the fund has still not been set up.

Initially the government had planned to launch the Gacaca system throughout the whole country in a comprehensive manner. However, on the recommendation of NGOs and donors, it was decided that the programme should be started on a smaller scale, resulting in only 79 cell courts taking up their work in June 2002. The pilot jurisdictions selected were all characterized by an above average number of confessions given by defendants within the competence of the jurisdictions.[68] Five months later, an additional 672 cell courts came into operation in 106 pilot sectors, with one per district.[69] The first task of the cell courts was to investigate the facts surrounding the genocide. Hence, these jurisdictions acted in the function of the prosecution.

The courts usually held their sessions weekly. During the first stage of the pilot phase, the judges, supported by the local population, gathered all the available information about the crimes committed as well as about both the victims and perpetrators. The second stage involved the jurisdiction drawing up case files for those who had committed crimes in the respective cell, and categorizing them according to the severity of their crimes. This work took much longer than anticipated, as the required quorum of 100 citizens present at the hearing[70] often could not be reached, resulting in the session having to be postponed. The amendment of the Gacaca Law in mid-2004 led to a further delay. It was only in January 2005, after a pilot phase lasting two and a half years, that the system became fully operational throughout the country.[71] At the time, the pilot jurisdictions had already finished the investigatory work and sent the files to the competent sector courts for judgment. Therefore, a number of 336 sector and appeal courts moved on to the judgment phase in March 2005.[72] By mid-2006 all of the sector and appeal courts had entered the judgment phase.[73]

One of the major challenges for the authorities supervising the Gacaca courts is to ensure the population's active participation. It is only by gathering as many eyewitnesses as possible that the courts are able to deal with the caseload in a swift manner. At the same time, Gacaca can only have a reconciliatory effect if the population is extensively involved in the process. Participation in the sessions is

[65] Art 32 of Organic Law No 08/96. [66] Arts 67(9), 90 of Organic Law No 40/2000.
[67] S. Vandeginste, 'Victims of Genocide' in J. Torpey (ed), *Politics and the Past* (2003) 262.
[68] LIPRODHOR, *Situation des droits de la personne au Rwanda en 2002* (2003) 59.
[69] PRI, *Report VII* (2005) 19. [70] Art 18 of the Gacaca Law.
[71] 'Investigations Begin for Gacaca Genocide Trials', *IRIN*, 18 January 2005.
[72] ASF, *Rapport analytique no 1* (2005) 7.
[73] 'General Opening of the Semi-Traditional Tribunals', *Hirondelle*, 3 January 2007.

therefore compulsory.[74] Every Rwandan has a pink card indicating whether he or she has participated in the Gacaca sessions within his or her home cell and sector. During the early stages of the courts' work, people were curious about the nature of the proceedings and turned up in great numbers at the Gacaca sessions. After a few weeks, however, many stayed away from the meetings, making it difficult for the required quorum of 100 people to be met.[75] Often local authorities used force to round up the necessary number of participants or imposed fines on absentees.[76] It goes without saying that this practice is completely at odds with Gacaca's voluntary and reconciliatory character. Nor is there a legal basis to sanction absence from Gacaca courts. An alternative way of convincing the people of the need to participate in the Gacaca project are 'sensitization' campaigns. While such campaigns may have been the only way to keep the Gacaca project running, their use is problematic, given that they may awaken unpleasant memories of similar campaigns in the early 1990s used to mobilize the population to participate in the genocide.[77] In addition, the top down approach of these campaigns reveals a fundamental weakness of the Gacaca system. Unlike their traditional antecedents, Gacaca courts are no longer a true grassroots mechanism administered by the population, but a system imposed on the people against their will or without their consent.

The government has always been anxious to conclude the Gacaca process within a few years. In 2005, it was proposed that the year 2007 be added to the Gacaca Law as a deadline for all Gacaca activities in order to put the courts under pressure to give their judgments more quickly. This led to protests from NGOs working in the field,[78] and the proposed amendment was never passed. The National Service of Gacaca Courts did, however, make repeated use of sensitization campaigns in order to inform the population and the judges of the need to deal with the caseload swiftly. In 2007, the Gacaca Law was modified so as to increase the capacity of the courts.[79] When I observed Gacaca in 2007, no trial lasted longer than three sessions, while most cases were processed within a single day. Nevertheless, completing the caseload still appeared to be a Sisyphean task. In its completion strategy, the National Service had not sufficiently taken the appeal and review cases still pending into account.[80] On top of that, the courts were faced with 12,000 first category cases that had only recently come under the jurisdiction of Gacaca courts. These brought about a range of new challenges, particularly in connection with cases of sexual offences, for which the judges required special training.[81] Finally, the patterns of criminal conduct revealed within the Gacaca proceedings proved so complex that testimonies often resulted in new suspicions.[82] Since 2007, deadlines

[74] Art 29(1) of the Gacaca Law.

[75] ISS, *The Gacaca Process* (2005) 4, 7.

[76] C. Honeyman, *Gacaca Jurisdictions* (2002) 26; PRI, *Report VII* (2005) 40; L. Waldorf, 'Rwanda's Failing Experiment in Restorative Justice' in D. Sullivan and L. Tifft (eds), *Handbook of Restorative Justice* (2006) 429 *et seq*.

[77] C. Honeyman, *Gacaca Jurisdictions* (2002) 26; see also PRI, *Report V* (2003) 49, 52.

[78] Position paper of 17 October 2005 by the NGOs ASF, PRI, RCN, and Danish Centre for Human Rights, on file with the author.

[79] See section B below.

[80] Telephone interview with Professor Sam Rugege, Deputy Chief Justice of the Republic of Rwanda, 19 August 2010.

[81] Ibid.

[82] Amnesty International, *Report 2010* (2010) 274; ASF, *Rapport annuel 2008* (2008) 21.

have been announced and postponed again and again. Currently, December 2011 is envisaged as the official closure date.[83] Once Gacaca has been officially brought to a close, any fresh accusations relating to the genocide must be brought before ordinary courts. Legislation to deal with such cases is being drafted at the moment of writing.[84] It seems that, in the long run, even amnesty for lower-ranking perpetrators is possible.[85]

B. The development of the legislation

The architecture of the Gacaca system was subject to far-reaching reforms in 2004, 2007, and 2008. The original Organic Law No 40/2000, which had been slightly amended by Organic Law No 33/2001, was repealed by Organic Law No 16/2004. This law, as modified by Organic Laws No 28/2006, No 10/2007, and No 13/2008, is the current legal basis for the Gacaca system. The judges were provided with a small book containing Organic Law No 16/2004 that indicates where modifications were made. Apart from that, however, no coordinated version of the law was published, making its use often fairly confusing for research purposes. A coordinated version, which I drew up myself, can be found in the appendix.

The original Organic Law No 40/2000 had adopted two major innovations of the 1996 law governing genocide trials in specialized chambers of ordinary courts: the confession procedure, which provides for considerable reductions in penalties when a confession is made; and the categorization of the suspects according to the severity of their crimes. Both elements have been retained throughout all amendments, albeit with modifications. The categorization under article 51 of Organic Law No 40/2000 essentially corresponds to article 2 of Organic Law No 08/96. Under this provision, the first category comprised those who planned the genocide, perpetrators in leading positions, those who had committed murders in a particularly 'zealous' or 'wicked' manner, and those who had committed sexual crimes. Category two encompassed murder or attempted murder; category three included those who had committed assaults without the intention to kill. The fourth category was reserved for crimes relating to property. This categorization has a dual function: the competent court and the penalty imposed are determined according to the category the defendant was assigned to.

Organic Law No 40/2000 provided for the establishment of Gacaca jurisdictions on four different administrative levels: the highest courts in the eleven provinces and the City of Kigali; 106 courts at the district level; 1,545 at the sector level; and 9,201 at the cell level.[86] The cell jurisdictions are in charge of investigating the facts and categorizing the suspects. They also hear cases pertaining to the fourth category,[87] thus playing the role of a court and of the prosecution at the same time.

[83] 'Official Closure of Gacaca Courts Set for December, Says Justice Minister', *Hirondelle*, 23 May 2011.

[84] 'Final Brief on Gacaca Trials Expected End of September', *Hirondelle*, 17 August 2010; telephone interview with Professor Sam Rugege, Deputy Chief Justice of the Republic of Rwanda, 19 August 2010.

[85] P. Clark, *The Gacaca Courts* (2010) 242, quoting from an interview with President Paul Kagame.

[86] PRI, *Report I* (2002) 10.

[87] Arts 33–34, 39 of Organic Law No 40/2000.

The third category was assigned to the sector courts.[88] The district jurisdictions were competent to try suspects of the second category and hear appeals against judgments of the sector courts.[89] Appeals against district court judgments were to be brought to the province or the City of Kigali jurisdictions.[90] The first category remained within the competence of the ordinary courts. The specialized chambers competent for genocide trials under Organic Law No 08/96 were repealed.[91] First category cases were heard by the Higher Instance Courts by judges without any specialization and were not given priority over other matters.[92] This led to a considerable slowdown in judgments of category one cases.[93] It has therefore been repeatedly suggested that the Gacaca tribunals also be entrusted with category one cases. In 2005, a proposal made by the National Service of Gacaca Courts to create a 'national Gacaca court' competent to hear these cases was withdrawn after protests from several NGOs.[94] A good number of the first category cases were eventually transferred to Gacaca courts following the 2008 amendment of the Gacaca Law.[95]

The first major modification of the structure of the Gacaca system was made in 2004, at a time when many Gacaca courts had not even become operational. The changes were adopted in response to the experiences of the pilot phase, and were part of a package of measures to reform the judiciary.[96] After almost two years of investigatory work, the authorities had enough data to extrapolate the approximate number of trials to be held at the different levels. The extrapolation showed that the 106 district courts would have to deal with nearly two thirds of the defendants, whereas the over 1,500 sector courts were competent for only a fraction of the cases.[97] It was therefore decided to abolish the province and district courts before they had even become operational and entrust the sector courts with the bulk of the cases. The new Organic Law No 16/2004 provided for three stages on two

[88] Art 40 of Organic Law No 40/2000.
[89] Art 41 of Organic Law No 40/2000.
[90] Art 42 of Organic Law No 40/2000.
[91] Art 96(1) of Organic Law No 40/2000.
[92] Art 72(3) of *Organic Law No 07/2004 of 25 April 2004 determining the organisation, functioning and jurisdiction of courts*, OGRR no 14 of 15 July 2004, as modified by art 44 of *Organic Law No 14/2006 of 22 March 2006 modifying and completing the Organic Law No 07/2004 of 25 April 2004*, OGRR no special of 23 March 2006. On the internal organization of the Higher Instance Courts, see arts 8 *et seq* of Organic Law No 07/2004 as modified by arts 9 *et seq* of Organic Law No 14/2006. Organic Law No 07/2004 has recently been replaced by *Organic Law No 51/2008 of 9 September 2008 determining the organisation, functioning and jurisdiction of courts*, OGRR no special of 10 September 2008. The Higher Instance Courts have been replaced with so-called Intermediate Courts that have a similar structure and jurisdiction, see arts 8–9 of Organic Law No 51/2008.
[93] Interview with a representative of ASF Rwanda, Kigali, 20 March 2007.
[94] Position paper of 17 October 2005 by the NGOs ASF, PRI, RCN, and Danish Centre for Human Rights, on file with the author.
[95] See arts 2, 51 of the Gacaca Law as modified by arts 1, 9 of Organic Law No 13/2008.
[96] The reform sought to make the judiciary more effective by reducing the number of judges and courts, providing better pay, requiring better education, and ensuring monitoring. In addition, new laws reorganized the structure and competence of the courts, and integrated common law elements in the legal system. For details, see A.O. Nsengiyumva, 'L'impact de la récente réforme juridique' in *RCN Bulletin no 16* (2006) 11 *et seq*; L. Waldorf, 'A Justice "Trickle-Down"' in E.L. Lutz and C. Reiger (eds), *Prosecuting Heads of State* (2009) 160 *et seq*.
[97] See the Progress Report of 2004 by the National Service of Gacaca Courts, Annex 3 to PRI, *Report VI* (2004) 76.

administrative levels only: the cell and sector courts remained in place as under the old law. In addition, a Gacaca court of appeal was created in each sector.[98] The former categories two and three were merged to a new second category, and all the cases in this category were assigned to the sector courts for judgment. The investigatory work and the cases of the former fourth, now third, category remained within the competence of the cell courts. Finally, the first category was extended to include torturers and those who had 'committed dehumanising acts on the dead body'.[99] These cases remained within the jurisdiction of the ordinary courts.

Another difficulty encountered during the pilot phase was the high dropout rate among judges. Many of them had not been aware what an enormous strain working as a judge would put on them. Others were disappointed that they did not receive any benefits for their commitment.[100] Close to five per cent of the judges in the pilot jurisdictions had to resign due to genocide charges against them.[101] In reaction to these experiences, Organic Law No 16/2004 reduced the number of judges per jurisdiction from 19 to 14.[102] The restructured system required about 70,000 fewer judges, necessitating new elections for the judges.[103] Eventually, Organic Law No 16/2004 repealed all previous legislation governing the prosecution of the *génocidaires*, in particular Organic Law No 08/96.[104]

In late 2005 the administrative entities within the republic were restructured.[105] The Gacaca jurisdictions, however, remained in place according to the boundaries of the old administrative entities. This was clarified in Organic Law No 28/2006, which modified the provisions relating to cells and sectors while making some other minimal changes to the Gacaca Law. In order to further speed up the trials and to relieve the still overcrowded prisons, the law was amended again in March 2007. The most important modification made by Organic Law No 10/2007 was to introduce yet another change with regard to how perpetrators were categorized, which had the effect of expanding the Gacaca courts' jurisdiction. The new law limited category one to those who had planned the genocide, those in leading positions, and those who had committed sexual offences. All other suspects who had formerly been grouped within category one—particularly 'zealous' murderers, torturers, and those who had committed dehumanizing acts on dead bodies—were moved to the second category.[106] This considerably extended the competence of the Gacaca courts at the sector level and reduced the caseload for the ordinary courts.

[98] Arts 3–4 of Organic Law No 16/2004. The structure and competences of the courts at the different levels will be described in more detail in the next section.

[99] Art 51 of Organic Law No 16/2004. This provision was modified again by art 11 of Organic Law No 10/2007 and art 9 of Organic Law No 13/2008.

[100] African Rights, *Gacaca Justice* (2003) 16.

[101] See the Progress Report of 2004 by the National Service of Gacaca Courts, Annex 3 to PRI, *Report VI* (2004) 76; PRI, *Report VII* (2005) 41.

[102] Nine judges and five deputies, arts 8, 13 of Organic Law No 16/2004, modified again by arts 1–2 of Organic Law No 10/2007.

[103] Interviews with a representative of ASF Rwanda, Kigali, 20 March 2007, and a representative of PRI Rwanda, Kigali, 29 March 2007; see also PRI, *Report VI* (2004) 6, fn 9.

[104] Art 105 of Organic Law No 16/2004.

[105] On the administrative reform, see ch 1, section V above.

[106] Art 51 of the Gacaca Law as modified by art 11 of Organic Law No 10/2007.

The reorganization of the categories also required that the provisions governing penalties be adapted. In former category one cases, which, following the reform, now fall under the jurisdiction of the Gacaca courts at the sector level, life sentences can be imposed. Most other penalties were slightly reduced. In the majority of cases a partial suspension of the sentence is standard.[107] In order to deal with the additional cases in a swift manner, a provision was made to allow Gacaca jurisdictions to form additional benches as necessary.[108] At the same time, the number of judges per bench was reduced again, this time from 14 to nine.[109]

A final amendment was made by Organic Law No 13/2008, by which point many Gacaca courts had already completed their trials. Even though the amendment modifies one in four provisions, it brought in only two significant changes, with the bulk of the amendments merely rephrasing modifications already made. Like the 2007 amendment, the 2008 one was intended to tackle the remaining caseload that would otherwise have been tried in ordinary courts. Organic Law No 13/2008 introduced a more detailed description of category one offenders[110] and conferred a good number of these defendants onto the jurisdiction of the Gacaca court at the sector level.[111] The defendants subsequently put under the jurisdiction of Gacaca courts were those suspected of incitement to genocide, the alleged supervisors and ringleaders of the genocide itself, less senior political officials, and perpetrators of sexual offences.[112] These cases were to be heard by approximately 2,000 newly formed Gacaca benches at the sector level and a similar number at the appeals level with around 18,000 new judges.[113] The new benches did not only hear new cases but also took over cases pending before ordinary courts.[114] Gacaca courts of appeal were even competent to resume appeals cases pending before the High Court of the Republic, the Military High Court, and the Supreme Court.[115]

Only the central core of those who planned and organized the genocide, as well as offenders in leading positions at the national and the prefecture[116] level remained with the Intermediate Courts[117] or the Military Tribunal.[118] The ordinary courts

[107] Art 73 of the Gacaca Law as modified by art 14 of Organic Law No 10/2007.

[108] Art 8(2) of the Gacaca Law as modified by art 1 of Organic Law No 10/2007.

[109] Seven persons of integrity and two substitutes, see art 8 of the Gacaca Law as modified by art 1 of Organic Law No 10/2007.

[110] Art 51 of the Gacaca Law as modified by art 9 of Organic Law No 13/2008.

[111] Art 2 of the Gacaca Law as modified by art 1 of Organic Law No 13/2008.

[112] Art 2(2) of the Gacaca Law as modified by art 1 of Organic Law No 13/2008, and art 51, category 1(3), (4), and (5) of the Gacaca Law as modified by art 9 of Organic Law No 13/2008.

[113] Interview with Denis Bikesha, Director of Training, Mobilisation, and Sensitisation, National Service of Gacaca Courts, Kigali, 16 September 2008. The judges were newly elected from all the judges serving in the respective sector, see art 11(1) of *Instructions No 16/2008 of 5 June 2008 issued by the Executive Secretary of the National Service of Gacaca Courts Concerning Persons Accused of Genocide and Other Crimes Against Humanity of the First Category Outside the Competence of the Ordinary and Military Courts and Review of Cases by Gacaca Courts.*

[114] Art 9(1) of Instructions No 16/2008.

[115] Art 9(2) and (3) of Instructions No 16/2008.

[116] The highest regional entity at the time of the genocide.

[117] Also referred to as Higher Instance Courts.

[118] Art 2(2) of the Gacaca Law as modified by art 1 of Organic Law No 13/2008, art 73(3) of Organic Law No 51/2008. Appeals before ordinary courts go to the High Court of the Republic, arts 87, 105(1) of Organic Law No 51/2008. Since 2004, a second appeal to the Supreme Court against

also remained competent to try defendants transferred to Rwanda from other states and from the ICTR in accordance with Rule 11*bis* of the tribunal's Rules of Procedure and Evidence,[119] regardless of the category of the defendant.[120] The competent court of first instance for 11*bis* cases will be the High Court of the Republic.[121] All in all, ordinary and military courts still have approximately 2,000 genocide cases in their jurisdiction,[122] which will require a concerted effort in order to reach judgments in a timely manner.

By expanding the jurisdiction of the Gacaca courts in accordance with the 2008 amendment, the Gacaca Law did away with a general precept governing the allocation of jurisdictions. It had been agreed that the political leadership, those responsible for planning or overseeing the genocide and those suspected of incitement to genocide should be tried by professional judges. As community courts, Gacaca courts were designed to try offences committed within and against the community. In contrast, the crimes of high-level perpetrators—planning or inciting genocide in particular—had repercussions far beyond the place where they were physically committed. In addition, bringing leadership offences to trial entailed legal and evidentiary challenges far too complex to be dealt with by lay judges and also required that defendants received legal representation. It was for this reason that the political leadership, those responsible for planning or overseeing the genocide and those suspected of incitement to genocide had originally been placed within the jurisdiction of ordinary courts.

Cases involving those who had committed sexual offences were also supposed to be tried by the professional judiciary, since they involved specific challenges which Gacaca judges would have lacked the necessary experience to deal with. According to the Gacaca Law, proceedings concerning charges of sexual crimes must be held

an appeals judgment by the High Court of the Republic is admissible in cases of blatant miscarriage of justice, or a sentence of at least 10 years' imprisonment (art 108 of Organic Law No 51/2008, art 43(2)(2)–(6) and (8) of *Organic Law No 01/2004 of 29 January 2004 establishing the organisation, functioning and jurisdiction of the Supreme Court*, OGRR no 3 of 1 February 2004, as modified by art 3 of *Organic Law No 58/2007 of 16 December 2007 modifying and complementing Organic Law No 01/2004 of 29 January 2004*, OGRR no 5 of 1 March 2008). Crimes committed by military personnel are tried by the Military Tribunal and appealed before the Military High Court. A second appeal can be lodged with the Supreme Court (arts 137(2), 138(2), 140 of Organic Law No 51/2008, art 43(2) of Organic Law No 01/2004 as modified by art 3 of Organic Law No 58/2007).

[119] As of 1 October 2009.

[120] Art 2(1) of *Organic Law No 11/2007 of 16 March 2007 concerning transfer of cases to the Republic of Rwanda from the International Criminal Tribunal for Rwanda and from other states*, OGRR no special of 19 March 2007, as modified by art 1 of *Organic Law No 03/2009/OL. of 26 May 2009 modifying and completing the Organic Law No 11/2007 of 16 March 2007*, OGRR no special of 26 May 2009.

[121] Ibid. The jurisdiction is the same for both civilians and military personnel. Appeals can be lodged with the Supreme Court, art 43(1) of Organic Law No 01/2004 as modified by art 3 of Organic Law No 58/2007. The first 11*bis* case was referred to Rwanda in June 2011, *Prosecutor v Uwinkindi*, ICTR, Referral Chamber, Decision of 28 June 2011 (ICTR-2011–75-R11*bis*). An appeal against this decision by the defendant is still pending.

[122] Information provided by Dieter Magsam, consultant on Rwanda for the German Technical Cooperation (GTZ), during a lecture given at the University of the Western Cape, Cape Town, South Africa, on 30 March 2009.

in camera.[123] In such closed trials, the usual mechanisms used in Gacaca courts to facilitate an investigation of the facts are not in place. In addition, taboo and trauma are always a problem in cases of sexual offences. While Gacaca judges were used to dealing with traumatized witnesses, they required extra training in order to be able to deal with victims of rape.[124]

The second important modification made by Organic Law No 13/2008 pertains to the execution of sentences. Defendants whose confessions were accepted by the Gacaca court usually incurred a sentence consisting of both a prison term and community service.[125] Article 21 of Organic Law No 13/2008[126] provided for those deemed to have carried out their community service 'well' to have their remaining prison term converted into community service. This amendment made it standard for those that had been sentenced to both community service and a prison term not to have to return to prison.[127]

III. The Structure of the Gacaca System

The structure of the Gacaca system implemented in 2004 was maintained via the 2006, 2007, and 2008 amendments of the underlying legislation:[128] 9,013 courts are in operation at the administrative level of the cell. During the first two phases of the Gacaca process, the investigation and categorization phases, these courts carried out the function of the prosecution. With the support of the local population, they investigated the crimes, drew up or completed case files, and categorized the suspects.[129] Now their task is to hear cases relating to offences against property.[130] At the sector level, 1,545 Gacaca courts have been set up to hear second category cases at first instance, and, since the amendment of 2008, also first category cases, except for those concerning the most senior offenders.[131] Cases on appeal and review are within the competence of the Gacaca courts of appeal.[132] One appeals court operates in each of the 1,545 sectors. The courts usually hold sessions once a week.[133]

[123] Art 38(3) as modified by art 6 of Organic Law No 13/2008.

[124] Telephone interview with Professor Sam Rugege, Deputy Chief Justice of the Republic of Rwanda, 19 August 2010. On rape cases before Gacaca courts, see also HRW, *Justice Compromised* (2011) 116–18.

[125] See Table 1 in section VIII below.

[126] Modifying art 80 of the Gacaca Law.

[127] Art 80(1) of the Gacaca Law as modified by art 21 of Organic Law No 13/2008. For details, see section VIII A below.

[128] Numbers taken from ASF, *Vade-mecum* (2004) 58, fnn 95–7. For a schematic overview of the structure of Gacaca courts, see C. Kirkby, 'Rwanda's *Gacaca* Courts' 50 *Journal of African Law* (2006) 104.

[129] Arts 33–34, 41(2) of the Gacaca Law. On information gathering and categorization, see section V below.

[130] Art 41(1) of the Gacaca Law.

[131] Art 42(1) of the Gacaca Law as modified by art 7 of Organic Law No 13/2008.

[132] Arts 43(1), 93(3) of the Gacaca Law, the latter as modified by art 24 of Organic Law No 13/2008.

[133] For the cell courts, this is stipulated in art 17(1) of the Gacaca Law. Under art 19(1) of the Gacaca Law, the sector and appeals courts only sit every three months. Yet given the enormous

Each court is made up of a seat (or bench),[134] a coordination committee, and a general assembly.[135] The seat is formed by seven *inyangamugayo* and two substitutes, five of whom must be present for the meeting held by the court to be legitimate. The coordination committee is elected by the judges from their own number and consists of a president, two vice presidents, and two secretaries.[136] The president convenes and chairs the sessions, the secretaries inter alia take the minutes and issue summonses.[137]

The composition of the general assembly differs for each of the respective administrative levels. For the cell jurisdictions it consists of all residents who are 18 years of age or over.[138] In order to complete the tasks allocated to them by the Gacaca Law, the cell courts are heavily dependent on popular participation. Article 18 of the Gacaca Law states that the court 'only meets legitimately if at least one hundred members are present'. During their investigatory work in the first two phases of the Gacaca process, the cell courts often had to rely exclusively on testimonies given by the local population. Participation is equally vital during the judgment phase, when cell courts are competent to hear civil cases concerning damaged or lost property relating to the genocide. The cell courts judge these cases with the support of the local population. If the parties are able to reach an out-of-court agreement, the cell court may then approve it, thus giving it legal effect.[139] Punitive sanctions cannot be imposed.[140] The cell Gacaca courts can therefore be regarded as a contemporary equivalent of the traditional Gacaca, much more so than the Gacaca courts dealing with more serious crimes.[141]

The sector and appeals jurisdictions do not rely on popular participation to the same extent, functioning as they do in a similar way to an ordinary court. Not only do they follow a pre-determined agenda and summon parties and witnesses, they also impose penalties in the same way a regular criminal court does. In the sector courts, the general assembly is intended to provide information on the case at bar rather than to actively help with the proceedings. In accordance with article 7, the assembly is therefore composed of all the Gacaca judges of the respective sector—the cell court judges of the cells within the sector, the sector court judges and the appeals court judges. The general assembly of the sector court must meet a quorum consisting of at least two thirds of all Gacaca judges in the sector in order that the session is legitimate.[142] In many courts, however, this requirement is hard to meet. Often, for example, all the courts within a particular sector hold their meetings the

caseload they have to deal with, they actually end up meeting once a week, some of them even twice a week (interview with a representative of ASF Rwanda, Kigali, 20 March 2007).

134 The term 'seat' is used in Organic Law No 16/2004, while Organic Law No 10/2007 uses the term 'bench'. The French version uses the term 'siège' throughout.

135 Art 5 of the Gacaca Law.

136 Art 11(1) of the Gacaca Law.

137 Arts 11(3), 17(2), 19(2), 82(1) of the Gacaca Law.

138 Art 6(1) of the Gacaca Law.

139 Arts 1(2), 2 of *Instructions No 14/2007 of 30 March 2007 issued by the Executive Secretary of the National Service of Gacaca Courts Concerning Compensation for Property Destroyed During the Genocide and Other Crimes Against Humanity Committed Between 1 October 1990 and 31 December 1994.*

140 Art 75 of the Gacaca Law.

141 See also M. Day, 'Alternative Dispute Resolution and Customary Law' 16 *Georgetown Immigration Law Journal* (2001/02) 249 *et seq.*

142 Art 20 of the Gacaca Law.

same day. The *inyangamugayo* of the cell are therefore unable to attend the sector court's sessions. Thus, in practice, the general assembly of the sector court is often made up of those interested in the case at bar. As the sector and appeals jurisdictions do not rely on the participation of the population to such a great extent, they usually sit without verifying the quorum. At the beginning of the national phase, lack of popular participation was a particular problem.[143] Sensitization schemes played a part in motivating people to attend the sessions in much greater numbers once the national phase had gathered momentum.[144] Yet as the Gacaca process dragged on through 2007 and beyond, their numbers dwindled again.[145]

Mindful of the objective to complete the genocide trials within just a few years, the 2007 amendment to the Gacaca Law enabled the jurisdictions to form additional benches within the same Gacaca court.[146] This was supposed to allow the courts to deal with the cases in their jurisdiction more swiftly. The modalities for this restructuring were laid down in instructions issued by the National Service of Gacaca Courts.[147] According to these instructions, courts were supposed to be organized in such a way that each bench was able to deal with at least 150 files.[148] The additional judges are either elected[149] or recruited from those let off following the reduction in the number of judges per bench. The creation of additional benches has speeded up the judgment process enormously.[150] Over 1,800 benches have been added to the existing 1,545 at the sector level and over 400 at the appeals level.[151] This has also changed the appearance of Gacaca. In many sectors, four or five additional benches have been set up. As there is often not enough space at the site where the Gacaca courts originally sat, they end up occupying the whole surrounding area.

IV. The Jurisdiction of Gacaca Courts and the Applicable Substantive Law

The jurisdiction of Gacaca courts as well as the substantive law applicable in the courts has to be determined according to the provisions of the Gacaca Law. Yet the jurisdiction and the law applied de facto sometimes depart from the provisions of

143 PRI, *Report VII* (2005) 39.

144 ASF, *Rapport analytique no 1* (2005) 8; ASF, *Rapport analytique no 2* (2006) 21; P. Clark, *The Gacaca Courts* (2010) 148; G. Hankel, 'Justice in Transition—The Case of Rwanda' in G. Werle (ed), *Justice in Transition* (2006) 182.

145 PRI, *Final Report* (2010) 17 *et seq*. For a detailed analysis of participation in Gacaca over time, see P. Clark, *The Gacaca Courts* (2010) 147 *et seq*.

146 Art 8(2) of the Gacaca Law as modified by art 1 of Organic Law No 10/2007.

147 *Instructions No 11/2007 of 2 March 2007 issued by the Executive Secretary of the National Service of Gacaca Courts Concerning the Creation and Coordination of Additional Benches in Gacaca Courts.*

148 Art 1(2) of Instructions No 11/2007.

149 Art 2(1) of Instructions No 11/2007.

150 According to statistical information published by the National Service of Gacaca Courts at the end of 2006 and 2007, just over 50,000 trials were completed between 15 July and 31 December 2006. By the end of 2007 nearly one million cases had been judged.

151 PRI, *Report X* (2007) 13.

the law itself. Therefore, the following section will take both the legal provisions as well as the factual conditions into account.

A. Temporal jurisdiction

The jurisdiction *ratione temporis* of Gacaca courts is defined in article 1 of the Gacaca Law as including offences 'committed between October 1, 1990 and December 31, 1994'. By extending its scope of application to the period since 1990, the law encompasses not only preparatory acts but also the massacres committed since the first RPA incursion on 1 October 1990;[152] this is a clear difference to the ICTR, whose jurisdiction is limited to acts committed in 1994.[153] The Gacaca Law does not apply to crimes committed after 1994. This excludes the massacres by Hutu militias acting from bases in the eastern Zairian refugee camps in 1997, for example. More importantly, it also excludes crimes committed by the RPA after 1994 during the campaign to disband the refugee camps and to stabilize the country.[154]

B. Territorial jurisdiction

The Gacaca Law does not say a great deal about the jurisdiction *ratione loci* of Gacaca courts. The context of the Gacaca Law, however, makes clear that its competence is essentially limited to crimes committed in Rwanda.[155] However, the prosecution of crimes outside the territory of Rwanda is possible. Article 44(3) of the Gacaca Law entrusts crimes 'committed beyond the borders of Rwanda' to the jurisdiction of the Gacaca court in the sector or cell where the suspect is resident. This provision covers crimes committed in refugee camps in Zaire in late 1994 in particular.[156] In practice, extraterritorial prosecution is virtually of no importance.[157] It appears that Gacaca judges are unaware of this particular option or eschew the problems associated with the investigation of crimes committed abroad. In any event, extraterritorial jurisdiction is permissible only within the reach of Rwandan criminal law. Under articles 6, 9, and 13 of the Penal Code, Rwandan criminal law applies only to crimes committed on Rwandan territory, by Rwandans, or against the Republic.[158]

[152] eg, the massacre of Kibilira on 11 October 1990 or the Bugesera, and other massacres, see P. Gourevitch, *We Wish To Inform You That Tomorrow We Will Be Killed With Our Families* (1998) 84, 93 *et seq.*

[153] Art 1 of the ICTR Statute.

[154] eg, the killing of thousands of people in the Kibeho refugee camp in April 1995, see G. Prunier, *The Rwanda Crisis* (1997) 362 *et seq.* On the prosecution of RPA crimes, see section C *(4)* below.

[155] eg, the Preamble makes reference to 'the crimes of genocide and the crimes against humanity committed *in Rwanda*' (para 7, italics added).

[156] Interview with Denis Bikesha, Director of Training, Mobilisation, and Sensitisation, National Service of Gacaca Courts, Kigali, 5 October 2007.

[157] I have neither witnessed a case involving crimes committed abroad, nor is any such case mentioned within the several hundred case transcripts made by ASF.

[158] See also W.A. Schabas and M. Imbleau, *Introduction to Rwandan Law* (1997) 49 *et seq.*

The territorial competence of each Gacaca court is determined on the basis of article 44(1) of the Gacaca Law. Under that provision, a crime falls within the jurisdiction of the Gacaca court in the cell or sector where it was committed. Where a suspect is accused of acts in different places, all the courts of the respective cells and sectors in question are competent.[159] During the investigation phase, this simply meant that the inquiry was made by the jurisdiction operating at the scene of the crime. If the defendant committed his or her crimes in several cells of a sector, the results of the investigation in the respective sector are combined in one file and the suspect is tried before the court of this sector. If the suspect committed his or her acts in different sectors, several files are drawn up and a trial then takes place for the same defendant in each sector court. At the end of this process, the sentence finally received by the defendant is the heaviest sentence of those which have been pronounced by the various different jurisdictions.[160] This quite peculiar system of competence is a tribute to Gacaca's reconciliatory and truth-telling function: 'Gacaca is not only justice, but also reconciliation. Therefore, Gacaca has to give the offender the chance to return to his community and to face his victims. It does not intend to separate the criminal from his community. It intends to sanction him and to bring him back and reintegrate him into his community'.[161]

C. Subject matter jurisdiction and applicable substantive law

The jurisdiction *ratione materiae* of Gacaca Courts is delineated in detail in article 1 of the Gacaca Law:

> La présente loi organique porte sur l'organisation, la compétence et le fonctionnement des Juridictions Gacaca chargées des poursuites et du jugement des infractions constitutives du crime de génocide et d'autres crimes contre l'humanité commis entre le 1er octobre 1990 et le 31 décembre 1994, ou des infractions prévues par le code pénal qui, selon les accusations du Ministère Public ou les témoignages à charge aussi bien que les aveux du prévenu, ont été commis dans l'intention de faire le génocide ou d'autres crimes contre l'humanité.[162]

This provision establishes the competence of the Gacaca tribunals. However, it does not allow any conclusion concerning the substantive criminal provisions applicable in the courts. The only such statement can be found in the Preamble to the Gacaca Law: '...prosecutions must be based on the penal code of Rwanda'.[163] In the early 1990s, genocide and crimes against humanity had not yet been incorporated

[159] Art 44(2) of the Gacaca Law.

[160] Interview with Domitilla Mukantaganzwa, Executive Secretary of the National Service of Gacaca Courts, Kigali, 8 August 2007.

[161] Ibid. The translation from French is my own.

[162] The English version of art 1 (see appendix) is phrased ambiguously. Therefore, I translated the following from the French version: 'This Organic Law governs the organization, the competence, and the functioning of Gacaca Jurisdictions, whose task is to undertake the prosecution and trial of perpetrators of the crime of genocide and other crimes against humanity committed between 1 October 1990 and 31 December 1994, or other crimes provided for in the Penal Code, which, according to the allegations of the Public Prosecution, incriminating testimonies, or the defendant's confessions, were carried out with the intention to commit genocide or other crimes against humanity.'

[163] Para 14. The principle of double incrimination, ie incrimination under international as well as domestic law, was also laid down in the former laws on genocide trials: an identical statement

into Rwandan criminal law, even though the country had ratified the Genocide Convention in 1975. In order to avoid retroactive punishment, the drafters of the legislation governing genocide trials therefore decided to rely exclusively on the crimes detailed in the Penal Code. However, the Gacaca courts do not actually impose the penalties provided for in the Penal Code, as the Gacaca Law contains its own penalty provisions.[164] Their application is determined according to the category the defendant was assigned to under article 51. The penalties imposed under the Gacaca Law are usually much more lenient than the ones imposed by the Penal Code. In some cases, however, the contrary is true: a defendant, for instance, who has caused a physical injury to someone without any aggravating circumstances, would be punishable under article 318(1) of the Penal Code and would incur a maximum penalty of one year in prison and a fine. Under articles 51 category 2(6) and 73(3)(1) of the Gacaca Law the sentence for the same crime ranges from five to seven years, subject to suspension or commutation. This amounts to retroactive aggravation of the penalty, which is only permissible under Article 15(2) of the ICCPR if the act qualifies as a crime under customary international law. In any event, it is at odds with the aim of Rwandan legislature to base prosecutions on the national criminal law applicable at the time.

Hence, Gacaca is competent to try genocide and crimes against humanity; however, it can only punish these crimes if they fulfil the preconditions of what constitutes a crime in the Penal Code.[165] This entails a further (factual) limitation to the competence of the courts: genocide and crimes against humanity can only be dealt with by Gacaca if they actually constitute a crime under the Penal Code.[166] Moreover, it must be noted that Gacaca is only competent to investigate these crimes. Whether Gacaca courts will also hear these cases depends on the categorization of the defendant: the most senior perpetrators remain within the competence of the ordinary or military courts.[167]

can be found in the Preamble to Organic Law No 40/2000, para 13. Arts 1 and 39 of Organic Law No 08/96 declared the Penal Code applicable in genocide trials.

164 Arts 72 *et seq*.

165 This is certainly the case for most acts constituting genocide or crimes against humanity. However, it is conceivable that acts punishable as one of these crimes do not amount to an offence under the Rwandan Penal Code, eg, certain acts of persecution; on the customary legal content of this crime, see G. Werle, *Principles of International Criminal Law*, 2nd edn (2009) paras 890 *et seq*.

166 In this respect, the wording of art 1 of Organic Law No 40/2000 was clearer: 'The purpose of this organic law is to organize the putting in trial of persons prosecuted for having, between October 1, 1990 and December 31, 1994, committed acts qualified and punished by the penal code and which constitute: a) either crimes of genocide or crimes against humanity...; b) or offences aimed at in the penal code which, according to the charges by the Public prosecution or the evidences for the prosecution or even what admits the defendant, were committed with the intention of perpetrating genocide or crimes against humanity.' J. Fierens, '*Gacaca* Courts' 3 *JICJ* (2005) 907 *et seq*, in contrast, argues that Organic Law No 16/2004 gave up the principle of double incrimination of crimes under international law and under the Rwandan Penal Code, but fails to take into account that paras 13 and 14 of the Preamble uphold that principle.

167 Art 51, category 1(1) and (2) as modified by art 9 of Organic Law No 13/2008, and art 2(2) of the Gacaca Law as modified by art 1 of Organic Law No 13/2008. Regardless of their category, those transferred to Rwanda from the ICTR and other states will be tried at the first instance by the High Court of the Republic, see art 2(1) of Organic Law No 11/2007 as modified by art 1 of Organic Law No 03/2009/OL.

(1) Genocide and crimes against humanity

The Gacaca Law does not define the terms genocide and crimes against humanity, although the Preamble does mention the Genocide Convention. The term 'genocide' in article 1 of the Gacaca Law can therefore be understood as a reference to the definition of the crime in Article II of the Genocide Convention, which corresponds to the common definition in international law[168] and to the one recently introduced into Rwandan law.[169] It thus appears that even though the Gacaca Law solely refers to 'the crime of genocide', the law is also meant to include the acts punishable under Article III of the Genocide Convention in the jurisdiction of the Gacaca courts.[170] Whether these acts can eventually be punished will depend on the Penal Code. Conspiracy and incitement to genocide[171] are not independently punishable under the Rwandan Penal Code.[172]

What exactly constitutes a crime against humanity under international law is much harder to define. Unlike with genocide, there is no internationally binding treaty to which Rwanda is a party that provides a definition of the term.[173] The core elements of the crime can be deduced from jurisprudence since World War II, as well as from statements of UN organs, and are thus widely acknowledged as customary international law today.[174] Crimes against humanity are commonly defined as crimes against any civilian population committed in the course of a widespread or systematic attack, or of an armed conflict, namely murder, extermination, enslavement, deportation, and persecution on political, racial, or religious grounds.[175]

[168] See, eg, Art 2(2) of the ICTR Statute, Art 6 of the *Rome Statute of the International Criminal Court* of 17 July 1998 (Rome Statute), 2187 UNTS 90, Art 4(2) of the *Statute of the International Tribunal for the Former Yugoslavia* (ICTY Statute), Annex to *Report of the Secretary General pursuant to Paragraph 2 of Security Council Resolution 808 (1993)*, UN Doc S/25704, as amended to date, see the tribunal's website, <http://www.icty.org/sid/135>, last visited June 2011.

[169] Art 2 of *Law No 33*bis*/2003 of 6 June 2003 repressing the crime of genocide, crimes against humanity and war crimes*, OGRR no 21 of 1 November 2003, is virtually identical to Art II of the Genocide Convention. The only difference is that it includes regional groups as protected groups. For a detailed discussion of the term in the Rwandan legal context, see ASF, *Vade-mecum* (2004) 93 *et seq.*

[170] On the similar legal situation under Organic Law No 08/96, see D. De Beer, *Loi rwandaise du 30 août 1996*, 2nd edn (1999) paras 10 *et seq.*

[171] Art III(b) and (c) of the Genocide Convention.

[172] The Genocide Convention also criminalizes preparatory acts at a very early stage, prior to the actual commission of the crime, even including cases in which genocide does not actually end up being committed, see G. Werle, *Principles of International Criminal Law*, 2nd edn (2009) paras 621 *et seq*, 766 *et seq.* Under domestic Rwandan criminal law, however, conspiracy and incitement to commit a crime are not independently punishable. Incitement (art 91(1) and (4) of the Penal Code), eg, is only punishable as a completed offence if the crime is actually committed; on the almost identical provisions of art 66(4) and (5) of the Belgian Penal Code, see F. Tulkens and M. van de Kerchove, *Introduction au droit pénal* (1993) 274; C. Van den Wyngaert, *Strafrecht, Strafprocesrecht & Internationaal Strafrecht* (2006) 338.

[173] At the time of research, Rwanda had not ratified the *Rome Statute of the International Criminal Court.*

[174] On the development of customary international law in this field, see G. Werle, *Principles of International Criminal Law*, 2nd edn (2009) paras 781 *et seq.*

[175] These elements can be found in all international codifications and draft codifications of crimes against humanity. Since *Control Council Law No 10* of 20 December 1945 (Official Gazette of the Control Council for Germany No 3, 31 January 1946, 50 *et seq*, extracts reprinted in G. Werle, *Principles of International Criminal Law*, 2nd edn (2009) 557 *et seq*), imprisonment, rape, and torture have also formed part of this definition in international codifications.

In order to clarify the use of the term in the Gacaca Law, the Preamble makes reference to the Convention on the Non-Applicability of Statutory Limitations to War Crimes and Crimes against Humanity of 26 November 1968.[176] This Convention does not provide a definition of crimes against humanity; Article I(b) merely refers to the definition of the crime in Article 6(c) of the Nuremberg Charter.[177] Other than the latter provision, however, Article I(b) of the Convention includes crimes 'whether committed in time of war or in time of peace'. Thus, the Convention expressly dispenses with the requirement that the crimes must be committed in relation to an armed conflict, as prescribed by Article 6(c) of the Nuremberg Charter.[178] In this respect, Article I(b) of the Convention reflects customary international law.[179] Nevertheless, the definition that can be gleaned from the Convention remains of a fragmentary nature; although the provision dispenses with the requirement of an armed conflict, it fails to define an additional contextual element, such as a widespread or systematic attack, which would serve to distinguish a crime against humanity from an ordinary crime.

It may therefore be argued that crimes against humanity have to be defined on the basis of what was acknowledged as customary international law between 1990 and 1994.[180] This is not always easy to ascertain, as customary law in this field was in constant flux in the run-up to the Rome conference on the creation of the International Criminal Court (ICC) in 1998.[181] Yet, strict adherence to the customary definition acknowledged at the time of the genocide is, in fact, not required here. The reference to crimes against humanity in the Gacaca Law was not made in order to define it as a substantive criminal offence within the Gacaca system.

176 754 UNTS 73, ratified by Décret-loi no 08/75.

177 *Charter of the International Military Tribunal*, Appendix to the *Agreement for the Prosecution and Punishment of the Major War Criminals of the European Axis* of 8 August 1945, 39 *AJIL* (1945), suppl. 257.

178 Art 6(c) literally required that crimes against humanity be committed 'in execution of or in connection with any crime within the jurisdiction of the Tribunal' (ie crimes against peace and war crimes). This element limited the scope of Art 6(c) to crimes committed during World War II, with the unsatisfactory result being that crimes against the Jewish population in the German Reich before the war could not be prosecuted by the tribunal, see International Military Tribunal Nuremberg, Judgment of 1 October 1946, in *The Trial of German Major War Criminals*, Part 22 (1950) 468.

179 Under the international customary rule that emerged after World War II, the nexus requirement was swiftly given up, for more details, see A. Cassese, *International Criminal Law*, 2nd edn (2008) 99; G. Werle, *Principles of International Criminal Law*, 2nd edn (2009) para 783.

180 On the customary content of the crime at the time, see M. Delmas-Marty, 'Le crime contre l'humanité, les droits de l'homme, et l'irréductible humain' *Revue de science criminelle et de droit pénal comparé* (1994) 477 *et seq*, 488. The customary nature of the definitions of crimes against humanity in the 1993 ICTY Statute and in the 1994 ICTR Statute has been confirmed in *Prosecutor v Tadić*, ICTY, Trial Chamber, Judgment of 7 May 1997 (IT-94–1-T) paras 618 *et seq* and *Prosecutor v Akayesu*, ICTR, Appeals Chamber, Judgment of 1 June 2001 (ICTR-96–4-A) paras 464 *et seq*, respectively.

181 Several of the acts enumerated in Art 7 of the Rome Statute appear for the first time as part of a conventional definition of crimes against humanity, namely forms of sexual violence other than rape, enforced disappearance, apartheid, and persecution on national, ethnic, cultural, gender, and other grounds impermissible under international law. On the customary content of Art 7, see A. Cassese, 'Crimes against Humanity' in A. Cassese, P. Gaeta and J.R.W.D. Jones (eds), *The Rome Statute of the International Criminal Court*, vol I (2002) 373 *et seq*; A. Cassese, *International Criminal Law*, 2nd edn (2008) 113, 123 *et seq*.

If it were, the *nullum crimen* principle would certainly require a definition based on the law at the time. Here, crimes against humanity are mentioned only to delineate the courts' subject matter jurisdiction. The substantive criminal offences according to which the courts pass their judgments are instead those of the Rwandan Penal Code. It therefore appears reasonable to understand the term crimes against humanity in the Gacaca Law as conforming to other Rwandan legislation on the subject. In 2003, genocide, crimes against humanity, and war crimes were incorporated into Rwandan criminal law by Law No 33*bis*/2003. Article 5[182] of this Law defines crimes against humanity closely following Article 7 of the Rome Statute. Unlike that provision and in divergence from customary international law, however, article 5 contains the additional requirement that the crime must be committed on grounds of nationality, political opinion, ethnic affiliation, or religion. This requirement is borrowed from Article 3 of the ICTR Statute. Law No 33*bis*/2003 was passed only a few months before Organic Law No 16/2004. It is therefore appropriate to interpret crimes against humanity in a uniform manner and to construe this term in the Gacaca Law as making reference to article 5 of Law No 33*bis*/2003.

(2) Crimes under the Penal Code and special intent

The courts also have jurisdiction over crimes detailed under the Penal Code of Rwanda. Unlike the crime of genocide and crimes against humanity, the provisions of the Penal Code are applied directly in Gacaca courts. In particular, they encompass murder (articles 312 *et seq*), inflicting physical injury (articles 318 *et seq*), rape (articles 360 *et seq*), deprivation of liberty (articles 388 *et seq*), as well as theft and other offences against property (articles 396 *et seq*).[183] Another important type of offence committed extensively during the genocide concerns the illegal possession, carrying, and distribution of arms—crimes which are not contained in the Penal Code. They are punishable under Décret-loi no 12/79 du 7 mai 1979,[184]

[182] The English version of the provision reads: 'The crime against humanity shall mean one of the following acts committed within the context of a widespread or systematic attack directed against the civilian population because of their nationality, political opinions, ethnic or religious origins: 1. murder; 2. extermination; 3. enslavement; 4. deportation or forcible transfer of population; 5. imprisonment or other severe deprivation of physical liberty in violation of fundamental rules of international law; 6. torture; 7. rape, sexual slavery, forced prostitution, forced pregnancy, forced sterilization, or any other form of sexual violence of comparable gravity; 8. persecution against any identifiable group or collectivity on political, racial, national, ethnic, cultural, religious reasons or any other form of discrimination; 9. forced disappearance of persons; 10. the crime of apartheid; 11. other inhumane acts of a similar character intentionally causing great sufferings, or serious injury to body integrity or to mental or physical health.' However, the English, French, and Kinyarwanda versions of that provision do not correspond entirely. In number 5, the French and Kinyarwanda versions refer to law in general, not to international law; neither includes forced pregnancy in number 7; the French version of number 8 does not encompass persecution for national and cultural reasons; the Kinyarwanda version does not refer to racial, national, and cultural reasons. The interpretation of the provision is left entirely to the judge, as Rwandan constitutional law does not determine an authoritative language for the interpretation of laws, see the second sentence of art 5 of the Rwandan Constitution.

[183] For a detailed discussion of the crimes under the Penal Code in the jurisprudence of the specialized chambers under Organic Law No 08/96, see ASF, *Vade-mecum* (2004), 109 *et seq*.

[184] *Journal officiel de la République Rwandaise* 1979, 343.

and therefore fall outside the scope of article 1 of the Gacaca Law. Nevertheless, for the identical legal situation under article 1 of Organic Law No 08/96, some specialized chambers declared themselves competent to try these offences, since they formed part of the general context of genocide and crimes against humanity.[185] This interpretation goes beyond the wording of article 1 of the Gacaca Law. The National Service of Gacaca Courts has repeatedly pointed out that Gacaca courts have no jurisdiction over these crimes.[186]

Article 1 of the Gacaca Law adds another, rather peculiar element to the definition of the offences Gacaca courts are competent for: crimes under the Penal Code only fall within the courts' jurisdiction if they were 'carried out with the intention to commit genocide or crimes against humanity'.[187] This additional subjective element is not a substantive precondition for punishment, but merely of a jurisdictional nature. The presumption of innocence does not apply to it, as is made clear by the phrase 'according to the allegations of the Public Prosecution, incriminating testimonies, or the defendant's confessions'. Nevertheless, a literal understanding of this element would considerably limit the Gacaca Law's scope of application. In any event, it cannot be applied literally to offences against property, such as looting. It is hardly conceivable, for example, that a person would steal some firewood from an abandoned house with the intention of committing genocide or crimes against humanity.[188] Instead, this additional subjective element is only meant to establish a nexus to the events in mid-1994 and to the massacres prior to that. This was clearly the case under article 1 of Organic Law No 08/96, where a mere link to the events surrounding genocide and crimes against humanity[189] was sufficient. It is therefore appropriate to interpret the additional subjective element to mean that the perpetrator is aware of the genocide and the widespread or systematic attacks in the context of which he or she is committing the individual acts in question. This awareness is subject to a rebuttable presumption, as follows from the reference to the allegations of the prosecution, testimonies, and confession.

(3) *The role of article 51 of the Gacaca Law*

Article 51 is a hybrid provision with jurisdictional as well as substantive repercussions. On the one hand, the categorization under article 51 is a precondition for determining who will be tried by Gacaca courts and who by ordinary courts as well as which particular Gacaca courts will be competent. All crimes under article 1 of

[185] TPI Kigali, *Affaire Théogène Rutayisire*, Judgment of 22 February 1999, in *Recueil de jurisprudence II*, 176; see also TPI Byumba, *Affaire François Kanyabugande et consorts*, Judgment of 2 May 1997 in *Recueil de jurisprudence III*, 53; contra TPI Gitarama, *Affaire Jean Baptiste Ntarwanda*, Judgment of 5 April 1999, in *Recueil de jurisprudence IV*, 117. See also ASF, *Vade-mecum* (2004) 135 *et seq*.

[186] Interview with Domitilla Mukantaganzwa, Executive Secretary of the National Service of Gacaca Courts, Kigali, 8 August 2007; interview with a representative of PRI Rwanda, Kigali, 15 October 2007.

[187] Quotations from art 1 of the Gacaca Law are taken from my own translation, see the quote in section IV C above and the note thereto.

[188] See also F. Digneffe and J. Fierens (eds), *Justice et gacaca* (2003) 87.

[189] '[I]nfractions... commises en relation avec les événements entourant le génocide et les crimes contre l'humanité.'

the Gacaca Law are investigated by Gacaca courts. However, the most senior perpetrators[190] are tried by ordinary courts. On the other hand, the penalty imposed depends upon the category assigned to a defendant. As Gacaca judges are not familiar with substantive criminal law and usually do not have a copy of the Penal Code at their disposal, article 51 is de facto applied as if it were a fully-fledged substantive provision, which is not the case. Article 51 does not describe a certain conduct, but rather different types of perpetrators. Moreover, it lacks the specificity required in criminal law. Finally, it does not cover all the crimes within the jurisdiction of the Gacaca courts. This has caused considerable problems: the fragmentary nature and the lack of specificity of article 51 have encouraged judges to try defendants for conduct which is not within the jurisdiction of Gacaca courts, such as illegal possession of arms,[191] or that is not even criminal, such as presence at a roadblock.[192]

(4) Crimes committed by the RPA?

The Gacaca system is construed as an instrument that deals exclusively with genocide and related crimes. It was repeatedly made clear by Rwandan officials that Gacaca shall not be competent to try perpetrators of crimes committed by the RPA troops during their offensive in mid-1994, let alone crimes committed by RPA forces after that. Demands to that effect were quashed by the government as attempts to minimize the genocide or to propagate the idea of a 'double genocide'.[193] Certainly the RPA crimes are a long way from reaching the dimensions of the genocide. Yet it is estimated that they accounted for tens of thousands of casualties and, according to the findings of a UNHCR commission, were carried out in a systematic and preordained manner.[194] Presumably, most of these crimes would be qualified as war crimes, which are not in the jurisdiction of the courts. Yet they would still, in most cases, fall within the competence of Gacaca courts since there is a considerable overlap between war crimes and crimes against humanity in many areas. Besides, most of these crimes could most certainly be punished under the Penal Code. Despite all this, these cases are not heard by Gacaca courts. Victims of these crimes have repeatedly addressed them in Gacaca courts, especially in the pre-trial phase, but have been turned down.[195] The government has

[190] All the perpetrators of the first category prior to the 2008 amendment; after that, only category 1(1) and (2) of art 51 as modified by art 9 of Organic Law No 13/2008 remained within the competence of the ordinary and military courts.

[191] Gacaca Court of the Sector of Butamwa, Butamwa District, *Case of Gasirikare Jean*, 11 May 2005; Gacaca Court of the Sector of Nyarugunga, Kanombe District, *Case of Karera Papias*, 27 May 2005; Gacaca Court of the Sector of Rwamaraba, City of Gitarama, *Case of Nahimana Samuel*, 30 June 2005; Gacaca Court of the Sector of Nyundo, Rubavu District, *Case of Karemera Jean Bosco*, 18 May 2006.

[192] Gacaca Court of the Sector of Rusororo, City of Kabuga, *Case of Rutagwenda Innocent*, 20 and 27 July 2005; Gacaca Court of the Sector of Maranyundo, Bugesera District, *Case of Rutayisire François*, 26 October 2006; see also ASF, *Rapport analytique no 1* (2005) 19 *et seq.*

[193] See R.M. Borland, 'The Gacaca Tribunals and Rwanda after Genocide' 8 *Swords and Ploughshares* (2003); PRI, *Report I* (2002) 48.

[194] Yet the commission never published its report, see N. Eltringham, *Accounting for Horror* (2004) 104 *et seq.* See also ch 1, section III above.

[195] P. Clark, *The Gacaca Courts* (2010) 211; L. Waldorf, 'Mass Justice for Mass Atrocities' 79 *TempLRev* (2006) 77 *et seq.*

admitted that occasional revenge killings occurred and reiterated that these were both prosecuted and punished with the necessary severity by military courts. Yet whatever scale the RPA crimes reached, it appears that RPA personnel largely enjoy impunity. In fact, only very few senior officers were tried. In 1998, an RPA major was sentenced to life imprisonment, but was eventually released on appeal.[196] As a reaction to the looming prosecution of RPA crimes by the ICTR, four officers, a general, a major, and two captains were indicted in 2008 for the revenge killing of 13 Catholic clergy members in the parish of Kabgayi, about 40 kilometres south-west of Kigali.[197] While the two senior officers were acquitted, the two captains each incurred a prison term of three years.[198]

(5) 'Annex' competence: offences against the administration of justice in Gacaca courts

Gacaca courts also have jurisdiction over offences relating to the testimonies given in Gacaca courts, cases of tampering with Gacaca judges or witnesses, and the disclosure of details of *in camera* proceedings. Under article 29(2) of the Gacaca Law, '[a]ny person who omits or refuses to testify on what he or she has seen or on what he or she knows, as well as the one who makes a slanderous denunciation'[199] in a Gacaca session is to be tried by the respective court where the offence took place. These offences can result in a prison sentence of up to six months, and in the case of a repeated offence up to one year. According to article 30(1) of the Gacaca Law, '[a]nyone who exercises pressures, attempts to exercise pressures or threatens the witnesses or the Seat members of the Gacaca Court shall incur a prison sentence from three (3) months to one (1) year. In case of repeat[ed] offence, the defendant risks a prison penalty from six (6) months to two (2) years'. Due to their connection with the cases heard, these offences are also tried by Gacaca courts. Only if a judge is threatened and this threat is put into action is the offence tried by an ordinary court.[200]

Articles 29 and 30 are the only provisions of the Gacaca Law that actually define certain offences which fall within the jurisdiction of the courts; they are the only provisions of the Gacaca Law that contain substantive criminal law. An omission to testify is committed when a person 'knew something on a given matter denounced by others in his or her presence, without expressing his or her own opinion' (article 29(3)). Refusal to testify is distinguished from the above in that the offender has been summoned by a Gacaca court or is already being examined as a witness

[196] For an overview of the prosecutions, also for those of lower ranking RPA staff, see N. Eltringham, *Accounting for Horror* (2004) 108 *et seq*.

[197] 'Trial of Rwandan Army Officers Accused of Murdering Bishops in 1994 Begins', *Hirondelle*, 20 August 2008.

[198] 'Gumisiriza Wins Appeal', *The New Times*, 26 February 2009.

[199] The offence is more appropriately described by the term perjury, which appears in the definition of 'slanderous denunciation' in para 5. See also the comments on the provision in the appendix.

[200] See (the not entirely unambiguous) art 30(2) of the Gacaca Law, second sentence, and interview with Denis Bikesha, Director of Training, Mobilisation, and Sensitisation, National Service of Gacaca Courts, Kigali, 5 October 2007.

(article 29(4)).[201] Perjury (or 'slanderous denunciation') is false testimony given on purpose and under oath (article 29(5)). A person, however, who commits any of these offences with respect to his or her own criminal conduct, cannot be prosecuted under article 29(2). This would go against the principle of *nemo tenetur se ipsum accusare*.[202] In such a case, the matter is governed by the special provisions relating to the confession procedure.[203] However, in practice, judges are often unaware of the defendants' right not to testify against themselves. Swearing in the accused before hearing them is a widespread practice in Gacaca courts,[204] although this may bring defendants into moral conflict when exercising their right not to testify against themselves. Cases of defendants having been convicted for refusing to incriminate themselves have even occurred.[205]

In practice, the application of article 29 in Gacaca courts has caused considerable problems. Perjury often goes unpunished, especially if committed by *rescapés*.[206] Other courts have taken immediate measures against offenders in contravention of the law. According to article 32, offences against the administration of justice must be dealt with in a separate hearing following the same procedure as any other case. A good number of Gacaca jurisdictions, however, followed a somewhat more drastic practice, sentencing offenders in the very same session where the offence was committed, often without giving them the chance to be heard.[207] Prompted by persistent criticism, the National Service of Gacaca Courts issued instructions stipulating that a sentence under article 29 can only be pronounced once a final judgment has been passed in the trial where the offence was committed.[208] Moreover, Gacaca practice has shown that consistent prosecution of the offences detailed in article 29

[201] Art 29(3) and (4) of the Gacaca Law both use the term 'refusing to testify'. Para 3, however, is meant to refer to the omission to testify, see the French version.

[202] The privilege against self-incrimination is not expressly included in the Rwandan Constitution. Yet it is an integral element of the right to a fair trial (art 19(1) of the Rwandan Constitution). It can also be found in Art 14(3)(g) of the ICCPR.

[203] Art 54 *et seq* of the Gacaca Law. For details, see section VI B below.

[204] Gacaca Court of Appeal, Gatenga, Kicukiro District, *Case of Hategekimana Jean and Ntambabazi Pacifique*, 4 and 18 June 2006; Gacaca Court of the Sector of Buhoro, Mudasomwa District, *Case of Semyavu*, 5 October 2005; Gacaca Court of the Sector of Nyarusovu, Nyaruguru District, *Case of Twagirumukiza Alphonse*, 9 June 2006; Gacaca Court of the Sector of Kigoma, Karongi District, *Cases of Munyandanguza Céléstin and Habineza Etienne*, 22 June 2006.

[205] Gacaca Court of the Sector of Rusagara, Rulindo District, *Cases of Musabyimana and Ndamyabahutu Védaste*, 3 and 10 June 2005; see also ASF, *Rapport analytique no 1* (2005) 15.

[206] PRI, *Report XI* (2008) 35. This was especially true in the later phase of Gacaca activities, when Gacaca courts were under increasing pressure to complete prosecutions. During my observations between August and October 2007, I only witnessed one instance of prosecution for perjury (Gacaca Court of the Sector of Gahondo, Nyanza District, 14 August 2007) despite a number of obvious cases.

[207] Gacaca Court of the Sector of Ruhunda, Muhazi District, *Case of Mukamarara*, 18 August 2005; Gacaca Court of the Sector of Rwabutenge, Kicukiro District, *Cases of Ndacyayisenga Emile and Nsanzimana*, 7 September 2006; Gacaca Court of the Sector of Kibeho, Nyaruguru District, *Case of Bicamumpaka*, 28 June 2007; See also ASF, *Rapport analytique no 2* (2006) 25 *et seq*.

[208] Art 4 of *Instructions No 10/2006 of 1 September 2006 issued by the Executive Secretary of the National Service of Gacaca Courts Concerning Arrests in Gacaca Courts*. A French translation can be found in Annex VII to ASF, *Rapport analytique no 2* (2006) 70 *et seq*. The courts' application of art 29 was also denounced by PRI, *Report VIII* (2006) 38, and in the position paper of 17 October 2005 by the NGOs ASF, PRI, RCN, and Danish Centre for Human Rights, on file with the author.

is impossible. If, for instance, a witness is summoned and deliberately fails to appear without due reason, this is considered a refusal to testify.[209] Absenteeism on the part of witnesses, however, is very common, and Gacaca courts simply lack the time and means to investigate all these cases.[210]

The offences of exercising pressure on the court and threatening judges or witnesses as laid down in article 30(2) and (4) cannot be clearly distinguished from one another:

> Is regarded as an act of *exercising pressures on a Court* [italics added], anything aiming at coercing the Seat into doing against its will, translated into actions, words or a behaviour threatening the Seat, and clearly meaning that if the latter fails to comply with, some of its members or the entire Seat may face dangerous consequences…
>
> Is regarded as an act of *threat on the Court or witnesses* [italics added], words and actions threatening the witnesses or the Seat members of a Gacaca Court, aiming at winning acceptance for his own wish at all costs.

Both require conduct threatening judges (paragraphs 2 and 4) or witnesses (paragraph 4) with the aim of coercing them into passing a certain decision or giving a certain testimony. According to paragraphs 3 and 5, attempting to exert pressure on the court or to threaten judges or witnesses is also punishable. Article 30 does not include the offence of bribing judges or witnesses. These cases are instead tried before ordinary courts. Gacaca courts can also order troublemakers to be detained for a period not exceeding 48 hours, even if the conduct in question does not fall within the scope of articles 29 and 30 of the Gacaca Law.[211]

Finally, in 2008, an additional offence was introduced to the jurisdiction of Gacaca courts. Since the 2008 amendment inter alia confers sexual offences to the jurisdiction of Gacaca courts, the legislator deemed it necessary for special protection to be provided for the victims of these offences. In order to ensure the confidentiality of these hearings, proceedings must be held *in camera*.[212] Any judge who reveals details of these proceedings will not only be dismissed, but also prosecuted in a separate hearing by the very same Gacaca court, and can be sentenced to a prison term of one to three years.[213]

(6) General principles of criminal law applicable in Gacaca courts

The Gacaca Law does not state clearly which general principles of criminal law are to be applied by the Gacaca courts. Other than under Organic Law No 08/96,[214]

[209] Art 29(4)(2) of the Gacaca Law.

[210] I attended several cases where witnesses failed to appear on summons, eg, Gacaca Court of Appeal, Kayanza, Nyanza District, *Case of Iyamuremye Martin*, 2 and 9 October 2007. Many witnesses do not appear because they live elsewhere and cannot afford the journey. While they may get some support from victim organizations, there is no official programme to provide witnesses with financial assistance, interview with Denis Bikesha, Director of Training, Mobilisation, and Sensitisation, National Service of Gacaca Courts, Kigali, 5 October 2007.

[211] Art 71(3) of the Gacaca Law.

[212] Art 38(3) of the Gacaca Law as modified by art 6 of Organic Law No 13/2008. Details on *in camera* hearings are laid down in arts 2–8 of Instructions No 16/2008.

[213] Art 16(2), (4), (5) of the Gacaca Law as modified by art 5 of Organic Law No 13/2008.

[214] Art 39.

there is no provision that declares the Penal Code to be generally applicable in Gacaca courts. Only the Preamble contains the statement 'that prosecutions must be based on the penal code'. In any event, there is no reason to believe that the drafters of the Gacaca Law intended to change the conditions prevailing under Organic Law No 08/96 with regard to the applicability of general criminal law. Instead, it would appear that a reference to the Penal Code was deemed obsolete and overly technical for the judges who were to apply the law, given their lack of training.

Yet the Gacaca Law does contain provisions relating to certain issues of general criminal law. It exempts children from prosecution (article 79), provides for lower penalties for minors (article 78), and gives guidelines for sentencing (articles 52, 57, 77, 81).[215] Another provision pertaining to general principles of criminal law can be found in article 53(1), which clarifies the terminology used in article 51. By defining complicity, article 53(1) de facto[216] dispenses with the provisions of the Penal Code in that field.[217] The definition of an accomplice is very broad and includes everyone who 'has, by any means, provided assistance to commit offences'. Apparently, however, the provision is aimed at the same modes of participation as the Penal Code, with one exception. Contrary to articles 91(5) and 257 of the Penal Code, the wording of article 53(1) of the Gacaca Law does not encompass assistance by obstructing criminal prosecution.[218]

Another provision containing general principles can be found in article 53(2) of the Gacaca Law. This article lays down the principle of superior responsibility, a concept developed in international criminal law.[219] Superior responsibility is unknown to Rwandan criminal law, and was first introduced for genocide perpetrators by article 3(2) of Organic Law No 08/96, a provision taken word for word from Article 6(3) of the ICTR Statute. Since then, it has also been included in article 18(2) of Law No 33*bis*/2003 repressing the crime of genocide, crimes against humanity, and war crimes. Its inclusion in the Gacaca Law entails that conduct not necessarily punishable under the Penal Code would be punishable under the Gacaca Law. Nevertheless, this is in line with the *nullum crimen* principle under Rwandan law. *Nullum crimen sine lege* as defined in article 20(1) of the Rwandan Constitution[220] does not prohibit the prosecution of acts punishable under international criminal law, even if they did not form part of Rwandan statutory law at the time of the crime. It appears, however, that superior responsibility has never been applied by ordinary courts.[221]

The question of the general principles of criminal law applicable in Gacaca courts also arises in cases where one person kills another under the threat of being

215 For details, see section VIII D below.

216 Just as with art 51, art 53(1) is not a fully-fledged provision of substantive criminal law. Yet we have seen that art 51 is de facto applied as a substantive provision, see section *(3)* above.

217 Namely art 91 of the Penal Code, which equally defines complicity.

218 This was different under art 3 of Organic Law No 08/96, which expressly included such subsequent assistance. On that, see D. De Beer, *Loi rwandaise du 30 août 1996*, 2nd edn (1999) paras 53 *et seq*.

219 On superior responsibility, see B. Burghardt, *Die Vorgesetztenverantwortlichkeit im völkerrechtlichen Straftatsystem* (2008); G. Werle, *Principles of International Criminal Law*, 2nd edn (2009) paras 497 *et seq*.

220 As amended by art 1 of Amendment No 4.

221 D. De Beer, *Loi rwandaise du 30 août 1996*, 2nd edn (1999) para 55.

killed himself, a situation that frequently occurred during the genocide. Solving these cases is controversial under Rwandan law. Traditionally, Rwanda's legal system is a civil law system where such duress is regarded as a ground for exoneration. The recent influence of lawyers trained in common law through the influx of exiles from Uganda has brought a degree of uncertainty into this issue, though. Under common law systems, duress cannot be used as excuse for killing an innocent person.[222] Rwandan jurisprudence on the issue since 1994 has therefore not been uniform.[223] The Gacaca Law does not contain any provisions relating to such situations. Often the courts refused to deal with the issue at all because they believed that defendants invoked duress systematically to order to absolve themselves of responsibility.[224] In other cases, the defence of duress did entail a mitigation of the sentence[225] or an acquittal.[226]

V. The Pre-Trial Phase: Investigation and Categorization

The competence of the Gacaca courts is not limited to trying those accused of the crimes under their jurisdiction. Gacaca is designed to deal comprehensively with genocide cases. One of its objectives is to reveal the truth about what happened during the genocide.[227] Gacaca courts are therefore also vested with powers that originally lay within the competence of the prosecution before the Gacaca system was put into practice.[228] In the first phase, they were entrusted with the task of gathering information on the crimes committed in their territory, and of putting

[222] The question was highly controversial in the *Erdemović* judgment of the ICTY appeals chamber (*Prosecutor v Erdemović*, Judgment of 7 October 1997 (IT-96–22-A) para 19, and Separate and Dissenting Opinions of Judge Cassese and Judge Stephen, paras 11 *et seq* and paras 23 *et seq*), and during the *travaux préparatoires* for the Rome Statute, see on the issue G. Werle, *Principles of International Criminal Law*, 2nd edn (2009) para 562 with further references.

[223] Some courts have found that a perpetrator under such duress is excused, TPI Gisenyi, *Affaire Félix Niyoniringiye et consorts*, Judgment of 27 October 2000 in *Recueil de jurisprudence V*, 112; others have found it to be only a mitigating circumstance, TPI Byumba, *Affaire François Kanyabugande et consorts*, Judgment of 2 May 1997 in *Recueil de jurisprudence III*, 86, 88; TPI Gitarama, *Affaire François Minani*, Judgment of 23 September 1997 in *Recueil de jurisprudence II*, 91. The matter may be regarded as settled since 2005, when the High Court of the Republic acquitted a defendant on grounds that he had acted under duress (Haute Cour de la République, *Affaire Emmanuel Ahashakiye et consorts*, Judgment of 29 April 2005 in *Recueil de jurisprudence VII*, 139, 154). However, uncertainty is likely to prevail, given that the judgment does not provide any reasoning.

[224] Gacaca Court of Appeal, Karehe A, Ngororero District, *Case of Samvura*, 8 November 2007; Gacaca Court of Appeal, Kanzenze, Rubavu District, *Case of Birihanze*, 6 December 2007; Gacaca Court of the Sector of Mataba, Gakenke District, *Case of Sebagande Joseph alias Hazita*, 3 May 2006.

[225] Gacaca Court of the Sector of Busanza, Kanombe District, *Case of Hagenimana Jean Claude*, 27 July 2005.

[226] Gacaca Court of the Sector of Rubona, City of Kibungo, *Cases of Kanigi Venuste and Daruha Emmanuel*, 14 June 2005; Gacaca Court of the Sector of Gicaca II, Gasabo District, *Case of Karegeya Thomas*, 11 August 2005; see also ASF, *Rapport analytique no 3* (2007) 58 *et seq*.

[227] For the publicly declared objectives of the Gacaca system, see the website of the National Service of Gacaca Courts, <http://www.inkiko-gacaca.gov.rw/En/EnObjectives.htm>, last visited June 2011. See also M. Sosnov, 'The Adjudication of Genocide' 36 *DenvJIntlL&Pol* (2008) 136 *et seq*.

[228] On the transition from ordinary prosecutions to the Gacaca system, see art 47 of Organic Law No 16/2004, arts 47–9 of Organic Law No 40/2000, and ASF, *Vade-mecum* (2004) 148 *et seq*.

together or completing the files on the suspects in their jurisdiction. This was done at the lowest level of the Gacaca system, in the Gacaca courts of the cell. The cell courts then determined the category to which the defendant was to be assigned.[229] This was, however, only a provisional decision. It has been mentioned that the court competent to hear a case is determined based on the category of the suspect. Therefore, a provisional categorization had to be made in the pre-trial phase. The trial court reviews the categorization, and declares itself incompetent if it finds that the defendant was assigned to the wrong category. A final decision about the categorization can, of course, only be taken once the charges against the defendant have been proven. If it turns out after consideration of all evidence that the categorization was incorrect, the case can still be referred to the respective competent jurisdiction. Once the categorization has been confirmed, it serves as a basis for determining the sentence.

A. The pilot phase

In mid-2002, the first pilot cell courts took up their investigatory work. Their activities during the pilot phase were governed by articles 33 and 34 of Organic Law No 40/2000.[230] More detailed guidelines were provided in the training manual for the judges.[231] The inquiry was to be organized into two stages, the first being the reconstruction of the events during the genocide, and the second involving the preparation of individual files and the categorization of the suspects. The third stage would then be formed by the judgment phase.[232] The first stage was to encompass six sessions, which were ideally to be completed within six weeks. During the opening session, the jurisdiction would discuss organizational issues, and the judges would answer questions from the local population. In the following sessions, the judges and the local population put together lists of those people living in the cell before the genocide, those killed in the cell, those who used to live in the cell and who were killed elsewhere, a list of damaged property, and a list of suspects.[233] With the seventh session, the jurisdictions then entered the second stage, in which it would draw up individual case files and categorize the suspects.

The pilot phase revealed some serious flaws in the system and forced the competent authorities to modify their approach. Gacaca depends heavily on popular participation, particularly during the inquiry phase. In theory, the massive presence of the local population enables the events of the genocide to be reconstructed in a swift, efficient, and balanced manner. The initial sessions of the pilot courts were received with a great deal of interest by the local population, who showed up in

[229] Art 34(6) of the Gacaca Law.

[230] The current Organic Law No 16/2004 only came into force after the pilot phase. Although arts 33 and 34 have been rephrased, the provisions of Organic Law No 40/2000 have essentially been maintained. The following section quotes the provisions of Organic Law No 40/2000, as they were the ones applied at the time.

[231] Department of Gacaca Jurisdictions, *Manuel explicatif* (2001) 33 *et seq*.

[232] Ibid, 33.

[233] Department of Gacaca Jurisdictions, *Les juridictions Gacaca comme solution alternative* (2003) 2; see also art 34(a) of Organic Law No 40/2000.

large numbers.[234] Yet people soon realized that testifying carried the risk of being threatened or accused themselves. Survivors and even perpetrators experienced feelings of trauma when recalling the events. Quick help was often not available in these cases. Others were discouraged when they discovered how much preparation the trials would need and that speedy results could not be expected. Sessions often had to be postponed when the quorum of 100 persons present in court was not reached. All this considerably delayed the work of the pilot courts and impaired the quality of its results.

B. The national phase

The National Service of Gacaca Courts therefore decided to no longer leave the information gathering process to the population alone, but rather to involve local authorities to a greater extent. Local authorities had already supported Gacaca judges previously by drawing up preliminary lists at the level of the *Nyumbakumi*.[235] In November 2004, the National Service published a manual on information gathering that required a much more substantial commitment from local authorities.[236] The process of data collection detailed in this manual differed substantially from the law, which does not foresee any role for administrative organs beyond organizational issues and sensitization.[237] According to the manual, the Gacaca courts would only play a secondary role in the process of information gathering, while the bulk of the work was entrusted to the *nyumbakumi*. The law required the courts to draw up eight lists which essentially were to contain only information on victims and perpetrators,[238] while the manual intended a much more extensive record of the genocide to be compiled.[239] At the first stage, the *nyumbakumi*, sometimes assisted by cell-level authorities, were supposed to complete these lists with the cooperation of the local population.[240] As set out by the manual, they usually rounded up all residents of their *Nyumbakumi*, and gathered all the necessary data in collaboration with them. Others chose to go from house to house and speak to the people separately.[241] The records were then passed on to the *inyangamugayo* of the cell court, who analysed the information. The second stage of the

234 PRI, *Report VII* (2005) 39.

235 C. Honeyman, *Gacaca Jurisdictions* (2002) 13. Before the administrative reform and the *imidugudu* programme (see ch 1, section V above), the *Nyumbakumi* was the lowest administrative entity, a group of 10 households. They are not mentioned anywhere in the law, but were de facto the last link in the chain of local authorities, PRI, *Report VIII* (2006) 4, fn 15. The number of *Nyumbakumi* in the country was estimated to be higher than 100,000, see ibid, 6, fn 22. Written with capital N, the term refers to the administrative entity, while *nyumbakumi* with lower case n refers to its leader.

236 National Service of Gacaca Courts, *Programme de la collecte d'informations* (2004) (translation from Kinyarwanda by PRI). See also National Service of Gacaca Courts, *Report on Data Collection* (2006).

237 See art 49 of the Gacaca Law.

238 Art 34(a) of Organic Law No 40/2000.

239 The manual mentions 26 lists supposed to provide detailed information on both the planning (eg, a list on planning meetings, on distribution of arms, and on roadblocks) and the implementation of the genocide (eg, lists of victims, perpetrators, damaged goods, a list on the whereabouts of dead bodies), National Service of Gacaca Courts, *Programme de la collecte d'informations* (2004) 6 *et seq*.

240 Ibid, 8 *et seq*. See also ASF, *Rapport analytique no 3* (2007) 46; G. Gahima, 'Alternatives to Prosecution' in E. Hughes, W.A. Schabas and R. Thakur (eds), *Atrocities and International Accountability* (2007) 164.

241 PRI, *Report VIII* (2006) 8.

process involved the cell courts convening their general assemblies and discussing the records with them in order to validate the information.

The practice of partially relieving the courts of their investigatory work and assigning this task to administrative authorities had one undeniable advantage: it considerably speeded up the process of information gathering. Data collection carried out using the conventional procedure during the pilot phase had taken more than two years, which had led people to believe that Gacaca was just another approach incapable of providing any sort of solution. Their motivation to support the process was thus at risk. Under the direction of the *nyumbakumi*, and thanks to the intensified commitment of all participants,[242] the pre-trial phase was concluded within one year.[243]

Yet the 'administratization' of the investigations also produced a number of problems. The *nyumbakumi* had merely been briefed on their new task by cell and sector authorities, and had never received any training.[244] In addition, the new strategy dispensed with one of the key features of the Gacaca system, the participatory nature of fact-finding. Although the *nyumbakumi* were still supposed to gather the residents of the households under their jurisdiction, at the *Nyumbakumi* level, this group would be much smaller and more intimate than at the cell level. In addition, some *nyumbakumi* carried out their duties in a different way, going from house to house in order to collect information. While the more private atmosphere of these meetings made it easier for many to speak out openly, it also prevented a public discussion about these statements from taking place and increased the risk of false testimonies.[245] During the validation stage before the Gacaca court of the cell, where a public discussion was supposed to take place subsequently, the information gathered by the *nyumbakumi* was often merely brought together without actually even being disputed. In most courts observed by the NGO Penal Reform International (PRI), judges refused to discuss whether the information gathered was correct, stating that this was to be verified during the judgment phase.[246] This resulted in records that merely listed alleged perpetrators and their crimes. The forms designed by the National Service did not provide any space for collecting defence testimonies.[247] PRI reports that, in most cases, the *nyumbakumi* did not note down the names of defence witnesses, or failed to collect any such testimonies at all.[248] The investigatory work of the Gacaca courts was terminated in early 2006. Nevertheless, in some places it was necessary to resume investigations and to reconvene the general assemblies at the cell level. This was particularly necessary in

[242] See PRI, *Report VIII* (2006) 20.

[243] Investigations on a national level started in early 2005 and were finished in early 2006, see ASF, *Rapport analytique no 2* (2006) 7; LIPRODHOR, *Situation des droits de la personne en 2005* (2006) 90; PRI, *Report VIII* (2006) 20.

[244] PRI, ibid, 7 *et seq.*

[245] See ibid, 27.

[246] Ibid, 21.

[247] Ibid, 31. Samples of these forms are reprinted in Appendices 2 to 4 of PRI's report.

[248] Interview with a representative of PRI Rwanda, Kigali, 15 October 2007. See also PRI, *Report X* (2007) 56. The National Service of Gacaca Courts contests this assertion, see Observations du Service National des Juridictions Gacaca au rapport du Penal Reform International sur les infractions contre les biens, Annex to the French version of PRI, *Report X* (2007) 103.

regions with very few *rescapés* where the public had proven more reluctant to reveal what had happened.[249]

C. Categorization

Once the information gathering process was complete, the cell courts proceeded to draw up individual case files. These contained a form giving detailed information on each suspect, listing the charges against him or her, and specifying the category he or she was assigned to according to article 51 of the Gacaca Law ('fiche de l'accusé').[250] The categorization was made on the basis of the information gathered during the pre-trial phase. As explained above, the categorization made at this stage was only a provisional decision taken in order to determine which court was competent for the case, with a final decision being taken by the trial court once the charges had been verified. If necessary, other information was also included in the files.[251] The other lists not included in files were retained at the cell level and remained accessible for further investigation.[252] After categorization, the files were passed on to the competent jurisdiction, or, for defendants of the third category, remained with the Gacaca court of the cell.

VI. The Trial Phase

A. Gacaca courts in operation

Gacaca was ubiquitous in Rwanda between 2002 and 2008. Travelling through the country, Gacaca courts were to be found along the entire route. Gacaca used to play a major role in the lives of most Rwandans. Many attended the sessions at least once a week. Radio stations and newspapers reported on Gacaca every day. It was not uncommon to find all the shops in a particular area closed and the streets deserted because everyone had gone to the Gacaca session. In the District of Nyanza, where I visited several Gacaca courts, it was hard even to find a place to buy drinking water on Tuesdays, the day on which Gacaca trials were held there. At around four pm, however, shops opened up again and bars filled up with people coming from the sessions.

[249] Interview with Domitilla Mukantaganzwa, Executive Secretary of the National Service of Gacaca Courts, Kigali, 8 August 2007.

[250] For a sample of this form, see the Annex of PRI's translation of National Service of Gacaca Courts, *Programme de la collecte d'informations* (2004).

[251] Art 2 of *Instructions No 03/2004 of 1 December 2004 issued by the Executive Secretary of the National Service of Gacaca Courts Concerning the Pilot Gacaca Jurisdictions of the Cell*; see also National Service of Gacaca Courts, *Programme de la collecte d'informations* (2004) 14.

[252] Interview with Denis Bikesha, Director of Training, Mobilisation, and Sensitisation, National Service of Gacaca Courts, Kigali, 5 October 2007.

Gacaca sessions usually took place on the premises of the local authorities, usually the sector office.[253] In urban areas, the courts were fairly well equipped, with comfortable benches for the judges and the audience. Sessions often took place inside buildings or at least under a rain shelter. In terms of appearances at least, Gacaca sessions held in the countryside had much more in common with their traditional antecedents. Here, people used to gather somewhere on a slope of a hill around a few trees to provide some shade. There was a bench for the judges, while the audience and the defendants would sit on the ground. The judges' outfits had blue, yellow, and green sashes, while the defendants' were pink or orange; these groups were then surrounded by hundreds of people sitting among banana plantations and eucalyptus trees—a very colourful spectacle, all in all. Although armed Local Defence Force[254] officers and prison guards were usually around to guarantee security, they would always stay discreetly in the background. Their mere presence was enough to preserve the peaceful nature of the scene. I never heard of any incidents of violence during Gacaca sessions.

At the beginning of each session, the president of the court would usually give a short introduction, reminding the audience of the eight rules to be observed when speaking before the court,[255] with the assembly then observing a minute's silence in memory of those killed in the genocide. Usually, between one and 10 defendants were present for their trial, depending on the nature of their crimes and the complexity of their cases. A case could be judged within one day, but it could also take several weeks. After the opening rituals, the court would call the defendants, victims, and witnesses to the bar to present their summonses and establish their identities. The president would then inform the defendants of the charges against them, and ask for their defence. Sometimes a previous confession would be read out, or the defendant would reiterate it himself. After that, the judges would go on to hear the victims and examine the witnesses. Sometimes, the defendant was asked to comment on testimonies, or would take the floor himself. After the examinations, the audience was called upon to give further information or their view on the case.[256] Depending on the authority and skills of the judges, these discussions could either yield valuable information or drift off into pointless discussions about side issues. Sometimes the discussion could get heated, and judges had a hard time calming everybody down. Yet, however charged the atmosphere was, it was interesting to observe that this animosity only lasted as long as the session itself did. Sometimes defendants, witnesses, and even victims would greet each other after the hearing. During the session, all statements made were taken down in the minutes by the secretary of the Gacaca court. When the judges had gathered all information

[253] The Gacaca Law obliges the local administration to provide the courts with premises where they can hold their sessions, see art 49.

[254] The LDF is an informal force set up to guarantee security within communities, see B. Baker, '"He Must Buy What He Stole and Then We Forgive"' *Acta Juridica* (2007) 177.

[255] These are rules to guarantee a constructive discourse, eg, that the discussion is moderated by the president of the court; that a speaker may not be interrupted; or that offensive or threatening statements are not allowed, and all statements must relate to the case at hand. For details, see Department of Gacaca Jurisdictions, *Manuel explicatif* (2001) 26; see also art 71 of the Gacaca Law.

[256] See art 64 of the Gacaca Law.

deemed necessary, they would proceed to another defendant, adjourn, or retire to deliberate. The judgment, along with the reasons for it, would be pronounced later that day or at the beginning of the next session.

B. The confession procedure

What is known as the procedure of confessions, guilt plea, repentance, and apologies is one of the principal tools used to establish a workable system of criminal prosecution in the aftermath of the genocide. Suspects are offered a considerable reduction in their sentence if they

1 give a detailed description of the confessed offence, how he or she carried it out and where, when he or she committed it, witnesses to the facts, persons victimized and where he or she threw their dead bodies and damage caused;
2 reveal the co-authors, accomplices and any other information useful to the exercise of the public action;
3 apologise for the offences that he or she has committed.[257]

Persons who confess usually enjoy a reduction of their sentence by two to eight years. In addition, they serve only part of the sentence in prison, while part is served as community service and up to one third is suspended.[258] The confession procedure is supposed to help obtain information otherwise hard to establish due to a lack of survivors or witnesses. By reducing the penalties for those willing to confess, the authorities also hoped to relieve the burden on the prisons at the same time. The confession procedure can also be seen as a tribute to those who called for a truth commission following the South African model. However, it has also brought about a number of unforeseen problems.

The confession procedure was first introduced by Organic Law No 08/96. Under article 4(1) of this law, confessions were to be given within 18 months after the law came into force. Yet initially, rumours circulated in prisons that the confession procedure was just a trick by the new regime and that all confessors would be swiftly executed. The number of confessions therefore remained low during the first two years, and the confession deadline had to be postponed.[259] Due to massive sensitization efforts in prisons by representatives of the Ministry of Justice (Minijust) and the Public Prosecution, most detainees subsequently became familiar with the benefits of the procedure. When Gacaca got underway in 2001, 15,000 suspects had given confessions.[260] In fact, collecting these confessions in compliance with the formal requirements of the 1996 law became a major logistical challenge for the officers in charge. The 2001 Gacaca legislation therefore included the confession procedure in a much less formalized manner. Despite this, however, explaining to the detainees the requirements according to which a confession would be accepted

[257] Art 54(3) of the Gacaca Law.
[258] For details, see Table 1 in section VIII below.
[259] See PRI, *Report IX* (2007) 28; S. Vandeginste, 'L'approche "vérité et réconciliation" du génocide et des crimes contre l'humanité au Rwanda' in F. Reyntjens and S. Marysse (eds), *L'Afrique des Grands Lacs 1997/1998* (1998) 100 *et seq*. See also G. Packer, 'Justice on a Hill' 49 *Dissent* (2002) no 2, 61.
[260] HRW, *World Report 2002* (2002) 78.

and registering every single account before the deadline remained a daunting task for the authorities. Under article 58(1) of Organic Law No 40/2000, confessions could only be given until March 2003, a date later postponed to 2004. With material and logistic support, particularly on the part of several NGOs,[261] more than 50,000 confessions were collected in prisons from the introduction of the Gacaca system in early 2001 until late 2003.[262] An additional motivation for detainees to admit to their crimes was the Presidential Communiqué of 1 January 2003 that ordered the provisional release of over 20,000 detainees, especially those who had confessed.[263] In 2004, the deadline for confessions was abolished altogether. Confessions continue to be given during trials before the sector courts.

Under the Gacaca Law, confessions can be made before a Judicial Police Officer, the Public Prosecution, the competent Gacaca court of the cell in the pre-trial phase, or the Gacaca court of the sector in the judgment phase.[264] Under Organic Laws No 40/2000 and No 16/2004, the defendant could wait until the appeal hearing to give his or her confession.[265] Since the amendment by Organic Law No 10/2007, the defendant has to confess before the first instance judgment. A confession on appeal has no mitigating effect on the penalty.[266] Confessions are supposed to be given publicly and can be made orally or in writing.[267]

The defendant only benefits from the confession if it conforms to the requirements of article 54 of the Gacaca Law. The major precondition for acceptance is, of course, that a comprehensive account of the crimes committed is given. The decision as to whether a confession conforms to the requirements is taken at different stages. If the confession was made before the Public Prosecution, the prosecutor attaches a note providing a preliminary assessment as to whether the confession meets the requirements.[268] However, the final decision is then made by the Gacaca court of the cell.[269] The sector court in charge of the judgment cannot review this decision. This means that an important part of the judgment on the merits is already anticipated in the pre-trial phase. However, if the cell court rejects a confession, the defendant has to be heard again during his trial before the sector court.[270] In this case, the sector court can examine whether the new confession conforms to the Gacaca Law.[271] If the confessant turns out to be a first category

[261] See ASF, *Projet 'Soutien au recueil des aveux'* (2003); RCN, *Rapport d'activités 2003* (2004) 15.

[262] RCN, ibid.

[263] Presidential Communiqué of 1 January 2003, see Annex 2 of PRI, *Report IV* (2003) 20. For details, see section II A above.

[264] Art 58(1) of the Gacaca Law. See also arts 34(2) and 36(2) of the Gacaca Law.

[265] See Department of Gacaca Jurisdictions, *Manuel explicatif* (2001) 117. He would in this case, however, not be guaranteed a reduction of his sentence, ibid.

[266] Art 58(3) of the Gacaca Law.

[267] Arts 61, 62(2) of the Gacaca Law as modified by arts 15, 16 Organic Law No 13/2008. Confessions relating to rape or 'torture against sexual parts', however, are not to be given publicly, see art 38(3) of the Gacaca Law as modified by art 6 of Organic Law No 13/2008.

[268] Art 60(1) and (2) of the Gacaca Law prior to the amendment by art 14 of Organic Law No 13/2008.

[269] Art 60(3) of the Gacaca Law prior to the amendment by art 14 of Organic Law No 13/2008.

[270] See art 62(1) of the Gacaca Law.

[271] ASF, *Vade-mecum* (2004) 166.

defendant, the cell court takes a preliminary decision and passes on the file to the competent court, which, in turn, re-examines the confession.[272]

The earlier a defendant gives a confession, the better his or her prospects are of receiving a considerable reduction in the sentence given. Those who confess before appearing on the list of suspects drawn up by the Gacaca court of the cell enjoy greater benefits than those who confess subsequently. It is of no importance whether a file has already been compiled on them or whether they appear on the list published by the Prosecutor General of the Republic;[273] it is only the cell court list that is decisive.[274] Reductions in sentences are thus determined according to a three-stage model: no reduction for those who refused to confess or whose confessions did not comply with article 54 of the Gacaca Law; a minor reduction for those who confess after being included on the list of suspects; and a major reduction for those who confessed before appearing on the list.[275]

The confession procedure undoubtedly plays a major role in fact-finding in Gacaca courts. In addition, the acknowledgement of one's own responsibility is the first condition for pardon. Nevertheless, the confession procedure has not remained undisputed. The Rwandan-Belgian scholar Charles Ntampaka is of the opinion that confession does, in fact, run counter to Rwandan tradition. According to him, confession represents a show of force by the perpetrator and therefore an additional offence against the victim.[276] Observations by Penal Reform International (PRI) seem to confirm Ntampaka's view. PRI reports that prisoners often behaved arrogantly, and demanded pardon in an aggressive manner after giving testimony before the victims.[277] A system that trades confession and pardon against personal benefit in a criminal trial is of limited use as an instrument for genuine reconciliation between offenders and victims anyway. For the majority of suspects, the confession procedure is little more than a means to an end. All too often, confessions are a mechanical recital of the facts followed by a mechanical statement of repentance.

In addition to this rather theoretical criticism, the confession procedure has, in fact, produced some adverse effects. Prisons full of genocide suspects provided a perfect breeding ground for collusion. In some cases, detainees in the same prisons prepared consistent, but incomplete or false confessions so as to minimize their

[272] Ibid, 172.

[273] See on that list art 51, category 1 of the Gacaca Law *in fine*. The list was available online until 2009.

[274] ASF, *Vade-mecum* (2004) 168.

[275] Under Organic Law No 16/2004, a first category defendant would only benefit if he or she gave his confession before appearing on the list of suspects, arts 55, 72(2) of Organic Law No 16/2004. This is no longer the case following the amendment of art 72 of Organic Law No 16/2004 by art 13 of Organic Law No 10/2007. For more details on the repercussions of confession on the sentences as well as on the modifications of the confession procedure since 1996, see section VIII below.

[276] C. Ntampaka, 'Le gacaca rwandais, une justice répressive participative' 6 *Actualité du droit international humanitaire* (2001) 220; PRI, *Report IV* (2003) 3; however, this statement was rejected by a Rwandan government official, Annex 5 to the said PRI Report, 25. On cultural communication barriers in Rwanda, see B. Ingelaere, 'Does the Truth Pass Across the Fire Without Burning?' 47 *Journal of Modern African Studies* (2009) 518 *et seq.*

[277] PRI, *Report III* (2002) 16; PRI, *Report VII* (2005) 23.

own and their relatives' involvement, and to place the blame on others.[278] Finally, the prospect of provisional release for those willing to confess did not just create an incentive to tell the truth, but also provided many suspects, innocent detainees in particular, with a reason to admit to crimes never actually committed. It was assumed that before Gacaca took up its work, a considerable number of those jailed for involvement in the genocide were innocent.[279] Even people jailed for other crimes have resorted to confessing that they participated in the genocide in order to benefit from provisional release.[280]

VII. The Appeals Phase

Given the severe sentences pronounced by Gacaca courts, remedies against judgments are of great practical importance. The Gacaca Law provides for three different remedies against judgments: opposition,[281] appeal, and review of judgment.[282] These are modelled upon the remedies provided by the Code of Criminal Procedure,[283] albeit in a simplified fashion. Gacaca judgments are not subject to review by ordinary courts. Under the 2001 Gacaca legislation, however, this possibility did originally exist; in the interest of the law, the Prosecutor General to the Supreme Court had the right to lodge an appeal against a Gacaca judgment before the Court of Cassation.[284] This provision was struck in the course of the 2004 amendment of the Gacaca Law.

A. Opposition

Opposition can be lodged against a judgment passed in the absence of a party to the case. It leads to a simple retrial in the presence of the party before the same court. The defaulting party is required to present a 'serious and legitimate reason'

[278] PRI, *Report I* (2002) 26; PRI, *Report VII* (2005) 22. See also A.T. Paul, 'Das Unmögliche richten' 34 *Leviathan* (2006) 49.

[279] Even Rwandan officials acknowledged that a high number of detainees are innocent. In 1998, the Public Prosecution of Ruhengeri province estimated that 15% of the jailed were innocent, Amnesty International, *Gacaca* (2002) 14. See also P.E. Harrell, *Rwanda's Gamble* (2003) 81.

[280] In January 2007, Dieter Magsam, consultant on Rwanda for the German Technical Cooperation (GTZ), informed me of the case of a woman jailed without a file for an illegal abortion. When provisional release of genocide detainees willing to confess was announced, she confessed to some minor involvement in the genocide. See also the case reported in P. Clark, *The Gacaca Courts* (2010) 209–10.

[281] The English version of the Gacaca Law sometimes uses the term 'objection' instead of opposition. The terminology used is the Kinyarwanda and French versions is consistent ('ibyerekeye gusubirishamo urubanza', 'opposition').

[282] Art 85 of the Gacaca Law.

[283] Arts 157–83 of the Code of Criminal Procedure (*Law No 13/2004 of 17 May 2004 relating to the Code of Criminal Procedure*, OGRR no special of 30 July 2004 as modified by *Law No 20/2006 of 22 April 2006 modifying and completing the Law No 13/2004 of 17 May 2004*, OGRR no special of 27 May 2006).

[284] Arts 88(1), 89 of Organic Law No 40/2000. Prior to the judicial reform of 2004, the Court of Cassation was one of the chambers of the Supreme Court. It was abrogated in 2004.

for his or her absence.[285] Unlike under the ordinary law of criminal procedure,[286] it is not only the defendant who can lodge an opposition. The victim also has the right to do so if a judgment was passed in his or her absence.[287] In case of a judgment passed *in absentia* of the defendant, a remedy against that judgment is an obvious requirement of procedural fairness.[288] In cases where the victim is absent, this is not so evident. In this case, the opposition takes the restorative dimension of the Gacaca system into account: it is just as important to give a floor to victims and offenders to tell their stories as it is to deliver justice. This is also in line with the approach of the Gacaca Law to treat the victim as a fully-fledged party to the trial.

B. Appeal

The most important remedy is the appeal. Appeals have been lodged in an estimated 14–15 per cent of the cases judged by sector courts.[289] It is admissible against the judgments of category two defendants, and against sentences for offences against the administration of justice in Gacaca courts (articles 29 and 30 of the Gacaca Law). According to article 89(1) of the Gacaca Law, cases concerning offences against property (category three) are not subject to appeal. The National Service of Gacaca Courts has, however, allowed such judgments to be reviewed.[290] A judgment relating to offences against the administration of justice passed by a cell court under articles 29, 30, and 32 of the Gacaca Law can be appealed against before the Gacaca court of the sector. Sentences imposed by the Gacaca court of the sector at first instance go to the Gacaca court of appeal.[291] If a person is convicted for offences against the administration of justice committed in the course of a hearing before an appeals court, this court convicts him or her under articles 29, 30, and 32 of the Gacaca Law. An appeal against such a conviction is heard by a nearby appeals court or, if there are several benches in the same court, by another bench.[292] Under the former Gacaca legislation, the right of appeal was confined to the parties to the case, defendant, and victim.[293] The supervising authorities found that this was too narrow however, especially in cases where the victims were deceased, and no appeal was possible against an overly mild judgment. It was

285 Art 86 of the Gacaca Law.

286 See art 158 of the Code of Criminal Procedure.

287 Interview with Denis Bikesha, Director of Training, Mobilisation, and Sensitisation, National Service of Gacaca Courts, Kigali, 5 October 2007; see also art 86(3) of the Gacaca Law.

288 See Art 14(3)(d) of the ICCPR, art 19(2) of the Rwandan Constitution.

289 This estimate is based on information by Alexis Habimana (Documentation and Archivist Officer, National Service of Gacaca Courts, Kigali, 8 October 2008) about the total number of cases before Gacaca courts of appeal as of December 2007, which amounts to 71,100 cases. Out of these, an estimated 7–8% are review cases (on that, see section C below). This leaves about 66,000 appeals cases out of a total of 444,455 cases.

290 Letter to all Gacaca Courts of 3 August 2006, quoted in PRI, *Report X* (2007), 59; see, eg, Gacaca Court of Appeal, Kanzenze, Rubavu District, *Case of Birihanze*, 6 December 2007.

291 Arts 89, 42(2), 43(1) of the Gacaca Law.

292 Art 31(2) of the Gacaca Law.

293 Art 90 of Organic Law No 16/2004 and art 84 of Organic Law No 40/2000. Under ordinary criminal procedural law, only 'the accused; the person liable to pay damages; the civil party or persons who have been automatically awarded damages but as regards their civil interests only; [and] the prosecution' can lodge an appeal (art 164 of the Code of Criminal Procedure).

argued that this had an adverse effect on the quality of the justice delivered.[294] The legislator therefore amended the provision and extended the right of appeal to 'any other interested person . . . , in the interest of justice'.[295] With this modification, the circle of potential appellants becomes boundless. The amendment did in fact result in a substantial increase in appeals being lodged.[296] In late 2007, the National Service of Gacaca Courts reacted to this by issuing a circular to all Gacaca courts, which stipulated that appeals made by those who were not a party to the trial were only admissible in cases where the victim's side was not represented or where the law had been wrongly applied in a blatant manner.[297]

A case on appeal must be judged in the same way as it is in the first instance, with a full inquiry made into the relevant facts. The only difference is that a confession no longer entails a reduction of the sentence.[298] In practice, however, the appeals courts often fail to conduct a full new inquiry, and decide the case essentially based on the files and the minutes of testimonies given at first instance.[299] An appeal is usually lodged in writing, meaning illiterate defendants have to rely on the help of others to lodge their appeal. If the appellant is in detention, the prison governor has to countersign the appeal. It is then subject to an admissibility procedure which is held *in camera*.[300] Under article 84(1) of the Gacaca Law, the parties have to declare their intention to lodge an appeal upon pronouncement of the first instance judgment. Yet this is usually not regarded as a precondition for admissibility of an appeal.[301] Both appeal and opposition have to be lodged within a period of 15 days.[302] The relevant provisions lay out a more uniform and simplified procedure compared to the provisions on deadlines in the Code of Criminal Procedure.[303]

An important precondition for preparing an appeal is that the accused is informed of the reasons for the verdict. The right to a reasoned judgment is a crucial element of a fair trial.[304] Knowing the reasons of a judgment is vital for the preparation of an appeal. The requirement to give reasons also counteracts the

[294] Interview with Denis Bikesha, Director of Training, Mobilisation, and Sensitisation, National Service of Gacaca Courts, Kigali, 21 September 2007.

[295] Art 90 of the Gacaca Law as modified by art 19 of Organic Law No 10/2007.

[296] Interview with Denis Bikesha, Director of Training, Mobilisation, and Sensitisation, National Service of Gacaca Courts, Kigali, 21 September 2007.

[297] Circulaire du 30 octobre 2007 du Secrétaire Exécutif du SNJG, Annex 11 to ASF, *Rapport analytique no 3* (2007) 123 *et seq.*

[298] Art 58(3) of the Gacaca Law.

[299] A judge expressly told me so in respect to an appeals trial I attended, Gacaca Court of Appeal, Kimihurura, Gasabo District, *Case of Gasasira Enock*, 30 September 2007. ASF has also pointed this out, *Rapport analytique no 1* (2005) 13; see also PRI, *Report XI* (2008) 38.

[300] Interviews with the president of the Gacaca Court of Appeal of Nyanza, Nyanza, 19 September 2007, and with the bench of the Gacaca Court of Appeal of Kimihurura, Kigali, 23 September 2007.

[301] Interview with the bench of the Gacaca Court of Appeal of Kimihurura, Kigali, 23 September 2007.

[302] Arts 87 and 91 of the Gacaca Law.

[303] In ordinary procedural law, opposition has to be lodged within 10 days, while the period for an appeal is 30 days, arts 158 and 165 of the Code of Criminal Procedure.

[304] Art 141(2) of the Rwandan Constitution as amended by art 27 of *Amendment of 13 August 2008 of the Constitution of the Republic of Rwanda of 4 June 2003*, OGRR no special of 13 August 2008.

danger of an arbitrary decision.[305] According to articles 67 and 69 of the Gacaca Law, every judgment has to be substantiated in writing. This requirement is a major challenge for many of the judges, who often have no or only very basic education. In practice, the reasons given are usually scanty; the written judgments consist of a form filled in by the judges that leaves only a few lines for explanations.[306] Instead, Gacaca courts produce lengthy minutes of all testimonies and other statements given during the hearing. The minutes are usually read out at the end of the trial, and in practice serve as the most important basis for the preparation of an appeal. This lack of appropriate reasoning has been pointed out by Avocats Sans Frontières in particular, who have repeatedly called upon the National Service of Gacaca Courts to instruct the judges accordingly.[307]

C. Review of judgment

Like many other systems of criminal procedure around the world, the Gacaca Law allows a review of a final judgment under certain circumstances. Review of judgment under the Gacaca Law means a new trial with a full inquiry and a new judgment. It was introduced by Organic Law No 16/2004. The provision was subject to amendments in 2007 and 2008. Review of judgment is also provided for in the Rwandan Code of Criminal Procedure, albeit only for the benefit of the convict.[308] The review provisions contained in the Gacaca Law go much further, however. Under the new version of article 93(1) of the Gacaca Law,[309] judgments by Gacaca courts can be reviewed in two cases, namely if '1 ... new evidence contradicting what [the original judgment] was based on is discovered; 2 an accused was given a sentence that is inconsistent with the law'. Under these conditions, review is admissible both for the benefit of the accused as well as to his detriment. Parallel to the appeals provisions, the 2007 amendment has extended the circle of potential applicants who can lodge a review. It is not just the defendant and the victim who are so entitled; 'any other person acting in the interest of justice' can also request that a judgement be reviewed.[310] The 2007 amendment has led to an increase in requests for review. The National Service has therefore issued clarifying instructions, which essentially repeat the provisions of article 93 of the Gacaca Law.[311] In fact, review occurs rarely—in less than

[305] S. Trechsel, *Human Rights in Criminal Proceedings* (2005) 102 *et seq*; see also ECtHR, *Hadjianastassiou v Greece*, Judgment of 16 December 1992, para 33.

[306] See the sample in Department of Gacaca Jurisdictions, *Manuel explicatif* (2001) 102 *et seq*.

[307] ASF, *Rapport analytique no 1* (2005) 32; ASF, *Rapport analytique no 2* (2006) 16 *et seq*; ASF, *Rapport analytique no 3* (2007) 21 *et seq*; ASF, *Rapport analytique no 4* (2009) 37 *et seq*.

[308] Art 180 of the Code of Criminal Procedure.

[309] As modified by art 24 of Organic Law No 13/2008.

[310] This provision has been retained in the course of the 2008 amendment, see art 93(2) of the Gacaca Law as modified first by art 20 of Organic Law No 20/2007, then by art 24 of Organic Law No 13/2008. The circular by the National Service mentioned above (section B) equally applies to review.

[311] Interview with Denis Bikesha, Director of Training, Mobilisation, and Sensitisation, National Service of Gacaca Courts, Kigali, 21 September 2007 referring to *Instructions No 12/2007 of 15 March 2007 issued by the Executive Secretary of the National Service of Gacaca Courts Concerning Cases on Review Before Gacaca Courts*.

two per cent of cases.[312] A request for review has to be submitted in writing.[313] The competent organ to decide on the admissibility of a review is the general assembly of the sector where the reviewed judgment was passed.[314] As a forum that brings together all *inyangamugayo* within one sector—those in charge of investigating and judging the case—the general assembly is the organ that can best assess whether the facts brought forth in the request for review warrant the reopening of the case. The review is then brought before the Gacaca court of appeal.[315] However, it cannot be heard by the same judges who rendered the reviewed judgment. The case must therefore be assigned either to another bench within the same court of appeal, or, if there is only one bench, to the nearest Gacaca court of appeal in another sector.[316]

The provisions on reviewing judgments have been subject to strong criticism, particularly before the 2008 amendment was made, providing narrower preconditions for review.[317] Prior to that, Gacaca courts could also review judgments rendered by ordinary courts.[318] It was even conceivable that a Gacaca court could overturn a final judgment pronounced by the Supreme Court.[319] In reaction to protests, in particular those made by Avocats Sans Frontières, in 2006 the National Service of Gacaca Courts ordered that all reviews concerning judgments by ordinary courts be suspended until all other genocide cases could be judged, and clearer requirements for the admissibility of these reviews could be defined.[320] The 2008 amendment finally abolished the review of ordinary or military court judgments by Gacaca courts and stipulated that such judgments could only be reviewed by the same courts.[321] Before the amendment, ordinary court judgments were in fact reviewed by a Gacaca court in a number of cases. In one particularly drastic case, a defendant who had been acquitted by an ordinary court was subsequently sentenced to 30 years in prison in a second trial before a Gacaca court.[322] Review in

312 Out of the 17 cases I observed in appeals courts, 16 defendants were on appeal; only one was on review. The ratio in ASF's observations between 2005 and 2007 was 21 to two, ASF, *Rapport analytique no 2* (2006) annex I; ASF, *Rapport analytique no 3* (2007) annex I. On the basis of the 71,100 judgments passed by appeals courts in both appeals and review cases cited above, and taking the confidence interval into consideration, this results in a percentage below 2.00%.

313 Art 4 of Instructions No 12/2007.

314 Art 6 of Instructions No 12/2007.

315 Art 93(3) of the Gacaca Law.

316 Art 7 of Instructions No 12/2007.

317 Both versions of art 93 of the Gacaca Law prior and subsequent to the 2008 amendment are reprinted in the appendix.

318 Art 93(1)(1) and (2) of Organic Law No 16/2004 and the same provision after the amendment by art 20 of Organic Law No 10/2007.

319 ASF, *Vade-mecum* (2004) 253. This is possible in cases where the Supreme Court has ruled on second appeal over a second category case opened before the implementation of Gacaca courts. On second appeal, see art 43(2)(2)–(6) and (8) of Organic Law No 01/2004 as modified by art 3 of Organic Law No 58/2007. However, this has apparently never occurred, interview with Denis Bikesha, Director of Training, Mobilisation, and Sensitisation, National Service of Gacaca Courts, Kigali, 5 October 2007.

320 Interview with two representatives of ASF Rwanda, Kigali, 12 October 2007; arts 2–3 of *Instructions No 09/2006 of 26 July 2006 issued by the Executive Secretary of the National Service of Gacaca Courts Concerning the Review of Judgments of Ordinary Courts*, art 11 of Instructions No 12/2007.

321 Art 93(3) of the Gacaca Law as modified by art 24 of Organic Law No 13/2008.

322 Gacaca Court of the Sector of Maranyundo, Bugesera District, *Case of Nturanyi Jean Bosco*, 2 November 2006, see also the case of *Rwamakuba Hamada*. This defendant had been sentenced to 10 years by an ordinary court and was then sentenced to 25 years in prison by the Gacaca court of

the case of new evidence coming to light and incorrect sentencing was not affected by the amendment.

Review to the detriment of the defendant is commonly considered to be in contravention of procedural safeguards against double jeopardy. Article 14(7) of the ICCPR prohibits a retrial 'for an offence for which [the defendant] has already been finally convicted or acquitted in accordance with the law and penal procedure of each country'. Even though Article 14(7) does not contain an express exception, the reference to 'the law and penal procedure' of the state parties suggests that the *ne bis in idem* rule can be derogated from. In fact, a fair number of states allow for retrials under narrow circumstances.[323] The Human Rights Committee has acknowledged the possibility of 'a resumption of a trial justified by exceptional circumstances',[324] possibly in cases where new evidence turns up.[325] The review procedure of the Gacaca Law is therefore not in contravention of the *ne bis in idem* principle of international human rights law per se. Yet some Gacaca courts have failed to properly examine the preconditions of a review, a practice that does not pay due regard to the principle of *ne bis in idem*. In a case I observed in Kigali, the grounds for review brought forth were that the sentence of 30 years pronounced in an earlier judgment was too mild. Even though there were no indications of new evidence or misapplication of the law, the case was admitted for review.[326]

VIII. Sanctions Imposed by Gacaca Courts

Even though the substantive criminal law applied by Gacaca courts is that of the Rwandan Penal Code, the penalties imposed differ from what the Code prescribes. The drafters of the Gacaca Law deemed it necessary to adapt the sanctions to the special situation of a post-genocide society with over half a million people suspected of participation in the crimes. In addition, the penalties are supposed to reflect, at least to some extent, the Gacaca system's reconciliatory approach. For the majority of the crimes, the penalties according to the Gacaca Law are considerably less harsh than those set out under the Penal Code.[327] The penalty provisions of the Gacaca Law are equally applicable in ordinary courts: article 72 of the Gacaca Law lists

the Sector of Gakenke (Gatsibo District, 18 March 2005). On appeal, he was reclassified to the first category with his case being referred back to the ordinary courts (Gacaca Court of Appeal, Gakenke, Gatsibo District, 26 May 2006). But a retrial by a Gacaca court can also result in an acquittal, as in the case of *Mutabazi Athanase* (Gacaca Court of Appeal, Gakenke, Gatsibo District, 26 May 2006), who had received a life sentence by an ordinary court in 1997; on retrials, see also ASF, *Rapport analytique no 3* (2007) 61.

[323] For instance, the UK in case of a 'tainted acquittal', *Criminal Procedure and Investigations Act 1996*, section 54; in Germany under the preconditions of § 362 of the *Strafprozessordnung*.

[324] General Comment 13/21 of 13 April 1984, para 19. Under the European human rights regime, an exception to that effect is provided for, see Art 4(2) of *Protocol No 7 to the Convention for the Protection of Human Rights and Fundamental Freedoms* of 22 November 1984, 1525 UNTS 195.

[325] *Almirati García v Uruguay*, Views of 25 July 1983 (no 92/1981) para 10.5.

[326] Gacaca Court of Appeal, Kimihurura, Gasabo District, *Case of Nyirabashitsi Françoise*, 16 September 2007. The jurisdiction, however, reduced the sentence to 19 years.

[327] For details, see section IV C above.

Table 1 Penalties according to articles 72, 73, 78 of the Gacaca Law

	No confession or confession rejected		Confession after appearing on the list of suspects		Confession before appearing on the list of suspects	
	adults	minors	adults	minors	adults	minors
Category 1	life imprisonment	10–20 years	25–30 years	8–9 years	20–24 years	6.5–7.5 years
Category 2(1)–(3)	30 years or life imprisonment	10–15 years	25–29 years (half in TIG, 1/6 suspended)	6.5–7.5 years (half in TIG, 1/6 suspended)	20–24 years (half in TIG, 1/3 suspended)	6–7 years (half in TIG, 1/3 suspended)
Category 2(4), (5)	15–19 years	4.5–5.5 years	12–14 years (half in TIG, 1/6 suspended)	4–5 years (half in TIG, 1/6 suspended)	8–11 years (half in TIG, 1/3 suspended)	2.5–3.5 years (half in TIG, 1/3 suspended)
Category 2(6)	5–7 years (half in TIG, 1/6 suspended)	2.5–3.5 years (half in TIG, 1/6 suspended)	3–4 years (half in TIG, 1/6 suspended)	1.5–2.5 years (half in TIG, 1/6 suspended)	1–2 years (half in TIG, 1/3 suspended)	0.5–1.5 years (half in TIG, 1/3 suspended)

the penalties for perpetrators classified in the first category, some of which are tried by regular courts. As explained above, the Gacaca Law offers reduced penalties to those who confess to their crimes, depending on whether the confession is given before or after a suspect appears on the list of alleged *génocidaires*.[328] Sanctions range from life imprisonment to community service (Travaux d'Intérêt Général or TIG). On top of that, convicts can incur the loss of civic rights. Those who merely committed offences against property are not subject to penal sanctions and are only liable to pay damages.[329] Table 1 gives an overview of the penalties.[330]

A. Imprisonment

Despite Gacaca's seemingly reconciliatory outward appearance and its (secondary) objective of providing a solution to prison overcrowding, the Gacaca Law does include the possibility of long prison sentences. It goes without saying that such sanctions are not inappropriate, given the nature of the crimes adjudged by Gacaca courts. In fact, most Rwandans perceive the penalties as very mild. This is compounded by the fact that many defendants in Gacaca courts have already completed their prison term in pre-trial detention and are immediately freed following their

[328] See section VI B above.

[329] Art 75 of the Gacaca Law.

[330] Similar tables relating to older versions of the Gacaca Law can be found in ASF, *Vade-mecum* (2004) 179 and F. Digneffe and J. Fierens (eds), *Justice et gacaca* (2003) 100–1.

Gacaca trial, even if found guilty.[331] Nevertheless, some of the penalties are harsh, especially if the shortcomings of the Gacaca system regarding the rights of the defence[332] are taken into account: it is certainly disturbing to see a person convicted to two decades in prison on grounds of two vague testimonies, one of which is only based on hearsay.[333] Gacaca courts can also impose prison terms of up to 15 years upon people aged between 14 and 17 years at the time of their crimes.[334]

The 2007 and 2008 amendments to the Gacaca Law conferred a number of cases to Gacaca courts that had previously been in the jurisdiction of ordinary courts.[335] In these cases, Gacaca courts are able to impose the harshest penalty in Rwandan law: life imprisonment with special provisions.[336] Although capital punishment was abolished in July 2007,[337] even before this date, it could not be imposed by Gacaca courts; however, an amendment to that effect was discussed in 2005. Yet Gacaca courts could make important preliminary decisions that could finally result in the death penalty being given: if the Gacaca court assigned a defendant to the first category and rejected his confession, there was a good chance that the trial court would impose the death penalty. Capital punishment was frequently imposed by regular courts in category one cases, but had not been carried out since 1998.[338] Since the abolition of the death penalty, death sentences have been converted to life imprisonment sentences with special provisions. This means that detainees cannot be pardoned before having served 20 years of their sentence. In addition, they are to be kept in an individual cell.[339] Initially, life imprisonment with special provisions was interpreted to exclude even visits by family members, despite this being inconsistent both with international standards[340] and the Rwandan law governing prison

331 See, eg, Gacaca Court of the Sector of Mataba, Gakenke District, *Case of Hategekimana*, 17 and 24 May 2006; Gacaca Court of the Sector of Rusororo, Gasabo District, *Cases of Munyurangabo Frédéric, Habyarimana Jean Claude, and Habineza Jean Claude*, 27 September 2006; Gacaca Court of the Sector of Musambira, Kamonyi District, *Case of Ndayisaba Elizaphan*, 26 June 2007.

332 These will be discussed in more detail in ch 3, section V below.

333 This was the case in a trial I witnessed in Kigali. The hearing lasted for about two and half hours and resulted in sentences of 19 years' imprisonment each for both defendants, Gacaca Court of Appeal, Kimihurura, Gasabo District, *Cases of Gasasira Enock and Ntamuvurira Mathias*, 30 September 2007.

334 Art 78 of the Gacaca Law as modified by art 16 of Organic Law No 10/2007.

335 'Zealous' murderers, torturers, and those who committed dehumanizing acts on the dead body in particular. For details, see section II B above.

336 Art 72(1) of the Gacaca Law. On life imprisonment with special provisions, see below in this section.

337 Art 2 of Organic Law No 31/2007.

338 See ch 1, section VI C above. In 2002, regular courts had imposed the death penalty in 9.5% of all genocide cases heard at that time, J. Busingye, *Reality and Challenges of Legal and Judicial Reconstruction in Rwanda* (2006) 21. Yet this figure is not very likely to be representative. On the one hand, the fairness of trials improved considerably over the years. On the other hand, the courts apparently started with the 'biggest fishes' before moving on to other, less severe cases (between 1997 and 2002, the percentage of death sentences fell from 30.8 to 3.4%). In 2006, 606 people sentenced to death were counted in Rwandan prisons, LIPRODHOR, *Situation des droits de la personne en 2005* (2006) 112.

339 Art 3 of *Law No 32/2010 of 22 September 2010 relating to serving life imprisonment with special provisions*, OGRR no special of 14 October 2010. See also art 4 of Organic Law No 31/2007 as modified by art 1 of *Organic Law No 05/2009/OL of 21 December 2009 modifying and completing Organic Law No 31/2007 of 25 July 2007*, OGRR no 4 of 25 January 2010.

340 See the recommendations by ASF, April 2008, on file with the author. International standards relating to prison conditions are laid down in Art 10 of the ICCPR. More detailed provisions are

conditions.[341] Life imprisonment with special provisions has been an obstacle for the transfer of ICTR cases to Rwanda.[342] It has therefore been clarified by law that life imprisonment with special provisions does not apply to defendants whose cases may be transferred to Rwanda by the ICTR in the future.[343]

When it comes to the situation in Rwandan prisons, Gacaca has not entirely lived up to the hopes of officials and activists. In fact, instead of reducing the prison population through expeditious trials, the information gathering process resulted in enormous numbers of new accusations. Instead of the over 120,000 detainees awaiting trial as cited before the introduction of Gacaca courts, suddenly numbers in excess of 800,000 suspects were mentioned.[344] Towards the end of the Gacaca process, this number had risen to around one million, with at least half a million people being suspected of grave crimes such as murder and assault.[345] The prison population that had ended up going down due to provisional releases was temporarily on the rise again and amounted to almost 100,000 detainees in mid-2007.[346] In view of these daunting figures, in 2004 community service had already become a compulsory penalty for those who had been sentenced to it.[347] In June 2007, following a cabinet decision to that effect, the National Service of Gacaca Courts decreed that convicts should perform community service before serving their prison term in order to avoid further pressure on the prison system.[348] Following that decision, almost 40,000 prisoners were released to do TIG.[349] Nevertheless,

included in the *Standard Minimum Rules for the Treatment of Prisoners* of 1955, approved by the UN Economic and Social Council.

[341] Art 28 of *Law No 38/2006 of 25 September 2006 establishing and determining the organisation of the National Prison Service*, OGRR no special of 23 October 2006. Life imprisonment with special provisions has also been challenged before the Rwandan Supreme Court, but was not declared unconstitutional, Supreme Court, Judgment no RS/Inconst/Pén.0002/08/CS of 29 August 2008.

[342] *Prosecutor v Munyakazi*, ICTR, Appeals Chamber, Decision of 8 October 2008 (ICTR-97-36-R11*bis*) paras 16–21; *Prosecutor v Kanyarukiga*, ICTR, Appeals Chamber, Decision of 30 October 2008 (ICTR-2002–78-R11*bis*) paras 12–17; *Prosecutor v Hategekimana*, ICTR, Appeals Chamber, Decision of 4 December 2008 (ICTR-00–55B-R11*bis*) paras 31–8. For details, see J.D. Mujuzi, 'Steps Taken in Rwanda's Efforts to Qualify for the Transfer of Accused from the ICTR' 8 *JICJ* (2010) 237 *et seq*.

[343] Art 1 of *Organic Law No 66/2008 of 21 November 2008 modifying and completing Organic Law No 31/2007 of 25 July 2007*, OGRR no 23 of 1 December 2008, which modified art 3 of Organic Law No 31/2007.

[344] National Service of Gacaca Courts, *Summary of Persons Prosecuted* (2006), which mentions a number of 818,564 suspects. See also Amnesty International, *The Enduring Legacy of the Genocide and War* (2004) 10.

[345] Information from Alexis Habimana, Documentation and Archivist Officer, National Service of Gacaca Courts, Kigali, 8 October 2008. See also National Service of Gacaca Courts, ibid.

[346] LIPRODHOR, *Rapport de monitoring des prisons au Rwanda* (2008) 15.

[347] Under art 75(1) of Organic Law No 40/2000, those convicted had the choice between serving a prison term or performing community service. This provision was taken out during the 2004 amendment.

[348] Preamble, para 1 and art 1(1) of *Instructions No 15/2007 of 1 June 2007 issued by the Executive Secretary of the National Service of Gacaca Courts Concerning the Completion of Sentences of Persons who Confessed, Repented and Asked for Forgiveness Before Gacaca Courts*. See also LIPRODHOR, *Rapport de monitoring des prisons au Rwanda* (2008) 4, 15. In 2008, this was also laid down in the Gacaca Law, see art 80(1) of the Gacaca Law as modified by art 21 of Organic Law No 13/2008.

[349] LIPRODHOR, *Rapport de monitoring des prisons au Rwanda* (2008) 15.

on average, the population of the country's 14 prisons still exceeds their actual capacity by more than half.[350]

This development demonstrates the dangers of attempting comprehensive prosecutions for large-scale mass atrocities, especially if they are to be effected by lay personnel.[351] Mass crimes are usually the result of a complex coaction of many people. Given that one incriminating testimony may often be sufficient prima facie evidence to justify a suspicion and an indictment, it is not surprising that the investigation phase has resulted in such astronomic numbers of new suspects. With several years having passed since the crimes, the situation became even more incalculable. While many suspects were eventually acquitted,[352] the suspicion in itself represents a stigma that innocent people had to carry with them for several years. It is difficult to foresee the impact of this situation on relations between the 10 per cent of the Rwandan population suspected of genocide, and the rest of Rwandan society, in particular the *rescapés*.

Rwandan officials are well aware of the problems caused by prison overpopulation, with considerable progress having been made regarding prison infrastructure over the last few years. Human rights activists report steady improvements, but conditions still fail to comply with international standards.[353] Due to overcrowding, neither a bed nor sufficient food can be provided for every detainee.[354] Most prisoners are therefore fed by their families. The development of the country's prison infrastructure in recent years enabled detainees from provisional detention facilities, where conditions were even worse, to be transferred to normal prisons.[355] These communal lock-ups (*cachots*) are designed only for temporary detention. In the late 1990s and early 2000s, they accommodated a great number of long-term detainees. In 2002, even after a large number of people had already been transferred to regular prisons, over 12,000 people were still being held in *cachots*.[356]

Another measure to relieve the prison service was introduced in 2007. Under the new penalty provisions, sentences for defendants who confessed are suspended in part.[357] For the time for which his or her penalty is suspended, the convict is on probation.[358] Finally, the 2008 amendment stipulated that those who carry out their community service well may also serve their remaining prison sentence

[350] At the time of research, the capacity of Rwandan prisons was at just over 38,000 compared to almost 60,000 actual prison inmates, LIPRODHOR, ibid, 14.

[351] On the problems Gacaca judges had in individualizing the contributions made by different defendants in large-scale crimes, see ch 3, section V C below.

[352] Up to 30%, for details, see ch 3, section V D below.

[353] LIPRODHOR, *Situation des droits de la personne en 2005* (2006) 107, 115; LIPRODHOR, *Rapport de monitoring des prisons au Rwanda* (2008) 4, 11; W.A. Schabas, 'The Rwanda Case' in M.C. Bassiouni (ed), *Post-Conflict Justice* (2002) 513 *et seq*.

[354] LIPRODHOR, *Situation des droits de la personne en 2005* (2006) 107, 110; LIPRODHOR, *Rapport de monitoring des prisons au Rwanda* (2008) 11, 19.

[355] LIPRODHOR, *Situation des droits de la personne en 2003–2004* (2004) 124.

[356] See LIPRODHOR, *Situation des droits de la personne au Rwanda en 2002* (2003) 52 *et seq*.

[357] One third or one sixth of the sentence, see Table 1 at the beginning of section VIII above.

[358] The term of suspension or 'sursis' in the Gacaca Law is used in the sense of arts 97–9 of the Penal Code, interview with Denis Bikesha, Director of Training, Mobilisation, and Sensitisation, National Service of Gacaca Courts, Kigali, 5 October 2007. On suspension of sentences under Rwandan law, see J. Gakwaya, *Les moyens d'adéquation de la peine en droit rwandais* (1993) 164 *et seq*.

in the form of community service.[359] As long as the convict works as expected and behaves appropriately, he or she will not have to go back to prison. This is to form the general rule, with any decision to the contrary having to be taken by the Gacaca court nearest to where the person in question is serving his or her service.[360] Such an amendment was suggested by the National Committee for Community Service, which realized that their efforts to rehabilitate the *tigistes*[361] would be frustrated if they had had to return to prison after their TIG.[362] This amendment makes community service another form of probation. A considerable number of those convicted of genocide, possibly a number exceeding 50,000 persons, are thus likely to serve a merely non-custodial penalty.[363]

A sentence of community service can also be transformed back into a term of imprisonment, such as when the convicted party commits another crime during the period of community service. In such a case, he or she is not only prosecuted for the new offence, but also sent back to prison for the whole period of his or her TIG sentence. The time already served is then not counted for the newly determined prison term. This rather drastic arrangement is laid down in article 74 of the Gacaca Law.[364] Although the English version does not state this so clearly, the French version is unambiguous:

> Si le condamné à une peine d'emprisonnement avec commutation de la peine en travaux d'intérêt général... se rend coupable d'une autre infraction, le sursis équivalent à toute la période de ces travaux encourus est de nul effet et le concerné rentre dans la prison pour y purger la totalité de la peine lui infligée par la juridiction et il est puni pour la commission de la nouvelle infraction.

This amounts to double punishment for the same offence: the time served already as TIG must be served again in prison, as if the defendant had been on probation while doing his TIG. Double punishment is expressly prohibited by Article 14(7) of the ICCPR.

359 Art 80(1) of the Gacaca Law as modified by art 21 of Organic Law No 13/2008. The Kinyarwanda and French versions merely require that the community service be carried out well ('neza', 'bien'). The English translation is inaccurate ('exemplary').

360 Interview with Denis Bikesha, Director of Training, Mobilisation, and Sensitisation, National Service of Gacaca Courts, Kigali, 16 September 2008.

361 Following the French term of *travaux d'intérêt général* or TIG, those doing community service are commonly referred to as *tigistes*.

362 Interview with Anastase Nabahire, Associate Executive Secretary of the National Committee for Implementing Community Service as an Alternative Penalty to Imprisonment, Kigali, 19 September 2008.

363 According to Anastase Nabahire, Associate Executive Secretary of the National Committee for Implementing Community Service as an Alternative Penalty to Imprisonment, 53,616 *tigistes* were registered with the Community Service Committee at the time of research. This number is very likely to increase given that Gacaca courts at the time of research had pronounced 94,466 community service sentences. However, this figure does not reflect the actual number of present and future *tigistes* since a sentence for the same person by different Gacaca courts, or a sentence at the trial and the appeals level are counted double, interview, Kigali, 19 September 2008.

364 In the original as well as in the version modified by art 18 of Organic Law No 13/2008.

B. Community service (TIG)

Faced with the problem of a considerable share of its population in prison, the Rwandan government was forced to develop alternative forms of sanctioning. A high prison population would not only lead to enormous costs; it would also seriously impair the country's economic development and drive thousands of families into poverty. Just like alternative forms of justice, non-custodial forms of sanctioning have also been discussed since shortly after the genocide.[365] Nevertheless, the 1996 law on genocide trials takes a conventional approach, and relies largely on the penalties provided in the Penal Code with reductions in penalties for confessants.[366] Community service as a supplementary penalty was introduced only by the first Gacaca Law in 2001. In theory, the community service programme appeared promising: it would relieve the prisons, it would make good use of the detainees' labour for economic development, it would foster the rehabilitation and reintegration of those who had confessed to their guilt,[367] and, ideally, it would enable those convicted to provide their victims with some form of direct compensation by rebuilding their houses or the infrastructure of their villages.

Having said that, many prisoners initially had reservations against community service. For years, anti-Tutsi propaganda had trained them to believe that the RPF would come to Rwanda with the express purpose of enslaving the Hutu population and re-establishing the forced labour regime. Community service appeared to fulfil this prophecy.[368] Moreover, the creation of an organizational framework to enable tens of thousands of people to work in a constructive manner was an enormous challenge for national and local authorities. The 2001 Gacaca Law mentioned community service as an alternative sanction, but did not contain details on how this sanction might be implemented. The actual modalities of community service were laid down in late 2001 by Presidential Order No 26/01/2001. As the pilot phase dragged on, however, the creation of an infrastructure for community service was delayed.[369] This infrastructure was finally created following Presidential Orders No 10/01/2005 and No 50/01/2005, which replaced the 2001 Order and slightly modified the framework provided therein.

These Orders set up a network of national and local authorities that are to organize the community service activities.[370] The most important functions are assigned to the district committees, which are supposed to identify the institutions that are to receive *tigistes* and subsequently allocate the convicted to these.[371] Community

[365] The above-mentioned 1995 conference (see ch 1, section VI B above) suggested '[a]ppropriate labor or service to the community in which their acts took place' as possible sanctions for *génocidaires*, Republic of Rwanda, Recommendations of the Conference Held in Kigali from November 1st to November 5th, 1995, 24.

[366] Arts 14 *et seq* of Organic Law No 08/96.

[367] Apart from category 2(6) convicts, TIG is reserved to those who confessed, see Table 1 at the beginning of section VIII above.

[368] See also PRI, *Report IX* (2007) 27.

[369] PRI, *Report III* (2002) 4; PRI, *Report VII* (2005) 18; PRI, *Report IX* (2007) 16.

[370] For details, see PRI, *Report IX* (2007) 18 *et seq*.

[371] Art 18 of Presidential Order No 10/01/2005. In reality, however, the decision which projects would benefit from TIG by receiving *tigistes* was often taken by the National Committee for Implementing Community Service as an Alternative Penalty to Imprisonment, see PRI, *Report IX* (2007) 19.

service can be carried out either in public institutions or in projects contributing to general welfare.[372] The strategy devised by the Presidential Orders intended that those convicted be sent to their home communities, where they would live at home and work three days a week in a TIG project until their sentence expired (so-called neighbourhood community service).[373] The community service sentence would thus gradually reintegrate those convicted into their former communities. The communities themselves would directly benefit from the work carried out by those who had originally caused them harm. However, implementing neighbourhood TIG encountered considerable difficulties. Given the great number of *tigistes*,[374] the programme proved extremely difficult to implement with regard to logistics. In particular, the distribution of *tigistes* among the regions ended up being very uneven. In addition, both the survivors and those convicted feared for their safety in the communities where the schemes had been set up.

As a result of this, the authorities increasingly resorted to setting up work camps.[375] Today, neighbourhood community service is done only by very few, while most *tigistes* work in camps. The convicts are interned in these camps, although they may leave the camp in exceptional circumstances, such as if one of their family members falls ill. At the time of research, there were 60 community service camps all over the country encompassing approximately 27,000 persons.[376] The camps can be monitored relatively easily and enable the work of the *tigistes* to be employed in a more concentrated manner, thus allowing infrastructural projects to be realized on a greater scale. Those convicted work for six days instead of the standard three days for neighbourhood community service. As a result, their term is halved, which is why many *tigistes* prefer the camps to neighbourhood community service, despite the fact that they are away from their homes and families.[377] The seventh day is reserved for family visits and sports. In addition, the *tigistes* are trained in manual skills, such as brick-making, terracing, or rational use of soil, which they can continue to make use of once they have served their sentence.[378]

While many expected community service to be a form of reparation for the survivors, it was, in fact, not devised with the benefit of the *rescapés* in mind, but rather for the general public as a whole: typical forms of TIG include measures for protecting the environment (erosion control, reforestation) and infrastructural

[372] Art 2(2) of Presidential Order No 10/01/2005.

[373] See arts 18(3), 30(1), 32(1) of Presidential Order No 10/01/2005, the latter as modified by art 7 of Presidential Order No 50/01/2005. The clarifying provision about the duration of TIG contained in art 32(2) of Presidential Order No 10/01/2005 no longer appears in the new version. See also M.A. Drumbl, *Atrocity, Punishment, and International Law* (2007) 88.

[374] For statistical data, see section A above.

[375] Work camps were introduced in addition to neighbourhood community service by art 7(2) of Presidential Order No 50/01/2005 modifying art 32(2) of Presidential Order No 10/01/2005.

[376] Interview with Anastase Nabahire, Associate Executive Secretary of the National Committee for Implementing Community Service as an Alternative Penalty to Imprisonment, Kigali, 19 September 2008.

[377] PRI, *Report IX* (2007) 1 *et seq*, 32 *et seq*; interview with Anastase Nabahire, Associate Executive Secretary of the National Committee for Implementing Community Service as an Alternative Penalty to Imprisonment, Kigali, 19 September 2008.

[378] Interview with Anastase Nabahire, Associate Executive Secretary of the National Committee for Implementing Community Service as an Alternative Penalty to Imprisonment, Kigali, 19 September 2008; PRI, *Report IX* (2007) 22 *et seq*.

improvements (construction and rehabilitation of schools, roads, etc).[379] They can also include the construction of housing for the needy.[380] However, community service has to provide some concrete benefit to the survivors of the genocide in order that it be accepted as an instrument for reconciliation.[381]

Nevertheless, the community service programme is one of the most promising elements of Rwanda's strategy for dealing with the crimes committed during the genocide. Community service presents a solution to prison overcrowding and creates much better conditions for the reintegration of *génocidaires* than imprisonment. The *tigistes* are not isolated from the public in the way prison inmates are. The camps are only loosely guarded and the *tigistes* move about freely in the surrounding area, allowing contact with the local population. In certain circumstances, the *tigistes* may even leave the camps for a longer period to visit their families, which helps them to gradually find their way back into their old communities. The manual skills they learn may help them earn a living once they return home. Rwandan authorities are aware of the potential of community service. TIG is very likely to become a possible sanction in the projected new Penal Code.[382]

C. Loss of civic rights

Article 76 of the Gacaca Law includes the loss of civic rights as an accessory penalty to imprisonment and community service. Those convicted under the Gacaca Law are deprived of their rights to be elected to public office and to serve in certain official functions. Depending on the gravity of their crimes and on their willingness to confess, these rights are suspended either on a permanent basis or for the duration of their sentence. In addition, the names of those convicted along with a short description of their crimes are published at genocide memorials, at the offices of their home sectors and on the Internet. The provision governing the loss of civic rights was initially modelled upon article 66 of the Penal Code.[383] In line with that provision, those convicted were not only to lose their right to be elected and to serve in official functions, but also their rights to vote and to carry firearms.[384] In the course of the 2007 amendment of the Gacaca Law, however, this sanction was mitigated. Instead, the new article 76(5) stipulates a more extensive and detailed publication of the identity of those convicted and their crimes.

379 See the list of possible measures in art 25 of Presidential Order No 10/01/2005.

380 PRI, *Report IX* (2007) 21.

381 According to a study conducted by the National Unity and Reconciliation Commission (NURC) conducted in 2003, 75% of the survivors believe that TIG will foster reconciliation if it is performed in their communities, PRI, *Report V* (2003) 16; see also C. Kirkby, 'Rwanda's *Gacaca* Courts' 50 *Journal of African Law* (2006) 114.

382 Draft Penal Code as approved by Cabinet decision in 2007, arts 47 *et seq* (on file with the author).

383 On that provision, see J. Gakwaya, *Les sanctions pénales en droit rwandais* (1993) 247 *et seq*.

384 Art 76 of Organic Law No 16/2004.

D. Sentencing

The Gacaca Law contains only very few isolated provisions on sentencing. One of these provisions pertains to the determination of a sentence in the case of multiple offences. While this issue is quite a complex and disputed one under many national criminal legal orders, the Gacaca Law has found a rather simple and elegant solution thereto. The categorization according to article 51 of the Gacaca Law entails that from the outset, the assessment of the defendant's criminal conduct depends solely on the gravest offence committed, regardless of any further offences. The sentence is thus determined according to articles 51 and 72–3, and 78 of the Gacaca Law. However, if the defendant has committed other offences, these are also reflected in the sentence; under article 77(1) of the Gacaca Law, '[w]hen there is a material combination of offences each of which classifies the offender in the same category, the maximum sentence provided in that specific category shall apply'. Yet it goes without saying that defendants in the second category, subcategories (4) to (6), do not incur the considerably higher sentences provided for subcategories (1), (2), and (3), but rather the penalty laid down for their respective subcategory. This is clarified by article 77(2).

The Gacaca Law contains some further guidelines for determining sentences. According to article 52, '[t]he person in the position of authority at the level of the Sector and Cell, at the time of genocide, are classified in the category corresponding to offences they have committed, but their positions of leadership exposes them to the most severe penalty within the same category'. Judges' discretion in determining penalties is equally limited for those who gave an incomplete confession, which was initially accepted, before additional crimes subsequently came to light. According to article 57 of the Gacaca Law, such a person 'is punishable by the maximum penalty provided for…'. This provision entails that a failure to confess is taken into account twice in the sentencing process: not only can the defendant not benefit from a reduction in his or her penalty, but the judge's discretion when sentencing is also limited to the harshest possible sanction. This situation is incompatible with the privilege against self-incrimination.[385] While offering benefits in return for confession is a well-established practice in courts all over the world,[386] prescribing the maximum possible sentence on top of that amounts to punishment for the exercise of the right to remain silent. A further provision on sentencing in the Gacaca Law is article 81, which clarifies that mitigating circumstances cannot justify any deviation from the penalties listed in articles 72–3 and 78 of the Gacaca Law, but can merely entail the minimum penalty provided. The provisions of the Penal Code, which offer substantial leeway for mitigation,[387] are thus declared inapplicable.

[385] Art 14(3)(g) of the ICCPR.

[386] See, eg, on the common plea bargaining practice at the ICTY and ICTR, W.A. Schabas, *The UN International Criminal Tribunals* (2006) 423 *et seq*. On the situation under US law, see J.B. Taylor, *Right to Counsel and Privilege against Self-Incrimination* (2004) 107.

[387] Arts 82 *et seq* of the Penal Code. See also J. Nzakunda, 'Les circonstances atténuantes' *Revue juridique du Rwanda* (2005) no 2, 41 *et seq*, 58.

IX. Civil Claims for Damage to or Loss of Property

During the genocide, all over Rwanda the killings were accompanied by looting. In order to carry out their 'work'[388] of killing the enemy, the killers had to abandon their fields. Regular economic activity was suspended. Looting therefore became an important factor in keeping the machinery of genocide running.[389] Compared to the atrocities committed during the genocide, looting may seem of negligible importance. Yet given the enormous poverty in which most Rwandans live, the economic dimension of the reconciliation process should not be underestimated. Looting deprived many people of their most basic possessions—a house, a cow, or their savings, which may make the difference between a life in extreme poverty and a life in modest economic security. Receiving restitution of or compensation for their property is often the only part of the Gacaca process of tangible importance for such people. For the present study, property-related cases before Gacaca courts are of particular interest, as they are a way of obtaining reparation for harm suffered during the genocide.

From the outset, the legislation on genocide trials has also covered offences against property committed in relation to the genocide. Initially, perpetrators of such offences were placed in the fourth category. In 2004, the fourth category became the third category. Since the introduction of Gacaca courts, property offences no longer entail punishment, but only reparation.[390] According to the law, the competent jurisdiction for trying third category defendants is the Gacaca court of the cell. Property offences committed by defendants classified in the second or first category must be brought as a civil action within the criminal trial before the respective jurisdiction that is competent.[391] De facto, however, this occurs rarely, as I myself was able to witness. Instead, property cases are usually adjudged by the Gacaca court of the cell, regardless of whether the accused has committed additional offences that would place him or her in a category other than the third.[392] This practice relieves the sector courts of the difficult task of determining forms of reparation, and thus prevents further complications in criminal trials. For the victims, it also makes access to justice easier. They can simply take the case to the Gacaca court of the cell without having to observe jurisdictional clauses or be up to date about criminal trials against those who have damaged their property. On the other hand, the separation of civil from criminal trials has complicated the logistics of the process. The authorities sometimes fail to inform offenders who are in prison or in TIG camps about their trial for looting before the cell court. In these

[388] During the genocide, the Hutu population was constantly incited to go to 'work', which meant to kill Tutsi, see A. Des Forges, *Leave None to Tell the Story* (1999) 8.

[389] See the study conducted by PRI, *Report X* (2007) 19 *et seq.*

[390] Art 75 of the Gacaca Law; art 71(1) of Organic Law No 40/2000; under art 14(d) of Organic Law No 08/96, penal sanctions could be imposed, but prison sentences were suspended.

[391] Art 94 of the Gacaca Law.

[392] This was confirmed to me by a representative of PRI Rwanda, interview, Kigali, 15 October 2007. See also PRI, *Report X* (2007) 56. For an exception, see Gacaca Court of the Sector of Mbyo, Gashoro District, *Case of Nteziryayo François*, 23 August 2005.

cases, judgments on damages are then passed in the absence of the offender, and it is up to his family to pay off the debt.[393]

The law acknowledges the possibility of an amicable settlement being made regarding reparation for damaged property. It stipulates that agreements reached prior to its enactment preclude the Gacaca court from hearing the case.[394] In practice, amicable settlements play an even more important role. The National Service of Gacaca Courts recognized their potential to relieve the burden on the courts, and as a form of reconciliation. In its instructions to Gacaca courts, it encouraged out-of-court agreements in all property cases and emphasized their primacy over judgments.[395] Since then, amicable settlements have been reached in nearly 40 per cent of all looting cases.[396] Settlements are to be brokered by local authorities, and approved by the Gacaca court of the cell.[397] The cell courts are thus similar to the new institution of *Abunzi*. If the parties cannot reach an agreement, they can take their case to the cell court. The court will then make a decision based on the testimonies and the information gathered during the investigation phase.

Field research by Penal Reform International (PRI) demonstrates the particular appeal of amicable settlements for both *rescapés* and offenders. These agreements result in lower damages but are much more likely to be respected. In the cell that PRI focused on, damages awarded through judgments amounted to three times more than those agreed upon in amicable settlements on average.[398] However, at the end of the three-month research period, more than half of the reparations agreed upon had been paid off. For damages awarded by courts, the rate was at just over one per cent. In addition, the stakeholders perceived agreements as an opportunity for pardon and reconciliation.[399]

Reparation for stolen or damaged property comes in the form of restitution whenever this is possible. Otherwise, the offender has to pay damages or perform work equivalent to the value of the lost property.[400] This work usually consists in helping in the fields, or comparable everyday jobs.[401] This is not to be confused with community service. Unlike TIG, it is not imposed as a penalty and a service

[393] PRI, *Report X* (2007) 67 *et seq*. The National Service of Gacaca Courts, however, contests this observation and states that defendants in prison are normally summoned for their trial, see Observations du Service National des Juridictions Gacaca au rapport du Penal Reform International sur les infractions contre les biens, Annex to the French version of PRI, *Report X* (2007) 104.

[394] Art 51, category 3 of the Gacaca Law; arts 51, category 4, 71(2) of Organic Law No 40/2000. Amicable settlement was also provided for in art 14(d) of Organic Law No 08/96. Interestingly, the provision encourages a participatory settlement ('règlement à l'amiable entre les parties intéressées avec le concours de leurs concitoyens'), which may be understood as a tribute to traditional dispute resolution.

[395] Letter to all Gacaca Courts of 3 August 2006, quoted in PRI, *Report X* (2007) 54; art 1(2) of Instructions No 14/2007. In addition, representatives of the National Service sensitized the population to seek amicable settlements, see PRI, *Report X* (2007) 54.

[396] In December 2007, 557,607 looting cases had been completed and 54,544 cases remained. Of the completed cases, 219,242 had been settled amicably, information obtained from Alexis Habimana, Documentation and Archivist Officer, National Service of Gacaca Courts, Kigali, 8 October 2008.

[397] Arts 1(2), 2 of Instructions No 14/2007.

[398] 74,428 FRw (approximately 135 US$) compared to 24,409 FRw (44 US$), PRI, *Report X* (2007) 60 *et seq*.

[399] Ibid, 61 *et seq*.

[400] Art 95(1) of the Gacaca Law.

[401] See PRI, *Report X* (2007) 85.

to the community, instead taking the form of individual reparation in favour of the injured party. Often the parties seeking to reach an amicable settlement prefer this form of reparation, as it is easier to comply with for offenders living in poverty. Judgments, on the other hand, impose mostly monetary damages.[402]

Judgments can be executed through seizure of the debtor's property by the local authorities at the cell and sector levels, or by a privately hired bailiff[403]—an arrangement corresponding to the general provisions on execution of judgments.[404] Interim protective measures can be ordered by the competent Gacaca court.[405] The most essential property is not subject to seizure.[406] Nevertheless, many families are impoverished through such seizures. The fear of poverty has, in fact, produced some adverse effects. Some offenders have randomly accused others in order to split the burden, or have conferred their property to family members or friends to protect it from seizure.[407] If the offender is deceased, reparation is paid by the heirs according to the extent to which they have inherited the deceased's property.[408] It is not clear, however, who is liable to pay damages if the offender is still at large, possibly outside the country. In these cases, Gacaca courts often resort to available family members, sometimes even distant ones, which may in turn cause conflicts within families.[409]

X. Monitoring Gacaca Activities

The entire Gacaca process, from the pilot phase to its completion, has been monitored by a number of different parties. The number of different monitoring programmes and the ensuing control density are quite impressive. Monitoring has been organized by Rwandan state agencies, namely the National Service of Gacaca Courts and the National Commission for Human Rights; by Rwandan NGOs and civil society organizations, such as the Ligue Rwandaise pour la Promotion et la Défence des Droits de l'Homme (LIPRODHOR) and the Projet d'Appui de la Société Civile au Processus Gacaca au Rwanda (PAPG); as well as by international NGOs such as Avocats Sans Frontières (ASF) and Penal Reform International (PRI). In addition, the Belgian organization Réseau des Citoyens Justice et

402 Ibid, 58.

403 Art 5(1) of Instructions No 14/2007; see also art 95(3) of the Gacaca Law.

404 See art 199 of *Law No 18/2004 of 20 June 2004 relating to the civil, commercial, labour and administrative procedure*, OGRR no special of 30 July 2004 as modified by art 8 of *Law No 09/2006 of 2 March 2006 modifying and completing Law No 18/2004 of 20 June 2004*, OGRR no special of 5 April 2006. For details on the execution of judgments and agreements, see PRI, *Report XII* (2009) 31 *et seq*.

405 Art 6 of Instructions No 14/2007.

406 These include, inter alia, two thirds of the debtor's crops, two thirds of his salary, one third of his pension, half of his land, his house, and tools he needs to earn his living, art 7 of Instructions No 14/2007. In essence, this corresponds to the provisions of the Code of Civil Procedure (art 260(2) of Law No 18/2004).

407 LIPRODHOR, *Situation des droits de la personne au Rwanda en 2006* (2007) 77 *et seq*.

408 Art 8(2) of Instructions No 14/2007. See also ASF, *Vade-mecum* (2004) 229 *et seq*.

409 PRI, *Report X* (2007) 65.

Démocratie (RCN) has observed prison Gacacas and supported the authorities in the collection of confessions.[410]

The monitoring programme of the National Service of Gacaca Courts essentially serves the purpose of identifying and remedying irregularities. There are approximately 120 district coordinators in the field, 70 per cent of whom hold a law degree, and each of whom is responsible for Gacaca activities in a certain area.[411] If they become aware of irregularities during Gacaca sessions, they are supposed to approach the *inyangamugayo* and advise them on the correct application of the law.[412] The National Service has 13 legal officers at their headquarters who receive reports drawn up by the Gacaca general assemblies together with the district coordinators.[413] If they come to the conclusion that certain provisions of the law or elements of the procedure require more explanation, the National Service can then issue instructions to all Gacaca courts.[414] In addition, the Executive Secretary and other staff regularly address the judges on the radio.[415] Besides its constant monitoring activities, the National Service has also organized training for the judges whenever the Gacaca Law was amended. Nevertheless, observers have deplored the lack of continuous training in order to prevent irregularities from occurring in the first place.[416] The National Service cooperates with the other organizations. The Executive Secretary usually meets all partners on a monthly basis.[417] The organizations have repeatedly managed to exert considerable influence on decision-making with regard to Gacaca.[418]

The National Commission for Human Rights operates a small monitoring programme that focuses on Gacaca and TIG. The commission has 24 agents in the field, each of whom holds a university degree. They observe Gacaca activities, collect background information relating to the human rights situation, and report back to the commission. On this basis, the commission issues reports every year. These are submitted to the National Service and the Ministry of Internal Security.[419]

[410] Interview with a representative of RCN Rwanda, Kigali, 20 September 2007.

[411] Interview with Domitilla Mukantaganzwa, Executive Secretary of the National Service of Gacaca Courts, Kigali, 8 August 2007.

[412] Interview with Denis Bikesha, Director of Training, Mobilisation, and Sensitisation, National Service of Gacaca Courts, Kigali, 21 September 2007.

[413] Interview with Domitilla Mukantaganzwa, Executive Secretary of the National Service of Gacaca Courts, Kigali, 8 August 2007, and with Denis Bikesha, Director of Training, Mobilisation, and Sensitisation, National Service of Gacaca Courts, Kigali, 21 September 2007. See also art 35(4) of the Gacaca Law.

[414] Art 50(2) of the Gacaca Law.

[415] Radios have been distributed to the judges to this end, interview with Domitilla Mukantaganzwa, Executive Secretary of the National Service of Gacaca Courts, Kigali, 8 August 2007.

[416] Interview with a representative of ASF Rwanda, Kigali, 20 March 2007.

[417] Interview with Joseph Shyirambere, Rapporteur in chief of the National Commission for Human Rights, Monitoring Project Gacaca and TIG, Kigali, 27 September 2007.

[418] Interview with two representatives of ASF Rwanda, Kigali, 12 October 2007, in which the two interviewees referred to the position paper of 17 October 2005 by the NGOs ASF, PRI, RCN, and Danish Centre for Human Rights, on file with the author.

[419] Interview with Joseph Shyirambere, Rapporteur in chief of the National Commission for Human Rights, Monitoring Project Gacaca and TIG, Kigali, 27 September 2007.

The Rwandan human rights organization LIPRODHOR, which was founded in 1991,[420] can look back on a fairly tumultuous history. In the 1990s and in the first years of the new century, LIPRODHOR was Rwanda's most active independent human rights organization. In 2003 and 2004, parliamentary commissions repeatedly accused the organization of divisionism and genocide ideology. In June 2004, parliament passed a resolution that called for the dissolution of LIPRODHOR. Its key staff had to leave the country for Uganda and Burundi, where they were also subject to harassment, which eventually led to their being granted asylum in Europe. LIPRODHOR continued to exist under a new leadership.[421] The organization issues yearly reports on the human rights situation in Rwanda. At the time of research, 20 people were working for the league all over the country. In addition, the organization had a further 440 contributing members. LIPRODHOR operates its own monitoring programme within the framework of their annual reporting activities. The league has six coordinators, who receive reports from volunteers in the field. There are 106 of these volunteers, so-called 'animateurs volontaires des droits de l'homme'.[422]

PAPG is an independent collective of several Rwandan civil society organizations,[423] and was founded in 2003 with funds from the Belgian government and the European Union. The network has 72 agents all over the country who observe Gacaca and TIG activities. The PAPG investigates human rights violations that are brought to its attention by those involved in the Gacaca and TIG process. It issues reports and recommendations twice every year and submits them to the National Service.[424]

The NGO Penal Reform International (PRI) was founded in 1989 and is registered in the Netherlands. It is based in London and currently has eight regional offices in Europe, Asia, Africa, and the United States. PRI focuses on the enforcement of human rights standards in criminal proceedings, prison conditions, the reduction of the use of imprisonment, and the development of non-custodial sanctions.[425] Its Kigali office was opened in 1997. The organization initially focused on improving prison conditions.[426] It began its research on Gacaca in 2001.[427] Their Gacaca project has 12 staff members in Kigali and five in the field.[428] PRI has issued 13 very insightful reports on the prosecution of the genocide with a focus on

[420] Interview with a representative of LIPRODHOR, Kigali, 30 October 2007.

[421] FIDH and OMCT, *Observatory for the Protection of Human Rights Defenders 2004* (2005) 86 *et seq*; Front Line, *Rwanda: Disappearances, Arrests, Threats, Intimidation and Co-Option of Human Rights Defenders 2001–2004* (2005) 45 *et seq*; see also Amnesty International, *Human Rights Organization Forced to Close Down* (2005).

[422] Interview with a representative of LIPRODHOR, Kigali, 30 October 2007.

[423] Namely the Collectif des Ligues et Associations de Défence des Droits de l'Homme (CLADHO), the Ligue des Droits de la Personne dans la Région des Grands Lacs (LDGL), the Conseil de Concertation des Organisations d'Appui aux Initiatives de Base (CCOAIB), *Ibuka*, and Pro Femme Twese Hamwe, see PAPG, *Rapport d'Activités, 1er semestre 2004* (2004) 2.

[424] Interview with a representative of PAPG, Kigali, 24 September 2007

[425] A. Chakravarty, 'Gacaca Courts in Rwanda' 1 *Yale Journal of International Affairs* (2005/2006) no 2, 136; PRI, *Annual Report 2002* (2003) 2.

[426] A. Othmani, 'La reconstruction du système criminel de justice' 43 *Revue de Droit Militaire et de Droit de la Guerre* (2004) nos 1–2, 146 *et seq*.

[427] PRI, *Annual Report 2002* (2003) 9.

[428] Interview with a representative of PRI Rwanda, Kigali, 15 October 2007.

Gacaca. The reports explore the Gacaca process from a sociological perspective and each focuses on a specific element of the process, following a methodology termed 'action research'.[429]

Avocats Sans Frontières (ASF) is an international NGO founded in 1992. The organization has its headquarters in Brussels. Besides Rwanda, it also runs programmes in Burundi, the DR Congo, Uganda, Algeria, and Israel/Palestine.[430] Its mission is to train and support lawyers, and to provide those defendants and victims who cannot afford it with legal assistance.[431] ASF has been active in Rwanda since 1996 and has followed the very first genocide cases before ordinary courts. After the introduction of Gacaca courts, ASF and the National Service of Gacaca Courts jointly organized the training of those who trained the Gacaca judges and participated in the supervision of the training sessions.[432] ASF has also supported the preparation of a manual for the judges, and has published a 'Vade-mecum' for the magistrates in ordinary courts who have to deal with genocide cases.[433] At the time of research, ASF had 35 staff members. Seven or eight observers, each with a law degree, regularly visited Gacaca sessions at the sector and appeals level, and drew up reports, which have been summarized in four analytic reports.[434]

The impact of monitoring on Gacaca can hardly be overstated. The various NGOs in particular and their meticulous reports have contributed to improvements being made to the Gacaca legislation. In addition, the presence of observers influences the proceedings, motivates the judges to investigate more thoroughly and to be more scrupulous in the application of the law. On the other hand, monitoring has been criticized for preventing Gacaca from realizing its potential as a restorative mechanism. It has been argued that the legalistic bias of international monitoring has modified Gacaca in the direction of a more retributive instrument.[435]

429 Action research differs from academic research in that its primary goal is not to collect and analyse data on the process being studied, but rather to support the process itself, see PRI, *Report VII* (2005) 1. For details on PRI's work, see also A. Meyerstein, 'Between Law and Culture' 32 *Law & Social Inquiry* (2007) 483 *et seq.*

430 Written information from a representative of ASF Rwanda, 4 November 2009.

431 A. Chakravarty, 'Gacaca Courts in Rwanda' 1 *Yale Journal of International Affairs* (2005/2006) no 2, 136 *et seq*; L. Walleyn, 'Justice as an Instrument of Conflict Prevention' 43 *Revue de Droit Militaire et de Droit de la Guerre* (2004) nos 1–2, 129 *et seq.*

432 Written information from a representative of ASF Rwanda, 5 November 2009.

433 Interview with two representatives of ASF Rwanda, Kigali, 12 October 2007; L. Walleyn, 'Justice as an Instrument of Conflict Prevention' 43 *Revue de Droit Militaire et de Droit de la Guerre* (2004) nos 1–2, 132. ASF, *Vade-mecum* (2004) and Department of Gacaca Jurisdictions, *Manuel explicatif* (2001).

434 Interview with two representatives of ASF Rwanda, Kigali, 12 October 2007.

435 M.A. Drumbl, *Atrocity, Punishment, and International Law* (2007) 94; for discussion of this argument, see ch 3, section IV below.

3

Transitional Justice Through Prosecution

After an analysis of Gacaca legislation and practice in the preceding chapter, we shall now go on to look at Gacaca from the angle of international law, more precisely of international criminal and human rights law. Both fields of law provide guidelines for states in transitional justice situations, as discussed in the introductory chapter. The example of the Rwandan transition is of particular interest for the discussion of these guidelines due to the unprecedented challenges that the country is facing in dealing with the enormous numbers of victims and perpetrators. In fact, Rwanda's situation calls the whole concept of transitional justice and its attempt to set universally applicable paradigms for similar situations into question. However, it is precisely this that makes Rwanda such a challenging topic for transitional justice research—all the more since the country has embarked on a highly ambitious policy of addressing its past. The centrepiece of Rwanda's efforts to address its past is the Gacaca system. While initial attempts to bring perpetrators to justice and to pay redress to victims proved inefficient, Gacaca was supposed to deal with both perpetrators and victims. It was introduced to prosecute genocide suspects in order to establish the truth about what happened, to identify the losses suffered by genocide survivors, and to allocate reparation to them. This was a highly ambitious project, given both the scale of the atrocities and the shortage of resources. It was clear Gacaca would never be able to live up to these high expectations entirely. Nevertheless, it remains a fascinating exercise in transitional justice. This chapter and the one that follows seek to evaluate the Gacaca process within the emerging international legal framework of transitional justice. By doing so, the study seeks to make a contribution to the clarification of this framework by identifying Rwanda's state practice with respect to its international obligations. While this chapter will examine Rwanda's international obligations with regard to the prosecution of the perpetrators of the genocide, and what Rwanda did to live up to these obligations, we shall look at the international legal framework and Rwanda's practice with respect to reparation for serious human rights violations in chapter four.

I. The Prosecution of Crimes under International Law: Rwanda's Obligations

It is a premise of international criminal law that certain values are so crucial to the international community that the law of state responsibility is not sufficient to protect them effectively. Respect for these values can only be ensured by holding the individuals who violate them criminally responsible. In order to enforce these international criminal norms, most international treaties defining crimes under international law obligate states to investigate and prosecute such crimes if committed on their territory.[1] The first treaty defining an obligation to prosecute crimes under international law was the Genocide Convention of 1948, whose Articles IV to VI require states to prosecute and punish perpetrators of genocide. This duty almost instantly acquired the status of customary international law.[2] It was soon followed by the obligation to prosecute war crimes in international armed conflict.[3] A treaty obligation to prosecute also exists with respect to torture.[4] Yet a duty to prosecute other crimes against humanity is nowhere to be found in international conventions. Whether Rwanda is under obligation to prosecute crimes against humanity committed during the genocide must therefore be determined on the basis of customary international law.

Even today, state practice with respect to the prosecution of crimes against humanity leaves a lot to be desired. Nonetheless, it is often implied that states are under a duty to prosecute such crimes.[5] This may appear a contradiction but is not. Existing practice, in fact, forms a solid basis for a customary duty to prosecute crimes against humanity. In the last few years in particular, prosecutions for crimes against humanity have gathered pace in many countries all over the world, even in places where amnesties had barred such efforts for a long time.[6] Examples include Argentina, Bosnia and Herzegovina, Cambodia, Chile, Croatia, East Timor, Ethiopia, Guatemala, Iraq, Peru, Serbia, and Uruguay.[7] Countless declarations and resolutions have proclaimed the duty to prosecute crimes against humanity.[8]

[1] For a discussion of the duty of third states to prosecute, see R. Cryer et al., *An Introduction to International Criminal Law and Procedure* (2007) 58 *et seq*; G. Werle, *Principles of International Criminal Law*, 2nd edn (2009) paras 197 *et seq* with further references.

[2] *Reservations to the Convention on the Prevention and Punishment of the Crime of Genocide*, ICJ, Advisory Opinion of 28 May 1951, ICJ Reports 1951, 15, 23. See also R. Cryer et al., *An Introduction to International Criminal Law and Procedure* (2007) 59; D.F. Orentlicher, 'Settling Accounts' 100 *Yale LJ* (1991) 2565; D. Robinson, 'Serving the Interest of Justice' 14 *EJIL* (2003) 490 *et seq*; G. Werle, *Principles of International Criminal Law*, 2nd edn (2009) para 194.

[3] Art 129 of the *(Geneva) Convention Relative to the Treatment of Prisoners of War* of 12 August 1949 (Third Geneva Convention) 75 UNTS 135; Art 146 of the *(Geneva) Convention Relative to the Protection of Civilian Persons in Time of War* of 12 August 1949 (Fourth Geneva Convention) 75 UNTS 287 (all ratified by Rwanda in 1964).

[4] Art 7 of the Torture Convention.

[5] See, eg, Rome Statute, Preamble, para 6; this view is shared by many experts in the field, see M.C. Bassiouni and E.M. Wise, *Aut dedere aut judicare* (1995) 20 *et seq*; R. Cryer et al., *An Introduction to International Criminal Law and Procedure* (2007) 60; D. Robinson, 'Serving the Interest of Justice' 14 *EJIL* (2003) 491 *et seq*; G. Werle, *Principles of International Criminal Law*, 2nd edn (2009) para 194.

[6] Already in 2003, D. Robinson detected a 'marked revolution in state practice', 'Serving the Interest of Justice' 14 *EJIL* (2003) 491 *et seq*.

[7] See the country profiles on <http://www.trial-ch.org>, last visited June 2011. See also G. Werle, *Principles of International Criminal Law*, 2nd edn (2009) paras 288 *et seq*, 297 *et seq* and the contributions in K. Ambos, E. Malarino and G. Elsner (eds), *Jurisprudencia latinoamericana sobre derecho penal internacional* (2008).

[8] See, eg, UN General Assembly Resolution 2840 (XXVI) of 18 December 1971; UN General Assembly Resolution 3074 (XXVIII) of 3 December 1973; Art 9 of the *Draft Code of Crimes against the Peace and Security of Mankind* of 1996; *Basic Principles and Guidelines on the Right to a*

A strong case for an obligation to prosecute crimes against humanity can also be made by reference to the practice of international human rights bodies. Since the 1980s, the duty to prosecute has been regarded as a corollary to the obligations imposed by international human rights conventions, in particular the ICCPR.[9] While that convention, unlike the Genocide and Torture Conventions, does not contain an express obligation to prosecute violations of the rights and prohibitions contained therein, the Human Rights Committee has implied the existence of such an obligation in the event of certain grave violations. In its authoritative interpretations of the ICCPR, the Committee has repeatedly found that states parties were under a duty to investigate and prosecute torture, severe ill-treatment, disappearance, or extra-legal execution.[10] With respect to amnesty legislation which barred the prosecution of crimes committed by the military dictatorship in Uruguay, it stated that 'amnesties for gross violations of human rights . . . are incompatible with the obligations of the State party', namely with the duty to provide effective remedies against violations as laid down in Article 2(3) of the ICCPR.[11] The Committee made this point even more clearly when it held with respect to the abduction and killing of a dissident by Colombian armed personnel that 'purely disciplinary and administrative remedies cannot be deemed to constitute adequate and effective remedies within the meaning of article 2, paragraph 3, of the Covenant, in the event of particularly serious violations of human rights, notably in the event of an alleged violation of the right to life'.[12] Instead, the state party was under a duty to prosecute criminally those responsible for the violation.[13]

Today, this interpretation of the obligations imposed by international human rights law is well established, as the jurisprudence of regional human rights courts has shown. The Inter-American Court of Human Rights, for instance, found in its landmark judgment in the *Velásquez-Rodríguez* case that states must investigate and punish violations in order to fulfil their obligation to ensure the enjoyment of human rights.[14] The European Court of Human Rights held that the duty to provide an effective remedy entailed an obligation to prosecute whenever applicants had an arguable claim that fundamental provisions of the Convention, such

Remedy and Reparation for Victims of Gross Violations of International Human Rights Law and Serious Violations of International Humanitarian Law, annex to UN General Assembly Resolution 60/147 of 16 December 2005, para 4 (hereinafter 'Basic Principles on the Right to a Remedy and Reparation').

[9] Rwanda has been a party to the ICCPR since 1975.

[10] HRC, *Bleier v Uruguay*, Views of 29 March 1982 (no 30/1978) para 15; *Dermit v Uruguay*, Views of 21 October 1982 (no 84/1981) para 11; *Quinteros v Uruguay*, Views of 21 July 1983 (no 107/1981) paras 15 *et seq*; *Muteba v Zaire*, Views of 24 July 1984 (no 124/1982) para 13; *Laureano v Peru*, Views of 25 March 1996 (no 540/1993) para 10; *Medjnoune v Algeria*, Views of 14 July 2006 (no 1297/2004) para 10; see also General Comment 31/80 of 29 March 2004, paras 8, 18.

[11] HRC, *Rodríguez v Uruguay*, Views of 19 July 1994 (no 322/1988) para 12.4.

[12] HRC, *Bautista v Colombia*, Views of 27 October 1995 (no 563/1993) para 8.2.

[13] Ibid, para 8.6.

[14] *Case of Velásquez Rodríguez v Honduras*, Judgment of 29 July 1988, paras 166, 176 *et seq*; see also *Case of Godínez-Cruz v Honduras*, Judgment of 20 January 1989, paras 182 *et seq*; *Case of the Rochela Massacre v Colombia*, Judgment of 11 May 2007, paras 146, 148, 225. The obligation to ensure the enjoyment of human rights is laid down in Art 1(1) of the *American Convention on Human Rights* of 22 November 1969 (ACHR), 1144 UNTS 123; the ICCPR contains an equivalent provision in Art 2(1).

as the right to life or the prohibition of torture, had been violated.[15] Against this backdrop, the failure to prosecute such crimes must be interpreted as a breach of an international obligation rather than as a manifestation of the conviction not to be under a duty to prosecute.[16]

In order to determine Rwanda's obligations with respect to the atrocities committed in the early 1990s, however, it is not sufficient to establish the existence of a duty to prosecute today. In fact, much of the practice quoted as proof of the duty to prosecute has developed quite recently. This is the case in particular with the prosecutions quoted above, most of which took place after 2000. On the other hand, many of these recent trials have addressed events dating back as far as the early 1970s. In Ethiopia, for instance, the Red Terror trials started in 1994, 20 years after the events in question.[17] Similarly, in Argentina, trials of the military junta have taken place with a delay of almost 25 years.[18] May we therefore conclude that the duty to prosecute once it crystallizes applies retroactively, that is, also with respect to crimes committed before it acquired customary status?

In general, it must be assumed that legal obligations when undertaken apply to future situations, but not to the past. With respect to treaty obligations, the Vienna Convention on the Law of Treaties of 22 May 1969[19] provides in its Article 28 that '[u]nless a different intention appears from the treaty or is otherwise established, its provisions do not bind a party in relation to any act or fact which took place or any situation which ceased to exist before the date of the entry into force of the treaty with respect to that party'.

The question of retroactive application of the obligation to investigate and prosecute has arisen several times before international human rights bodies. In 1990, the UN Human Rights Committee was called upon to decide whether Argentina had violated its obligation under Article 2(3) of the ICCPR to provide effective remedies against human rights violations. The authors of the communication had submitted that their children and other close relatives had been abducted or detained by security forces of the military regime in 1976. An investigation into their whereabouts had never occurred. In 1987, Argentina had enacted two laws effectively barring investigation and prosecution of crimes committed under military rule. The Committee found that the right to a remedy laid down in Article 2(3) of the ICCPR was an accessory right that could only be claimed in conjunction with the violation of another right guaranteed in the Covenant. Since Argentina had only ratified the Covenant in 1986, the Committee held itself incompetent to examine

[15] See, eg, ECtHR, *Aksoy v Turkey*, Judgment of 18 December 1996, para 98; *Aydın v Turkey*, Judgment of 25 September 1997, para 103; *Nasukhanova v Russia*, Judgment of 18 December 2008, paras 141 *et seq*. The right to a remedy is laid down in Art 13 of the *(European) Convention for the Protection of Human Rights and Fundamental Freedoms* of 4 November 1950 (ECHR), 213 UNTS 222.

[16] See *Case Concerning Military and Paramilitary Activities in and against Nicaragua (Nicaragua v USA)*, ICJ, Judgment of 27 June 1986, ICJ Reports 1986, 14, para 186. See also the more detailed discussion on the formation of customary human rights law in ch 4, section I A below.

[17] On the Mengistu trial for genocide and crimes against humanity, eg, see F.K. Tiba, 'The *Mengistu* Genocide Trial in Ethiopia' 5 *JICJ* (2007) 513 *et seq*.

[18] N. Roht-Arriaza, 'Prosecutions of Heads of State in Latin America' in E.L. Lutz and C. Reiger (eds), *Prosecuting Heads of State* (2009) 46 *et seq*.

[19] 1155 UNTS 331.

the original violations occurring in 1976 and declared the communications inadmissible.[20] The Committee thus refused to extend the obligation to provide remedies so as to apply to violations that had occurred before the ICCPR came into force. The Inter-American Court of Human Rights, in contrast, found no bar to its jurisdiction in comparable circumstances.[21] The UN Committee against Torture held in a case involving torture committed by the regime of Hissène Habré in Chad between 1982 and 1990 that Senegal, where Habré resided, was under an obligation to prosecute or extradite him. It did not address the issue that many of Habré's crimes had actually occurred before the Torture Convention came into force in 1987.[22]

While the two latter cases may militate in favour of a retroactive application of the duty to prosecute, state practice does not supply conclusive evidence to that effect. In many countries, prosecutions of crimes against humanity have certainly taken place long after the crimes were committed. Yet given that crimes against humanity are often committed with the participation of state actors or at least with their tacit approval, their prosecution is often delayed until a new government begins its work. The fact that states today prosecute crimes against humanity committed decades ago thus does not necessarily imply that they regard their obligation to prosecute to have a retroactive effect. In fact, many states are not willing to address wrongs from the more distant past. Uganda, for instance, may today be regarded as a state that generally supports international criminal justice, despite the conflicts between the government and the ICC. Nevertheless, there have never been serious attempts made to prosecute the crimes committed in the 1970s and 1980s under the rule of Idi Amin or Milton Obote. In Peru, former President Alberto Fujimori has recently been sentenced to a long prison term for crimes against humanity committed from 1991 onwards.[23] Internal strife before that time, however, has not been addressed.[24] Finally, Rwanda itself may be quoted as an example against a retroactive effect of the duty to prosecute. The government has often expressed its willingness to prosecute crimes against humanity

[20] HRC, *R.A.V.N. v Argentina*, Views of 26 March 1990 (nos 343, 344, and 345/1988) paras 5.2 *et seq*; *S.E. v Argentina*, Views of 26 March 1990 (no 275/1988) paras 5.2 *et seq*. See also the similar cases, HRC, *Acuña-Inostroza* et al. *v Chile*, Views of 23 July 1999 (no 717/1996) para 6.4; *Vargas Vargas v Chile*, Views of 26 July 1999 (no 718/1996) para 6.4; *Menanteau Aceituno and Carrasco Vasquez v Chile*, Views of 26 July 1999 (no 746/1997) para 6.4. However, it is quite possible that the Committee would decide differently today. In more recent views, the Committee found that while the right to a remedy is an accessory right and must be claimed in conjunction with another violation, this original violation does not actually have to be established. Instead, it is sufficient that the author of the communication presents an arguable claim of the original violation, see HRC, *Kazantzis v Cyprus*, Views of 7 August 2003 (no 972/2001) para 6.6; *Faure v Australia*, Views of 31 October 2005 (no 1036/2001) para 7.2.

[21] IACtHR, *Case of the Serrano-Cruz Sisters v El Salvador*, Judgment of 23 November 2004 (Preliminary Objections) paras 76 *et seq*; *Case of Almonacid-Arellano* et al. *v Chile*, Judgment of 26 September 2006, paras 45 *et seq*.

[22] CAT, *Guengueng* et al. *v Senegal*, Views of 17 May 2006 (no 181/2001) paras 9.7 *et seq*.

[23] See Fujimori's profile on <http://www.trial-ch.org>, last visited June 2011.

[24] On that, see E. González Cueva, 'The Peruvian Truth and Reconciliation Commission' in N. Roht-Arriaza and J. Mariezcurrena (eds), *Transitional Justice in the Twenty-First Century* (2006) 70 *et seq*.

committed in the course of the genocide, while there has been no mention of previous genocidal violence in 1972 and before.

Instead this practice suggests that a failure to prosecute such crimes was incompatible with international law even at the time. Even though practice was not sufficiently consistent then, the recent trials of crimes committed in 1970s, '80s and '90s are evidence that the duty to prosecute crystallized into a customary obligation at some point in time before 1990.[25] This assumption is confirmed by the jurisprudence of international human rights bodies quoted above. Since the 1980s, these bodies have derived the duty to prosecute from the obligations to ensure human rights and to provide effective remedies against violations. In fact, states today acknowledge that their practice of impunity was inconsistent with their international obligations. In 2005, the Supreme Court of Argentina, for instance, declared the Argentinian amnesty legislation unconstitutional, inter alia on the ground of its being inconsistent with the duty under Article 2(3) of the ICCPR to provide effective remedies against violations.[26] The Supreme Court of Uruguay recently passed a similar decision overriding the country's amnesty legislation.[27]

II. The Limits of Prosecution

We have seen that international law requires prosecution as the standard reaction to genocide, war crimes, and crimes against humanity. Yet little has been said about the scope of such prosecutions. This question is of great practical relevance. After all, crimes under international law are by their very nature committed on a large scale involving many perpetrators and accessories, while prosecutions have often focused on a relatively small number of suspects, usually those high up in the command chain. In fact, the evidence provided for a duty to prosecute in the previous section suggests that selective prosecutions are sufficient to comply with the duty. One particularly graphic example of a selective prosecution practice is provided by the Extraordinary Chambers in the Courts of Cambodia competent for the Khmer Rouge trials. To date, these chambers have only dealt with five defendants while further prosecutorial activity is controversial among judges and prosecutors. It is unclear whether further cases will be followed through.[28]

A rather different example of limited prosecutions is post-apartheid South Africa. During the negotiated transition from apartheid to democracy, the parties agreed to establish a Truth and Reconciliation Commission (TRC) which had the power to

[25] See also D.F. Orentlicher, 'Settling Accounts' 100 *Yale LJ* (1991) 2593; N. Roht-Arriaza, 'State Responsibility to Investigate and Prosecute' 78 *CalLR* (1990) 466 *et seq*; contra C. Tomuschat, 'The Duty to Prosecute International Crimes Committed by Individuals' in H.-J. Cremer et al. (eds), *Tradition und Weltoffenheit des Rechts* (2002) 337.

[26] Corte Suprema de Justicia de la Nación (Argentina), *Case of Julio Héctor Simón y otros*, Judgment of 14 June 2005, para 33.

[27] Suprema Corte de Justicia (Uruguay), *Case of Nibia Sabalsagaray*, Judgment of 19 October 2009.

[28] Amnesty International, *UN-Cambodia Court: Excessive Secrecy, Exclusion and Fears of Inappropriate Interference* (2011). See also P. Kroker, 'Auf gutem Weg' 122 *ZStW* (2010) 685 *et seq*; P. Kroker, 'Transitional Justice Policy in Practice' 53 *GYIL* (2011) 753 *et seq*.

grant amnesty for offences associated with a political objective and committed since 1960, on the condition that the perpetrator made a full disclosure of all relevant facts.[29] This arrangement included all societal factions and was widely welcomed among the international community. Most analysts found no contradiction between conditional amnesty and South Africa's duty to prosecute acts amounting to crimes under international law.[30] In fact, neither state practice nor jurisprudence allows the conclusion that conditional amnesty is necessarily inconsistent with international law. While international courts and other bodies have repeatedly declared amnesty for crimes under international law impermissible, this jurisprudence does not apply to conditional amnesty as enacted in South Africa. These bodies have usually based their rejection of amnesty on its effect of foreclosing any form of judicial action or investigation.[31] The TRC legislation, however, did not preclude access to remedies, but instead provided victims with a forum to have their cause heard.[32] In addition, it left room for prosecution of those suspects who had not successfully applied for amnesty, even though very few such prosecutions have taken place up to this day.[33] On the other hand, international approval for the South African amnesty process may also have its roots in a sense of political realism. The South African transition took place in a tense climate where a failure of the negotiations was likely to spark outbreaks of serious internal violence or even a civil war. Against this backdrop, the international community refrained from calling for unconditional prosecution of crimes under international law. It has therefore been argued that a narrow exception from the duty to prosecute exists on grounds of necessity in cases where criminal trials of former elites amount to a threat to internal peace.[34]

Refraining from prosecution can also be permissible from another point of view. States in transition have often emerged from protracted periods of violent conflict. The aftermath of these conflicts is not only characterized by political instability, but also by weak state institutions. Often states in transition are confronted with mass atrocities involving great numbers of perpetrators at a time when the judicial system, which would normally have to deal with such crimes, is severely damaged.

[29] See section 20(1) of the *Promotion of National Unity and Reconciliation Act* No 34 of 1995.

[30] See A. du Bois-Pedain, *Transitional Amnesty in South Africa* (2007) 319–22; R.C. Slye, 'The Legitimacy of Amnesty under International Law and General Principles of Anglo-American Law' 43 *Virginia Journal of International Law* (2002/03) 246–7.

[31] AfrComHPR, *Malawi African Association* et al. *v Mauritania*, Decision of 11 May 2000 (nos 54/91, 61/91, 98/93, 164–196/97, 210/98) paras 82 *et seq*; HRC, *Rodríguez v Uruguay*, Views of 19 July 1994 (no 322/1988) para 12.4; *Prosecutor v Furundžija*, ICTY, Trial Chamber, Judgment of 10 December 1998 (IT-95–17/1-T) para 155. In Latin America, a more restrictive practice with respect to amnesty has evolved, see IACtHR, *Case of Barrios Altos v Peru*, Judgment of 14 March 2001, paras 41 *et seq*; *Case of Almonacid-Arellano* et al. *v Chile*, Judgment of 26 September 2006, para 110.

[32] See section 11 of the Promotion of National Unity and Reconciliation Act.

[33] See O. Bubenzer, *Post-TRC Prosecutions in South Africa* (2009); A. du Bois-Pedain, *Transitional Amnesty in South Africa* (2007) 54–9; L. Fernandez, 'Post-TRC Prosecutions in South Africa' in G. Werle (ed), *Justice in Transition* (2006) 65–73.

[34] K. Ambos, *Internationales Strafrecht*, 2nd edn (2008) 193; G. Werle, *Principles of International Criminal Law*, 2nd edn (2009) para 216. See also K. Ambos, 'The Legal Framework of Transitional Justice' in K. Ambos, J. Large and M. Wierda (eds), *Building a Future on Peace and Justice* (2009) 49 *et seq*; C. Tomuschat, 'The Duty to Prosecute International Crimes Committed by Individuals' in H.-J. Cremer et al. (eds), *Tradition und Weltoffenheit des Rechts* (2002) 347.

Given the range of other challenges most states in transition normally face, comprehensive prosecution of all perpetrators may exceed the state's capacities. In such cases, a limited programme of prosecutions targeting the most senior perpetrators is sufficient in order for a state to fulfil its obligations.[35] The duty to prosecute cannot be considered in order to require states to perform the impossible.[36] Obligations under international law must be construed 'so as to exclude situations of both absolute and relative impossibility'.[37]

In practice, the discretion to decide what is impossible would lie with the prosecuting state, thus allowing for a certain leeway in deciding to what extent it allocates resources to criminal prosecution. Impossibility in this context may be understood as a situation in which the provision of vital public services and other crucial state functions is in danger. Consequently, if the judiciary ceased functioning for years due to prosecutions, or if schools had to be expelled from public buildings in order that they be turned into courthouses, it could be asserted that the state had taken its obligation to prosecute too seriously. On the other hand, the impossibility argument does not allow a state to refrain from prosecution altogether.

Limiting prosecutions is also in line with the rationale of international duties to prosecute certain crimes. These duties serve the purpose of enforcing a universal system of values inter alia by deterring other potential perpetrators of such crimes. Selective prosecutions of high-level perpetrators usually receive worldwide publicity, while trials concerning lower ranks often go unnoticed. It is therefore justifiable with regard to the need for effective deterrence to refrain from comprehensive prosecutions. In the case of Rwanda, the fact that over half a million people were suspected of genocide and crimes against humanity[38] would suggest that comprehensive prosecutions would have been impossible anyway. Therefore, a limited programme of prosecution would have been sufficient for Rwanda to comply with its international obligations. There are no criteria in international law to determine exactly how many cases would have been necessary. Given the magnitude of the crimes committed in Rwanda and the number of victims, a very serious effort, trials of 8,000 or 10,000 of the most senior suspects, for example, would have been appropriate.

III. The Implementation of the Duty to Prosecute: Trials and Local Mechanisms

While the existence of international obligations to prosecute is a widely discussed issue, international law does not provide much guidance as to what conditions

[35] Similarly, Justice Robertson of the Special Court for Sierra Leone in his Separate Opinion to *Prosecutor v Kondewa*, Appeals Chamber, Decision of 25 May 2004 (SCSL-2004–14-AR72(E)) para 33.

[36] D.F. Orentlicher, 'Settling Accounts' 100 *Yale LJ* (1991) 2600; see also N.J. Kritz, 'Coming to Terms with Atrocities' 59 *LCP* (1996) no 4, 134.

[37] G. Schwarzenberger, *International Law*, vol 1, 3rd edn (1957) 539; see also D.F. Orentlicher, ibid.

[38] According to data provided by the National Service, the number of first and second category suspects amounts to 509,826 people, National Service of Gacaca Courts, *Summary of Persons Prosecuted* (2006).

domestic prosecutions must fulfil in order to comply with prosecution duties. Criminal trials must, of course, be in line with the procedural guarantees provided by international human rights law, in particular the right to a fair trial.[39] Some further guidance is provided by the conventions that stipulate duties to prosecute. The Genocide and Geneva Conventions require that states provide 'effective' penalties for perpetrators.[40] The Torture Convention obligates states to try torture cases in the same manner as all other cases of serious offences[41]—a clause inserted in order to avert the potential dangers that can arise from the political nature of the crime of torture. It entails that defendants should not be privileged, as is often the case with police or military personnel.[42] Nor should they be treated with excessive severity.[43]

Another valuable instrument for interpreting international duties to prosecute is the Rome Statute, in particular Articles 1 and 17. These stipulate that the ICC is complementary to national jurisdictions. Other than the ICTR, for instance, the ICC does not have primacy over national organs. Instead, it only steps in if national courts fail to prosecute crimes that are within the jurisdiction of the ICC. Article 17 defines that failure to prosecute must, inter alia, be assumed if a state is unwilling to do so. The definition of unwillingness in paragraph 2 of the said provision may be regarded as the reflection of the obligation to prosecute in the jurisdictional system of the ICC. Article 17(2) stipulates, for instance, that if 'proceedings... are being conducted in a manner which... is inconsistent with an intent to bring the person concerned to justice', the state conducting such proceedings will be regarded as unwilling to genuinely prosecute. The aim of bringing a person to justice mentioned in Article 17(2) reveals that prosecutions for crimes under international law must, in general, follow the traditional model of a criminal trial as a retributive, perpetrator-centred instrument. This paradigm of international criminal justice implies that national prosecutions must be capable of resulting in an appropriate sentence.

In fact, the panoply of instruments to address gross human rights violations in different cultural settings goes far beyond criminal trials. We have seen in the introduction to this study that states increasingly resort to neo-traditional local mechanisms in order to come to terms with a violent past. Gacaca is an example of this. Yet what is the role of such mechanisms under the criminal justice paradigm? When it comes to crimes under international law falling within the jurisdiction of the International Criminal Court, there is limited room for local non-punitive mechanisms to address these crimes. This becomes clear with regard to the Uganda situation before the ICC. Following a referral of the situation concerning the Lord's Resistance Army (LRA) by the Ugandan government to the ICC, the Court has

[39] Art 14 of the ICCPR or Arts 7(1)(b), (c), (d), 26 of the Banjul Charter. See also Art 7(3) of the Torture Convention and M.C. Bassiouni, *Introduction to International Criminal Law* (2003) 344.

[40] Art V of the Genocide Convention, Art 129(1) of the Third and Art 146(1) of the Fourth Geneva Convention.

[41] Art 7(2) of the Torture Convention.

[42] See, eg, the *Bautista* case, HRC, *Bautista v Colombia*, Views of 27 October 1995 (no 563/1993).

[43] See M. Nowak and E. McArthur, *The United Nations Convention against Torture* (2008) Art 7 paras 70 *et seq*.

issued arrest warrants against five senior leaders of the LRA. This has upset local leaders in northern Uganda, who fear that their efforts to enter a peace agreement with the LRA are in danger. They argue that local mechanisms, in particular the Acholi rite *mato oput*, would be sufficient to ensure accountability.[44] *Mato oput* is a ritual employed to reconcile the clans of the offender and the victim, inter alia, through the payment of compensation.[45] Even though *mato oput* may be preceded by the caning of the perpetrator,[46] it is not a form of prosecution in terms of international law. Therefore, it would most probably fall short of the complementarity test under Article 17 of the Rome Statute.

Nevertheless the international criminal justice paradigm is not incompatible with local initiatives to come to terms with past atrocities. It has been argued above that states have discretion in implementing their duty to prosecute in the aftermath of mass atrocities. They may, under certain circumstances, limit prosecutions to the most senior perpetrators. The international criminal justice paradigm as understood here may thus be described as a regime that intervenes only in cases where universal rights and values are most threatened. Local approaches to tackle a violent past are welcome and necessary complements to international justice. The introduction of the principle of complementarity into the Rome Statute reflects the increasing openness of international justice towards pluralistic local approaches. The complementarity test allows the ICC to examine local measures taken and gives the Court the opportunity to step back if it sees no need for intervention. There was no room for such an examination under the Nuremberg tribunal's exclusivity model or the ad hoc tribunals' primary jurisdiction.[47]

IV. Locating Gacaca between Retributive and Restorative Justice

Despite Gacaca's neo-traditional and restorative elements, the stakeholders in the process have always understood Gacaca to be an innovative form of retributive criminal prosecution. In fact, Gacaca's record as a criminal justice mechanism is quite impressive in terms of the cases completed and the numbers of convictions and acquittals. Rwanda has taken its duty to prosecute genocide and crimes against humanity so seriously that it has more than fulfilled its international obligations to bring those responsible for the genocide to justice.

[44] T. Allen, 'The International Criminal Court and the Invention of Traditional Justice in Northern Uganda' 107 *Politique Africaine* (2007) 148; E.K. Baines, 'The Haunting of Alice' 1 *International Journal of Transitional Justice* (2007) 101 *et seq.*

[45] For details, see T. Allen, ibid, 149 *et seq*; J.O. Latigo, 'Tradition-Based Practices in the Acholi Region' in L. Huyse and M. Salter (eds), *Traditional Justice and Reconciliation after Violent Conflict* (2008) 103 *et seq*; J.R. Quinn, 'Social Reconstruction in Uganda' 8 *Human Rights Review* (2007) 398 *et seq.*

[46] Beyond Juba, *Tradition in Transition* (2009) 19 *et seq.*

[47] M.A. Drumbl, *Atrocity, Punishment, and International Law* (2007) 187 *et seq.* On the different models governing the relationship between international and national justice, see G. Werle, *Principles of International Criminal Law*, 2nd edn (2009) paras 223 *et seq.*

Nevertheless, Gacaca is often discussed in connection with restorative justice.[48] This concept refers to various forms of alternative justice in all parts of the world, whether traditional or modern. Definitions of restorative justice reflect the cultural diversity that it entails and are often not particularly tangible in nature. Characteristics commonly ascribed to restorative justice include a focus on the disrupted social fabric and the priority of repairing this social fabric over sanctioning.[49] Crime is being understood as a conflict between the offender and the victim, as well as the community. A restorative process therefore brings together all stakeholders including the community. An important element of a restorative process is often the 'reintegrative shaming' of the offender.[50] Punishment is commonly regarded as incompatible with restorative justice.[51]

Traditional Gacaca can be viewed as a prototype of restorative justice in many respects. It gave priority to reintegration over retribution and even over redress. Offences were regarded as being of concern to the entire community. Shaming the offender, it seems, helped ensure respect for whatever Gacaca imposed.[52] By contrast, modern Gacaca has very different preconditions that undermine its potential to deliver restorative justice. To begin with, restorative justice implies that there is a community ready to reintegrate an offender. Given that Rwandan society has been deeply divided and affected by mutual distrust within communities for a long time and given the massive displacement of the population brought about by the genocide, communities often lack the social coherence that facilitates reintegration. Shaming offenders in these communities is unlikely to provide an effective tool for reconciliation.[53] Especially in communities where perpetrators outnumber the survivors, offenders are much less likely to actually feel ashamed of their conduct.[54]

In addition, restorative justice is often regarded as an inappropriate reaction to the crimes that occurred in Rwanda. Many survivors are, unsurprisingly, opposed to the idea of a restorative process, given the demands that such a process makes on them by requiring their forgiveness and their willingness to reintegrate perpetrators

[48] M.R. Amstutz, 'Is Reconciliation Possible after Genocide?' 48 *Journal of Church and State* (2006) 556; J.B. Fink, 'Deontological Retributivism and the Legal Practice of International Jurisprudence' 49 *Journal of African Law* (2005) 129; P.E. Harrell, *Rwanda's Gamble* (2003) 85 *et seq*; P.E. Nantulya, 'The Gacaca System in Rwanda' *Conflict Trends* (2001) no 4, 55; A.E. Tiemessen, 'After Arusha' 8 *African Studies Quarterly* (2004) 60 *et seq*. For a detailed overview and critique, see P. Clark, *The Gacaca Courts* (2010) 245 *et seq*.

[49] J. Brathwaite, 'Restorative Justice and De-Professionalization' 13 *The Good Society* (2004) no 1, 28; H. Strang and J. Brathwaite (eds), *Restorative Justice and Civil Society* (2001) 1.

[50] J. Brathwaite, *Crime, Shame and Reintegration* (1989) 81, 119 *et seq*.

[51] J. Brathwaite, 'Principles of Restorative Justice' in A. von Hirsch et al. (eds), *Restorative Justice and Criminal Justice* (2003) 2; D. Roche, *Accountability in Restorative Justice* (2003) 27.

[52] See ch 2, section I above; see also M.A. Drumbl, 'Punishment, Postgenocide' 75 *NYULR* (2000) 1264.

[53] See also L. Waldorf, 'Mass Justice for Mass Atrocities' 79 *TempLRev* (2006) 75–7.

[54] For a critical discussion of deviance and conformity during mass atrocities and the consequences for individual criminal responsibility, see M.A. Drumbl, *Atrocity, Punishment, and International Law* (2007) 23 *et seq*.

into their communities.[55] Finally, Gacaca's punitive elements may defeat its restorative objectives and prove to be an obstacle to sincere truth-telling, reconciliation, and reintegration. With the prospect of punishment looming, offenders are more likely to behave defensively towards the victim and the community. The logic of the criminal trial leaves little room for restorative concepts. After all, the defendants' primary interest is getting off the hook, not reconciliation.[56] Drumbl argues that Gacaca's move away from its restorative origins into a more retributive mechanism is in part due to the criticism of Gacaca voiced by donors and international NGOs. Accordingly, these critics have prompted a modification of the system towards 'liberal legalist process and sanction, in which guilt instead of responsibility is the goal'.[57] This is not entirely convincing in my view. Most modifications that compromised Gacaca's restorative potential or made it a more retributive mechanism were implemented in opposition to the recommendations of the international observers involved. These include, for instance, the decision to entrust the *nyumbakumi* with the investigation or the expansion of the jurisdiction of Gacaca courts to encompass the majority of the legally complex category one cases.

In fact, notwithstanding Gacaca's retributive focus, communities and individuals have made use of it for restorative purposes. Gacaca has provided an opportunity for survivors to participate in shaping the process in a way that would not have been possible in an ordinary criminal trial. As Clark argues, Gacaca offers a vital forum for discourse that may provide a nucleus for broader dialogue outside Gacaca.[58] He also shows that many individual participants in Gacaca have made it a platform for individual reconciliation that exceeds, and is a precondition for, group-to-group reconciliation.[59] This is in line with my own experience. While the majority of defendants show little emotion, candid displays of remorse do at times occur and are likely to be received positively. I was able to observe a case where the victims' relatives had forgiven the accused and even testified in her favour. The case was heard upon a motion for review lodged by two applicants not related to the victims arguing that the sentence was too lenient. According to the testimonies, the accused had participated in a raid in which a couple had been killed. After that, the accused had undressed the dead bodies and put their dead dog between them, a gesture the audience regarded as highly reprehensible. It was apparent that the defendant was deeply embarrassed. She made no effort to deny any of the charges and said that she had no defence for what she had done. She was unable to stop crying while giving her statement. The victims' relatives both stated that they opposed the motion for review since they had accepted the defendant's apologies. The testimony given by one of them for her defence resulted in a reduction of her sentence.[60]

[55] P. Clark, *The Gacaca Courts* (2010) 242–5; L. Waldorf, 'Rwanda's Failing Experiment in Restorative Justice' in D. Sullivan and L. Tifft (eds), *Handbook of Restorative Justice* (2006) 429.

[56] See also L. Waldorf, 'Mass Justice for Mass Atrocities' 79 *TempLRev* (2006) 72 *et seq.*

[57] M.A. Drumbl, *Atrocity, Punishment, and International Law* (2007) 94.

[58] P. Clark, *The Gacaca Courts* (2010) 213.

[59] Ibid, 313, 333.

[60] Gacaca Court of Appeal, Kimihurura, Gasabo District, *Case of Nyirabashitsi Françoise*, 16 September 2007.

V. Gacaca Courts and International Law

Indeed, Gacaca courts are much more similar to ordinary courts than their outward appearance might suggest. Article 39 of the Gacaca Law contains a list of powers the courts have in order to fulfil their tasks:

They may in particular:

1 Summon any person to appear in a trial;

2 Order and carry out a search of [the defendant]. This search must, however, respect the defendant's private property and basic human rights;

3 Take temporary protective measures against the property of those accused of genocide crimes;

4 Pronounce sentences and order the convicted person to compensate;

5 Order the withdrawal of the distraint for the acquitted person's property;

6 Prosecute and punish trouble makers in the court;

7 Summon, if necessary, the Public Prosecution to give explanatory information on files it has investigated;

8 Issue summons to the alleged authors of offences and order detention or release on parole, if necessary.

As discussed above, Gacaca courts may hand down long prison sentences and regularly do so in fact. Gacaca tribunals must therefore respect due process standards.

Some authors have downplayed the importance of due process in Gacaca given its traditional roots, its unique setup, its restorative elements, and the general lack of judicial infrastructure. They argue that the formal approach of human rights critiques and their insistence on a catalogue of requirements modelled upon Western-style courts fails to take into account the distinctive nature of customary legal systems and ultimately challenges the idea of universality of human rights.[61] Amnesty International and Human Rights Watch in particular have been criticized for their formalist, one-size-fits-all approach to assessing Gacaca courts.[62]

To some extent this criticism is valid. Fair trial provisions in international law, such as Article 14 of the ICCPR, are modelled upon Western-style courts and do not allow for a great deal of flexibility in accommodating traditional, less formalized

[61] T. Longman, 'Justice at the Grassroots?' in N. Roht-Arriaza and J. Mariezcurrena (eds), *Transitional Justice in the Twenty-First Century* (2006) 213. Similarly, P. Clark, 'The Rules (and Politics) of Engagement' in P. Clark and Z.D. Kaufman (eds), *After Genocide* (2008) 311 *et seq*; P.E. Harrell, *Rwanda's Gamble* (2003) 92. See also J.E. Alvarez, 'Crimes of States/Crimes of Hate' 24 *Yale JIntlL* (1999) 414; C. Kirkby, 'Rwanda's *Gacaca* Courts' 50 *Journal of African Law* (2006) 108; A. Megwalu and N. Loizides, 'Dilemmas of Justice and Reconciliation' 18 *African Journal of International and Comparative Law* (2010) 15; C. Mibenge, 'Enforcing International Humanitarian Law at the National Level' in T.L.H. McCormack (ed), *Yearbook of International Humanitarian Law*, vol 7 (2006) 422; R. Nagy, 'Traditional Justice and Legal Pluralism in Transitional Context' in J.R. Quinn (ed), *Reconciliation(s)* (2009) 97 *et seq*; A.E. Tiemessen, 'After Arusha' 8 *African Studies Quarterly* (2004) 64.

[62] P. Clark, ibid, 308 *et seq*; A. Meyerstein, 'Between Law and Culture' 32 *Law & Social Inquiry* (2007) 467 *et seq*.

institutions. The fact that a customary, traditional, or neo-traditional institution dispenses with certain formalities does not mean that the outcome of processes conducted within them is necessarily unjust. Cultural relativists correctly argue that the fair trial principle as laid down in human rights conventions is a Western concept tailored to the formal procedures used in Western-style courts. Yet the basic tenets of fairness, independence and impartiality can also be ensured in an informal context.[63] They are particularly vital where an institution like Gacaca is capable of imposing drastic sanctions borrowed from Western criminal law. After all, the basic principles underlying the right to a fair trial also ensure that the outcome of the prosecutions is perceived as credible and just, and that prosecution is accepted as a step towards future stability and reconciliation.[64]

The fair trial principle is laid down in two Conventions to which Rwanda is a party: the ICCPR,[65] which contains a detailed listing of all important guarantees associated with that principle; and the Banjul Charter,[66] that includes a less comprehensive listing, but is understood to encompass essentially the same guarantees.[67] In addition, the Rwandan Constitution and the Code of Criminal Procedure contain various provisions to guarantee fair trials.[68] Some particular issues relating to fairness have already been addressed in the preceding chapter in connection with the respective provisions of the Gacaca Law examined there—namely the introduction of provisions amounting to retroactive aggravation of penalties in certain cases;[69] the *ex post facto* criminalization of superior responsibility;[70] the aggravation of the penalty in certain cases of defendants exercising their right not to testify against themselves;[71] and the power of Gacaca courts to reopen completed cases in violation of the *ne bis in idem* principle.[72] The following sections will try to complete the picture by discussing the major structural shortcomings of the Gacaca system when it comes to fairness and due process of law.

A. Independence and impartiality

Independence and impartiality are crucial characteristics of a court and its judges. A court that does not live up to the standard of an 'independent and impartial tribunal' (Article 14(1) of the ICCPR) can never conduct a fair trial. A comparable standard for criminal tribunals can be deduced from Articles 7(1)(b), (d), and 26 of the Banjul Charter, and from articles 19, 60(2), and 140(2) of the Rwandan

[63] P. Clark does not take this into account when he argues that greater respect for the rights of the defendant would inevitably require a more formalized procedure and the presence of lawyers, *The Gacaca Courts* (2010) 160 *et seq.*

[64] See S. Trechsel, 'Why Must Trials Be Fair?' 31 *IsLR* (1997) 99. See also A. Corey and S.F. Joireman, 'Retributive Justice' 103 *African Affairs* (2004) 84 *et seq.*

[65] Arts 14–15.

[66] Arts 7, 26.

[67] See AfrComHPR Resolution 4(XI)92 of March 1992.

[68] Arts 16–20, 60(2), 140, 141 of the Rwandan Constitution (art 20 as amended by art 1 of Amendment No 4; art 141 as amended by art 27 of the Amendment of 13 August 2008); and, eg, art 1(2) of the Code of Criminal Procedure as modified by art 1 of Law No 20/2006.

[69] See ch 2, section IV C above.

[70] See ch 2, section IV C *(6)* above.

[71] Art 57 of the Gacaca Law, see ch 2, section VIII D above.

[72] See ch 2, section VII C above.

Constitution. Independence and impartiality are two closely interrelated guarantees that are not always clearly distinguishable from one another. Independence is not only an individual right, but also an institutional guarantee: courts must not be subordinated to other state organs, and they must be free from undue interference by private actors.[73] In contrast, impartiality refers to a specific court and its judges: these 'must not harbour preconceptions about the matter put before them, and . . . they must not act in ways that promote the interests of one of the parties'.[74]

The Gacaca Law contains a number of provisions to ensure the independence and impartiality of Gacaca courts. Judges must be persons of integrity—'*inyangamugayo*'.[75] Those elected to be *inyangamugayo* are often people who enjoy special respect and authority in the community. Anyone who holds an official position is not eligible to become a Gacaca judge.[76] Judges can be removed from office for a number of reasons, inter alia for harbouring genocide ideology.[77] According to article 10, an *inyangamugayo* may not sit in judgment on a relative, a close friend or a person with whom he or she has had a longstanding enmity. Article 30 provides for sanctions against persons who exercise pressure on Gacaca judges or attempt to do so.

(1) The vulnerability of Gacaca judges

Obviously, Gacaca courts are still highly susceptible to outside influence. The judges are laymen who may not even be aware of attempts to affect their independence. While many judges do in fact enjoy considerable respect, others lack the authority to withstand interference. Instances of intervention by local authorities and other state officials in order to influence the process, and sometimes even to have a person convicted or acquitted, have been reported regularly.[78] Local authorities, in particular the *nyumbakumi*, have, in practice, conducted many of the inquiries preceding the trials by collecting testimonies and drawing up case files, even though the law assigned this task to the cell courts.[79] A further source of interference stems from the coordinators of the National Service of Gacaca Courts, who work in the field to monitor the activities of Gacaca courts. There are about 120 coordinators, each of whom is allocated a particular territory. If they observe irregularities, they may assemble the judges to explain to them how the law is to be applied correctly. They are only supposed to give advice.[80] Although constant monitoring is essential

[73] H.N.A. Noor Muhammad, 'Due Process of Law for Persons Accused of Crime' in L. Henkin (ed), *The International Bill of Rights* (1981) 147; S. Trechsel, *Human Rights in Criminal Proceedings* (2005) 53.

[74] HRC, *Karttunen v Finland*, Views of 23 October 1992 (no 387/1989) para 7.2.

[75] Art 14 of the Gacaca Law as modified by art 3 of Organic Law No 10/2007.

[76] Art 15 of the Gacaca Law as modified by art 4 of Organic Law No 28/2006.

[77] Art 16 of the Gacaca Law as modified by art 5 of Organic Law No 13/2008.

[78] See, eg, Gacaca Court of the Sector of Gashali, Karongi District, *Case of Sibomana Emmanuel*, 11 September and 2 October 2007; ASF, *Rapport analytique no 4* (2009) 45–6; PRI, *Report XI* (2008) 38–42. P. Clark questions the overall effect of outside interference on the process, but concedes that interference occurs, *The Gacaca Courts* (2010) 157.

[79] See ch 2, section V B above.

[80] Interview with Denis Bikesha, Director of Training, Mobilisation, and Sensitisation, National Service of Gacaca Courts, Kigali, 21 September 2007.

in order to ensure a minimum standard in the administration of justice by Gacaca tribunals, it does also put the independence of the courts at risk.

The danger of Gacaca activities being interfered with is particularly high in rural areas. I witnessed several instances where judges in the countryside were confused by comments made by a person with a higher standard of education than their own. In one appeals hearing that I attended in Nyanza District, a coordinator of the National Service was present as a representative of the victim side. Although the court hearing the case was outside his territorial competence, he still openly displayed his district coordinator's badge. When the accused challenged his classification as a second category suspect in order to be reclassified into the first category and, consequently, to be tried by an ordinary court, the district coordinator called upon the judges in no uncertain terms to dismiss this claim and to retire for deliberation. The judges followed his request and returned with a decision rejecting the defendant's request. After further discussion, the district coordinator called for an adjournment due to the absence of several witnesses for the prosecution. The judges complied without hesitation. The week after, the bench pronounced a life sentence without any further hearing on the merits.[81] In another case I witnessed in Nyanza District, the mother of a rich and influential businessman from Kigali was accused of killing a woman. During the trial, rumours were rife that the outcome was highly disputed among the *inyangamugayo*. After an adjournment of the hearing, the coordinator of the National Service had allegedly rounded up all *inyangamugayo* and had instructed them to acquit the defendant. The acquittal was eventually pronounced by only three out of the five judges sitting in the case.[82] This experience is in line with the findings of various NGOs whose reports testify to the particular danger of interference by the coordinators of the National Service.[83] Undue interference with the work of Gacaca courts has even been openly criticized by National Commission for Human Rights.[84]

The independence and impartiality of Gacaca jurisdictions is put at even greater risk by the corruption of judges. Corruption was already a problem in the trials conducted by the specialized chambers of the ordinary courts, and was one of the reasons why the government decided to assign genocide cases to Gacaca courts.[85] Yet Gacaca judges seem even more prone to corruption than ordinary judges. The vast majority of the *inyangamugayo* are farmers with minimal income.[86] For them,

[81] Gacaca Court of Appeal, Kayanza, Nyanza District, *Case of Iyamuremye Martin*, 2 and 9 October 2007. A similar case involving a representative of the victim organization *Ibuka* was reported to me by a representative of PRI Rwanda, interview, Kigali, 15 October 2007. See also ASF, *Rapport analytique no 4* (2009) 46; P. Clark, *The Gacaca Courts* (2010) 146.

[82] Gacaca Court of Appeal, Muyira, Nyanza District, *Case of Mukarubayiza Marie*, 23 and 30 October 2007.

[83] ASF, *Rapport analytique no 4* (2009) 45–6; HRW, *Justice Compromised* (2011) 110–1; PRI, *Report XI* (2008) 38–42.

[84] PRI, ibid, 44.

[85] G. Gahima, 'Alternatives to Prosecution' in E. Hughes, W.A. Schabas and R. Thakur (eds), *Atrocities and International Accountability* (2007) 170; U.A. Karekezi, 'Juridictions gacaca' in E. Ntaganda (ed), *Cahiers du Centre de Gestion des Conflits no 3* (2001) 27 *et seq*.

[86] According to a census conducted by the Belgian Technical Cooperation (BTC) in 2005, 92.7% of the *inyangamugayo* were farmers. 81.1% of them earned less than 5,000 FRw (less than 10 US$) per month, PRI, *Report XI* (2008) 50.

Gacaca means one or even two days a week away from their fields without any compensation for the lost income incurred as a result, let alone any payment. At the same time, the position of *inyangamugayo* involves considerable power that some may abuse by accepting payment for certain decisions. All this renders the judges highly vulnerable to corruption.[87]

Although isolated instances of bribery are reported regularly,[88] its overall impact on the Gacaca process is hard to assess. The frequent allegations of corruption expressed by the victims, defendants, and the population may be regarded as an indication of the scope of the problem. Penal Reform International has conducted a number of interviews with Gacaca judges that reveal disturbing insights. One of the interviewees reported cases where *inyangamugayo* sought to incriminate wealthy persons in order to offer them acquittal in return for payment. In general, the report suggests that bribes are paid and accepted in a systematic manner in many Gacaca courts.[89] Rwandan officials regularly highlight corruption as one of Gacaca's major problems, although it is usually regarded as a systematic attempt by the *génocidaires* and their families to prevent justice from being done. Corruption as a danger for the defendant is being widely ignored.[90]

Even more difficult to prove is the effect of personal bias on the outcome of Gacaca proceedings. Almost every Rwandan has either lost family members or has relatives that were themselves involved in the killings.[91] The vast majority of the population has witnessed violence. This history represents a huge burden for any attempt to come to terms with what happened, even for highly professional and well-trained judges. The scale of the problem becomes evident when the fact that, by mid-2006, 45,000 Gacaca judges (more than 30 per cent) had already been replaced due to genocide charges against them is taken into consideration.[92] On the other hand, the mechanisms for the replacement of *inyangamugayo* practically encourage the removal of unwanted judges from the bench. Article 16 of the

[87] ASF, *Rapport analytique no 4* (2009) 47; PRI, *Report XI* (2008) 50 *et seq*.

[88] See Gacaca Court of Appeal, Karambi, Ruhango District, *Case of Mbihayimana Nkwaya Aaron*, 17 and 24 April 2008; a representative of the National Commission for Human Rights told me that his working group had found nine recent cases where corruption could be proven, interview with Joseph Shyirambere, Rapporteur in chief of the National Commission for Human Rights, Monitoring Project Gacaca and TIG, Kigali, 27 September 2007; see also 'A Gacaca Judge Affirms to Have Been Bribed by a Member of Parliament', *Hirondelle*, 31 August 2007; 'Seven Gacaca Judges of a Same Court Arrested in Southern Rwanda', *Hirondelle*, 7 December 2007; 'Gacaca Judge Caught Bribing a Witness', *Hirondelle*, 21 January 2008; 'Eight Gacaca Judges Arrested over Corruption Allegations', *Hirondelle*, 11 September 2009; 'Corrupt Gacaca Judge Caught Red-Handed', *Hirondelle*, 18 November 2009. See also the four cases reported in PAPG, *Rapport d'Activités, mai–juin 2006* (2006) 15; PAPG, *Rapport d'Activités, juillet–août–septembre 2006* (2007) 15.

[89] PRI, *Report XI* (2008) 50 *et seq*; ASF comes to a similar conclusion, *Rapport analytique no 4* (2009) 47. See also C.J. Le Mon, 'Rwanda's Troubled Gacaca Courts' 14 *Human Rights Brief* (2007) Issue 2, 17.

[90] Interview with a representative of PRI Rwanda, Kigali, 15 October 2007.

[91] See the data in S. Gabisirege and S. Babalola, *Perceptions about the Gacaca Law in Rwanda* (2001) 5 *et seq*; for a discussion on the problem of personal bias, see P. Clark, 'Hybridity, Holism, and "Traditional" Justice' 39 *The George Washington International Law Review* (2007) 808 *et seq*.

[92] G. Hankel, 'Verordnete Versöhnung' 65 *Internationale Politik* (2010) no 1, 46. See also B. Ingelaere, 'The Gacaca Courts in Rwanda' in L. Huyse and M. Salter (eds), *Traditional Justice and Reconciliation after Violent Conflict* (2008) 48 *et seq*.

Gacaca Law,[93] which lists grounds for replacement, refers inter alia to sectarianism and genocide ideology—both terms that are often used in public debate to disqualify opponents.[94]

(2) The lack of effective safeguards for independence and impartiality

The Gacaca system does not provide for effective checks and balances to prevent outside interference or biased decisions, or to mitigate the repercussions of these. This is exemplified by the case of François-Xavier Byuma, a well-known author and human rights activist. Byuma was tried in 2007 by the Gacaca court of the sector of Biryogo in Kigali for attempted murder of a Tutsi woman during the genocide. Before and during the trial, Byuma had challenged the impartiality of the presiding judge. He alleged that the judge might be biased due to an investigation regarding the rape of a girl that Byuma's organization for children's rights had conducted against him. The court, however, had rejected the request. Byuma was subsequently convicted and sentenced to 19 years in prison. The judgment was based on contradictory evidence; one of Byuma's co-defendants accused of the same offence was acquitted even though he had confessed to it.[95] The verdict was strongly criticized by local and international human rights organizations as well as international media. Some observers even went so far as to suspect the government of a plot against Byuma. Criticism of the verdict was so widespread that the National Service of Gacaca Courts felt obliged to issue a statement dismissing all concerns.[96] The conviction was upheld on appeal, even though seven witnesses had testified in Byuma's defence.[97] In 2009, the case was heard upon review by a Gacaca court from Eastern Province. The trial was held on the premises of the Biryogo sector authorities in Kigali. Avocats Sans Frontières had appointed a defence counsel for Byuma. The attorney, who appeared in plain clothes, was not allowed to sit next to the accused and was repeatedly prevented from speaking on behalf of his client.[98] During the hearings, a considerable number of exonerating testimonies were given. Nevertheless, Byuma was convicted again.[99]

Although it is only possible to speculate about the background of Byuma's conviction, it is safe to say that there were striking and inexplicable irregularities present which were never addressed at any stage of the proceedings. This is in itself enough to seriously compromise the fairness of the trial. Despite Gacaca's potential for abuse, there are no effective safeguards against biased judgments. Appeals and review courts are often not sufficiently independent to address irregularities at the

[93] As modified by art 5 of Organic Law No 13/2008.

[94] See also G. Gahima, 'Alternatives to Prosecution' in E. Hughes, W.A. Schabas and R. Thakur (eds), *Atrocities and International Accountability* (2007) 170.

[95] 'A Rwandan Militant for Human Rights Sentenced to 19 Years Imprisonment', *Hirondelle*, 28 May 2007; HRW, *Gacaca Trial Condemns Activist to Prison*, 30 May 2007.

[96] National Service of Gacaca Courts, *Byuma François Xavier's Case* (2007); Byuma's conviction was the object of several 'urgent actions', inter alia, by Amnesty International.

[97] 'Verdict Saturday in the Appeal of a Famous Human Rights Activist', *Hirondelle*, 9 August 2007; 'Sentence Confirmed in Appeal for a Human Rights Militant', *Hirondelle*, 20 August 2007.

[98] Written information from a representative of ASF Rwanda, 4 November 2009.

[99] LIPRODHOR, *Byuma François-Xavier condamné à 17 ans de prison*, 16 March 2009.

trial stage. The judges sitting on appeal or review have gone through the same training as the trial judges.[100] They enjoy no more respect or authority, and are often not willing to question the findings of the trial court.[101] In order to ensure mutual control among *inyangamugayo*, the law requires that a certain number of judges sit for each case.[102] Yet the quorum of judges was reduced from an initial 14 to seven in 2004 and to five in 2007.[103] Judicial control of Gacaca decisions by ordinary courts, which was seen by some commentators as an essential safeguard for the quality of the trials,[104] was repealed in 2004. Effective monitoring and accountability for blatant disregard of procedural rules could help improve standards. But the National Service lacks the resources for such an undertaking. In isolated cases, however, the National Service agreed on an immediate solution in order to correct the outcome of a faulty trial: following complaints by the Rwandan human rights organization LIPRODHOR, the National Service ordered the release of a number of people who had been falsely convicted by Gacaca courts despite clear evidence of their innocence.[105]

B. Equality of arms and the rights of the defence

Equality of arms is an essential element of the right to a fair trial.[106] In order to guarantee it, 'each party must be afforded a reasonable opportunity to present his case under conditions that do not place him at a disadvantage *vis-à-vis* his opponent'.[107] This definition suggests that equality in the context of the fair trial guarantee differs from other equality clauses. Usually, equal treatment would mean that the accused must only be granted the rights and opportunities that the prosecution has. Yet this does not correspond to the reality of criminal proceedings, where the accused may invoke the presumption of innocence in his favour, while the prosecution has a number of special powers, such as search and seizure or wire-tapping, to collect evidence.[108] Equality of arms in a criminal trial is thus best understood through the minimum rights of the defence spelled out in Article 14(3) of the ICCPR. These ensure that both prosecution and accused appear before the court on an equal footing.

[100] Interview with two representatives of ASF Rwanda, Kigali, 12 October 2007.

[101] See ch 2, section VII B above.

[102] Art 23(1) of the Gacaca Law as modified by art 5 of Organic Law No 10/2007; J. Raper, 'The Gacaca Experiment' 5 *Pepperdine Dispute Resolution Law Journal* (2005) 50 *et seq.*

[103] Art 21(4) of Organic Law No 40/2000, art 23(1) of Organic Law No 16/2004, and art 5 of Organic Law No 10/2007, which modified art 23 of Organic Law No 16/2004.

[104] P. Ironside, 'Rwandan *Gacaca*' 15 *New York International Law Review* (2002) no 2, 50 *et seq.* See also M.A. Drumbl, 'Punishment, Postgenocide' 75 *NYULR* (2000) 1266. On the possibility of judicial review by ordinary courts under the old legislation, see ch 2, section VII above.

[105] Interview with a representative of LIPRODHOR, Kigali, 30 October 2007.

[106] HRC, *Morael v France*, Views of 28 July 1989 (no 207/1986) para 9.3; *Fei v Colombia*, Views of 4 April 1995 (no 514/1992) para 8.4; ECtHR, *Jasper v UK*, Judgment of 16 February 2000, para 51.

[107] ECtHR, *Bulut v Austria*, Judgment of 22 February 1996, para 47. See also M. Nowak, *CCPR Commentary*, 2nd edn (2005) Art 14 CCPR, para 29.

[108] S. Trechsel, *Human Rights in Criminal Proceedings* (2005) 96.

Unlike ordinary criminal proceedings, Gacaca trials often do not oppose two competing parties. There is a defendant, sometimes a victim, but no defence lawyer, and no prosecution. The functions of the prosecution at the pre-trial stage were exercised by the Gacaca courts of the cell, in practice with substantial support by local authorities.[109] During the trial, representatives of the cell court that investigated the case may be present in the general assembly, but they do not figure as a party to the trial. In cases that were investigated by the Public Prosecution before Gacaca came into being, representatives of the prosecution can be summoned as witnesses.[110] The various functions normally represented by the prosecution are taken on by the general assembly of the Gacaca court, the victim, and by the trial judges themselves, who read out the charges, call the witnesses and examine them. This may be regarded as an archaic, inquisitorial confusion of the prosecution's and the court's tasks.[111] But such an observation is beside the point. Despite the fact that the court may act as a mouthpiece for the prosecution during the trial, the court still remains distinct from the prosecution, as a clear institutional division exists. The trial is conducted by the sector court, while the investigation is carried out by the cell court. The tasks carried out by the judges during the trial are similar to those of a criminal judge in a continental legal system.[112]

Proponents of the Gacaca system tend to argue instead that the absence of a suitably trained prosecutor and the absence of trained lawyers in general represents an advantage for the defendant. Accordingly, fairness in Gacaca courts does not depend on particular procedural rights. Gacaca is 'a justice of truth rather than a justice of evidence and procedure'.[113] They also argue that the defendant is not put to trial by judges and prosecutors who have received standard legal training. Instead, he is judged by his own peers.[114] Fairness is ensured through the presence of a whole range of eyewitnesses, which allows an instant oral reconstruction of all facts relevant to the case. The general assembly acts as prosecution and defence at the same time and thus ensures equality between the two.[115] The presence of a professional in a Gacaca court would jeopardize this balance, confuse the witnesses, and contravene the spirit of the Gacaca system.[116] Therefore the Gacaca Law does not acknowledge the right to counsel.[117] This is not to say that lawyers

[109] See ch 2, section V B above. [110] Art 39(7) of the Gacaca Law.

[111] See J. Fierens, '*Gacaca* Courts' 3 *JICJ* (2005) 911; S. Vandeginste, 'Dealing with Genocide' in N. Biggar (ed), *Burying the Past* (2001) 245.

[112] On that, see C.J.M. Safferling, *Towards an International Criminal Procedure* (2001) 217.

[113] '[P]lutôt une justice de vérité qu'une justice de preuve ou qu'une justice procédurale', interview with Domitilla Mukantaganzwa, Executive Secretary of the National Service of Gacaca Courts, Kigali, 8 August 2007.

[114] See C.R.M. Dlamini, 'The Effects of Customs, Religions and Traditions on the Right to a Fair Trial in Africa' 33 *The Comparative and International Law Journal of Southern Africa* (2000) 328.

[115] P. Uvin, 'The Gacaca Tribunals in Rwanda' in D. Bloomfield, T. Barnes and L.Huyse (eds), *Reconciliation after Violent Conflict* (2003) 119. See also L.D. Tully, 'Human Rights Compliance and the Gacaca Jurisdictions in Rwanda' 26 *BCIntl&CompLRev* (2002) 410.

[116] J. Mucyo, '*Gacaca* Courts and Genocide' in C. Villa-Vicencio and T. Savage (eds), *Rwanda and South Africa in Dialogue* (2001) 53. See also E.H. Thelle, 'The Gacaca Jurisdictions' 13 *Human Rights in Development* (2001) 95.

[117] While art 36 of Organic Law No 08/96 acknowledged the right to counsel, albeit not at the expense of the state, the Gacaca Law is silent on the matter.

are prohibited from visiting Gacaca sessions. On the contrary, as Rwandans, they are even obliged to attend.[118] They may even defend an accused party as long as they do not interfere with the proceedings by displaying their superior legal knowledge.[119]

In practice, however, Gacaca's participatory elements do not make up for the disadvantage of the defence vis-à-vis the prosecution. Providing a defence lawyer for every single person accused is, of course, virtually impossible. The number of persons suspected of capital crimes during the genocide amounts to around 500,000.[120] In 2007, there were only 300 judicial defenders in the country, many of whom were not willing to defend genocide suspects.[121] The absence of lawyers can also be explained by Gacaca's character as a form of justice administered by ordinary people.[122] However, even beyond this, the rights of the defence are in any event minimal: defendants do not have access to their own case files,[123] are usually only informed about the charges against them during the trial itself, and are not given sufficient time to rebut the charges.[124] Moreover, detainees have been sensitized to confess to such an extent that many are no longer aware of their right to remain silent.

Compared to the defence, the prosecution is well equipped. The investigating Gacaca courts have powers similar to those of ordinary courts, such as the power to order search and seizure, for example.[125] The case files contain detailed information about witnesses for the prosecution while usually omitting any information on defence witnesses.[126] This failure to collect exonerating evidence not only represents a major disadvantage during the trial, but has also prevented the immediate release of detainees who were clearly innocent, something I myself witnessed firsthand.[127]

[118] Art 29(1) of the Gacaca Law.

[119] Interview with Domitilla Mukantaganzwa, Executive Secretary of the National Service of Gacaca Courts, Kigali, 8 August 2007. She reported five recent cases in Kigali where the defendant brought a lawyer.

[120] See National Service of Gacaca Courts, *Summary of Persons Prosecuted* (2006).

[121] Information from an official of the Ministry of Justice, October 2007; I.T. Gaparayi, 'Justice and Social Reconstruction in the Aftermath of Genocide in Rwanda' 1 *African Human Rights Law Journal* (2001) 97.

[122] P. Clark, *The Gacaca Courts* (2010) 160–3.

[123] M. Goldstein Bolocan, 'Rwandan Gacaca' *Journal of Dispute Resolution* (2004) 388 *et seq*; E. Kirs, 'Introduction and Critical Remarks Regarding the *Gacaca* System in Rwanda' 5 *Miskolc Journal of International Law* (2008) no 1, 55; LIPRODHOR, *Problématique des informations et témoignages devant les juridictions gacaca* (2006) 31 *et seq*; L. Werchick, 'Prospects for Justice in Rwanda's Citizen Tribunals' 8 *Human Rights Brief* (2001) Issue 3, 17.

[124] ASF, *Rapport analytique no 2* (2006) 14; ASF, *Rapport analytique no 3* (2007) 19 *et seq*; interview with two representatives of ASF Rwanda, Kigali, 12 October 2007; interview with a representative of PRI Rwanda, Kigali, 15 October 2007. See also N.A. Jones, *The Courts of Genocide* (2010) 70.

[125] Art 39(2) and (3) of the Gacaca Law.

[126] Such information has often not been collected during the investigation phase, interview with a representative of PRI Rwanda, Kigali, 15 October 2007. On the problems of files prepared by the Public Prosecution, see U.A. Karekezi, A. Nshimiyimana and B. Mutamba, 'Localizing Justice' in E. Stover and H.M. Weinstein (eds), *My Neighbor, My Enemy* (2004) 81.

[127] In the case of *Nshimuyuremyi Zacharie* I attended before the Gacaca court of appeal in Nyanza (Nyanza District, 18 and 25 September 2007), I was surprised that the defendant had been held in pre-trial detention even though there was virtually no credible evidence against him. Before his acquittal, he had spent 14 years in prison, interview with the president of the Gacaca Court of Appeal of Nyanza, Nyanza, 19 September 2007. On the logistical challenges in connection with Gacaca, see J. Raper, 'The Gacaca Experiment' 5 *Pepperdine Dispute Resolution Law Journal* (2005) 40.

Having said that, the judges in the trials I visited were normally responsive to the requests of the defendants when it came to summoning specific witnesses, even though this right is not expressly granted in the Gacaca Law.[128] Nevertheless, useful testimonies were often not available. Time constraints often prevented the judges from adjourning in order to summon additional witnesses. Gacaca courts are constantly pressurized by the National Service to hold expeditious trials,[129] with judgments often pronounced after just one day in court. Even if a court decides to adjourn to hear further testimonies, witnesses often fail to show up. For many witnesses, the lack of regular financial assistance for travelling makes it difficult to appear upon summons.[130] Article 29(4)(2) of the Gacaca Law does impose penalties for non-appearance without good reason, but most courts are too busy to enforce this provision. In addition, violence against witnesses, *rescapés*, and judges[131] has created a climate of fear among participants in Gacaca trials and has discouraged many from actively participating.[132] In 2006, the government instituted a Witness Protection and Victims Empowerment Unit under the supervision of the Prosecutor General. The sheer number of requests in connection

[128] In the case of *Nziyumvira Sylver*, eg, the president of the court offered the defendant 'as much time as he needs' to come up with defence witnesses, Gacaca Court of Appeal, Kimihurura, Gasabo District, 16 September 2007.

[129] Interview with two representatives of ASF Rwanda, Kigali, 12 October 2007. See also PRI, *Report XI* (2008) 26.

[130] In some cases, victim organizations have supported witnesses with travelling funds, interview with Denis Bikesha, Director of Training, Mobilisation, and Sensitisation, National Service of Gacaca Courts, Kigali, 5 October 2007. It also frequently occurs that summonses are delayed or not delivered at all, PRI, *Report XI* (2008) 26.

[131] 'Assassination of a Gacaca Court President', *Hirondelle*, 18 October 2007; 'Ibuka Report: 167 Genocide Survivors Murdered since 1995', *Hirondelle*, 15 July 2008. According to Dieter Magsam, consultant on Rwanda for the German Technical Cooperation (GTZ), 145 killings of witnesses have been registered (information provided during a lecture at the University of the Western Cape, Cape Town, South Africa, 30 March 2009).

[132] S. Buckley-Zistel, '"The Truth Heals"?' 80 *Friedenswarte* (2005) 120 *et seq*; A. Corey and S.F. Joireman, 'Retributive Justice' 103 *African Affairs* (2004) 85; A. Molenaar, *Gacaca* (2005) 110 *et seq*; M. Rettig, 'Gacaca' 51 *African Studies Review* (2008) no 3, 43 *et seq*; see also M.-E. Desrosiers, 'Quand justice et réconciliation ne font qu'un' in Y. Conoir and G. Verna (eds), *Faire la paix* (2005) 133; HRW, *Killings in Eastern Rwanda* (2007); Redress and African Rights, *Survivors and Post-Genocide Justice in Rwanda* (2008) 6 *et seq*. According to a study carried out by LIPRODHOR, only 48.5% of all testimonies are given voluntarily, LIPRODHOR, *Problématique des informations et témoignages devant les juridictions gacaca* (2006) 57, 79. In contrast, Rwandan officials argue that the effect of violence on the outcome of Gacaca is minimal and cannot distort the truth, interview with Ombudsman Tito Rutaremara, 19 March 2007. The insufficient availability of testimonies due to security concerns had been the major reason for the ICTR to reject the referral of cases to the Rwandan judiciary, see *Prosecutor v Munyakazi*, Appeals Chamber, Decision of 8 October 2008 (ICTR-97–36-R11*bis*) paras 37 *et seq*; *Prosecutor v Kanyarukiga*, ICTR, Appeals Chamber, Decision of 30 October 2008 (ICTR-2002–78-R11*bis*) paras 23 *et seq*; *Prosecutor v Hategekimana*, ICTR, Appeals Chamber, Decision of 4 December 2008 (ICTR-00–55B-R11*bis*) paras 21 *et seq*; *Prosecutor v Gatete*, ICTR, Trial Chamber, Decision of 17 November 2008 (ICTR-2000–61-R11*bis*) paras 54 *et seq*; *Prosecutor v Kayishema*, ICTR, Trial Chamber, Decision of 16 December 2008 (ICTR-01–67-R11*bis*) paras 39 *et seq*. See also *Prosecutor v Uwinkindi*, ICTR, Referral Chamber, Decision of 28 June 2011 (ICTR-2011–75-R11*bis*) paras 84 *et seq*, in which the tribunal decided to refer a case to Rwanda for the first time.

to the Gacaca proceedings, however, has more than exceeded the programme's capacity.[133]

In addition to all this, the mechanisms in place to ensure equilibrium in Gacaca trials often fail. The general assembly, which is supposed to function as a corrective element by playing the part of both the prosecution and the defence, is generally much too passive. In the cities, the public has proven reluctant to attend the trials; those implicated in the trial usually show up only when summoned. In the countryside, where the turnout is generally good, people do not actively participate in the process.[134] Moreover, the creation of additional benches in Gacaca courts has made it impossible for the local population to be present during all the hearings. Often, those who may have information on a particular case are attending another hearing at the same time.[135] All this has substantially undermined the moderating potential of the general assembly.

C. Problems in apportioning individual criminal responsibility

As discussed in the previous sections, the 'proximity' of Gacaca courts to the ordinary population carries enormous risks for the quality of justice. This is true not only for procedural justice, but also for substantive justice. International human rights law is largely limited to procedural justice. When courts and other bodies competent to hear cases under international human rights law are called upon to judge the fairness of a trial, they will only examine the procedural aspects and refrain from reviewing the national jurisdiction's findings on the merits.[136] The only narrow exception to this is the *nullum crimen* principle, which is more than a mere procedural guarantee.[137]

Guidelines for substantive justice in a criminal trial can also be derived from general principles of international criminal law, such as the principle of personal culpability.[138] Classically, this principle is believed to encompass two elements. On the one hand, people may only be held accountable for their own conduct, while the conduct of others may be imputed only within a narrow set of conditions.[139]

[133] In 2007, the unit received over 1,000 requests for protection, PRI, *Report XI* (2008) 18; UNDP, *Annual Report Rwanda 2007* (2008) 9; see also Redress and African Rights, *Extraditing Genocide Suspects From Europe to Rwanda* (2008) 36.

[134] For details, see ch 4, section II B *(3)* below.

[135] PRI, *Report XI* (2008) 25, 27–8.

[136] ECtHR, *Edwards v UK*, Judgment of 16 December 1992, para 34; HRC, *Pinkney v Canada*, Views of 29 October 1981 (no 27/1977) para 20; *Mbenge v Zaire*, Views of 25 March 1983 (no 16/1977) para 15.

[137] On that, J.A. Frowein and W. Peukert, *EMRK-Kommentar*, 2nd edn (1996) Art 7 paras 2 *et seq*; M. Nowak, *CCPR Commentary*, 2nd edn (2005) Art 15 CCPR para 4.

[138] The terminology with regard to this principle is not uniform. Notions of the principle outlined here are also referred to under the heading of 'principle of individual responsibility', 'individual liability', or 'individual guilt'.

[139] Or, in the words of the ad hoc tribunals, 'nobody may be held criminally responsible for acts or transactions in which he has not personally engaged or in some other way participated', *Prosecutor v Mpambara*, ICTR, Trial Chamber, Judgment of 11 September 2006 (ICTR-01–65-T) para 26; *Prosecutor v Tadić*, ICTY, Appeals Chamber, Judgment of 15 July 1999 (IT-94–1-A) para 186. For a summary, see B. Burghardt, *Die Vorgesetztenverantwortlichkeit im völkerrechtlichen Straftatsystem* (2008) 287 *et seq*; A. Cassese, *International Criminal Law*, 2nd edn (2008) 33 *et seq*; H.-H. Jescheck,

In addition, personal culpability entails that criminal liability is not merely objective, but requires a criminal state of mind.[140] The ad hoc tribunals have added yet another notion to the principle of individual culpability: they have underscored the importance of meting out punishment according to the respective contribution of each participant to the criminal activity in question,[141] an idea also reflected in the ICC's Rules of Procedure and Evidence.[142]

While this principle is acknowledged in international criminal law, it does not have a directly binding effect on national courts. However, certain blatant contraventions of the principle of individual culpability are likely to amount to arbitrariness, with an ensuing prison sentence becoming arbitrary detention in breach of Article 9(1) of the ICCPR.[143] It is argued here that this threshold is reached if a person is sentenced in connection with a collective crime without any regard to his or her role in the collective and his or her state of mind. Thus, a sentence is arbitrary if it neither reflects whether the conduct of an individual in the collective was even criminal, nor makes any discernible distinction between the mastermind of the crime and a mere bystander.[144]

'The General Principles of International Criminal Law Set out in Nuremberg' 2 *JICJ* (2004) 43 *et seq*. For a critical discussion, see G. Simpson, 'Men and Abstract Entities' in A. Nollkaemper and H. van der Wilt (eds), *System Criminality in International Law* (2009) 87 *et seq*. See also G.P. Fletcher, *The Grammar of Criminal Law* (2007) 298 *et seq*.

140 A. Cassese, ibid; C. Damgaard, *Individual Criminal Responsibility for Core International Crimes* (2008) 237; S. Manacorda, 'Culpability' in A. Cassese (ed), *The Oxford Companion to International Criminal Justice* (2009) 288 *et seq*. However, strict liability offences are common in many legal systems, see, eg, on US criminal law, W.R. LaFave, *Criminal Law*, 4th edn (2003) 272 *et seq*.

141 *Prosecutor v Obrenović*, ICTY, Trial Chamber, Judgment of 10 December 2003 (IT-02–60/2-S) paras 64, 78; see also *Musema v Prosecutor*, ICTR, Appeals Chamber, Judgment of 16 November 2001 (ICTR-96–13-A) paras 382 *et seq*; *Muhimana v Prosecutor*, ICTR, Appeals Chamber, Judgment of 21 May 2007 (ICTR-95–1B-A) para 233; *Prosecutor v Rutaganda*, ICTR, Trial Chamber, Judgment of 6 December 1999 (IT-96–3-T) para 469. For discussion, see B. Burghardt, *Die Vorgesetztenverantwortlichkeit im völkerrechtlichen Straftatsystem* (2008) 384 *et seq*.

142 Of 9 September 2002, Rule 145(1)(c). This is referred to as a 'general principle of law' already in Art 67 of the Fourth Geneva Convention, which states that the courts of an occupying power shall impose penalties 'proportionate to the offence'.

143 For details, see M. Nowak, *CCPR Commentary*, 2nd edn (2005) Art 9 CCPR paras 28 *et seq*.

144 This does not mean that wide concepts of commission, such as those applied by the UN ad hoc tribunals are arbitrary. In particular the ICTY's concept of joint criminal enterprise has attracted much criticism, also with respect to the principle of individual culpability (see, eg, V. Haan, 'The Development of the Concept of Joint Criminal Enterprise' 5 *International Criminal Law Review* (2005) 167 *et seq*). Yet the threshold for participation in a joint criminal enterprise is still relatively high; on the *mens rea* requirements, see *Prosecutor v Stakić*, ICTY, Appeals Chamber, Judgment of 22 March 2006 (IT-97–24-A) para 65; *Prosecutor v Brđanin*, ICTY, Appeals Chamber, Judgment of 3 April 2007 (IT-99–36-A) paras 411, 416; *Prosecutor v Martić*, ICTY, Appeals Chamber, Judgment of 8 October 2008 (IT-95–11-A) para 168. Nor does it mean that a differentiated concept of individual liability with different modes of participation must be applied. In fact, quite a few legal systems, such as those of Austria, Denmark, Norway, and to a limited extent, Italy, rely on a unitary perpetrator concept. In these systems, no normative distinction is drawn between the different participants, but the weight of each one's contribution is taken into account at the sentencing stage, see A. Eser, 'Individual Criminal Responsibility' in A. Cassese, P. Gaeta and J.R.W.D. Jones (eds), *The Rome Statute of the International Criminal Court*, vol I (2002) 781; K. Hamdorf, *Beteiligungsmodelle im Strafrecht* (2002) 25 *et seq*; D. Kienapfel, *Der Einheitstäter im Strafrecht* (1971); B. Schünemann in H.W. Laufhütte, R. Rissing-van Saan and K.Tiedemann (eds), *Leipziger Kommentar StGB*, vol 1, 12th edn (2006) Vor § 25 paras 17 *et seq*.

Arguably, the most striking shortcoming of Gacaca trials from the point of view of a legally trained observer is the inability of the courts to individualize criminal responsibility. One of the most common charges against a defendant who is accused before a Gacaca court is 'participation in an attack' that took place in a particular village or neighbourhood. In such cases, the judges often fail to investigate the specific part that the defendant played in the attack, with it remaining unclear as to whether the accused was a mere bystander or the actual ringleader of the attack. Testimonies often remain inconclusive. My experience was that the discussion instead centred on the defendant's general attitude at the time and on circumstantial evidence, such as the fact that the accused sold machetes in his shop or was seen carrying a gun, for example.[145] Another frequent allegation and grounds for conviction has been the fact that the accused was present at a roadblock,[146] even though this alone does not amount to criminal participation. Avocats Sans Frontières reported on a case which illustrated all too well the inability of many judges to assess the weight of a person's responsibility: in the southern city of Butare (Huye), a woman was sentenced to 25 years in prison for giving food to *Interahamwe* soldiers who were involved in killings.[147] The organization has frequently pointed out difficulties with respect to proving criminal participation.[148] The National Service of Gacaca Courts is aware of the problem and has issued informal instructions to the judges to clarify that having been present at a roadblock does not in itself constitute criminal participation or a criminal offence.[149] The Executive Secretary has also pointed this out several times on the radio. Since then, the number of convictions on unspecified charges may have diminished, but they have not stopped altogether.[150]

Convicting suspects without determining their share in the commission of the crime and the weight of their participation goes against the principle of individual culpability and, if the conduct in question is below the threshold of criminal participation, the *nullum crimen* principle. In addition, it carries the risk of frustrating an important purpose of the criminal prosecution of mass atrocities: the individualization of responsibility. Breaking down macro-criminality to the individual perpetrators precludes the assignment of collective responsibility to certain groups and is

[145] Gacaca Court of Appeal, Kimihurura, Gasabo District, *Case of Ntamuvurira Mathias*, 30 September 2007. The verdict was 19 years' imprisonment.

[146] Gacaca Court of Appeal, Nyanza, Nyanza District, 21 August 2007; Gacaca Court of the Sector of Rusororo, City of Kabuga, *Case of Rutagwenda Innocent*, 20 and 27 July 2005; Gacaca Court of the Sector of Maranyundo, Bugesera District, *Case of Rutayisire François*, 26 October 2006. See also ASF, *Rapport analytique no 3* (2007) 46.

[147] Gacaca Court of the Sector of Rukira, City of Butare, *Case of Nyirabapfizina Joyce*, 21 April 2005, quoted in ASF, *Rapport analytique no 1* (2005) 20. A parallel case occurred in the Gasabo District of Kigali in 2009, ASF, *Rapport analytique no 5* (2010) 53.

[148] ASF, *Rapport analytique no 1* (2005) 20; ASF, *Rapport analytique no 3* (2007) 46–8; ASF, *Rapport analytique no 5* (2010) 53.

[149] Interview with the president of the Gacaca Court of the Sector of Nyanza, Nyanza, 19 September 2007.

[150] Interview with two representatives of ASF Rwanda, Kigali, 12 October 2007; interview with a representative of PRI Rwanda, Kigali, 15 October 2007.

therefore a crucial precondition for reconciliation.[151] Whenever judges ignore the difference between criminal participation and mere sympathizing, Gacaca risks failure in its objective to individualize culpability. This leads not only to a considerable increase in the number of convictions, but will also amount to a summary conviction of those who were on the wrong side. This is a manifestly unjust outcome, and may generate the impression that the entire Hutu population comes under general suspicion.[152] This is compounded by the fact that the repressive actions of RPA soldiers against genocide suspects in the immediate aftermath of 1994, which continued into the late 1990s, have created a feeling among many Hutu that they are collectively presumed to be guilty.[153]

It would, of course, be naive to expect too much from Gacaca courts in that respect. Mass crimes are much too complicated to be adjudged by lay courts in a satisfactory manner. Hearing category one cases that came under the jurisdiction of Gacaca courts in 2008 is an even greater challenge. Cases concerning the ranks of the leadership are more complicated than all other cases. Files of category one cases newly in the jurisdiction of Gacaca courts have often been compiled by professional prosecutors and are much thicker than those compiled by the Gacaca court of the cell. It is a particular challenge for judges to deal with these files. While there is more evidence at their disposal in such files, drawing the appropriate conclusions from it is much more difficult than in ordinary category two cases.

Regrettably, the Gacaca Law actually adds to the difficulties in assigning individual responsibility. It even appears to encourage uniform, across the board punishment for all those who provided any kind of assistance to a crime.[154] Article 51 of the Gacaca Law, which governs the categorization, systematically equates the 'person who committed' a crime with 'his or her accomplices'. Article 53(1) defines an accomplice as 'the person who has, by any means, provided assistance to commit offences with the persons referred to in article 51 of this organic law'. It would have been necessary to sensitize the *inyangamugayo* to the need for a thorough examination of the involvement of each individual defendant in a large-scale attack. Yet this would also have required more time than Gacaca courts were granted. It would at least have been desirable to insert a general provision on sentencing in the law, which would have clarified that the weight of the individual share in the commission of the crime must be reflected in the sentence.

[151] M. Minow, *Between Vengeance and Forgiveness* (1998) 40; G. Werle, *Principles of International Criminal Law*, 2nd edn (2009) para 102. Others, in contrast, question the possibility of individualizing responsibility and the point in doing so, H. Cobban, 'The Legacies of Collective Violence' 27 *Boston Review* (2002) no 2; E. Daly, 'Between Punitive and Reconstructive Justice' 34 *NYUJIntlLaw&Pol* (2002) 384; M.A. Drumbl, 'Law and Atrocity' 31 *Ohio NULRev* (2005) 67 *et seq*.

[152] See also ASF, *Rapport analytique no 1* (2005) 18; L. Waldorf, 'Rwanda's Failing Experiment in Restorative Justice' in D. Sullivan and L. Tifft (eds), *Handbook of Restorative Justice* (2006) 431.

[153] P. Clark challenges the conclusion of collectivized guilt by arguing that many *génocidaires* actually do not feel guilty, *The Gacaca Courts* (2010) 250. Yet, arguably, the problem about collectivized guilt is not that a group actually *feels* collectively guilty, but that it perceives itself as being *blamed* collectively.

[154] See also ASF, *Rapport analytique no 1* (2005) 20.

D. Conclusion

The preceding discussion has pointed out the structural deficiencies of the Gacaca system. These deficiencies prevent it from being considered a fair mechanism in the formal or procedural sense of the word, which underlies Article 14 of the ICCPR and the corresponding provisions of the Banjul Charter. In addition, the discussion has shown that these shortcomings are not only of a procedural nature, but that they also pose a concrete threat to the outcome of Gacaca trials. It is not necessary to visit many Gacaca sessions to recognize that this threat is, in fact, very real. On the other hand, I had the impression that most judges did perceive their task as an honour, and that the majority of them were very committed and acted in good faith. While people were often frustrated with a certain judgment, it appears that, astonishingly, Gacaca still enjoys a great deal of general support.[155] This may be due to the widespread fatalism among Rwandans that there is no choice other than to accept and support what the government imposes on them as a solution. It also seems to reflect the attitude that something had to be done and that among all options available, Gacaca represents the lesser evil, or, in many cases, even a 'fair' solution. In fact, Gacaca has helped address one of the major problems in the aftermath of the genocide: the enormous number of detainees awaiting trial. In the late 1990s, over 120,000 persons were being held in prison on genocide charges without any prospects for a trial.[156] This number even included people who were children under the age of criminal responsibility at the time of their crimes.[157] Some of the suspects finally tried by Gacaca courts had spent up to 14 years in prison. Gacaca courts have acquitted an estimated number of over 100,000 genocide suspects[158] and have rehabilitated thousands of innocent detainees.[159] The situation before the introduction of the Gacaca system was arguably just as serious as the lack of fairness during the trials themselves is now.

Nevertheless, it is no solution to address the problem of heavily overcrowded prisons and thousands of pending cases by holding swift trials that are unfair. However ardent the desire for justice may be, it is still not a justification to deviate from the principle that criminal trials must be fair. From a legal point of view, a shortage of resources does not allow departure from the minimum guarantees of

[155] In a recent survey, 74.4% of the respondents expressed the opinion that Gacaca 'was doing a good job in delivering justice', A. Megwalu and N. Loizides, 'Dilemmas of Justice and Reconciliation' 18 *African Journal of International and Comparative Law* (2010) 14.

[156] See ch 1, section VI B above.

[157] P. Clark, 'The Rules (and Politics) of Engagement' in P. Clark and Z.D. Kaufman (eds), *After Genocide* (2008) 301 *et seq*. On the situation of minors, see C.F. Morrill, 'Reconciliation and the Gacaca' 6 *The Online Journal of Peace and Conflict Resolution* (2004) Issue 1, 1 *et seq*.

[158] A representative of PRI Rwanda whom I interviewed (Kigali, 15 October 2007) estimated that the number of acquittals in Gacaca courts amount to about 30%. According to the Executive Secretary of the National Service of Gacaca Courts, about 20% of the trials result in acquittals. According to data quoted by LIPRODHOR (*Situation des droits de la personne au Rwanda en 2006* (2007) 66 *et seq*), 28.8% of the defendants tried between July and December 2006 were acquitted (10,723 out of 51,649). P. Clark estimates the number of acquittals to amount to 25%, *The Gacaca Courts* (2010) 155.

[159] However, cases are reported where detainees acquitted by Gacaca courts were not liberated, LIPRODHOR, *Rapport de monitoring des prisons au Rwanda* (2008) 25.

the fair trial principle.[160] Moreover, the right to a fair trial was not subject to an express derogation by Rwanda under Article 4(1) of the ICCPR.[161] Nor were the preconditions for a derogation fulfilled. On the contrary, in fact, Rwandan officials have always attempted to argue that Gacaca does provide the basic judicial safeguards to ensure fairness.

[160] The obligation to provide a fair trial is not one of progressive implementation (Art 2(2) of the ICCPR), see HRC, *Lubuto v Zambia*, Views of 31 October 1995 (no 390/1990) paras 5.1, 5.2, 7.3; M. Nowak, *CCPR Commentary*, 2nd edn (2005) Art 2 CCPR paras 58 *et seq*, 14 CCPR para 54.

[161] See also M. Capellà i Roig, 'Jurisdicciones *gacaca*' 56 *Revista Española de Derecho Internacional* (2004) 775.

4

Transitional Justice Through Reparation

The second important set of international legal rules for states in transition pertains to the issue of reparation for human rights violations and violations of humanitarian law. While the duty to prosecute and the fair trial principle are essentially laid down in international treaties, there are very few definite rules regarding the right to reparation. The issue of reparation for the violation of individual rights appeared on the agenda of the UN human rights bodies some 20 years ago.[1] Since then, it has been closely linked to the field of transitional justice, and many publications on the issue deal with reparation in the specific context of a period of political transition. The United Nations has worked on the subject with a particular focus on reparation in transitional periods.

The following section will deal with the right to reparation under international law and its implementation in Rwanda. To begin with, the sources of a general right to reparation will be examined. Then the study will go on to discuss the different forms of reparation under international law. As we will see, most of the legal rules pertaining to reparation for human rights violations are still largely unsettled and in need of clarification. Therefore, we will then focus on Rwanda's approach to the issue of reparation, and will try to draw conclusions for the development of the law from Rwanda's state practice. The discussion on Rwanda's approach to the issue of reparation will follow the same structure as the preceding discussion on reparation under international law: first, a general overview on Rwanda's reparation policy will be given; then, the different forms of reparation and their implementation in post-genocide Rwanda will be examined. In the two final sections, we will address the question of who is entitled to reparation under international law and who is liable to pay reparation. Here as well, we will attempt to draw conclusions from Rwanda's state practice regarding the development of the law.

Reparation for breaches of humanitarian law shall not be addressed in the following discussion. The Rwandan approach does not allow any conclusions regarding humanitarian law since most violations committed primarily qualify as human rights violations. Examining the Rwandan reparation policy would therefore not allow any conclusions to be made as to the existence of a right to redress for violations of humanitarian law. In addition, the existence of a right to reparation for

[1] In 1989, UN Commission on Human Rights initiated a study on reparation for gross human rights violations, *Resolution 1989/13 of the Sub-Commission on Prevention of Discrimination and Protection of Minorities*, UN Doc E/CN.4/Sub.2/1989/13 of 31 August 1989.

violations of humanitarian law remains highly disputed. It is still widely argued that the law of armed conflict, unlike international human rights law, merely obliges states without conferring rights to individuals and that, consequently, individual reparation lacks a legal basis.[2]

I. The Right to Reparation for Human Rights Violations under International Law

A. The sources of a general right to reparation

'[I]t is a principle of international law, and even a general conception of law, that any breach of an engagement involves an obligation to make reparation'.[3] This oft-quoted finding of the Permanent Court of International Justice (PCIJ) describes what has been the undisputed standard in the relations among states for a long time now. Regarding reparation claims of individuals against states under international law, however, the situation is not so clear-cut. Despite the fact that the right to reparation appears virtually as a matter of course in the language used by the PCIJ, its existence in the relations between individuals and states is still controversial. In fact, a provision that expressly lays down a comprehensive right to reparation for the violation of individual rights is nowhere to be found in international human rights law.[4] Certainly, there are numerous references to the issue of reparation in human rights conventions. The ICCPR, the ECHR, and the Torture Convention, to name just a few, do require reparation, but merely with regard to violations of specific rights, that is in case of unlawful arrest, false conviction, or torture.[5] The European and American Conventions even provide for their respective courts to grant 'just satisfaction',[6] or 'fair compensation'[7] for any human rights violation. These provisions, however, merely authorize the courts to afford some form

[2] N. Ronzitti, 'Access to Justice and Compensation for Violations of the Law of War' 16 *Collected Courses of the Academy of European Law* (2007) Book 4, 109 *et seq*; similarly, P. d'Argent, *Les réparations de guerre en droit international public* (2002) 779 *et seq*; R. Hofmann, 'Victims of Violations of International Humanitarian Law' in P.-M. Dupuy et al. (eds), *Common Values in International Law* (2006) 345 *et seq*, 356. See also Bundesverfassungsgericht, Decision of 13 May 1996, BVerfGE 94, 329; Bundesgerichtshof, Decision of 26 June 2003, BGHZ 155, 291, 42 *ILM* (2003) 1037; Tokyo High Court, *X* et al. *v Government of Japan*, Judgment of 8 February 2001, 45 *Japanese Annual of International Law* (2002) 145; US Supreme Court, *Argentine Republic v Amerada Hess*, Judgment of 23 January 1989, 81 *ILR* (1990) 668. Yet a right to reparation for violations of international humanitarian law may be evolving given the more recent developments in this field, such as the creation of the Victims' Trust Fund at the ICC or the work of the UN Commission on Human Rights on reparation discussed in section I A below.

[3] *Case Concerning the Factory at Chorzów (Germany v Poland)*, PCIJ, Judgment of 13 September 1928, PCIJ Series A no 17, 29.

[4] C. Tomuschat, 'La protection internationale des victimes' 18 *Revue universelle des droits de l'homme* (2006) 4.

[5] Arts 9(5), 14(6) of the ICCPR, Art 5(5) of the ECHR, Art 14(1) of the Torture Convention; for an exhaustive listing, see UN Commission on Human Rights, *Study concerning the right to restitution, compensation and rehabilitation for victims of gross violations of human rights and fundamental freedoms*, UN Doc E/CN.4/Sub.2/1993/8 of 2 July 1993, paras 27 *et seq*.

[6] Art 41 of the ECHR, formerly Art 50.

[7] Art 63(1) of the ACHR.

of reparation, and give them a large degree of discretion in doing so. The norms are not constitutive of a comprehensive right to reparation.

In recent years, a general right to reparation for human rights violations has been inferred from the right to a remedy laid down in various human rights conventions.[8] This understanding is backed by the practice of the Human Rights Committee, which has repeatedly interpreted the right to a remedy as encompassing some form of reparation.[9] In a series of cases involving illegal detention, disappearance, ill-treatment, and extra-legal executions by Uruguayan police in the late 1970s and early 1980s, the Committee found that the state party was under a duty to investigate the violations, to bring those responsible to justice, and to award compensation to the victims; often, however, without specifying the legal basis for this finding.[10] In recent years, the Committee has adopted a more differentiated approach on the basis of Article 2(3) of the ICCPR, and has developed specific forms of reparation tailored to individual cases.[11]

Yet despite this practice it remains questionable whether the right to a remedy provides a sufficient basis for a comprehensive right to reparation for human rights violations. In general, the right to a remedy is a procedural, not a substantive right. States must provide effective access to courts or comparable bodies for individuals claiming a violation of their rights. Whether the remedy results in any form of reparation for the victims is irrelevant, provided it is theoretically capable of doing so.[12] In fact, while the term 'remedy' may warrant a broader interpretation, its French, Spanish, and Russian equivalents ('recours', 'recurso', 'средство правовой защиты' respectively) appear to refer to a merely procedural guarantee.[13] Regarding the right to a remedy as the basis for inferring specific individual

[8] eg, Art 2(3) of the ICCPR, Art 13 of the ECHR, Art 25 of the ACHR. See also Art 7(1)(a) of the Banjul Charter.

[9] See also HRC, General Comment 31/80 of 29 March 2004, para 16. The ECtHR has also recognized that the right to a remedy entails 'the payment of compensation where appropriate', *Aksoy v Turkey*, Judgment of 18 December 1996, para 98; *Kaya v Turkey*, Judgment of 19 February 1998, para 107; *Akdeniz v Turkey*, Judgment of 31 May 2005, para 139.

[10] HRC, *Santullo v Uruguay*, Views of 26 October 1979 (no 9/1977) para 13; *Bleier v Uruguay*, Views of 29 March 1982 (no 30/1978) para 15; *Quinteros v Uruguay*, Views of 21 July 1983 (no 107/1981) paras 15 *et seq*. The practice of the African Commission on Human and Peoples' Rights is similar, see the operative parts of *Union Inter Africaine des Droits de l'Homme* et al. *v Angola*, Decision of 11 November 1997 (no 159/96); *Malawi African Association* et al. *v Mauritania*, Decision of 11 May 2000 (nos 54/91, 61/91, 98/93, 164–196/97, 210/98).

[11] For instance, restitution for arbitrarily confiscated assets (*Äärelä v Finland*, Views of 24 October 2001 (no 779/1997) para 8.2); reinstatement of an unlawfully dismissed civil servant and payment of compensation equivalent to what he would have received (*Vargas-Machuca v Peru*, Views of 22 July 2002 (no 906/2000) para 9); for other examples, see M. Nowak, *CCPR Commentary*, 2nd edn (2005) Art 2 CCPR paras 78 *et seq*; C. Tomuschat, 'Reparation in Favour of Individual Victims of Gross Violations of Human Rights and International Humanitarian Law' in M.G. Kohen (ed), *Promoting Justice, Human Rights and Conflict Resolution through International Law* (2007) 584 *et seq*.

[12] ECtHR, *Boyle and Rice v UK*, Judgment of 27 April 1988, paras 67, 75; M. Seegers, *Das Individualrecht auf Wiedergutmachung* (2005) 87; M. Traßl, *Die Wiedergutmachung von Menschenrechtsverletzungen im Völkerrecht* (1994) 38 *et seq*.

[13] See also C. Tomuschat, 'Reparation for Victims of Grave Human Rights Violations' 10 *Tulane Journal of International and Comparative Law* (2002) 168; contra E. Klein, 'Individual Reparation Claims under the International Covenant on Civil and Political Rights' in A. Randelzhofer and C. Tomuschat (eds), *State Responsibility and the Individual* (1999) 33.

rights to reparation and the corresponding state obligations would therefore overstretch the provision. In order to establish a right to reparation, it is therefore necessary to resort to customary law.

A glance at the 'general practice accepted as law', as the Statute of the International Court of Justice[14] circumscribes custom, often only allows a few universally accepted principles to be established; while, regarding the details, merely emerging rules of customary law can already be found. This is hardly different in the field of reparation for human rights violations. Before proceeding to the discussion of the current status of the right to reparation and to the analysis of the Rwandan approach to the reparation issue, we need to briefly review the conditions for the formation of customary international law in the field of human rights in order to evaluate the status of the right to reparation under customary international law.

Customary human rights law is formed in the same manner as any other customary law: through consistent state practice accompanied by the belief that this practice corresponds to a legal obligation (*opinio juris*).[15] This brings about considerable difficulties: states are not uniform entities acting uniformly; they have complex structures with different organs and thousands of persons acting on their behalf. Uniform practice and *opinio* are therefore often hard to establish. This is especially true in the field of human rights law, where the relevant practice does not take place at the level of high politics, but rather in the relations between state officials and millions of individuals.[16]

A solution to these problems lies in a flexible understanding of the elements of custom. While state practice need not necessarily consist of the physical acts carried out by a state, it can also manifest itself in official statements, a state's voting in the organs of international organizations, the enactment of domestic legislation, or in domestic jurisprudence. Today, this broad understanding of state practice enjoys wide support.[17] The International Court of Justice has even stated that contrary state practice does not necessarily undermine the customary rule, but can, under certain circumstances, be regarded as a violation of the rule.[18] That is especially true if the rule is supported by a strong *opinio juris*: in 1951, the Court held that the Genocide Convention, which had been adopted only two and a half years before and had been in force for just one year, formed part of customary law. The

[14] Art 38(1)(b) of the *Statute of the International Court of Justice* of 26 June 1945, 15 UNCIO 355.

[15] For an overview of the discussion on customary human rights law, see T. Meron, *Human Rights and Humanitarian Norms as Customary Law* (1989) 79 *et seq*; B. Simma, 'International Human Rights and General International Law' 4 *Collected Courses of the Academy of European Law* (1993) Book 2, 223 *et seq*; B. Simma and P. Alston, 'The Sources of Human Rights Law' 12 *AustYBIL* (1988/89) 90 *et seq*.

[16] See C. Tomuschat, *Human Rights* (2003) 34.

[17] The ICJ has, eg, relied on official statements as state practice, *Fisheries Jurisdiction Case (UK v Iceland)*, ICJ, Judgment of 25 July 1974, ICJ Reports 1974, 3, para 58 and the Separate Opinions, ibid, 47, 120; see also I. Brownlie, *Principles of Public International Law*, 7th edn (2008) 6 *et seq*; A. Pellet in A. Zimmermann et al. (eds), *The Statute of the International Court of Justice* (2006) Art 38 para 212. However, this wide interpretation of practice used to be controversial, see M. Akehurst, 'Custom as a Source of International Law' 47 *BYBIL* (1974/75) 1 *et seq*.

[18] *Case Concerning Military and Paramilitary Activities in and against Nicaragua (Nicaragua v USA)*, ICJ, Judgment of 27 June 1986, ICJ Reports 1986, 14, para 186.

Court based this finding on the fundamental acceptance of the need to outlaw, prevent and punish genocide.[19] Thus, if official statements, laws, jurisprudence, and voting practice of states are sufficiently consistent to give rise to a customary rule, contrary action can simply be regarded as a breach of that rule. In the field of human rights in particular, there are several reasons for resorting to such 'soft' practice.[20] Physical acts—what state officials actually do or do not do in their everyday contacts with citizens—occur in such great numbers that they are not easily subject to empirical registration. In addition, states with a bad human rights record are usually anxious to conceal their practice from the public or to circulate false information about this practice.[21] Against this backdrop, it seems quite obvious that states that consistently pledge adherence to a certain rule of human rights law in order then to act in breach of this rule cannot invoke such contrary practice in order to deny the rule's existence.

As regards the right to reparation for gross human rights violations, there are a number of examples of physical practice. The South African Truth and Reconciliation Commission, for example, has identified approximately 20,000 victims of apartheid. Today, almost all of them have received some compensation for the wrongs they suffered.[22] Although the payments have often been insufficient, they testify to the increasing conviction that human rights violations must not go unredressed. For some decades already, the victims of Nazi Germany have received compensation.[23] After the fall of the Berlin Wall, victims of unlawful imprisonment or professional bans in the former German Democratic Republic were rehabilitated and have received compensation.[24] The same is true for the victims of the military dictatorships in Chile and Argentina.[25] While there has certainly been contrary practice,[26] these examples provide strong indications for the customary character of the right to reparation.[27]

19 *Reservations to the Convention on the Prevention and Punishment of the Crime of Genocide*, ICJ, Advisory Opinion of 28 May 1951, ICJ Reports 1951, 15, 23.

20 See also Special Tribunal for Lebanon, Order of 15 April 2010 (CH/PRES/2010/01) para 30. Similarly, B. Simma, 'International Human Rights and General International Law' 4 *Collected Courses of the Academy of European Law* (1993) Book 2, 224 *et seq*; see also T. Meron, *Human Rights and Humanitarian Norms as Customary Law* (1989) 94.

21 For the comparable situation under international humanitarian law, see *Prosecutor v Tadić*, ICTY, Appeals Chamber, Decision of 2 October 1995 (IT-94-1-A) para 99.

22 B. Hamber, 'Reparations as Symbol' in J. Miller and R. Kumar (eds), *Reparations* (2007) 255 *et seq*.

23 See Bundesminister der Finanzen and W. Schwartz (eds), *Die Wiedergutmachung nationalsozialistischen Unrechts durch die Bundesrepublik Deutschland*, vol III (1985).

24 G. Werle and M. Vormbaum, 'After the Fall of the Berlin Wall' (forthcoming 2012).

25 P.B. Hayner, *Unspeakable Truths* (2001) 172 *et seq*.

26 See C. Tomuschat, 'Reparation for Victims of Grave Human Rights Violations' 10 *Tulane Journal of International and Comparative Law* (2002) 175 *et seq*.

27 The South African TRC has stated that '[a]lthough no consistent reparation policy has evolved in international human rights law, there is nevertheless reasonable consensus about the obligations of states to make reparations for violations of human rights', *Truth and Reconciliation Commission of South Africa Report*, vol 6 (2003) 102. Similarly, IACtHR, *Hilaire, Constantine and Benjamin* et al. *v Trinidad and Tobago Case*, Judgment of 21 June 2002, para 202 and S. Peté and M. du Plessis, 'Reparations for Gross Violations of Human Rights in Context' in M. du Plessis and S. Peté (eds), *Repairing the Past?* (2005) 13 *et seq*; M. Seegers, *Das Individualrecht auf Wiedergutmachung* (2005) 204; D. Shelton, 'The

In recent years, reparation claims for violations of international human rights law have increasingly been acknowledged in national jurisprudence.[28] Since the late 1980s, the issue of reparation for gross human rights violations has been discussed within the framework of the UN Commission on Human Rights. Their work initially resulted in several proposals being put forward for a set of principles regarding reparation.[29] In 2005, the UN General Assembly finally adopted the Basic Principles on the Right to a Remedy and Reparation. The principles are not considered to create new obligations, but are designed to specify existing legal obligations.[30] The resolution was adopted without a vote. The document provides a wide range of measures, many of which are not framed as binding obligations. Nonetheless, it reveals that there is general acceptance of the principle of reparation.[31]

Beyond these more recent developments, there are indications that the right to reparation has already been recognized for some time. In particular, the examination of the law relating to individual claims against the state under domestic legal orders provides a strong case for the right to reparation under international law. The principle that the state is liable for violations of the rights of individuals has been almost universally recognized for some decades already.[32] Even though its actual enforcement may be difficult or even entirely elusive, the principle certainly does exist. Governmental liability is also provided for under Rwandan law. There is no specific law governing state responsibility for individual harm, but such responsibility is inferred from the general provisions on liability for tort.[33] For these reasons,

Right to Reparations for Acts of Torture' 17 *Torture* (2007) no 2, 116; contra C. Tomuschat, 'La protection internationale des victimes' 18 *Revue universelle des droits de l'homme* (2006) 4.

[28] See the *obiter dictum* by the Bundesverfassungsgericht, Decision of 13 May 1996, BVerfGE 94, 329 *et seq*; another example is the jurisprudence of US American courts under the Alien Tort Claims Act (ATCA), 28 USC § 1350, which requires a violation of the law of nations. Courts have repeatedly awarded damages for violations of international human rights law, G.P. Fletcher, *Tort Liability for Human Rights Abuses* (2008); D. Shelton, *Remedies in International Human Rights Law*, 2nd edn (2005) 160 *et seq*.

[29] *Study concerning the right to restitution, compensation and rehabilitation for victims of gross violations of human rights and fundamental freedoms*, UN Doc E/CN.4/Sub.2/1993/8 of 2 July 1993, para 137; *Revised set of basic principles and guidelines on the right to reparation for victims of gross violations of human rights and humanitarian law*, UN Doc E/CN.4/Sub.2/1996/17 of 24 May 1996; *Basic principles and guidelines on the right to a remedy and reparation for victims of violations of international human rights and humanitarian law*, annex to UN Doc E/CN.4/2000/62 of 18 January 2000.

[30] Para 7 of the Preamble to the Basic Principles on the Right to a Remedy and Reparation.

[31] In para 15, it is stated that 'a State *shall* provide reparation' (italics added) for human rights violations, a wording that suggests that a binding norm is referred to. Regarding the particular measures of reparation, however, the principles use 'should' instead of 'shall' (paras 19 *et seq*).

[32] H.-W. Bayer, 'Der Ausschluß der Staatshaftung' in H. Mosler (ed), *Haftung des Staates für rechtswidriges Verhalten seiner Organe* (1967) 768; G. Eörsi, 'Private and Governmental Liability for the Torts of Employees and Organs' in A. Tunc (ed), *International Encyclopedia of Comparative Law XI-1* (1983) ch 4, para 166; M. Traßl, *Die Wiedergutmachung von Menschenrechtsverletzungen im Völkerrecht* (1994) 53 *et seq*.

[33] Art 258 of the Code Civil, livre III (*Décret du 30 juillet 1888*, Bulletin Officiel du Congo Belge 1888, 109), written information from an official of the Ministry of Justice, 24 July 2008. State liability has also been dealt with within the context of the genocide trials before ordinary courts, section IV C below.

it is safe to conclude that the victims of genocide and crimes against humanity in Rwanda have a right to reparation under customary international law.

B. Forms of reparation under international law

While the right to reparation is acknowledged in principle, there still remains a great deal of uncertainty regarding its content and the details of its implementation. Commonly, reparation in human rights law is divided into the following categories: restitution, that is restoration of the status quo ante where this is possible; compensation of financially assessable damages; satisfaction, which covers symbolic measures such as apology or acknowledgment of the violation; and rehabilitation, which includes access to medical and psychological care. These categories are common in domestic legal orders[34] as well as being recognized under the law of state responsibility.[35] As regards human rights law, they are regularly referred to in decisions made by international courts as well as in the statements issued by UN bodies.[36] The forms of reparation which have to be awarded to victims can only be determined with regard to the specific situation. It is argued here that, in general, all human rights violations entail an obligation to provide reparation. In cases of less serious abuses, the mere acknowledgment of the violation may constitute sufficient reparation. Conversely, in the event of serious violations, a programme that fails to provide any form of compensation is unlikely to satisfy the victims' right to reparation.

(1) Restitution

Restitution is commonly defined as wiping out all consequences of the violation by restoring the situation before.[37] It can consist of the release of an unlawfully detained person, or in the restoration of property. In cases of mass killings, however, restitution is obviously impossible. Nevertheless, it can play a crucial role in transitions from violent conflict: the common side effects of mass atrocities are the displacement of great numbers of persons and the occupation of their land and houses by others, which may deprive those who have fled of their most essential belongings, thus plunging them into poverty. Restitution of their property is therefore crucial in the aftermath of the conflict. In international human rights

[34] See H. Stoll, 'Consequences of Liability' in A. Tunc (ed), *International Encyclopedia of Comparative Law XI-2* (1986) ch 8, para 9.

[35] See Arts 34–9 of the *Articles on the Responsibility of States for Internationally Wrongful Acts* (ILC Articles on State Responsibility), annex to UN General Assembly Resolution 56/83 of 12 December 2001; see also *Preliminary Report on State Responsibility by Mr. Gaetano Arangio-Ruiz, Special Rapporteur*, *YBILC* (1988) II-1, 21 *et seq*; *Report of the International Law Commission*, 53rd session, *YBILC* (2001) II-2, 95 *et seq*, which all refer to restitution, compensation, and satisfaction.

[36] See IACtHR, *Case of Garrido and Baigorria v Argentina*, Judgment of 27 August 1998, para 41; *Case of Loayza Tamayo v Peru*, Judgment of 27 November 1998, para 85. See also UN Commission on Human Rights, *Study concerning the right to restitution, compensation and rehabilitation for victims of gross violations of human rights and fundamental freedoms*, UN Doc E/CN.4/Sub.2/1993/8 of 2 July 1993, para 137; Basic Principles on the Right to a Remedy and Reparation, para 19. For a summary, see M. Nowak, *CCPR Commentary*, 2nd edn (2005) Art 2 CCPR paras 78 *et seq*.

[37] *Case Concerning the Factory at Chorzów (Germany v Poland)*, PCIJ, Judgment of 13 September 1928, PCIJ Series A no 17, 47.

litigation, the lack of a right to property in most human rights conventions has often made restitution of property difficult. Only in the African and the European system is property guaranteed in the applicable treaties.[38]

(2) Compensation

Compensation attempts to qualify and quantify the harm suffered in economic terms.[39] As such, it plays an important, or maybe even central, role as the form of reparation that produces the most tangible results. However, it also involves considerable difficulties, such as how to assess the value of a human life, or a person's physical or mental health. Measuring such suffering in financial terms trivializes the loss, and may even be perceived as an insult. Nevertheless, compensation is an important remedy, and many domestic legal orders contain rules for determining the amounts to be paid out for loss of life or damage to health. At the international level, the jurisprudence of the Inter-American Court of Human Rights in particular contains many examples of extensive compensation awards for gross human rights violations.[40] The European Court of Human Rights has taken a more cautious approach.[41] At the level of global human rights law, neither the Human Rights Committee nor the Committee against Torture has ever specified any amounts of compensation.[42] European and Inter-American jurisprudence does not allow any general conclusions to be drawn as to the modalities and amounts of compensation—regardless of the fact that their jurisprudence is not authoritative at the level of global human rights law. Compensation awards in the jurisprudence of both courts are the result of a case-to-case assessment. The courts usually make reference to their discretion under the Conventions and do not elaborate on any guidelines regarding the amounts fixed.[43]

States in transition will often not be able to award sums comparable to those awarded in individual cases.[44] Particularly in cases where the transitional society

[38] Art 14 of the Banjul Charter, Art 1 of the *(First) Protocol to the (European) Convention for the Protection of Human Rights and Fundamental Freedoms* of 20 May 1952, 213 UNTS 262. Nevertheless, the HRC has called for restoration of property in some of its views. In *Des Fours Walderode v Czech Republic* (Views of 30 October 2001 (no 747/1997) para 9.2), eg, withholding the property amounted to a violation of the prohibition of discrimination.

[39] See P. de Greiff, 'Justice and Reparations' in P. de Greiff (ed), *The Handbook of Reparations* (2006) 452.

[40] See, eg, IACtHR, *Case of the Ituango Massacres v Colombia*, Judgment of 1 July 2006, paras 383 *et seq*; *Case of La Cantuta v Peru*, Judgment of 29 November 2006, paras 216 *et seq*; *Case of the Rochela Massacre v Colombia*, Judgment of 11 May 2007, paras 253 *et seq*; for an overview of the Court's jurisprudence regarding reparation, see D. Cassel, 'The Expanding Scope and Impact of Reparations Awarded by the Inter-American Court of Human Rights' in K. De Feyter et al. (eds), *Out of the Ashes* (2005) 198.

[41] C. Tomuschat, 'Just Satisfaction under Article 50 of the European Convention on Human Rights' in P. Mahoney et al. (eds), *Protecting Human Rights* (2000) 1409 *et seq*.

[42] Yet in *Vargas-Machuca v Peru*, Views of 22 July 2002 (no 906/2000) para 9, the HRC held that an unlawfully dismissed civil servant was entitled to compensation equivalent to what he would have received as a salary.

[43] See, eg, IACtHR, *Case of the Rochela Massacre v Colombia*, Judgment of 11 May 2007, paras 268–9, 271; ECtHR, *Nasukhanova v Russia*, Judgment of 18 December 2008, para 158.

[44] In the *Case of the Rochela Massacre v Colombia* (Judgment of 11 May 2007), the IACtHR awarded a total amount of 7.8 million US$ to the next of kin of 12 persons killed.

has suffered mass violations of human rights, the burden of having to award full compensation could jeopardize the very foundations of the new order.[45] A way to make compensation available in these situations is through the creation of funds that victims can then apply to in order to receive compensation. Such administrative compensation mechanisms define victims and violations in standardized terms. Those who fulfil the requirements are awarded compensation in the form of a lump sum. It cannot be said that administrative compensation is the rule in transitional states, since too many states have completely ignored their violent past. Quite a few such states have, however, enacted procedures that allow victims to obtain compensation as a lump sum. Such compensation has, for example, been paid to the victims of Nazi atrocities,[46] to those of the communist regime in the former German Democratic Republic,[47] to the victims of the military regimes in Chile[48] and Argentina,[49] of the South African apartheid state,[50] and recently to the victims of paramilitary and rebel groups in Colombia as well.[51] In addition to this, truth commissions in several countries have also recommended such forms of compensation.[52] These compensation systems were not without their flaws, however: they excluded certain categories of victims;[53] victims often faced a long, degrading fight with a reluctant bureaucracy in order to obtain compensation in the first place;[54] and the sums awarded were often insufficient.

Nevertheless, administrative compensation can represent a sound option in cases of mass human rights violations. For victims, it offers relatively simple access to reparation without their having to risk a civil suit for compensation. For the state, they make compensation quantifiable.[55] Given the number of cases where administrative compensation has been awarded, or where such compensation has

[45] C. Tomuschat, 'Individual Reparation Claims in Instances of Grave Human Rights Violations' in A. Randelzhofer and C. Tomuschat (eds), *State Responsibility and the Individual* (1999) 19; C. Tomuschat, 'Reparation for Victims of Grave Human Rights Violations' 10 *Tulane Journal of International and Comparative Law* (2002) 175 *et seq*, referring to South Africa and Guatemala.

[46] For details, see K. Schwerin, 'German Compensation for Victims of Nazi Persecution' 67 *Northwestern University Law Review* (1972) 479 *et seq*; W. Tappert, 'Die Wiedergutmachung von Staatsunrecht im 20. Jahrhundert' 70 *Friedenswarte* (1995) 220 *et seq*.

[47] G. Werle and M. Vormbaum, 'After the Fall of the Berlin Wall' (forthcoming 2012).

[48] See P.B. Hayner, *Unspeakable Truths* (2001) 172 *et seq*; E. Lira, 'The Reparations Policy for Human Rights Violations in Chile' in P. de Greiff (ed), *The Handbook of Reparations* (2006) 55 *et seq*.

[49] See P.B. Hayner, ibid, 174 *et seq*.

[50] See C.J. Colvin, 'Overview of the Reparations Program in South Africa' in P. de Greiff (ed), *The Handbook of Reparations* (2006) 176 *et seq*.

[51] For details, see section IV B below.

[52] For instance, the UN backed truth commission for El Salvador, see *Report of the Commission on the Truth for El Salvador*, annex to UN Doc S/25500 of 1 April 1993, 186; the Guatemalan commission, see *Report of the Commission for Historical Clarification* (1999) 50 *et seq*; the Liberian commission, *Final Report of the Truth and Reconciliation Commission of Liberia*, vol I (2009) 77 *et seq*; or the Sierra Leonean commission, *Report of the Sierra Leone Truth and Reconciliation Commission*, vol 2 (2004) 124 *et seq*.

[53] As in the case of Holocaust, eg, the next of kin of euthanasia victims, or victims of forced sterilization, A. Lehmann-Richter, *Auf der Suche nach den Grenzen der Wiedergutmachung* (2007) 134 *et seq*, on 'gypsies', ibid, 252 *et seq*.

[54] N. Roht-Arriaza, 'Reparations in the Aftermath of Repression and Mass Violence' in E. Stover and H.M. Weinstein (eds), *My Neighbor, My Enemy* (2004) 124.

[55] See J.E. Malamud-Goti and L.S. Grosman, 'Reparations and Civil Litigation' in P. de Greiff (ed), *The Handbook of Reparations* (2006) 543 *et seq*.

at least been proposed by internationally acknowledged bodies, it can be assumed that such lump sum payments are sufficient to discharge states from the obligation to provide access to a remedy. In addition, these cases are evidence of an emerging customary right to compensation, which can come in the form of a lump sum payment. International law does not give any guidance regarding the calculation of monetary compensation for human rights violations, and it is not likely that it ever will, given the variety of approaches for the assessment of damages under domestic legal systems. The Human Rights Committee has also accepted lump sum payment and has refused to comment on the amounts to be awarded for violations carried out by states parties.[56]

(3) Satisfaction

Given the difficulties of monetary reparation for mass violations of human rights, satisfaction is of particular importance in the aftermath of mass atrocities. Satisfaction comprises different forms of moral reparation, in particular public apologies or measures aimed at the restoration of the victim's dignity.[57] It also includes obligations that are commonly associated with the right to know, such as an investigation into the circumstances of the violation, and commemoration for the victims.[58]

The value and importance of apology as a form of reparation is relatively undisputed.[59] Paradoxically, however, it is not taken very seriously as a means of reparation. In criminal trials all around the world, apology plays a marginal role and rarely figures in publications about remedies under international human rights law.[60] Apology is a statement of regret and acknowledgment of one's conduct, ideally accompanied by sincere repentance. However, the concept of apology varies in different cultural contexts. Some may stress the importance of an external acknowledgement of misconduct, while others may regard sincere regret as the central requirement of an apology.[61] In any event, it is questionable whether apology can be subject to an obligation in a reparations context. Such an institutionalized form of apology would carry the risk of becoming a mechanical act amounting to

[56] See HRC, *Summary Record of the First Part (Public) of the 1611th Meeting*, UN Doc CCPR/C/SR.1611 of 4 August 1997, para 4 and E. Klein, 'Individual Reparation Claims under the International Covenant on Civil and Political Rights' in A. Randelzhofer and C. Tomuschat (eds), *State Responsibility and the Individual* (1999) 40; see also F.H. Paolillo, 'On Unfulfilled Duties' in V. Götz, P. Selmer and R. Wolfrum (eds), *Liber Amicorum Günther Jaenicke* (1998) 306 *et seq.*

[57] Basic Principles on the Right to a Remedy and Reparation, para 22 (d), (e).

[58] Ibid, para 22(b), (c), (g), (h); see also UN Commission on Human Rights, *Question of the impunity of perpetrators of human rights violations*, UN Doc E/CN.4/Sub.2/1997/20 of 26 June 1997, paras 17 *et seq*, which, however, understands the right to know as a separate right of victims apart from the right to reparation.

[59] See C. Tomuschat, 'Reparation for Victims of Grave Human Rights Violations' 10 *Tulane Journal of International and Comparative Law* (2002) 176; C. Tomuschat, 'Ein umfassendes Wiedergutmachungsprogramm für Opfer schwerer Menschenrechtsverletzungen' 80 *Friedenswarte* (2005) 162.

[60] See C. Jenkins, 'Taking Apology Seriously' in M. du Plessis and S. Peté (eds), *Repairing the Past?* (2007) 60.

[61] See the discussion ibid, 57 *et seq.*

nothing more than mere lip service, or may encourage wrongdoers to believe that they can make up for their deeds simply by stating that they are sorry.

Other forms of satisfaction mentioned above have received much more attention in academic writing and international jurisprudence. A particularly important form of satisfaction for victims is to know exactly what happened to them or to their loved ones. It was in the context of disappearances and extra-legal executions under the Latin American military dictatorships of the 1970s and '80s that human rights bodies, confronted with violations carried out by military and police acting with impunity, started calling upon states to officially investigate the circumstances of these violations.[62] Since then, the right to truth has developed various facets, which go far beyond a mere secondary right to satisfaction. Today the right to the truth can be regarded as an emerging customary human right.[63]

Initially, the duty to investigate was applied as a corollary of the obligation to ensure the enjoyment of human rights.[64] Investigation was an instrument to secure compliance by obligating the state to expose its conduct. Soon, however, the human rights bodies went one step further and stated that in the event of disappearances or extrajudicial killings, the victims' next of kin were entitled to know what had happened to their loved ones. This followed not only from the right to a remedy. The bodies even found that, in cases of particularly serious violations, withholding information about the fate of the victim from his or her next of kin amounted to cruel or inhuman treatment of these persons.[65]

Remedial truth is more than mere knowledge of the facts. Using the terms of the South African Truth and Reconciliation Commission,[66] truth has a personal or narrative component: victims may experience relief at having a place where their story can be heard or where they can exchange their experiences with others. In the aftermath of mass atrocities, dictatorship, or war, truth also consists of the interaction between different accounts, in public discussion and debate ('social truth').[67] This has been recognized by the Inter-American Commission on Human Rights: the Commission suggested that the right to the truth could be inferred from the

[62] See UN General Assembly Resolutions on the protection of human rights in Chile 34/179 of 17 December 1979, para 7 and 35/188 of 15 December 1980, para 7; UN Commission on Human Rights, *Report of the Working Group on Enforced or Involuntary Disappearances*, UN Doc E/CN.4/1435 of 26 January 1981, para 187; HRC, *Bleier v Uruguay*, Views of 29 March 1982 (no 30/1978) para 15.

[63] For a detailed discussion of the right to truth as a customary human right, see Y. Naqvi, 'The Right to the Truth in International Law' 88 *International Review of the Red Cross* (2006) 254 *et seq.* The right to the truth has also been expressly articulated in international instruments, eg, Arts 32–3 of the *(First) Additional Protocol to the Geneva Conventions of 12 August 1949, and Relating to the Protection of Victims of International Armed Conflicts* of 8 June 1977 (1125 UNTS 3), and Art 24(2) of the *International Convention for the Protection of All Persons from Enforced Disappearance* (annex to UN General Assembly Resolution 61/177 of 20 December 2006), which has, however, not yet entered into force.

[64] eg, Art 2(1) of the ICCPR.

[65] Art 7 of the ICCPR; HRC, *Quinteros v Uruguay*, Views of 21 July 1983 (no 107/1981) para 14; *Schedko v Belarus*, Views of 3 April 2003 (no 886/1999) para 10.2; *Sankara v Burkina Faso*, Views of 28 March 2006 (no 1159/2003) para 12.2; General Comment 20/44 of 3 April 1992, para 14. See also ECtHR, *Kurt v Turkey*, Judgment of 25 May 1998, paras 130 *et seq.*

[66] *Truth and Reconciliation Commission of South Africa Report*, vol 1 (1999) 111 *et seq.*

[67] See A. Sachs, in A. Boraine and J. Levy (eds), *The Healing of a Nation?* (1995) 105; *Truth and Reconciliation Commission of South Africa Report*, vol 1 (1999) 113.

freedom to seek, receive, and impart information, particularly in cases of systematic violations of human rights.[68] This component of the right to the truth has its origin in the idea of a society having an interest in being duly informed about its own history. Correspondingly, states are called upon to preserve memory of such events.[69]

As for the individual victims of human rights violations and their families, the right to truth entails a right to all relevant information regarding the violation. This right need not necessarily be given effect through a judicial investigation and a trial of those responsible for the violations. States may have a duty to prosecute gross human rights violations in order to fulfil their obligation to respect and ensure the enjoyment of human rights. However, victims do not have an individual right to see another person be prosecuted.[70] The facts of the violation can also be brought to light outside of courts, for example by a truth commission. The investigation, whether judicial or not, must lead to the reasons and circumstances of the violation being revealed and publicly acknowledged, and must identify those responsible.[71] Depending on the particular case, an investigation into the whereabouts of those who have disappeared or been killed, and their place of burial can be required.[72]

(4) Rehabilitation

Another vital remedy in cases of grave human rights violations is free access to medical and psychological care. These forms of reparation are commonly discussed in terms of 'rehabilitation' but can also be regarded as a form of compensation.[73] The importance of medical and psychological care for victims of human rights violations has been stressed in several statements by United Nations organs.[74] In

[68] Art 13(1) of the ACHR or Art 19(2) of the ICCPR; IAComHR, *Ellacuría* et al. *v El Salvador*, Report no 136/99 of 22 December 1999, para 221; see also T.M. Antkowiak, 'Truth as Right and Remedy in International Human Rights Experience' 23 *MichJIntlL* (2002) 993.

[69] See the UN Commission on Human Rights, *Updated set of principles for the protection and promotion of human rights through action to combat impunity*, UN Doc E/CN.4/2005/102/Add.1 of 8 February 2005, Principles 2 and 3; see also T.M. Antkowiak, 'Truth as Right and Remedy in International Human Rights Experience' 23 *MichJIntlL* (2002) 993 *et seq.*

[70] HRC, *H.C.M.A. v The Netherlands*, Views of 30 March 1989 (no 213/1986) para 11.6; *R.A. V.N. v Argentina*, Views of 26 March 1990 (nos 343, 344, and 345/1988) para 5.5; *S.E. v Argentina*, Views of 26 March 1990 (no 275/1988) para 5.5; *Rodríguez v Uruguay*, Views of 19 July 1994 (no 322/1988) para 6.4; contra, eg, the preparatory work of the UN Commission on Human Rights on the question of impunity for perpetrators of human rights violations, *Question of the impunity of perpetrators of human rights violations*, UN Doc E/CN.4/Sub.2/1997/20 of 26 June 1997, para 26. See also J.E. Méndez and J. Mariezcurrena, 'Accountability for Past Human Rights Violations' 26 *Social Justice* (1999) no 4, 89; M. Nowak, *CCPR Commentary*, 2nd edn (2005) Art 2 CCPR para 70; J.M. van Dyke, 'The Fundamental Human Right to Prosecution and Compensation' in J.D. White and A.J. Marsella (eds), *Fear of Prosecution* (2007) 189 *et seq.*

[71] IAComHR, *Ellacuría* et al. *v El Salvador*, Report no 136/99 of 22 December 1999, para 226; J.E. Méndez, 'The Right to Truth' in C.C. Joyner (ed), *Reigning in Impunity* (1998) 268 *et seq*; M. Nowak, *CCPR Commentary*, 2nd edn (2005) Art 2 CCPR para 80.

[72] HRC, *Schedko v Belarus*, Views of 3 April 2003 (no 886/1999) para 12; *Staselovich v Belarus*, Views of 3 April 2003 (no 887/1999) para 11; *Sankara v Burkina Faso*, Views of 28 March 2006 (no 1159/2003) para 14.

[73] D. Shelton, *Remedies in International Human Rights Law*, 2nd edn (2005) 35.

[74] See Basic Principles on the Right to a Remedy and Reparation, para 21; *Declaration of Basic Principles of Justice for Victims of Crime and Abuse of Power*, annex to UN General Assembly Resolution

their jurisprudence, human rights bodies have also identified medical and psychological care for victims as a crucial form of reparation and regularly award it as such.[75] State practice in that field, however, is scarce. Although access to medical or psychological care for victims of mass atrocities has often been called for,[76] only very few states in transition have actually enacted programmes to cover the costs of medical or psychological care for victims. Among the ones that have done so are Germany,[77] South Africa,[78] and Chile.[79] Apart from that, it appears that no examples of rehabilitation on a larger scale exist.[80] In developing states in particular, this is hardly surprising. Such states usually lack the infrastructure to provide such services, and creating such facilities would go way beyond a standard reparation policy.

II. Reparation for Human Rights Violations in Post-Genocide Rwanda

A. Overview

To begin with, it is worth mentioning that only very few genocide survivors in Rwanda have received any payment for their sufferings. Certainly, reparation can also come in other, non-material, forms, some of which have been implemented during the Gacaca process. When it comes to material reparation however, the actual achievements have been meagre to say the least. There is no doubt that this

40/34 of 29 November 1985, para 14 (hereinafter 'Basic Principles of Justice for Victims of Crime and Abuse of Power'); *Conclusions and Recommendations of the Committee against Torture*: Indonesia, 22 November 2001, UN Doc CAT/C/XXVII/Concl.3, para 10(n) and Zambia, 23 November 2001, UN Doc CAT/C/XXVII/Concl.4, para 8(g). See also Art 14(1) of the Torture Convention.

[75] This is particularly true for the IACtHR that awards rehabilitation on a regular basis, *Case of Villagrán Morales* et al. *('Street Children') v Guatemala*, Judgment of 26 May 2001 (Reparations) para 80; *Case of 19 Tradesmen v Colombia*, Judgment of 5 July 2004, paras 275 *et seq*; *Case of the Pueblo Bello Massacre v Colombia*, Judgment of 31 January 2006, paras 274 *et seq*; *Case of Vargas-Areco v Paraguay*, Judgment of 26 September 2006, paras 159 *et seq*; *Case of the Rochela Massacre v Colombia*, Judgment of 11 May 2007, paras 298 *et seq*. The ECtHR and the HRC seldom refer to it expressly, but apparently recognize it as an important form of reparation, see HRC, *Vasilskis v Uruguay*, Views of 31 March 1983 (no 80/1980) para 12; *R.S. v Trinidad and Tobago*, Views of 2 April 2002 (no 684/1996) para 9; ECtHR, *Aksoy v Turkey*, Judgment of 18 December 1996, paras 111, 113.

[76] See the recommendations of the truth commissions for Guatemala, *Report of the Commission for Historical Clarification* (1999) 50; see also *Report of the Sierra Leone Truth and Reconciliation Commission*, vol 2 (2004) 124 *et seq*.

[77] See section 29 of the Federal Compensation Law (*Bundesgesetz zur Entschädigung für Opfer der nationalsozialistischen Verfolgung* vom 18. September 1953, BGBl I 1953, 1387). On that, see Bundesminister der Finanzen and W. Schwartz (eds), *Die Wiedergutmachung nationalsozialistischen Unrechts durch die Bundesrepublik Deutschland*, vol III (1985).

[78] L. Fernandez, 'Reparation for Human Rights Violations Committed by the *Apartheid* Regime in South Africa' in A. Randelzhofer and C. Tomuschat (eds), *State Responsibility and the Individual* (1999) 185; P.B. Hayner, *Unspeakable Truths* (2001) 146.

[79] N. Roht-Arriaza, 'Reparations in the Aftermath of Repression and Mass Violence' in E. Stover and H.M. Weinstein (eds), *My Neighbor, My Enemy* (2004) 124.

[80] M.B. Lykes and M. Mersky, 'Reparations and Mental Health' in P. de Greiff (ed), *The Handbook of Reparations* (2006) 590.

lack of actual practice is a setback for the customary right to reparation. At the same time, it cannot be denied that, for a long time now, the Rwandan government has taken its duty to provide reparation for gross human rights violations seriously. There have been several efforts to implement an operable reparations policy, initially through damage awards within genocide trials, then through financial assistance and lump sum compensation paid out by funds. While the implementation of these policies proved impossible, the attempts demonstrate that the Rwandan state acknowledges the right to reparation in principle.

When discussing payments to genocide survivors in Rwanda, a distinction between compensation and assistance needs to be made. Compensation is supposed to make up for the loss suffered via the payment of a sum, which, in one way or another, seeks to reflect the value of the lost good. Assistance, in contrast, is aimed only at the neediest. It does not reflect the losses suffered, but is rather geared to the needs of the survivors. Nevertheless, assistance can also be regarded as a measure of reparation.[81] This will be discussed in more detail below.[82] In any event, the implementation of the assistance fund (FARG, later FSARG) can be regarded as a manifestation of the government's conviction that reparation must be paid.

(1) Reparation within genocide trials

A highly persuasive example of state practice in favour of the right to reparation is provided by the extensive jurisprudence of ordinary Rwandan courts in genocide trials. Under Organic Law No 08/96, the specialized chambers were given the competence to adjudicate the victims' reparation claims within the criminal trial[83]—a power the ICTR does not have. Civil liability under Organic Law No 08/96 lay jointly with the offender and the Rwandan state (liability *in solidum*).[84] Perpetrators of the first category incurred civil liability for all damages suffered during the genocide throughout the whole country.[85] The law also provided for the creation of a compensation fund (FIND), which was to be governed by another law. Under article 32 of Organic Law No 08/96, damages awarded to unidentified victims upon request by the Prosecution were to be allocated to that fund once it had been set up.[86] There is extensive jurisprudence with respect to damage claims by genocide victims under Organic Law No 08/96. The courts regularly condemned the

[81] Similarly, H. Rombouts, *Victim Organisations and the Politics of Reparation* (2004) 402 *et seq.* At the same time, Rombouts points out that, due to its selectivity, assistance may produce conflicts and may therefore frustrate the goal to repair. On that, see also L. Waldorf, 'Goats & Graves' in C. Ferstman, M. Goetz and A. Stephens (eds), *Reparations for Victims of Genocide, War Crimes and Crimes Against Humanity* (2009) 522.

[82] See section B *(4)*.

[83] For details on the procedure and on the concept of victimhood under Organic Law No 08/96, see section III B below. For an overview, see V. Thalmann, 'Rwandan Genocide Cases' in A. Cassese (ed), *The Oxford Companion to International Criminal Justice* (2009) 505.

[84] Not all courts accepted this, for details see section IV C below.

[85] Art 30(1) of Organic Law No 08/96. eg, in TPI Kigali, *Affaire Euphrasie Kamatamu et consorts*, Judgment of 17 July 1998, in *Recueil de jurisprudence I*, 139 *et seq*, two defendants were condemned jointly with the Rwandan state to pay three billion FRw (about nine million US$ at the time) and 700 million FRw (2.1 million US$), respectively, as compensation for damages in the whole country. In general, however, this form of comprehensive liability was hardly applied.

[86] On the attempts to create a compensation fund, see below in this section.

Rwandan state *in solidum* with the perpetrator to pay enormous amounts of compensation to the victims. The government, however, was reluctant to comply with these judgments. When the Gacaca proposals took shape towards the end of the 1990s, the government had given up on the idea of individualized compensation awards by courts and was instead looking at solutions involving administrative compensation distributed by a fund. It hoped to create this fund in the wake of the introduction of the Gacaca system.

The provisions on damages in the first Gacaca Law, Organic Law No 40/2000, were less ambitious than in the previous legislation. It was clear that the issue could not be put aside completely, as Gacaca was supposed not only to punish, but also to restore peaceful co-existence. On the other hand, the question of reparation was considered too complex to be addressed by lay courts. In that regard, Organic Law No 40/2000 found a compromise that has, in essence, been retained throughout the various amendments of the Gacaca Law: as described above, Gacaca courts are able to award material damages for destroyed or stolen property;[87] when it comes to determining damages for death or injury, they were to investigate the losses suffered and to fix the amount of damages according to a scale provided in the projected law on the compensation fund (FIND).[88] They were to pass on all relevant information on damage claims to the FIND.[89] At the same time, Organic Law No 40/2000 did acknowledge the civil liability of the perpetrators. Like Organic Law No 08/96, it provided for 'comprehensive' liability of first category convicts for all damages suffered in the country over the course of the genocide.[90] Even though Organic Law No 08/96 remained in force for first category cases until its abrogation in 2004, its reparation regime was factually repealed by Organic Law No 40/2000; the new provisions were to be applied not only to future trials, but also to pending cases and cases where a final judgment had not yet been handed down.[91]

As we have seen above, Organic Law No 40/2000 was replaced in 2004 before the beginning of the judgment phase, and before the provisions on damages could be applied. The new Organic Law No 16/2004 reflects the increasing resignation regarding the reparation issue on the part of the Rwandan government. The provisions, which have remained unchanged throughout the 2006, 2007, and 2008 modifications, deal almost exclusively with property damages. For all other forms of reparation, the law refers to another law yet to be enacted.[92] This leads to the somewhat absurd situation that victims of looting may be compensated through the Gacaca courts, while victims of violent crimes end up not receiving anything.

[87] Art 71(1) of Organic Law No 40/2000. See also art 75 of the Gacaca Law; these damages are not supposed to be dealt with by the FIND, even though art 90 of Organic Law No 40/2000 seems to suggest that they should be, see also Department of Gacaca Jurisdictions, *Manuel explicatif* (2001) 97. On Gacaca trials relating to property offences, see ch 2, section IX above.

[88] Art 67(9) of Organic Law No 40/2000.

[89] Art 90 of Organic Law No 40/2000. For details on the FIND, see sections II A *(3)*, B *(2)*, and III B below.

[90] Art 91(1) of Organic Law No 40/2000.

[91] Art 91(4) of Organic Law No 40/2000 (the English version is incorrect, see the French version).

[92] Art 96 of the Gacaca Law.

In general, the introduction and implementation of Gacaca actually marked a shift away from material redress towards moral forms of reparation. Repentance, apology, and unveiling the truth are crucial elements of the Gacaca system.[93]

(2) *The assistance fund (FARG/FSARG)*

Initial attempts to create a fund for the victims of the genocide as envisaged in Organic Law No 08/96 date back to 1996–97. This fund was to grant compensation for harm suffered as well as additional assistance to the needy, but the legislation governing that particular fund never got beyond the drafting stage.[94] In 1998, the government decided to create an independent assistance fund, the Fonds national d'assistance aux victimes les plus nécessiteuses du génocide et des massacres (FARG), and to put off dealing with the compensation issue to a later stage.[95] The fund has a largely social character: its beneficiaries are 'survivors... in need, especially orphans, widows, and handicapped persons'.[96] Assistance mostly comes in the form of education, health, housing, and income-generating programmes.[97] The beneficiaries have, for example, received vouchers for medical treatment and support for their *minerval* (secondary school fees). The FARG has also organized the construction of houses for families whose homes were destroyed during the genocide.[98]

The FARG has an annual budget of approximately 10 million US$.[99] It is financed by the Rwandan government, which contributes five per cent of its annual budget. All adult Rwandans have to pay at least one per cent of their annual salary to the fund.[100] In addition, substantial funding comes from the US and the Dutch governments.[101] The Rwandan government has recently identified that there are approximately 119,000 *rescapés* in need of assistance.[102] Yet, as the fund is permanently underfinanced, only a fraction of those entitled to receive assistance actually end up receiving it.[103] Implementing the FARG has brought about various difficulties. The selective allocation process of the fund is reported to have fuelled

[93] On that see section B *(3)* below.

[94] H. Rombouts, *Victim Organisations and the Politics of Reparation* (2004) 372.

[95] The fund was created by *Law No 02/98 of 22 January 1998 establishing a National Assistance Fund for needy victims of genocide and massacres committed in Rwanda between October 1, 1990 and December 31, 1994*, OGRR no 3 of 1 February 1998. The fund is commonly referred to as Fonds d'Assistance aux Rescapés du Génocide, from which the acronym FARG is derived.

[96] Art 14(1) of Law No 02/98.

[97] V. Sinsebyimfura, 'Le Fonds d'Assistance' in ASF and Minijust (eds), *Séminaire sur la réparation* (2000) 28; see also art 14(1) of Law No 02/98.

[98] H. Rombouts, *Victim Organisations and the Politics of Reparation* (2004) 375 *et seq.*

[99] C. Mgbako, '*Ingando* Solidarity Camps' 18 *HarvHRJ* (2005) 216.

[100] For details, see art 12(1) of Law No 02/98.

[101] H. Rombouts, *Victim Organisations and the Politics of Reparation* (2004) 378; J. Sarkin, 'Reparations for Gross Human Rights Violations in Africa' in M. du Plessis and S. Peté (eds), *Repairing the Past?* (2007) 214.

[102] 'Government Appointees Have to Start Accepting Responsibility', *The New Times*, 17 January 2009. A census in 1998 had identified that there were still 282,804 potential beneficiaries of the FARG, C. Mibenge, 'Enforcing International Humanitarian Law at the National Level' in T.L.H. McCormack (ed), *Yearbook of International Humanitarian Law*, vol 7 (2006) 421; H. Rombouts, *Victim Organisations and the Politics of Reparation* (2004) 381.

[103] See H. Rombouts, *Victim Organisations and the Politics of Reparation* (2004) 378, 382.

social envy.[104] What is more, the fund has been notorious from its very inception for its corrupt management.[105] In early 2009, several senior officials, including the executive secretary, were suspended and 17 people were charged with fraud and embezzlement—a measure seen as long overdue.[106]

For some years now, there have been plans to tackle these shortcomings. In April 2009, a new law on the Fund for the Support and Assistance to the Survivors of the Genocide (FSARG) entered into force.[107] The new fund will have an increased budget.[108] The contribution of the Rwandan state, for instance, is being increased from five to six per cent.[109] In addition, the fund is given the exclusive power to sue first category defendants for damages.[110] However, like the FARG, its remit will still be made up by only the neediest *rescapés*.[111] The forms of assistance envisaged in the new law are similar to those by the FARG.[112] At the time of research, the new fund had not yet been implemented and no assessment of its functioning could be made.

(3) The compensation fund (FIND)

As we have seen, the creation of a compensation fund (Fonds d'indemnisation, FIND) was already announced in Organic Law No 08/96.[113] The first Gacaca legislation, Organic Law No 40/2000, stipulated that compensation paid out of the fund should be allocated by Gacaca courts.[114] Details on the beneficiaries of the fund, contributors to it, and its organization were to be determined by another specific law to this end. In 2001 and 2002, parallel to the implementation of the Gacaca system, two different drafts for a FIND law were under consideration. The Rwandan state was supposed to contribute part of its budget to the FIND, which would exempt it from any further liability.[115] Additional contributions were supposed to come from those convicted of genocide, and from the international community and individuals on a voluntary basis. In addition, the profits from the community service programme would also be passed on to the fund.[116]

104 NURC, *Nation-Wide Grassroots Consultations Report* (2001) 15 *et seq*; H. Rombouts, ibid, 399 *et seq*.

105 NURC, *Report on the Evaluation of National Unity and Reconciliation* (2002) 17 *et seq*; H. Rombouts, ibid, 380.

106 '17 under Investigation for Alleged Embezzlement of Funds', *Hirondelle*, 8 January 2009; 'Government Sacks FARG Leaders', *The New Times*, 15 January 2009; 'Government Appointees Have to Start Accepting Responsibility', *The New Times*, 17 January 2009.

107 *Law No 69/2008 of 31 December 2008 relating to the establishment of the Fund for the Support and Assistance to the Survivors of the Tutsi Genocide and other crimes against humanity committed between 1st October 1990 and 31st December 1994, and determining its organisation, competence and functioning*, OGRR no special of 15 April 2009.

108 PRI, *Report X* (2007) 95 *et seq*.

109 Art 22(2)(1) of Law No 69/2008. A previous draft of the FSARG law stipulated that the Rwandan state, due to its contribution to the fund, was to be exempted from all reparation claims by genocide victims (see IRDP, *Cahier No 2* (2007) 31 *et seq* referring to art 5 of the draft law)—a provision that would undoubtedly have marked a conclusive end to all efforts to provide comprehensive compensation.

110 Arts 4(2)(2), 20 of Law No 69/2008.

111 Art 26 of Law No 69/2008.

112 See art 4(2) of Law No 69/2009.

113 Art 32.

114 Arts 67(9), 90 of Organic Law No 40/2000.

115 Art 91(3) of Organic Law No 40/2000.

116 On the FIND law drafts and their contents, see H. Rombouts, *Victim Organisations and the Politics of Reparation* (2004) 411 *et seq*; S. Vandeginste, 'Victims of Genocide' in J. Torpey (ed), *Politics and the Past* (2003) 262 *et seq*.

The first draft in particular attracted great public attention and support, and was intensively discussed between officials and civil society organizations. The drafts contained detailed provisions on the potential beneficiaries of the projected fund, and on amounts to be awarded.[117] The implementation of the Gacaca system may still have been a priority, but the efforts undertaken to devise an operable victims' fund are evidence of the government's commitment to the issue of compensation at the time. In the wake of the 2003 elections, however, the process came to a standstill and has not been taken up again since. The 2003 Constitution reflects the government's resignation regarding compensation; it contains a provision on the 'welfare of the survivors of the genocide', but at the same time states that this is possible only 'within the limits of [the state's] capacity'.[118] Organic Law No 16/2004 no longer mentions the creation of a compensation fund, but merely states that compensation is to be governed by another law.[119] In 2005, Minister of Justice Edda Mukabagwiza stated that compensation was 'impractical', but later backpedalled on this.[120] Her successor Tharcisse Karugarama announced that the law was still under consideration and to be voted upon by Parliament soon.[121] Most observers, however, no longer believe in the introduction of a compensation fund.[122]

B. The forms of reparation in post-genocide Rwanda

(1) Restitution

Restitution of property in the aftermath of the Rwandan genocide has mostly been effected outside of courts. Most refugees who returned to their homes after the genocide to find them occupied reclaimed their property before the genocide trials had even begun. Occupants often vacated houses and returned assets voluntarily or under pressure from local authorities or RPA soldiers. In some cases, suits were filed before First Instance Courts. Penal Reform International (PRI) reported on a case where the court refused to pass a judgment and referred the dispute to the local population for settlement.[123] In general, those who had fled from the RPA invasion in the north and the east of the country were much less likely to be given back their lands after their return. This was also due to the fact that many of them were afraid of being charged and arrested if they voiced their claims.[124] The Gacaca Law in its article 95(1) acknowledges the right to restitution and proclaims it as the primary mode of reparation. However, restitution has always played a minor role in Gacaca courts and in genocide trials before regular courts, while compensation for lost property has played a much more prominent one.

[117] For details on that, see section B *(2)* below.

[118] Art 14 of the Rwandan Constitution. The provision was amended by art 2 of the Amendment of 13 August 2008, but the quoted parts were maintained.

[119] Art 96 of the Gacaca Law.

[120] J. Sarkin, 'Reparations for Gross Human Rights Violations in Africa' in M. du Plessis and S. Peté (eds), *Repairing the Past?* (2007) 214.

[121] Redress and African Rights, *Survivors and Post-Genocide Justice in Rwanda* (2008) 101.

[122] Interview with Benoit Kaboyi, Executive Secretary of *Ibuka*, Kigali, 4 October 2007, and with two representatives of ASF Rwanda, Kigali, 12 October 2007.

[123] PRI, *Report X* (2007) 46.

[124] PRI, ibid, 45 *et seq*.

(2) Compensation

Up to this day, there have been various attempts to make compensation available to genocide victims in Rwanda, none of which have borne fruit. Payments to survivors have only been made by the assistance fund. These payments cannot, however, be regarded as compensation, given that assistance does not reflect the damage suffered. Initial approaches by the ordinary courts to award compensation to civil parties in genocide trials under Organic Law No 08/98 were as ambitious as they were divorced from reality. A major flaw of the reparations system set out by Organic Law No 08/96 was the lack of any guidelines for the courts in determining which sort of damages should entail reparation or how reparation was to be calculated. In the majority of the cases dealing with reparation, 'moral' damages were awarded for the loss of family members, which would sometimes entail a detailed breakdown of the potential future income of the person killed.[125] The courts granted material damages on a regular basis for the destruction of houses, pillage of assets, or killing of cattle.[126] Compensation for physical or mental harm suffered was requested and granted only in exceptional cases.[127] The amounts were usually fixed *ex aequo et bono*. In a small number of cases, courts relied on a Ministerial Instruction relating to damages resulting from traffic accidents.[128] It has also been reported that an informal scale for the calculation of sums was circulated in First Instance Tribunals.[129] Nevertheless, no uniform practice has emerged in that respect. While some courts awarded 10 million FRw for the loss of a spouse and eight million for a child,[130] others granted only two and one million FRw, respectively.[131] Compensation was mostly claimed and granted for the

[125] eg, Cour d'Appel Nyabisindu, *Affaire Joseph Murindangabo et consorts*, Judgment of 27 September 2002, in *Recueil de jurisprudence IV*, 307 *et seq*; Conseil de Guerre, *Affaire Caporal Joseph Ukurikiyimfura et consorts*, Judgment of 17 April 2001, in *Recueil de jurisprudence V*, 378; TPI Kibungo, *Affaire François Twahirwa*, Judgment of 16 June 1999, in *Recueil de jurisprudence I*, 48 *et seq*; TPI Kigali, *Affaire Euphrasie Kamatamu et consorts*, Judgment of 17 July 1998, in *Recueil de jurisprudence I*, 138.

[126] eg, Cour d'Appel Cyangugu, *Affaire Emmanuel Ntagozera et consorts*, Judgment of 30 June 1999, in *Recueil de jurisprudence II*, 233; TPI Cyangugu, *Affaire Védaste Rwanteli et consorts*, Judgment of 8 October 1997, in *Recueil de jurisprudence IV*, 76; TPI Nyamata, *Affaire André Ndererehe et Elie Rwakibibi*, Judgment of 21 October 1999, in *Recueil de jurisprudence II*, 188.

[127] eg, Cour d'Appel Ruhengeri, *Affaire Faustin Ntaganda et consorts*, Judgment of 24 June 1998, in *Recueil de jurisprudence I*, 185 (injuries suffered); TPI Cyangugu, *Affaire Védaste Rwanteli et consorts*, Judgment of 8 October 1997, in *Recueil de jurisprudence IV*, 76, 80 (fear, flight, 'leading a miserable life', 66, 70); TPI Gisenyi, *Affaire Tharcisse Gakuru et consorts*, Judgment of 12 February 1999, in *Recueil de jurisprudence II*, 84 (rape). See also S. Vandeginste, 'Victims of Genocide' in J. Torpey (ed), *Politics and the Past* (2003) 258.

[128] *Instruction Ministérielle no 01/87 du 14 septembre 1987 portant détermination des dommages et intérêts matériels pour perte de revenus et des dommages et intérêts moraux en cas d'accidents de la circulation*, Journal officiel de la République Rwandaise 1987, 1573, see ASF, *Vade-mecum* (2004) 219.

[129] H. Rombouts, *Victim Organisations and the Politics of Reparation* (2004) 452.

[130] Conseil de Guerre, *Affaire Caporal Joseph Ukurikiyimfura et consorts*, Judgment of 17 April 2001, in *Recueil de jurisprudence V*, 378 (about 21,000 and 17,000 US$ at the time).

[131] Cour d'Appel Nyabisindu, *Affaire Joseph Murindangabo et consorts*, Judgment of 27 September 2002, in *Recueil de jurisprudence IV*, 307 *et seq*; TPI Kibungo, *Affaire François Twahirwa*, Judgment of 16 June 1999, in *Recueil de jurisprudence I*, 48 *et seq* (about 4,200 and 3,000 US$ at the respective times).

loss of family members and for damage to or loss of property.[132] Compensation for physical or mental injury was seldom claimed. In some cases, however, victims were awarded payments for physical injury,[133] fear,[134] or rape.[135]

Yet the value of this jurisprudence as state practice in the field of compensation should not be overrated. While some courts took their power to award compensation seriously, others refused to rule on the issue. It is estimated that only half of the trials resulted in damages being awarded.[136] This was often due to the fact that no one had actually filed a civil action. In other cases, the court ordered that the civil action be separated from the criminal trial. The victims would have had to pursue their claims before civil courts, which they rarely did, as they were usually not familiar with the proceedings and feared the costs of another trial. In many cases, state representatives were summoned to the trials because the state was jointly liable for damages together with the perpetrators. After a while, these representatives did not appear at the trials any more, which often prompted the courts to no longer rule on damage claims. It seems that, soon after the genocide trials had started, the government realized that the reparations system set up by Organic Law No 08/96 was inoperable. The convicts were usually unable to pay the damages, and neither was the Rwandan state. In an act of obvious interference with the judiciary, the minister of justice instructed the courts to suspend all cases where government participation was required.[137] However, even in cases where damages were actually awarded, the victims did not end up receiving anything. In the few cases involving wealthy defendants, execution was not ordered.[138] The state also refused to pay the damages it had been condemned to.

The efforts to create the compensation fund (FIND) more persuasively show the government's conviction that it had a duty to pay compensation. Both the 2001 as well as the 2002 drafts of FIND law already contained detailed provisions on the individual amounts to be awarded. The approaches taken in the two drafts were very different, however. The 2001 draft included highly detailed scales listing

[132] eg, Cour d'Appel Cyangugu, *Affaire Emmanuel Ntagozera et consorts*, Judgment of 30 June 1999, in *Recueil de jurisprudence II*, 233; Cour d'Appel Nyabisindu, *Affaire Joseph Murindangabo et consorts*, Judgment of 27 September 2002, in *Recueil de jurisprudence IV*, 307 *et seq*; Conseil de Guerre, *Affaire Caporal Joseph Ukurikiyimfura et consorts*, Judgment of 17 April 2001, in *Recueil de jurisprudence V*, 378.

[133] Cour d'Appel Ruhengeri, *Affaire Faustin Ntaganda et consorts*, Judgment of 24 June 1998, in *Recueil de jurisprudence I*, 185.

[134] TPI Cyangugu, *Affaire Védaste Rwanteli et consorts*, Judgment of 8 October 1997, in *Recueil de jurisprudence IV*, 76, 80.

[135] TPI Gisenyi, *Affaire Tharcisse Gakuru et consorts*, Judgment of 12 February 1999, in *Recueil de jurisprudence II*, 84.

[136] H. Rombouts and S. Vandeginste, 'Reparation for Victims in Rwanda' in K. De Feyter et al. (eds), *Out of the Ashes* (2005) 318. Statistical data comes from an unspecified study undertaken by ASF, which included 159 convictions. Extracts from that study can be found in ASF, *Rapport semestriel, janvier–juin* (2000) 37.

[137] H. Rombouts, *Victim Organisations and the Politics of Reparation* (2004) 451 *et seq*; H. Rombouts and S. Vandeginste, 'Reparation for Victims in Rwanda' in K. De Feyter et al. (eds), *Out of the Ashes* (2005) 318.

[138] The only apparent exception to this was the case of Froduald Karamira; on the trial see ch 1, section VI C above. Yet Karamira had other creditors who had priority over the victims of his crimes, see H. Rombouts, ibid, 454, fn 243; on the reasons for the non-execution of judgments, see ibid, 455.

categories of damages. Compensation was envisaged for immediate next of kin. If these happened to be deceased, more distant family members would then be able to make a subsidiary claim.[139] The scales also covered injury suffered and damage to property. The draft went as far as to list specific items damaged or destroyed and fixed particular sums for each of them.[140] The amounts listed in the draft were more than merely symbolic. In fact, they could have made a real difference, especially for the poorest among the victims: for instance, a victim would receive three million FRw (approximately 6,300 US$ in 2001) for the death of a spouse.[141]

Apparently, the government was concerned that these detailed provisions were too complex. After all, untrained Gacaca judges were to be responsible for the inventory of all damages and the allocation of compensation sums.[142] Therefore, in close cooperation with a taskforce of the victim collective *Ibuka*,[143] the Ministry of Justice (Minijust) developed a different approach which was incorporated in the 2002 FIND draft. According to this approach, all beneficiaries were to receive one payment of 12 million FRw,[144] which would cover all damages.[145] While the lack of implementation of these drafts certainly represents a setback for a customary right to compensation, the sustained efforts of the Minijust to set up a framework for compensation are evidence of the conviction that victims of human rights violations have a right to compensation. In addition, they confirm the trend towards lump sum compensation for mass atrocities.

(3) Satisfaction

The genocide trials in Rwanda do offer a framework for apology. The confession procedure requires not only an account of the crime committed and the circumstances surrounding it, but also a public apology to the victims and to Rwandan society.[146] Yet such apologies are hardly perceived as constituting reparation. Apology is propagated not as a means of reparation, but as a precondition for reconciliation. The institutionalization of apology and forgiveness by the Gacaca Law has almost trivialized the concept.[147] For many victims, apology is part of a trade-off to their detriment. The victims receive a simple 'sorry' from those who have done them wrong and are then expected to grant them their forgiveness in return. The defendants, in contrast, have the prospect of an official pardon, a reduction of their prison term and, in some cases, preliminary release.[148] The behaviour of the defendants, who

[139] S. Vandeginste, 'Victims of Genocide' in J. Torpey (ed), *Politics and the Past* (2003) 262.

[140] H. Rombouts, *Victim Organisations and the Politics of Reparation* (2004) 422.

[141] S. Vandeginste, 'Victims of Genocide' in J. Torpey (ed), *Politics and the Past* (2003) 263.

[142] Arts 67(9), 90 of Organic Law No 40/2000. The forms Gacaca courts had to fill out are reprinted in Department of Gacaca Jurisdictions, *Manuel explicatif* (2001) 49 *et seq.*

[143] *Ibuka* is a collective of several organizations and the most important representative of victims' interests. 'Ibuka' is Kinyarwanda for 'remember'. For details, see H. Rombouts, *Victim Organisations and the Politics of Reparation* (2004) 284 *et seq.*

[144] About 25,000 US$ at the time.

[145] H. Rombouts, *Victim Organisations and the Politics of Reparation* (2004) 423 *et seq.*

[146] Art 54(2), (3) of the Gacaca Law. This was already the case under the previous legislation on Gacaca and genocide trials, art 54(2) of Organic Law No 40/2000, art 6(1) of Organic Law No 08/96.

[147] S. Buckley-Zistel, '"The Truth Heals"?' 80 *Friedenswarte* (2005) 125.

[148] See interview with Benoit Kaboyi, Executive Secretary of *Ibuka*, Kigali, 4 October 2007.

often act as if they are entitled to pardon, adds to the frustration of the victims.[149] In practice, apology is often a mere annex to the confession and is rarely followed by a dialogue between the victim and the offender. There are exceptions to this, but they are not the rule: I attended the trial of a woman who had participated in a raid on a man's house, who was also present. Before the trial, she approached the man and apologized. He accepted this and went on to give a statement in her favour during the trial, which resulted in a reduction of the sentence.[150]

In Rwanda, truth-telling and truth recovery have increasingly come into the focus of interest in recent years. The major concern of the new government in the immediate aftermath of the genocide was not truth but justice, as is reflected in a statement of a cabinet member in 1997: 'we don't need truth, we know who did what'.[151] Investigation and truth recovery were by-products of the trials conducted under Organic Law No 08/96. The popularization of truth-telling began only with the implementation of the Gacaca system, which lists revealing the truth among its declared objectives.[152] By obliging every Rwandan citizen to participate, Gacaca provides a broad forum for truth-telling and truth recovery. In addition, Gacaca jurisdictions are vested with powers similar to those of ordinary courts when it comes to investigating the truth: they can summon persons and order property to be searched.[153] However, at the same time, the 'de-professionalization' of investigation and prosecution, and the ensuing arbitrariness of the proceedings weaken the persuasive power of fact-finding by Gacaca courts and undermine their capacity to recover the truth.

Gacaca's major potential in fact-finding lies in the investigation stage. During this stage, each Gacaca court of the cell was supposed to gather at least 100 people each week to collect information on the genocide.[154] The Gacaca Law prescribes a systematic reconstruction of the facts with the support of the population.[155] The lack of active participation in these sessions, and the increasing involvement of local leaders (*nyumbakumi*) in the process of information gathering,[156] however, essentially undermined Gacaca's truth-finding potential at the investigation stage.

During my field research, I found that trials in the countryside were well attended. Usually far more than 100 people were present. However, active participation was limited to very few people, mostly survivors, defendants, and their

[149] See PRI, *Report VI* (2004) 57. See also G. Hankel, '"Wir möchten, dass ihr uns verzeiht."' in N. Paech (ed), *Völkerrecht statt Machtpolitik* (2004) 368; A. Richters, C. Dekker and K. de Jonge, 'Reconciliation in the Aftermath of Violent Conflict in Rwanda' 3 *Intervention* (2005) 213; L. Waldorf, 'Remnants and Remains' in R.A. Wilson and R.D. Brown (eds), *Humanitarianism and Suffering* (2009) 298.

[150] Gacaca Court of Appeal, Kimihurura, Gasabo District, *Case of Nyirabashitsi Françoise*, 16 September 2007. See also PRI, *Report VI* (2004) 57 *et seq*; P. Uvin and C. Mironko, 'Western and Local Approaches to Justice in Rwanda' 9 *Global Governance* (2003) 228.

[151] Quoted in J. Sarkin, 'Promoting Justice, Truth and Reconciliation in Transitional Societies' 2 *International Law Forum* (2000) 117; J. Sarkin, 'The Tension Between Justice and Reconciliation in Rwanda' 45 *Journal of African Law* (2001) 154.

[152] See, eg, Discours de Paul Kagame à l'occasion du lancement officiel des travaux des juridictions gacaca, le 18 juin 2002, Annex to PRI, *Report III* (2002) 34 and <http://www.inkiko-gacaca.gov.rw/En/EnObjectives.htm>, last visited June 2011.

[153] Art 39 of the Gacaca Law.

[154] Thus, ideally, the 9,013 Gacaca courts of the cell would have brought together almost one million people each week!

[155] Arts 33–4 of the Gacaca Law. See also ch 2, section V A above.

[156] On that, see ch 2, section V B above.

respective families.[157] At the sessions I visited in Kigali, the picture was different. Trials were very badly attended, but those who came usually got actively involved in the proceedings. This was also due to the fact that the jurisdiction made extensive use of its power to summon witnesses. The president of the court was very eager to find out what had actually happened. Yet her efforts to hear everyone who had information were often defeated by witnesses failing to turn up.[158]

In general, the shortage of useful testimonies was a major obstacle for recovering the truth in many of the trials I attended. Often, only vague information based on hearsay was available and the judges had to rely on their gut feeling.[159] The reasons for this were manifold. Time is one important factor here. The Gacaca process started in 2002, eight years after the genocide. It was only in 2006 that the judgment phase began nationwide. This has obviously had an adverse effect on the ability of many potential witnesses to remember the events they experienced in an accurate way.[160] But even if potential witnesses do have accurate memories, their voices are often not heard anyway. Gacaca trials are too short for all witnesses to be heard. This was particularly dramatic in category one cases, which were placed under the jurisdiction of the Gacaca courts in 2008.[161] In general, people are much more reluctant to speak out and testify than the government had anticipated. In some cases, it is even reported that *rescapés* chose to keep quiet in return for being paid 'compensation' from wealthy genocide suspects.[162]

Beside testimonies, an important instrument for fact-finding is the confession procedure. The confession procedure creates an incentive for the defendant to give a complete and truthful account of what he or she did by offering a substantial reduction in the penalty. However, linking procedural benefits to confession may compromise the value of confession as an instrument for truth-finding. This is reflected in the general dissatisfaction of victims with confessions.[163] Many of them doubt the truthfulness of the defendants' accounts. The victims' frustration is fuelled by reports of collusion between prison inmates to present consistent, mutually exonerating

157 Reporting the same: B. Baker, '"He Must Buy What He Stole and Then We Forgive"' *Acta Juridica* (2007) 184; A. Molenaar, *Gacaca* (2005) 106 *et seq*, who reports that in the area of his field research, the small group of survivors accounted for 90% of all testimonies, 164.

158 In the case of *Ntampaka Adrien* (Gacaca Court of Appeal, Kimihurura, Gasabo District, 16 and 23 September 2007), eg, the court summoned 21 witnesses, but only 11 were present. For details on participation in Gacaca sessions over time, see the discussion and references in ch 2, section III above.

159 PRI, *Report XI* (2008) 25–8, comes to the same conclusion.

160 Given the long tradition of memory being based on oral accounts, it has also been argued that, over the years, Rwandans may tend to confuse what they actually witnessed themselves with hearsay, see O. Lin, 'Demythologizing Restorative Justice' 12 *ILSA Journal of International and Comparative Law* (2005/06) 82; see also M.A. Drumbl, 'Rule of Law amid Lawlessness' 29 *ColHRLR* (1998) 606; G. Hankel, 'Justice in Transition—The Case of Rwanda' in G. Werle (ed), *Justice in Transition* (2006) 182; J. Sarkin, 'The Tension Between Justice and Reconciliation in Rwanda' 45 *Journal of African Law* (2001) 163; L. Waldorf, 'Mass Justice for Mass Atrocities' 79 *TempLRev* (2006) 71.

161 PRI, *Eight Years On...* (2010) 63 *et seq*.

162 HRW, *Justice Compromised* (2011) 109; PRI, *Report XI* (2008) 46–7.

163 In the trials I observed, it was very common for victims to doubt the truthfulness of a confession, see, eg, Gacaca Court of Appeal, Kayanza, Nyanza District, *Case of Nkurunziza Appolinaire*, 9 October 2007; Gacaca Court of the Sector of Kayanza, Nyanza District, *Case of Semakware Daniel*, 25 September, 2 and 9 October 2007. Mistrust of the results of the Gacaca court investigations is widespread in general, see the case study by M. Rettig, 'Gacaca' 51 *African Studies Review* (2008) no 3, 39.

confessions.[164] Given the lack of testimonies, the risk of incomplete confessions is even greater. It appears that the confession procedure is more likely to add to the resignation of the victims than to recover truth in such a way as to comfort victims.

Another important factor for truth recovery in Gacaca courts is the overall political climate in Rwanda. It is quite common in public debates for one side to accuse the other of divisionism or genocide ideology.[165] These labels are often used for statements that deviate from the official narrative of the genocide, or from the general policy that denies that ethnic divides actually exist. I have also witnessed allegations of divisionism in Gacaca courts.[166] Divisionist statements or genocide ideology can entail prosecution under the corresponding catch-all offences.[167] Another taboo is the responsibility of RPA soldiers for massacres committed during their campaign to stop the genocide and to restore stability after the genocide. The government has recognized that such 'excesses' did occur but has always been anxious to prevent investigations into these crimes. Prosecutions for these crimes have only occurred in very small numbers. The government has repeatedly stated that the appropriate forum for these crimes is not Gacaca, but the military judiciary. It is true that investigating these cases would have been extremely difficult for Gacaca courts, since it is not very likely that the military would have respected the authority of the judges and thus cooperated.[168] However, the government's refusal to let Gacaca investigate revenge crimes reveals a fundamental mistrust of the system on the part of the authorities. Quite a few Gacaca judges were themselves surprised when they found out that they were not supposed to investigate revenge crimes.[169] The fact that no one knows what happened during the RPA advance in 1994 makes it possible for the idea of a countergenocide committed against the Hutu population to be spread—a provocation for genocide survivors. The government's refusal to tackle RPA crimes also frustrates many Hutu. They perceive Gacaca as victors' justice and prefer to opt for *ceceka* (keeping quiet).[170]

[164] PRI, *Report I* (2002) 26; PRI, *Report VII* (2005) 22. See also ch 2, section VI B above.

[165] See G. Gahima, 'Alternatives to Prosecution' in E. Hughes, W.A. Schabas and R. Thakur (eds), *Atrocities and International Accountability* (2007) 170; B. Ingelaere, 'Does the Truth Pass Across the Fire Without Burning?' 47 *Journal of Modern African Studies* (2009) 521; L. Waldorf, 'Mass Justice for Mass Atrocities' 79 *TempLRev* (2006) 39.

[166] Gacaca Court of the Sector of Kayanza, Nyanza District, *Case of Minani*, 25 September 2007.

[167] See arts 1, 3, 5 of Law No 47/2001 and arts 2–4 of Law No 18/2008. On that, see Amnesty International, *Safer to Stay Silent* (2010); L. Waldorf, 'Censorship and Propaganda in Post-Genocide Rwanda' in A. Thompson (ed), *The Media and the Rwanda Genocide* (2007) 404 *et seq*. See also C.J. Le Mon, 'Rwanda's Troubled Gacaca Courts' 14 *Human Rights Brief* (2007) Issue 2, 19; D. Magsam, 'Coming to Terms with Genocide in Rwanda' in W. Kaleck (ed), *International Prosecution of Human Rights Crimes* (2007) 164; A. Richters, C. Dekker and K. de Jonge, 'Reconciliation in the Aftermath of Violent Conflict in Rwanda' 3 *Intervention* (2005) 213. The prognosis of A. Wierzynska that Gacaca may foster a pluralism of opinions ('Consolidating Democracy Through Transitional Justice' 97 *NYULR* (2004) 1957 *et seq*) is therefore far too optimistic.

[168] G. Gahima, 'Alternatives to Prosecution' in E. Hughes, W.A. Schabas and R. Thakur (eds), *Atrocities and International Accountability* (2007) 174.

[169] African Rights, *Gacaca Justice* (2003) 28 *et seq*.

[170] On the phenomenon of *ceceka*, see PRI, *Final Report* (2010) 17; J.F. Burnet, 'The Injustice of Local Justice' 3 *Genocide Studies and Prevention* (2008) 179; M. Rettig, 'Gacaca' 51 *African Studies Review* (2008) no 3, 40 *et seq*.

While Gacaca is a flawed instrument for the recovery of forensic or factual truth, it must not be overlooked that Gacaca has brought the discourse about the genocide to the grassroots level and made it an everyday matter in a way that no formalized mechanism would have been capable of doing. These grassroots discourses have produced valid versions of the truth in many cases and are accepted among victims as a means of bringing what happened to light.[171] It is therefore important to preserve the Gacaca records, to archive judgments, minutes and other documents, and make them accessible to the public. In December 2010, the National Commission for the Fight against Genocide launched the Genocide Archive Rwanda, which catalogues Gacaca files and judgments.[172] In the long run, the Gacaca records might be able to make a contribution to a more differentiated narrative of the genocide that goes beyond the current interpretation.[173]

In summary, the Gacaca trials, despite all misgivings regarding the quality of truth-finding, are an affirmative state practice acknowledging the customary right of victims of human rights violations to know the truth about what happened to them or their next of kin. At the same time, the refusal to investigate RPA crimes is an act of blatant disregard of the victims' right to the truth and a violation of their right to an effective remedy. Nevertheless, it is safe to say that, in general, truth recovery plays a very central role in Rwanda's efforts to come to terms with the genocide. In Gacaca courts, truth is not only a by-product, but an essential outcome of the process, something to which the victims are entitled: any victim who was absent during a trial of one of its tormentors has a right to a retrial in his or her presence.[174] In fact, Gacaca does achieve a great deal in the field of truth recovery, especially with respect to social truth.[175] It is unavoidable that the truth unveiled is often distorted or incomplete. After all, any investigation can end up failing to disclose what happened. The reasons for this often lie beyond the control of the investigating authorities.

(4) Rehabilitation

Rehabilitation in the form of access to medical and psychological care is an urgent need of many genocide survivors. The effects of the genocide on mental and physical health in Rwanda are devastating and noticeable up to the present day. Yet expertise is lacking, especially in the field of psychological assistance. Since shortly after 1994,

171 Interview with Benoit Kaboyi, Executive Secretary of *Ibuka*, Kigali, 4 October 2007. Similarly P. Clark, *The Gacaca Courts* (2010) 153, 213.

172 'Genocide Archives Launched', *The New Times*, 11 December 2010. The archive can be found online at <http://www.genocidearchiverwanda.org.rw>, last visited June 2011. See also P. Clark, *The Gacaca Courts* (2010) 218; A. Lollini, 'L'istituzione delle giurisdizioni *Gacaca*' *Diritto pubblico comparato ed europeo* (2004) 1531.

173 See on that S. Buckley-Zistel, 'Remembering to Forget' 76 *Africa: The Journal of the International African Institute* (2006) 140; S. Buckley-Zistel, 'We Are Pretending Peace' in P. Clark and Z.D. Kaufman (eds), *After Genocide* (2008) 128 *et seq*; P. Clark, *The Gacaca Courts* (2010) 218–19.

174 The victim must then lodge an opposition against the judgment, arts 86–8 of the Gacaca Law, see ch 2, section VII A above.

175 On social truth, see section I B *(3)* above.

various initiatives have been set up by various different actors to improve access to medical and psychological services in the aftermath of the genocide. The Rwandan Ministry of Health and the National University of Rwanda have developed programmes to offer training in psychological assistance; NGOs have provided similar services.[176] Another specific focus is on trauma counselling during Gacaca sessions. Testifying or hearing testimonies often results in trauma among victims, witnesses, and even perpetrators.[177] Several organizations have deployed their counsellors to Gacaca sessions to provide quick assistance in such cases.[178] Nevertheless, Rwanda remains a third world country that only provides access to very basic medical services in rural areas. There are also cultural obstacles to overcome. Traumatic experiences are often concealed. Many are afraid of talking about their mental problems for fear of stigmatization.[179]

Medical and psychological assistance are provided free of charge through a voucher system run via the FARG. Similar measures are to be expected from the newly created FSARG, which replaced the FARG in 2009. A handful of persons were even sent to Europe or South Africa for medical treatment with the costs being covered by FARG.[180] Like all FARG measures, access to medical aid is limited to those in greatest need only. FARG assistance is available for the handicapped, for example.[181] Vouchers for medical treatment were handed out to a great number of people.[182] Some hospitals, however, no longer accept FARG vouchers, as the fund has proven to be an unreliable debtor.[183] FARG assistance usually only covers very basic services; antiretroviral treatment for persons who were raped and infected with HIV is not provided, for example,[184] but might be in the future.[185] All in all, these measures are evidence that the Rwandan government is aware of the need to provide medical assistance to victims of gross human rights violations. However, the country is still far from ensuring that its citizens have a right to access to such services. The Rwandan approach can therefore hardly be regarded as supportive state practice.

[176] See K. Groninger et al., *Gacaca and Trauma* (2007) 4; A. Richters, C. Dekker and K. de Jonge, 'Reconciliation in the Aftermath of Violent Conflict in Rwanda' 3 *Intervention* (2005) 216.

[177] See K. Brounéus, 'Truth-Telling as Talking Cure?' 39 *Security Dialogue* (2008) 55 *et seq*; B. Oomen, 'Rwanda's *Gacaca*' in R. Haveman and O. Olusanya (eds), *Sentencing and Sanctioning in Supranational Criminal Law* (2006) 178.

[178] See K. Groninger et al., *Gacaca and Trauma* (2007) 5 *et seq*; PRI, *Report III* (2002) 14.

[179] A. Richters, C. Dekker and K. de Jonge, 'Reconciliation in the Aftermath of Violent Conflict in Rwanda' 3 *Intervention* (2005) 215 *et seq*.

[180] For instance 24 people in 1998 and 12 in 2000, H. Rombouts, *Victim Organisations and the Politics of Reparation* (2004) 377.

[181] See art 14(1) of Law No 02/98.

[182] In 2000, over 60,000 people received a voucher, H. Rombouts, *Victim Organisations and the Politics of Reparation* (2004) 377.

[183] Ibid.

[184] HRW, *Struggling to Survive* (2004) 42.

[185] See art 4(2)(6) of Law No 69/2008 on the newly created FSARG. On the FSARG, see also L. Waldorf, 'Goats & Graves' in C. Ferstman, M. Goetz and A. Stephens (eds), *Reparations for Victims of Genocide, War Crimes and Crimes Against Humanity* (2009) 523.

III. Who Is Entitled to Reparation?

A. Victimhood under international law

Those entitled to reparation under international human rights law are the victims of the violation.[186] The 'Basic Principles on the Right to a Remedy and Reparation' define victims as:

> persons who individually or collectively suffered harm, including physical or mental injury, emotional suffering, economic loss or substantial impairment of their fundamental rights, through acts or omissions that constitute gross violations of international human rights law... Where appropriate, and in accordance with domestic law, the term 'victim' also includes the immediate family or dependants of the direct victim and persons who have suffered harm in intervening to assist victims in distress or to prevent victimization.[187]

This definition refers to the common differentiation between the direct victims of a violation and indirect victims, that is family members of the direct victim. Where reparation for serious human rights violations is concerned, the direct victims are usually easily identified. Regarding indirect victims, however, there are no clear criteria under international human rights law to determine which exact relationships entail victimhood, nor does a comparative glance at domestic legal systems make the picture any clearer.[188] To a large extent, such questions depend on the case in question and on cultural factors. While uncles and aunts may be regarded as more remote members of the family in Western cultures, this may not be the case in Africa. The European Court of Human Rights has put forward some criteria for determining whether a family member can be regarded a victim:

> Whether a family member is such a victim will depend on the existence of special factors which gives the suffering of the applicant a dimension and character distinct from the emotional distress which may be regarded as inevitably caused to relatives of a victim of a serious human rights violation. Relevant elements will include the proximity of the family tie—in that context, a certain weight will attach to the parent-child bond—, the particular circumstances of the relationship, the extent to which the family member witnessed the events in question, the involvement of the family member in the attempts to obtain information about the disappeared person and the way in which the authorities responded to those enquiries.[189]

[186] For the complex procedural issues related to victimhood as a precondition for admissibility of a complaint to the HRC see P.R. Ghandhi, *The Human Rights Committee and the Right to Individual Communication* (1998) 91 *et seq*. See also H. Rombouts, P. Sardaro and S. Vandeginste, 'The Right to Reparation for Victims of Gross and Systematic Violations of Human Rights' in K. De Feyter et al. (eds), *Out of the Ashes* (2005) 466 *et seq*.

[187] Para 8. The definition goes back to the one in the Basic Principles of Justice for Victims of Crime and Abuse of Power, paras 1, 2.

[188] H. McGregor, 'Personal Injury and Death' in A. Tunc (ed), *International Encyclopedia of Comparative Law XI-2* (1986) ch 9, para 226.

[189] *Çakıcı v Turkey*, Judgment of 8 July 1999, para 98.

Human rights courts have found parents, children, spouses, companions, sisters, and brothers of a deceased person to be entitled to reparation.[190] In some cases, even uncles or nephews were included.[191]

B. Victims and *rescapés* in Rwanda

The different laws and draft laws governing genocide trials and reparation in Rwanda are not based on a uniform approach to victimhood. While the earlier laws and drafts tend to define victimhood similarly to the definition under international law cited above, in recent years the narrower notion of *rescapé* or survivor[192] has gained ground. Under international law the decisive criterion is loss or harm: those who have been harmed themselves are direct victims; indirect victims are those whose family members have been harmed, or those who have lost family members. In contrast, a *rescapé* is a person who was persecuted, but survived. The term is commonly understood to include survivors of the genocide and of the persecution of the Hutu who were opposed to the genocide. On the other hand, it excludes Hutu who lost Tutsi family members, but who were not themselves persecuted, and persons outside the country, even if they lost their family during the genocide.[193]

The notion of *rescapé* has dominated public debates for some years and is increasingly being used in legislation, while the term victim is usually understood to refer exclusively to those who were killed. Whether a person is a *rescapé* or not cannot always be clearly ascertained, meaning the term is, as such, unsuitable as a legal category. It cannot always be determined whether a person has been persecuted or not, as this may sometimes depend on the person's own perception of the situation. Killings were often indiscriminate and random, and could also target persons who were neither Tutsi nor particularly opposed to the genocide. In addition, granting reparation to survivors instead of victims means that reparation is effectively separated from the actual damages suffered. Being a *rescapé* does not necessarily mean that that person was harmed, while people who did suffer losses may not qualify as *rescapés*.

The first reparations regime under Rwandan law was that of Organic Law No 08/96, which governed genocide trials before specialized chambers in ordinary courts. According to that law and in line with general criminal procedural law, a victim could file a civil action within a criminal trial in order to be awarded

[190] IACtHR, *Case of the Pueblo Bello Massacre v Colombia*, Judgment of 31 January 2006, para 235; ECtHR, *Tanrıkulu v Turkey*, Judgment of 8 July 1999, para 118. See also HRC, *Quinteros v Uruguay*, Views of 21 July 1983 (no 107/1981) para 14.

[191] IACtHR, *Case of La Cantuta v Peru*, Judgment of 29 November 2006, para 206; ECtHR, *Yaşa v Turkey*, Judgment of 2 September 1998, para 66.

[192] According to a census conducted in 2008, there are still 309,368 *rescapés*, 'Genocide Survivors Estimated to Be 300,000', *Hirondelle*, 28 August 2008.

[193] For a detailed discussion of the term of *rescapé* in public debate, see H. Rombouts, *Victim Organisations and the Politics of Reparation* (2004) 197 *et seq*. For a slightly different interpretation of the term, see LIPRODHOR, *Rescapés et droits humains* (2002) 9.

damages.[194] In departure from general procedural law, article 29(2) of Organic Law No 08/96 also allowed victim associations to claim compensation on behalf of the victims. This provision, however, has not been of great practical importance.[195] The legislation did not give any indications as to the circle of potential beneficiaries who might be awarded reparation in civil actions. The chambers therefore relied on general principles in order to determine who was entitled to reparation. Civil actions were frequent and the chambers awarded reparation to a broad circle of the deceased's relatives, thus subscribing to the common distinction under international law between direct and indirect victims: spouses, parents, children, siblings, aunts, uncles, nephews, nieces, in-laws,[196] and even girlfriends ('concubines')[197] were found to be indirect victims and thus entitled to damages. There were also cases, however, where the chambers found the relationship too distant.[198] Beside reparation for killing, damages were also awarded to persons whose property had been damaged or stolen, or to those who had been injured.[199]

The term *rescapé* became a legal one with the introduction of the FARG law[200] in 1998. The term is defined narrowly therein, namely as 'a person who survived genocide and massacres committed in Rwanda between October 1, 1990 and December 31, 1994'.[201] It encompasses both people persecuted for their ethnic origin and for their dissident opinions.[202] The reform of the fund in 2008–09 entailed a further limitation of the *rescapé* definition to 'survivors of the Genocide against the Tutsi and other crimes against humanity committed between 1st October 1990 and 31st December 1994'.[203] Persons opposed to the genocide are no longer taken into account as *rescapés*, at least not expressly.

The first draft legislation on the compensation fund (FIND) of 2001 did not include the concept of *rescapé*. Instead, its article 13 embraced the distinction of direct and indirect victims common in international law. It envisaged all victims of genocide and crimes against humanity as potential beneficiaries, and in the case of the direct victim's death, his or her next of kin too. This would include the spouses,

194 Art 29(1) of Organic Law No 08/96 in connection with art 71 of the former Code of Criminal Procedure.

195 D. De Beer, *Loi rwandaise du 30 août 1996*, 2nd edn (1999) para 116, who is not aware of a single case.

196 See, eg, the list in Conseil de Guerre, *Affaire Caporal Joseph Ukurikiyimfura et consorts*, Judgment of 17 April 2001, in *Recueil de jurisprudence V*, 378.

197 TPI Kigali, *Affaire Wellars Kayinamura*, Judgment of 13 October 1997, in *Recueil de jurisprudence I*, 102.

198 Regarding a damage claim for the killing of the plaintiff's cousins, TPI Cyangugu, *Affaire Védaste Rwanteli et consorts*, Judgment of 8 October 1997, in *Recueil de jurisprudence IV*, 66, 76.

199 eg, Cour d'Appel Cyangugu, *Affaire Emmanuel Ntagozera et consorts*, Judgment of 30 June 1999, in *Recueil de jurisprudence II*, 233; Cour d'Appel Ruhengeri, *Affaire Faustin Ntaganda et consorts*, Judgment of 24 June 1998, in *Recueil de jurisprudence I*, 185.

200 Law No 02/98. Confusingly, the official name of the law refers to 'victims', but the text itself only mentions survivors or *rescapés* as beneficiaries. The common acronym FARG also contains the notion of *rescapé*.

201 Art 14(2) of Law No 02/98.

202 Ibid.

203 Art 3(1) of Law No 69/2008.

parents, and children of a deceased person. Siblings, grandchildren, aunts, and uncles only had a subsidiary claim if all closer relatives were deceased.[204]

Even though the 2001 FIND draft was widely welcomed, the government came up with a new draft in 2002. This project had been developed in close cooperation with *Ibuka*, but without any consultation with other victim organizations.[205] The group of beneficiaries of the fund is defined on the basis of the term *rescapé*. Article 17 of the draft identified three different categories of beneficiaries:

> [1] toute personne qui était pourchassé en raison de son ethnie ou de ses idées non favorable au génocide et aux massacre ;
> [2] les enfants, le conjoint, les frères et sœurs ainsi que le père et mère de la personne qui a été tuée en raison de son ethnie ou de ses idées non favorable au génocide et aux massacre ;
> [3] toute personne qui était domiciliée au Rwanda mais qui, pendant le génocide et les massacres, se trouvait en dehors du pays et dont les enfants, le conjoint, les frères et sœurs ainsi que le père et la mère qui étaient restés au Rwanda... dans ce temps ont été tuée en raison de leur ethnie ou de leurs idées précitées.[206]

The first category is congruent with the notion of *rescapé* as explained above. The second appears to correspond to indirect victims as recognized under international law. However, according to the Ministry of Justice (Minijust), this group did not comprise the indirect victims of genocide and massacres, but rather those persecuted for the ethnicity or political opinions of their close family members.[207] The third group extends the *rescapé* definition to those who were temporarily outside the country during the genocide. The 2002 FIND draft thus rejects the international law approach to victimhood, instead limiting reparation to *rescapés*.

Gacaca grants victims the status of a party to the trial ('plaintiff'). The notion of *rescapé* does not figure in the Gacaca legislation. The victims' role is limited to their immediate interests, such as claiming reparation, telling their story, or seeing justice done. Thus, their participation is comparable to that of a *partie civile*[208] to the trial, with the difference that, in the Gacaca trial, the victim acquires this status automatically. The first Gacaca law, Organic Law No 40/2000, does not give any indication about who qualifies as a plaintiff in the trial. Organic Law No 16/2004, which still applies today in amended form, refers only to victims in its Kinyarwanda ('uwahohotewe') and French versions ('victime'),[209] while the English version uses the terms plaintiff as well as victim. In contrast to the former Gacaca legislation, Organic Law No 16/2004 defines a victim as anybody who was 'killed, hunted to be killed but survived, suffered acts of torture against his

[204] S. Vandeginste, 'Victims of Genocide' in J. Torpey (ed), *Politics and the Past* (2003) 262. For more details, see H. Rombouts, *Victim Organisations and the Politics of Reparation* (2004) 415 *et seq.*

[205] H. Rombouts, ibid, 413, 417 *et seq*, 423 *et seq.*

[206] Reprinted ibid, 418.

[207] Ibid, 419 *et seq.*

[208] The possibility of an *action civile* or *Nebenklage* within the criminal trial is common in continental criminal procedure. It is provided for in the Rwandan Code of Criminal Procedure, arts 9 *et seq.* Quite tellingly, the French version of the first Gacaca law, Organic Law No 40/2000, refers to *parties civiles* whereas the English version speaks of the plaintiff.

[209] Only twice, in arts 19 and 20 of Organic Law No 10/2007 that modified arts 90 and 93 of Organic Law No 16/2004, do the Kinyarwanda and French versions refer to 'urega' or 'le plaignant'.

or her sexual parts, suffered rape, injured or victim of any other form of harassment, plundered, and whose house and property were destroyed because of his or her ethnic background or opinion against the genocide ideology'[210] or whose next of kin were killed. This latter group does not figure in the English version of the provision. The Kinyarwanda and French versions, however, do list the relatives as victims.[211] In Gacaca practice, the family members of persons killed are the most common representatives of the victim side, irrespective of whether they were in or outside the country during the genocide or whether they are Hutu, Tutsi, Twa, or anything else. When the members of a victim's immediate family are dead or cannot appear in court for some other reason, more distant family members often take their place.[212] This sometimes even includes relatively remote family members. The victim definition included in the Gacaca Law thus essentially corresponds to that of international law. However, it is important not to forget that Gacaca is not a forum for compensation claims with regards to loss of family members or bodily injury.

In sum, the approaches to victimhood under Rwandan law in the aftermath of the genocide are too inconsistent to indicate any telling state practice. Essentially, two tendencies can be observed: that of limiting the group of potential beneficiaries of reparation to those who were themselves persecuted (*rescapés*)—a particularly Rwandan approach to victimhood—and, in contrast, the tendency to extend the group of potential beneficiaries of reparation to include remote family members, as exemplified in particular by the jurisprudence of the specialized chambers under Organic Law No 08/96.

IV. Who Is Liable to Pay Reparation?

The issue of liability for mass violations and abuses of human rights is a very complex one. The scale of these crimes necessarily involves a great number of perpetrators, from presidents and commanders in chief all the way down to privates, from powerful warlords to child soldiers. The events during the genocide in Rwanda exemplify this complexity: a good number of the crimes were committed by state organs such as the police, the army, or the Presidential Guard. That said, the whole operation would never have been so viciously effective without the mass participation of ordinary people. For weeks, thousands ravaged and killed; some of their own volition, others only reluctantly and under threat, some after being instigated to do so by politicians or radio reporters. Paramilitary groups, especially *Interahamwe*, also played a crucial part in the killings. These groups, in turn, also received support from outside the country.

210 Art 34 of the Gacaca Law *in fine*.

211 '[U]muntu wese wiciwe', 'toute personne dont les siens ont été tués'. But they leave out those who were killed themselves. In fact, the definition only makes sense in the context of the Gacaca Law if it includes both those who were killed themselves as well as those whose next of kin were killed.

212 Interview with Denis Bikesha, Director of Training, Mobilisation, and Sensitisation, National Service of Gacaca Courts, Kigali, 5 October 2007.

Criminal liability under international law covers all these forms of participation, regardless of whether the suspect is a state actor or not.[213] Civil liability under international law, however, only arises in connection with state responsibility. Claims based on violations by private persons are not covered by the international legal rules on reparation, as these rules do not apply all the way down to the level of private relations.[214] In cases of state-sponsored mass violence in particular, however, even a human rights violation committed by a private person can, depending on the circumstances, be attributed to the state and can thus entail an obligation on the part of the state to pay reparation.

A. State responsibility under general international law and human rights law

To begin with, the liability of the state is to be determined on the basis of the general rules regarding state responsibility. Accordingly, a state is primarily responsible for the conduct of its organs.[215] The conduct of non-state actors can also be attributed to the state, for example if the state directed or controlled their conduct.[216] If the issue is genocide, as in the case of Rwanda, responsibility can also be incurred by complicity in genocide,[217] or the failure to prevent and punish genocide.[218] International human rights law further extends the categories of the general law on state responsibility by obliging states to ensure or secure human rights.[219] The Inter-American Court of Human Rights has elaborated on that in its famous *Velásquez-Rodríguez* judgment:

> Article 1(1) [the duty to respect and ensure human rights] is essential in determining whether a violation of the human rights recognized by the Convention can be imputed to a State Party... [I]n principle, any violation of rights recognized by the Convention carried out by an act of public authority or by persons who use their position of authority is imputable to the State. However, this does not define all the circumstances in which a State is obligated to prevent, investigate and punish human rights violations, nor all the cases in which the State might be found responsible for an infringement of those rights. An illegal act which violates human rights and which is initially not directly imputable to a State (for example, because it is the act of a private person or because the person responsible has not

213 For a discussion of the different modes of participation under international criminal law, see G. Werle, 'Individual Criminal Responsibility in Article 25 ICC Statute' 5 *JICJ* (2007) 953 *et seq*; G. Werle, *Principles of International Criminal Law*, 2nd edn (2009) paras 442 *et seq*.

214 E. Klein, 'Individual Reparation Claims under the International Covenant on Civil and Political Rights' in A. Randelzhofer and C. Tomuschat (eds), *State Responsibility and the Individual* (1999) 33.

215 See Art 4 of the ILC Articles on State Responsibility. The Articles are applicable to inter-state relations, not to the relations between states and individuals. However, Arts 4–11 contain customary law principles, which can be transferred to international human rights law.

216 See Art 8 of the ILC Articles on State Responsibility.

217 *Case Concerning the Application of the Convention on the Prevention and Punishment of the Crime of Genocide (Bosnia and Herzegovina v Serbia and Montenegro)*, ICJ, Judgment of 26 February 2007, para 416, referring to Art III(e) of the Genocide Convention.

218 ICJ, ibid, paras 425 *et seq* referring to Art I of the Genocide Convention.

219 Art 2(1) of the ICCPR, Art 1(1) of the ACHR, Art 1 of the ECHR; Art 1 of the Banjul Charter is formulated differently, but amounts to the same standard.

been identified) can lead to international responsibility of the State, not because of the act itself, but because of the lack of due diligence to prevent the violation or to respond to it as required by the Convention.[220]

The Court has since frequently applied this principle in order to establish state responsibility for violations, which are at first glance not imputable to a state actor. In recent years, the Court has repeatedly found the state of Colombia responsible for human rights violations by paramilitary groups and liable to pay extremely high amounts of damages, not only for the state's historic role in encouraging the formation of these groups, but also by attributing the abuses the state failed to prevent to the state: 'The Court has also recognized that the State's international responsibility may arise from attribution to the State of human rights violations committed by third parties or individuals, within the framework of the State's obligations to guarantee respect for those rights between individuals'.[221]

The European Court of Human Rights has followed a similar approach: '[T]he responsibility of a State is engaged if a violation of one of the rights and freedoms defined in the Convention is the result of non-observance by that State of its obligation . . . to secure those rights and freedoms in its domestic law to everyone within its jurisdiction'.[222] In order to determine the state's responsibility for violations of the right to life, the Court has, however, developed some additional criteria. Accordingly, the state holds the responsibility for a killing by a non-state actor if the authorities 'did not do all that could be reasonably expected of them to avoid a real and immediate risk to life of which they have or ought to have knowledge'.[223] In its more recent jurisprudence, the Court has repeatedly found the state responsible for abuses committed by private persons.[224]

The opinions expressed by the Inter-American and European Courts of Human Rights are obviously authoritative only for their highly developed regional human rights systems and cannot be directly transferred to human rights law at the global level. The UN Human Rights Committee has taken a much more cautious approach. While it has acknowledged an obligation on the part of the state to protect human rights, it has not been so clear-cut in attributing the responsibility of a third party to the state merely because the state failed to prevent the abuse from

[220] *Case of Velásquez Rodríguez v Honduras*, Judgment of 29 July 1988, paras 164, 172. See also para 182 and D. Shelton, 'Private Violence, Public Wrongs, and the Responsibility of States' 13 *Fordham IntlLJ* (1989/90) 1 *et seq*.

[221] IACtHR, *Case of the Pueblo Bello Massacre v Colombia*, Judgment of 31 January 2006, para 113. See also *Case of 19 Tradesmen v Colombia*, Judgment of 5 July 2004, paras 141 *et seq*; *Case of the 'Mapiripán Massacre' v Colombia*, Judgment of 15 September 2005, paras 110 *et seq*; *Case of the Rochela Massacre v Colombia*, Judgment of 11 May 2007, paras 66 *et seq*, 101 *et seq*.

[222] *Costello-Roberts v UK*, Judgment of 25 March 1993, para 26.

[223] *Osman v UK*, Judgment of 28 October 1998, para 116.

[224] *Ergi v Turkey*, Judgment of 28 July 1998, para 79, concerning a civilian woman killed by an unidentified bullet during a counter-terrorist operation; *Akkoç v Turkey*, Judgment of 10 October 2000, paras 79 *et seq*, concerning a Kurdish activist who had received death threats; see also *X and Y v The Netherlands*, Judgment of 26 March 1985, paras 21 *et seq*; *Costello-Roberts v UK*, Judgment of 25 March 1993, para 26. For further references, see A. Clapham, *Human Rights Obligations of Non-State Actors* (2006) 352; T. Meron, *Human Rights and Humanitarian Norms as Customary Law* (1989) 166 *et seq*.

occurring. Instead, the Committee found that the obligation to protect individual rights leads to a shift in the burden of proof. Several times, the Committee has found a state responsible for a violation even though the involvement of a state agent could not be proven.[225]

The initial jurisprudence of the African Commission on Human and Peoples' Rights appears to adopt the more cautious approach taken by the Human Rights Committee.[226] In recent years, however, the Commission has gone further, relying extensively on the jurisprudence of the Inter-American Court. On the basis of Article 1 of the Banjul Charter and the ensuing obligation to protect human rights, the Commission has found that a violation committed by a private individual may be imputed to the state because of the state's lack of due diligence to prevent it.[227] At the same time, the Commission applied a high standard for proving the state's failure to exercise due diligence: 'Responsibility must be demonstrated by establishing that the state condones a pattern of abuse through pervasive non-action'.[228] In a decision taken in 2009, the Commission departed from this line of reasoning and rather obscurely declared that the obligation to protect human rights was one of result. Accordingly, violations committed by private actors give rise to state responsibility merely for the failure 'to implement all measures required to produce the result of protecting... individuals'.[229] The responsibility of the state is precluded only in cases of *force majeur*.[230] In fact, this is a case of circular reasoning: the question whether a violation is imputable to the state depends upon whether the violation occurred.

B. Liability to pay reparation

State responsibility for a violation of international law does not automatically entail the duty to pay reparation. In principle, this is only the case if there is a causal link between the violation and the injury.[231] In cases of genocide, this nexus is easily established if a state agent has himself committed acts of genocide, or if the state

[225] *Herrera Rubio v Colombia*, Views of 2 November 1987 (no 161/1983) paras 10.3, 10.5; *Jiménez Vaca v Colombia*, Views of 25 March 2002 (no 859/1999) para 7.3. This is in line with the Committee's constant jurisprudence regarding the burden of proof, *Bleier v Uruguay*, Views of 29 March 1982 (no 30/1978) para 13.3; *Jegatheeswara Sarma v Sri Lanka*, Views of 16 July 2003 (no 950/2000) para 9.8; *Boucherf v Algeria*, Views of 30 March 2006 (no 1196/2003) para 9.4; *Medjnoune v Algeria*, Views of 14 July 2006 (no 1297/2004) para 8.3. On the duty to protect human rights, see also General Comment 31/80 of 29 March 2004, para 8, which takes an approach similar to the ECtHR.

[226] *Commission Nationale des Droits de l'Homme et des Libertés v Chad*, Decision of October 1995 (no 74/92) para 22.

[227] *Zimbabwe Human Rights NGO Forum v Zimbabwe*, Decision of May 2006 (no 245/2002) para 143; *Sudan Human Rights Organisation, Centre on Housing Rights and Evictions v The Sudan*, Decision of May 2009 (no 279/2002, 296/2005) para 148. See also *The Social and Economic Rights Action Center and the Center for Economic and Social Rights v Nigeria*, Decision of October 2001 (no 155/96) para 57.

[228] *Zimbabwe Human Rights NGO Forum v Zimbabwe*, Decision of May 2006 (no 245/2002) para 160.

[229] *Association of Victims of Post Electoral Violence and Interrights v Cameroon*, Decision of November 2009 (no 272/2003) para 115.

[230] Ibid, para 117.

[231] See Art 31(1) of the ILC Articles on State Responsibility.

is in direct control of a paramilitary group that engaged in such acts. Regarding the obligation to prevent genocide, things are more complicated. This obligation is one of conduct, not of result. States are under a duty to 'employ all means reasonably available', but cannot be blamed if they are unable to actually prevent the genocide.[232] In the case concerning the genocide against Bosnian Muslims during the Yugoslavian civil war, the International Court of Justice required proof that the killings would have been prevented had the Federal Republic of Yugoslavia taken the necessary measures. As Bosnia failed to prove such a causal nexus, the Court denied its reparation claim.[233]

Yet regarding the issue discussed here, namely the individual right to reparation for human rights violations, the premises are different than those in the dispute between Bosnia and Serbia. In that case, Bosnia sought reparation from Serbia (the former Federal Republic of Yugoslavia) for genocide committed on Bosnian territory. Individual human rights were not discussed in that case, as the violations were committed neither on the territory of, nor on a territory under the jurisdiction of, the Federal Republic of Yugoslavia.[234] The obligation to respect and ensure the rights of the Bosnian Muslims was therefore not considered. Certainly, whether a state has a duty to prevent atrocities outside its borders or to protect individual rights inside its borders represents a fundamental difference. In the latter case, the requirements of international law are evidently much stricter—not only because the violations occur on the state's territory, but also because the obligation to protect is further-reaching than the obligation to prevent. Consequently, the international human rights courts readily award damages without elaborating on the causality requirement and without distinguishing between violations by a state agent and abuses due to the state's failure to protect.[235] Thus states which violate their duty to protect individual rights incur unlimited liability to pay damages.

It has been observed above that there is a tendency in transitions to entrust the compensation for mass human rights violations to funds that pay lump sum compensation. This tendency is in line with the approach of human rights courts to define state responsibility for such violations in a broad way—so as to encompass not only violations committed by state actors, but also by non-state actors where the state has neglected its duty to protect victims' rights. A telling example is that of Colombia, which was repeatedly condemned to reparation for its failure to prevent violations by rebel or paramilitary groups. In 2008, a framework was created

[232] *Case Concerning the Application of the Convention on the Prevention and Punishment of the Crime of Genocide (Bosnia and Herzegovina v Serbia and Montenegro)*, ICJ, Judgment of 26 February 2007, para 430.

[233] Ibid, para 462. For criticism of this approach, see A. Gattini, 'Breach of the Obligation to Prevent and Reparation Thereof in the ICJ's Genocide Judgment' 18 *EJIL* (2007) 706 *et seq*; A. Gattini, 'Evidentiary Issues in the ICJ's *Genocide* Judgment' 5 *JICJ* (2007) 890 *et seq*; C. Tomuschat, 'Reparation in Cases of Genocide' 5 *JICJ* (2007) 907 *et seq*.

[234] See Art 2(1) of the ICCPR.

[235] ECtHR, *Ergi v Turkey*, Judgment of 28 July 1998, para 110; *Tanrıkulu v Turkey*, Judgment of 8 July 1999, para 138; *Akkoç v Turkey*, Judgment of 10 October 2000, para 136; IACtHR, *Case of 19 Tradesmen v Colombia*, Judgment of 5 July 2004, paras 219 *et seq*; *Case of the 'Mapiripán Massacre' v Colombia*, Judgment of 15 September 2005, paras 242 *et seq*; *Case of the Pueblo Bello Massacre v Colombia*, Judgment of 31 January 2006, paras 226 *et seq*; *Case of the Rochela Massacre v Colombia*, Judgment of 11 May 2007, paras 226 *et seq*.

for the compensation of persons who fell victim to human rights violations by these groups.[236]

C. State responsibility and liability to pay reparation for the Rwandan genocide

It is hard to deny that the Rwandan government in power at the time of the genocide bears the full responsibility for it. Other than in the ICJ case cited above, the government of the early 1990s not only failed to prevent and punish genocide, but was also actively engaged in it.[237] Those de facto in charge after President Habyarimana's fatal plane crash and the assassination of Prime Minister Uwilingiyimana, namely Colonel Théoneste Bagosora, as well as the interim government set up on 8 April 1994, openly subscribed to the eradication of the Tutsi. Maybe the clearest example of the government's intentions was the speech given by interim President Théodore Sindikubwabo in the southern town of Butare on 19 April 1994. The President called upon people to take up their 'work', a term that unambiguously referred to killing Tutsi. This speech, along with the installation of a new prefect in Butare, is generally believed to have sparked the massacres in the region, which had, until then, withstood the pressure to implement the government's policy of genocide.[238]

It is not only the events in 1994 that were imputable to the government, however; there are various indications that the Habyarimana regime played an active part in the massacres that took place before 1994. The 1993 International Commission of Investigation[239] found that Rwandan authorities had been actively involved in the Kibilira and Bugesera massacres in 1991 and 1992, and had subsequently failed to effectively prosecute those responsible.[240] Another example is the infamous speech of Léon Mugesera, which was inter alia broadcast on national radio. Mugesera was the MRND vice president in the Prefecture of Gisenyi and an official in the Ministry for the Family. In his speech in November 1992, he encouraged his fellow Hutu in shockingly unambiguous language to exterminate the Tutsi. He claimed

[236] *Decreto 1290 de 22 de abril 2008 por el cual se crea el Programa de Reparación Individual por vía administrativa para las víctimas de los grupos armados organizados al margen de la ley.* On that, see J. Guerrero Orozco and M. Goetz, 'Reparations for Victims in Colombia' in C. Ferstman, M. Goetz and A. Stephens (eds), *Reparations for Victims of Genocide, War Crimes and Crimes Against Humanity* (2009) 456 *et seq.*

[237] Engaging in genocide is not expressly mentioned among the obligations and prohibitions of the Genocide Convention. Art I only mentions the failure to prevent and punish. However, engaging in genocide breaches the Convention a fortiori.

[238] A. Des Forges, *Leave None to Tell the Story* (1999) 456 *et seq.* The state's responsibility has not only been proved by historical research, see, eg, the above cited work by A. Des Forges, but was also accepted by the ICTR. The Court, for instance, found that Colonel Bagosora used his authority to commit genocide, *Prosecutor v Bagosora* et al., Trial Chamber, Judgment of 18 December 2008 (ICTR-98–41-T) paras 2015 *et seq*, 2158; it also convicted interim Prime Minister Jean Kambanda (*Prosecutor v Kambanda*, Trial Chamber, Judgment of 4 September 1998 (IT-97–23-S), confirmed by *Kambanda v Prosecutor*, Appeals Chamber, Judgment of 19 October 2000 (IT-97–23-A)), and a number of other leading figures of the interim government for their role in the genocide.

[239] On the commission, see ch 1, section VI A above.

[240] *Rapport de la Commission internationale d'enquête sur les violations des droits de l'homme au Rwanda depuis le 1er Octobre 1990* (1993) 17 *et seq.*

repeatedly that he was speaking for President Habyarimana. The President made no efforts to dissociate himself from Mugesera. The judiciary undertook a half-hearted attempt to prosecute him, but members of the army helped him escape to Canada where he has lived to the present day.[241]

All of this shows that the Habyarimana regime tolerated and even endorsed massacres against Tutsi. The interim government in 1994 vigorously pursued a genocidal policy and openly encouraged the Hutu population to take up arms and kill the Tutsi. Therefore, even though the genocide was not only committed by government forces, but also by great numbers of ordinary people, it can be attributed to the state. Starting from 1990 and culminating in April 1994, the government created a climate in which violence against Tutsi was acceptable, or even the duty of every good citizen, up to the point where anyone who refused to join in was in danger him or herself. It is uncontested that government and government-sponsored propaganda played a critical part in mobilizing ordinary Rwandans to assault their Tutsi neighbours. Following the approach of international human rights bodies expounded above, a virtually comprehensive attribution of the genocide to the Rwandan state is therefore possible. The fact that the responsible regime is no longer in power, and that its fiercest adversaries rule the country today, does not relieve the Rwandan state from its current responsibility to pay reparation to the victims of the genocide.[242] In addition, the state is responsible for the crimes committed by the RPA during their campaign to free the country from the genocidal regime.[243]

While the government denies any responsibility for crimes by RPA soldiers, Rwandan state practice since 1994 reflects a growing acceptance of the country's responsibility for the genocide. Organic Law No 08/96 deliberately omitted the question of state liability to pay damages. The early jurisprudence of the specialized chambers was not entirely uniform in that regard. Some chambers found the state and the accused liable *in solidum* to pay damages, accepting the state's general responsibility for the genocide.[244] In other cases, for no apparent reason, the state was not condemned to reparation, while the accused was.[245] Other courts examined whether the conduct of a state agent was imputable to the state in the specific case, and rejected the state's liability on the ground that the crimes were not committed in an official capacity.[246]

[241] A. Des Forges, *Leave None to Tell the Story* (1999) 83 *et seq*; for details on the *Mugesera* affair, see W.A. Schabas, 'Justice, Democracy, and Impunity in Post-Genocide Rwanda' 7 *CLF* (1996) 555 *et seq*; extracts from the speech in French are reprinted in *Rapport de la Commission internationale d'enquête sur les violations des droits de l'homme au Rwanda depuis le 1er Octobre 1990* (1993) 23 *et seq*.

[242] See I. Brownlie, *Principles of Public International Law*, 7th edn (2008) 80.

[243] See Art 10(1) of the ILC Articles on State Responsibility.

[244] Cour d'Appel Ruhengeri, *Affaire Faustin Ntaganda et consorts*, Judgment of 24 June 1998 in *Recueil de jurisprudence I*, 185; TPI Kigali, *Affaire de Froduald Karamira*, Judgment of 14 February 1997 in *Recueil de jurisprudence I*, 80, 91; F. Digneffe and J. Fierens (eds), *Justice et gacaca* (2003) 69; H. Rombouts, 'Women and Reparations in Rwanda' in R. Rubio-Marín (ed), *What Happened to the Women?* (2006) 198.

[245] TPI Gisenyi, *Affaire Wellars Banzi et consorts*, Judgment of 25 May 2001 in *Recueil de jurisprudence VI*, 146 *et seq*. See also S. Vandeginste, 'Victims of Genocide' in J. Torpey (ed), *Politics and the Past* (2003) 257.

[246] See the references to unpublished jurisprudence in D. De Beer, *Loi rwandaise du 30 août 1996*, 2nd edn (1999) para 127 and F. Digneffe and J. Fierens (eds), *Justice et gacaca* (2003) 70.

Apparently the government, while being aware of its duty to pay reparation, considered this jurisprudence unrealistic, and practised an empty chair policy during the trials. Some claimants therefore decided to suspend their claims against the state.[247]

The state's acceptance of its responsibility for the genocide and its liability to pay reparation has repeatedly been voiced in legislation. The Preamble of the 1998 FARG law[248] speaks of the government's 'essential role in the commission of' the genocide and the ensuing 'obligations of the Rwandese State'.[249] Another such statement is found in the first Gacaca law, Organic Law No 40/2000. Its article 91(3) abolishes the framework for damage claims under Organic Law No 08/96 and declares civil actions against the state inadmissible on the ground that the state pays 'a percentage of its annual budget' to the FIND 'in compensation' for 'its role in the genocide'. Given that the FIND was never created, in practice this provision did nothing but curtail the rights of victims to compensation. It still, however, contains an express acknowledgement of comprehensive state responsibility for the genocide.

Beside Rwanda, one may also wonder whether the international community, the United Nations, or the governments of certain countries are under a duty to pay reparation. This question goes beyond the scope of this study, but it may play an important role in the future. The United Nations has been quick to recognize its failure to act and its ensuing moral obligation to make up for this failure. President Nicolas Sarkozy of France only admitted to 'mistakes' having occurred during the genocide in 2010, but refused to offer a full apology for his country's involvement.[250] A duty of these external actors to pay individual reparation is hard to establish under international human rights law. The responsibility for the protection of human rights in Rwanda lies with the Rwandan state, not with the UN or a foreign government. It is therefore questionable whether a violation committed outside their jurisdiction can be attributed to them. Nevertheless, they bear responsibility for what happened in Rwanda. Victim organizations have therefore repeatedly called upon the UN, foreign countries, and the international community as a whole to help finance a compensation fund. In this context, a representative of the most important victims' organization, *Ibuka*, told me: 'I think this should not be done by Rwanda alone; it should be a concern of the international community. Genocide is a crime against humanity. Mankind as a whole should feel wronged, and should call for reparation. That is why *Ibuka* requested the United Nations to create this fund'.[251]

V. Conclusion

From the point of view of the victims, the outcome of the Rwandan government's efforts to provide reparations is disappointing. Admittedly, Gacaca has in many

[247] TPI Cyangugu, *Affaire Védaste Rwanteli et consorts*, Judgment of 8 October 1997 in *Recueil de jurisprudence IV*, 66.
[248] Law No 02/98, repealed by art 29 of Law No 69/2008.
[249] Preamble, para 4.
[250] 'Nicolas Sarkozy Admits Rwanda Genocide "Mistakes"', *BBC*, 25 February 2010.
[251] Interview with Benoit Kaboyi, Executive Secretary of *Ibuka*, Kigali, 4 October 2007. The translation from French is my own.

cases provided them with official or semi-official recognition of their suffering and with explanations about the fate of their loved ones. On a collective level, the Rwandan government regularly honours those who died and acknowledges the plight of the survivors. The community service (TIG) programme can also be regarded as a collective form of reparation, especially where TIG is carried out as 'neighbourhood community service' in the convict's home community. However, more tangible forms of reparation to the individual victims have not followed.

From the perspective of international law, Rwanda's reparation policy allows a number of conclusions to be drawn. First, the state's duty to pay reparation for human rights violations and the corresponding right to claim reparation are acknowledged in principle. Even though physical practice has not followed in the case of Rwanda, this acknowledgment does represent state practice in favour of a right to reparation. Secondly, investigation and truth recovery are increasingly recognized as crucial interests of the victims that must be ensured. The introduction of Gacaca courts in Rwanda testifies to this trend. Thirdly, the state is responsible for human rights violations by private persons if it has encouraged them; the state is also responsible for violations that it failed to prevent in a climate of violence and impunity brought about by the state itself. The Rwandan government has expressly acknowledged this wide notion of state responsibility with respect to the genocide. On the other hand, the Rwandan example also demonstrates the limits of the right to reparation. If an old regime is replaced by a new one, the issue of reparation is always subject to the logic of the transition. In Rwanda, the perpetrator regime was ousted by its fiercest enemies, many of whom had also been potential targets of the genocide. It is therefore quite obvious that this new government attaches importance to the needs of the victims and at least attempts to provide them with reparation. At the same time, the RPF government has always refused to deal with the crimes of its own army during the civil war and its aftermath. It has certainly never made any sort of effort to provide the victims of these crimes with reparation.

Conclusion

I. Summary of the Study's Principal Results

This study has attempted to make a contribution to transitional justice research by exploring the legal framework for political transitions and by examining Rwanda's Gacaca courts against the backdrop of these legal rules. It has demonstrated that international legal rules governing transitions from a dictatorship to a democracy or from war to peace essentially cover two areas of concern: the issue of whether and how to prosecute serious human rights violations committed by an old regime or by opposition forces; and the question of whether the victims of the violations have a right to reparation. Regarding the first issue, states are under a duty to prosecute crimes under international law. With respect to genocide and war crimes, this duty originates from treaty law; for crimes against humanity, it is of a customary nature. In addition, it can be inferred from the duty to respect and ensure human rights, as laid down, for instance, in Article 2(1) of the ICCPR. In cases of mass atrocities, the obligation to prosecute crimes under international law can, however, be fulfilled by selective prosecution of the most senior perpetrators. Regarding less senior perpetrators, states are free to rely on mechanisms other than prosecution. A trial that may entail punishment must always respect the fair trial principle.

Regarding the issue of reparations, it has been shown that the right to reparation for human rights violations does not have a sufficient legal basis in the different human rights conventions. However, it can be inferred from customary international law. State practice, statements of UN bodies, and general acceptance among states testify to the customary status of the right to reparation. Yet its enforcement is difficult since there is little certainty regarding the content of this right under customary international law. The common forms of reparation under international law are restitution, compensation, satisfaction, and rehabilitation. It has been demonstrated that restitution is required where possible. Regarding compensation, it is difficult to determine clear guidelines under customary international law. Given the crucial importance of compensation as a form of reparation, however, a reparations programme that does not include compensation at all falls short of the requirements of international law. Compensation, however, may be made available as a lump sum payment. Satisfaction as a form of reparation comprises inter alia an acknowledgment of the violation suffered and truth recovery with respect to the violation. More recent practice shows in particular the increasing recognition of the victims' right to the truth. Rehabilitation of the victims in the form of medical and psychological care is a critical remedy for grave human rights violations. In state practice, however, it plays only a minor role.

In applying these rules to Gacaca, the study has shown that Gacaca tribunals are courts in terms of international criminal law and international human rights law. Through prosecutions by Gacaca courts, Rwanda discharges its duty to prosecute crimes under international law. Admittedly, Gacaca tribunals differ considerably from ordinary courts. These differences are owed to traditional elements in Gacaca, such as the involvement of the community in the process, and to its restorative aims, such as truth recovery, reparation, and reconciliation. While there is no prosecutor in Gacaca courts, the victims are granted the role of a party in the proceedings. This is reflected in certain procedural rights, such as the right to a new hearing if the victim was absent from the trial ('opposition').[1] Nevertheless, the parallels to traditional restorative dispute settlement are only superficial. Gacaca courts are organs of the Rwandan judiciary, act according to law, and have powers similar to ordinary courts. In accordance with the ICCPR and the Banjul Charter, they must therefore fulfil the fair trial standard.

When it comes to the fairness of Gacaca proceedings, the system has a number of structural weaknesses that jeopardize the outcome of the trials. Gacaca judges do not receive payment and have hardly enjoyed any education, which makes them highly susceptible to corruption or manipulation and threatens the independence of Gacaca courts. Moreover, the hardly trained judges have difficulties in dealing with complex crimes involving great numbers of perpetrators. In particular, they often fail to draw appropriate distinctions between ringleaders and bystanders. This leads to unspecified convictions for participation in a crime or even to convictions for acts that do not reach the threshold of a criminal offence.

The accused in the Gacaca trial often finds him or herself in a weak position. Defendants do not have access to their case files, they are not informed of the charges against them before their hearing, and they are not granted the right to counsel. These shortcomings are supposed to be compensated through the presence of a neutral public and of eyewitnesses to the alleged crimes. The public acts as prosecution and defence at the same time. In practice, however, popular participation in Gacaca has not had that effect; instead the public usually remained passive during the sessions. Some of Gacaca's other drawbacks are attributable to legislative weaknesses. For instance, article 93 of the Gacaca Law allows a retrial under broad conditions for offences already adjudged in a final manner. Review occurs rarely, but the provision of article 93 represents a threat to legal certainty. In practice, retrials have occurred without due regard to the principle of *ne bis in idem*.

In the field of reparation, Gacaca has provided a forum for restitution or compensation of property looted or destroyed during the genocide. Gacaca proceedings have brought about an official acknowledgment of the suffering of the victims. Finally, Gacaca has helped reveal the circumstances of many of the crimes, even though it has not lived up to its potential in truth recovery. Altogether, Rwanda's reparation policy was not very successful. Paradoxically, Gacaca courts award compensation only for damage and loss of property, while the efforts to make compensation available for victims of more serious crimes were not followed by results. The

[1] Arts 86 *et seq* of the Gacaca Law. On that, see ch 2, section VII A above.

projected compensation fund has never seen the light of day and it is unlikely ever to do so. Nevertheless, Rwanda's persistent attempts to provide reparation testify to the government's conviction that the victims have a right to reparation.

Regardless of the many problems just mentioned, Gacaca has produced a number of very notable results, especially given the situation in the immediate aftermath of 1994. The courts have completed over a million cases in only a few years,[2] often concerning suspects who had spent years in prison awaiting trial. While some speculated that Gacaca was introduced as a reaction to the rising number of acquittals in ordinary courts,[3] Gacaca jurisdictions have themselves pronounced a considerable number of acquittals[4]—an indicator that the trials were not entirely one-sided. All this has been achieved in a remarkably peaceful climate. Only isolated, relatively minor instances of violence have been reported.

Beside these obvious results, the effects of the Gacaca experiment in the future require more detailed discussion. Gacaca is a grassroots mechanism based on popular participation. It encourages communities to gather on a regular basis and to address crimes that haunt them up to the present day. In the cases where the population takes this opportunity and actively participates, Gacaca has an enormous potential to rebuild the shattered communities.[5] Gacaca has even been praised as the nucleus of democracy in Rwanda.[6] It appears, however, that Gacaca has only partially lived up to its community-building potential. One important factor is the general lack of active participation, one of the crucial conditions for Gacaca's success.[7] Another factor is the limited sense of ownership of Gacaca among the population. Gacaca was never really what it pretended to be and what the sensitization programmes attempted to suggest: a grassroots mechanism used by ordinary people for ordinary people. Instead, it was imposed by the government and operated under the permanent control of local authorities. What kept Gacaca running was often not the conviction that it was responding to the actual needs of communities, but rather that it was an obligation imposed by the government. The culture of obedience, which is often quoted as an important factor for the widespread participation in the genocide, is also likely to have made mass participation in Gacaca possible. At the same time, obedience to authority has undermined its potential as a grassroots mechanism. In fact, Gacaca failed to trigger broad-based public debates about the reasons for the genocide and the future of Hutu-Tutsi relations beyond the official narrative promoted by the government.

[2] 'Gacaca Courts: 1.4 Million Cases Handled in Past Two Years', *Hirondelle*, 6 February 2009. Apparently cases on the trial and the appeals level as well as property cases were counted separately.

[3] See P. Ironside, 'Rwandan *Gacaca*' 15 *New York International Law Review* (2002) no 2, 50.

[4] Up to 30%, for details, see ch 3, section V D above.

[5] P. Clark, 'Hybridity, Holism, and "Traditional" Justice' 39 *The George Washington International Law Review* (2007) 815 *et seq*; E. Daly, 'Between Punitive and Reconstructive Justice' 34 *NYUJIntlLaw&Pol* (2002) 378.

[6] A. Wierzynska, 'Consolidating Democracy Through Transitional Justice' 97 *NYULR* (2004) 1957 *et seq*. See also E. Staub, 'Justice, Healing, and Reconciliation' 10 *Peace and Conflict* (2004) 30. For criticism, see P. Clark, *The Gacaca Courts* (2010) 152.

[7] See the quote by former Minister of Justice Jean de Dieu Mucyo in P. Clark, 'Hybridity, Holism, and "Traditional" Justice' 39 *The George Washington International Law Review* (2007) 809.

Nevertheless, Gacaca has established a culture of discourse in Rwanda. While this discourse is essentially limited to the survivors, every week hundreds of thousands listen to it nonetheless. Talking about one's suffering can lead to retraumatization, but it can also be a cathartic experience. In societies that have suffered egregious atrocities, it is not self-evident that the victims speak about what they have been through. The *Eichmann* trial in Jerusalem in 1961 was so shocking and formative for Israeli society precisely because it was the first time that survivors had spoken about their suffering. As Hannah Arendt observed, the experiences of the survivors were not new to most in the audience.[8] What was new was the fact that people were talking about them and the cathartic effect on the whole nation that came about as a result.[9] The discourse about the past in Gacaca sessions may be flawed in many respects: the truth is elusive, especially if there are no survivors to testify; victims are often frustrated when having to tell their story to an effective wall of silence; finally, the specific suffering of women remains largely unaddressed in Gacaca courts.[10] Still, a society with a history of violence will not escape the need to hold a discourse about the past. Even though individual victims may perceive talking about their experiences as agonizing, it is an essential and eventually inevitable element of the collective process of coming to terms with the past. This culture of discourse could only be achieved through a grassroots mechanism, a forum accessible to everyone such as Gacaca.[11]

II. Outlook

The pivotal question about Gacaca in the long run is whether it will contribute to Rwanda's future stability.[12] Rwandan officials are in no doubt that accountability is necessary in order to allow Rwandans to find reconciliation. They have inspired enormous hope among the population that truth-telling will heal the wounds and that perpetrators and victims will be able to live side by side peacefully once justice is done. With these expectations still partly unfulfilled, the completion of the Gacaca process will leave a huge vacuum. The closure of the last genocide case will not mean that there is no need to continue the discourses Gacaca has triggered.

[8] H. Arendt, *Eichmann in Jerusalem* (1963) 6.

[9] See A. Assmann, *Der lange Schatten der Vergangenheit* (2006) 100; L. Douglas, *The Memory of Judgment* (2001) 109; T. Segev, *The Seventh Million* (1991) 343.

[10] It is estimated that over 200,000 rapes occurred during the genocide, D. Magsam, 'Coming to Terms with Genocide in Rwanda' in W. Kaleck (ed), *International Prosecution of Human Rights Crimes* (2007) 162. A figure of 250,000 to 500,000 women raped is quoted in S.L. Wells, 'Gender, Sexual Violence and Prospects for Justice at the Gacaca Courts in Rwanda' 14 *Southern Californian Review of Law and Women's Studies* (2004/05) 182; see also K. Brounéus, 'Truth-Telling as Talking Cure?' 39 *Security Dialogue* (2008) 57; C.C. Feliciati, 'Restorative Justice for the Girl-Child in Post-Conflict Rwanda' 7 *International Women's Studies* (2006) no 4, 14 *et seq*; H. Rombouts, 'Women and Reparations in Rwanda' in R. Rubio-Marín (ed), *What Happened to the Women?* (2006) 194 *et seq*.

[11] Similarly A.T. Paul, 'Das Unmögliche richten' 34 *Leviathan* (2006) 53 *et seq*, 60. See also S. Schilling, *Gegen das Vergessen* (2005) 358.

[12] For a recent case study of Gacaca's repercussions on peace and security, see M. Rettig, 'Gacaca' 51 *African Studies Review* (2008) no 3, 25 *et seq*.

We have seen that various factors have impaired the emergence of truth in Gacaca courts. Against this backdrop, there can be no doubt that there is an ongoing need for truth-telling. The continuation of a non-formalized Gacaca facilitating further grassroots discourse has been suggested.[13] It appears that Rwanda has become yet another example of steady-state transitional justice.

Beyond the vital grassroots discourses that Gacaca has initiated, it is difficult to assess its repercussions on inter-ethnic relations. Gacaca is part of the government's crusade against ethnic divisions in Rwandan society. This policy has become manifest in the disappearance of the categories of Hutu and Tutsi from public debate. In private, people lower their voice when talking about them. However, in the last few years, a different tendency that goes against this trend has emerged. Faced with accusations of revenge crimes, the government has started to modify the term used for the events in 1994: while laws and public statements used to refer to 'genocide and other crimes against humanity', or to 'genocide and massacres', suddenly the term used is 'genocide against the Tutsi'.[14] This illustrates a tendency that many Hutu also see in the Gacaca process. According to them, Gacaca means punishment for Hutu. Their impression is that people are convicted not only because they have committed crimes, but also for their sympathy with the killers. In fact, there are many troubling examples of severe sentences being given to mere bystanders.[15] Gacaca may thus create the perception among Hutu that they are being collectively blamed, which is further compounded by the fact that the crimes of the RPA forces are not addressed in Gacaca and largely ignored by regular courts. Therefore, instead of creating a common Rwandan identity, Gacaca may deepen the divide between the different groups in society.[16]

On the other hand, what else could have been done about the atrocities committed in Rwanda? From a human rights perspective, it would have been appropriate to limit prosecutions to trials of no more than 10,000 of the most senior perpetrators. These could have been determined on the basis of a refined categorization provision with category one suspects liable to prosecution. With a comparable number of trials, it would have been possible to ensure respect for all procedural safeguards required by the ICCPR, the Banjul Charter, and the Rwandan Constitution. Rwandan courts have demonstrated this in the trials under Organic Law No 08/96. These prosecutions would not necessarily have taken longer than the Gacaca process, given that by 2002 over 7,000 trials had already been completed.[17] All other

[13] See PRI, *Final Report* (2010) 46 *et seq.*

[14] See, eg, Law No 69/2008.

[15] See ch 3, section V C above.

[16] B. Baker, '"He Must Buy What He Stole and Then We Forgive"' *Acta Juridica* (2007) 183; A. Corey and S.F. Joireman, 'Retributive Justice' 103 *African Affairs* (2004) 86 *et seq*; E. Daly, 'Between Punitive and Reconstructive Justice' 34 *NYUJIntlLaw&Pol* (2002) 385; G. Gahima, 'Alternatives to Prosecution' in E. Hughes, W.A. Schabas and R. Thakur (eds), *Atrocities and International Accountability* (2007) 175 *et seq*; B. Ingelaere, 'The Gacaca Courts in Rwanda' in L. Huyse and M. Salter (eds), *Traditional Justice and Reconciliation after Violent Conflict* (2008) 56 *et seq*; A. Molenaar, *Gacaca* (2005) 163 *et seq*; M. Rettig, 'Gacaca' 51 *African Studies Review* (2008) no 3, 42 *et seq.*

[17] On the standard and the speed of the trials before ordinary courts, see ch 1, section VI C and D above. A similar suggestion was made by J. Sarkin, 'The Tension Between Justice and Reconciliation in Rwanda' 45 *Journal of African Law* (2001) 172.

cases could have been investigated, but not prosecuted, by institutions similar to the Gacaca courts. Such a limited programme of prosecution would have been sufficient for Rwanda to discharge its duty to prosecute.

However, the potentially destabilizing effects of a partial amnesty in the mid- or late 1990s and the ensuing mass release of prisoners that would have accompanied such an amnesty should not be overlooked.[18] We have seen that in the 1990s, Rwandan prisons were overcrowded with genocide suspects. Many of them believed they were prisoners of war and that they had done nothing wrong except for losing the war. It appears that individual accountability was necessary in that situation in order to reinstate the normative standards necessary for peaceful co-existence of perpetrators and victims in Rwanda. In addition, it is important for detainees that their individual accountability be determined. After having spent years in prison, there was a need for some sort of 'official' act in order for them to be able to make sense of their situation. Those innocently detained in particular would still carry the stigma of suspicion had they not been acquitted.

Nevertheless, it appears that a greater reliance on Gacaca's restorative components would have helped limit the negative consequences of the system and would thus have been advantageous in the long run. Had punishment played a less prominent role in the Gacaca system, it goes without saying that the due process shortcomings associated with it would also have been of less concern. As we have seen above, Gacaca often takes place in a climate where people avoid testifying for fear of violence or of being charged themselves. A more restorative approach could have helped dispel such fears. In addition to this, it would have allayed the impression among the Hutu that they are being held collectively responsible. Accountability as well as an acknowledgment of an unlawfully imprisoned person's innocence could also have been established through a well-devised truth and reconciliation process. This could have been realized by offering individual amnesty on the condition that a person found guilty perform certain reconciliatory measures, either for the victims and their families, or for the community. These measures could have included voluntary work similar to the community service programme.[19] Such measures would not necessarily have been perceived as punishment. Official monitoring would possibly not have been necessary to the same extent as it is in the community service camps. This would have strengthened the sense of ownership of the process among the population.

The victims' support for such a process could have been secured through the implementation of a compensation programme. Such a programme could have been implemented through a fund, which would have paid lump sum compensation to victims. Payments would have been low, but they would have given the victims a chance to escape poverty. A compensation programme could also have been understood as a stimulus to the national economy. Beneficiaries of compensation could have been encouraged to build up small businesses with the allowances

[18] See P. Akhavan, 'Beyond Impunity' 95 *AJIL* (2001) 23; in fact, Rwandans often voice such concerns, see the comment quoted in G. Packer, 'Justice on a Hill' 49 *Dissent* (2002) no 2, 61 *et seq*.

[19] For a similar model, see E. Daly, 'Between Punitive and Reconstructive Justice' 34 *NYUJIntlLaw&Pol* (2002) 388 *et seq*.

received, similar to a microcredit programme. This would have required a great deal of support being provided for the beneficiaries. Given the enormous amounts spent on prosecutions, however, such a programme is not entirely unrealistic.[20] It appears that a paradigm change towards stronger reliance on reparation is necessary. Instead, national politicians and donors in particular are highly motivated to allocate considerable resources to criminal trials. Prosecution of high-level perpetrators is necessary and obligatory under international law. Yet the international community has a tendency to overcharge it with expectations for reconciliation and development that courts and judges are unable to meet.

III. Learning Lessons from the Gacaca Experience

By attempting to ensure comprehensive prosecution of those responsible for the genocide, Rwanda has entered new territory in transitional justice. This gives rise to the question of what we can learn from the Rwandan experience. While the previous discussion has shown that Gacaca as a complete model is certainly not suitable for application in other contexts, the Gacaca process has nonetheless proved to be invaluable with regards to assessing the potential of using traditional forms justice in transitional settings. Given that local mechanisms have increasingly come into the focus of transitional justice research, this issue warrants further discussion.

Rwanda has chosen to create a hybrid mechanism incorporating both traditional and modern elements. It is due to the hybrid nature of this mechanism that Gacaca has few features specific to one particular culture, quite unlike other more 'genuine' forms of traditional justice employed after mass atrocities. The practices used in Sierra Leone in order to reintegrate former child soldiers, for example, rely upon rites that can only be properly understood within a specific cultural context.[21] Another example is the Acholi rite *mato oput* practised in northern Uganda to reintegrate former LRA fighters. While *mato oput* has attracted a lot of interest and support in this context, it enjoys little acceptance among the other ethnic groups of the region, which have also suffered from the LRA incursion.[22] In contrast, the informal setting of Gacaca courts is largely unspecific and could just as

[20] Just to illustrate: the ICTR's budget for the 2010/11 biennium is 245.3 million US$, see <http://www.unictr.org/AboutICTR/GeneralInformation/tabid/101/Default.aspx>, last visited June 2011. On the basis of a number of around 310,000 survivors (see 'Genocide Survivors Estimated to Be 300,000', *Hirondelle*, 28 August 2008), a comparable amount alone would have sufficed for lump sum payments of close to 800 US$ to each of them.

[21] J.A.D. Alie, 'Reconciliation and Traditional Justice' in L. Huyse and M. Salter (eds), *Traditional Justice and Reconciliation after Violent Conflict* (2008) 141 *et seq*; *Report of the Sierra Leone Truth and Reconciliation Commission*, vol 3B (2004) 440.

[22] T. Allen, 'The International Criminal Court and the Invention of Traditional Justice in Northern Uganda' 107 *Politique Africaine* (2007) 153; T. Murithi, 'African Approaches to Building Peace and Social Solidarity' 6 *African Journal on Conflict Resolution* (2006) no 2, 24 *et seq*; J.R. Quinn, 'Social Reconstruction in Uganda' 8 *Human Rights Review* (2007) 399.

easily be practised in other cultural contexts too. This flexibility is another reason why Gacaca is being discussed as a model for transitional justice.[23]

Yet the hybrid nature of Gacaca courts, which brings together grassroots justice and legal procedure, is also one of its drawbacks in comparison to other traditional systems. Traditional mechanisms usually generate a strong feeling of ownership among the participants, which helps ensure compliance with their decisions.[24] Gacaca, in contrast, was imposed by law and has always been under close official control. It therefore lacks the legitimacy of a true grassroots mechanism. In addition, the introduction of formal legal elements into Gacaca threatens to marginalize its restorative objectives of reintegration and reparation.[25] Many traditional systems, including ancient Gacaca, attach great importance to consensus when it comes to solving disputes.[26] Gacaca trials, however, are inevitably adversarial to some extent and often end in highly contentious verdicts. The verdict itself is likely to become the pivotal issue of the process, with the focus being removed from the victim and the community.[27] Gacaca has demonstrated once more that formal legal elements are often likely to dominate and undermine an informal system.[28]

Rwanda's approach has also revealed the limits of informal community justice in dealing with serious crimes. Gacaca courts have a strong focus on the local communities in their respective jurisdictions—much like most other traditional mechanisms. Traditional Gacaca, for instance, would usually only deal with petty offences, while capital crime was regarded as being of concern beyond the local community.[29] Most other traditional or informal mechanisms are similar in this regard.[30] The Gacaca courts' community focus is also reflected in their structure. Their organs are made up exclusively of residents of the respective sector. By sitting in judgment over crimes committed in the community, the original idea was that Gacaca courts would help the local population to reach reconciliation and come to terms with their own experiences. This idea makes sense whenever the crime in question was committed by a local in his or her home community. Yet in cases of higher-level crimes, the criminal act is likely to have repercussions far beyond the place where it was physically committed. This is especially true for category

[23] See, eg, P.E. Harrell, *Rwanda's Gamble* (2003); A. Wierzynska, 'Consolidating Democracy Through Transitional Justice' 97 *NYULR* (2004) 1967.

[24] See J.O. Latigo, 'Tradition-Based Practices in the Acholi Region' in L. Huyse and M. Salter (eds), *Traditional Justice and Reconciliation after Violent Conflict* (2008) 113.

[25] On the potential of informal justice with regards to this see E. Wojkowska, *Doing Justice* (2006) 17.

[26] See, eg, J.O. Latigo, 'Tradition-Based Practices in the Acholi Region' in L. Huyse and M. Salter (eds), *Traditional Justice and Reconciliation after Violent Conflict* (2008) 111; A. Molenaar, *Gacaca* (2005) 149; A. Naniwe-Kaburahe, 'The Institution of Bashingantahe in Burundi' in L. Huyse and M. Salter (eds), *Traditional Justice and Reconciliation after Violent Conflict* (2008) 157.

[27] See also N. Christie, 'Conflicts as Property' 17 *BJCrim* (1977) 7 *et seq*; L. Waldorf, 'Mass Justice for Mass Atrocities' 79 *TempLRev* (2006) 72 *et seq*.

[28] On the experiences made by many African states during and after colonization, see PRI, *Access to Justice in Sub-Saharan Africa* (2000) 129 *et seq*.

[29] OHCHR, *Gacaca: Le droit coutumier au Rwanda: Rapport final de la première phase d'enquête sur le terrain* (1996) 10.

[30] E. Wojkowska, *Doing Justice* (2006) 23. On similar reservations against *mato oput* among locals in northern Uganda, see T. Allen, 'The International Criminal Court and the Invention of Traditional Justice in Northern Uganda' 107 *Politique Africaine* (2007) 153.

one cases, namely offences relating to incitement to genocide and overseeing massacres, and the crimes committed by the sub-prefecture leadership, all of which came under the jurisdiction of Gacaca courts in 2008.[31] The community is not an appropriate forum for cases such as these. The proximity of the Gacaca court to the site of the crime was of little use here, as the witnesses to and victims of these offences were very often not among the local population. In order to be dealt with properly, such cases would have required more time in order that witnesses and victims could be summoned and that the complex repercussions of leadership offences be brought to light. Instead, category one cases were tried in the same manner as all other cases, with far too little time being dedicated to gathering and examining the necessary evidence.[32]

On the other hand, some of Gacaca's other features may well be suitable for use in other settings. Gacaca is likely to have strengthened the role of women in many communities, given the crucial role women played as judges.[33] In that regard, modern Gacaca is very progressive in comparison both to its antecedent and to other forms of traditional justice practised elsewhere.[34] A similar effect may occur in other contexts, given that women often take on a strong role in families and communities after violent conflict, since men are more likely to have been killed or involved in the atrocities.[35] In addition, it has been argued in the previous section that the discursive elements in Gacaca have produced notable achievements. In cultures with a tradition of addressing conflict through ongoing discussions, as is often the case in Africa, encouraging community-based truth-telling suggests itself as a cheap and culturally appropriate response to communal violence. Taken as a whole however, Gacaca cannot ultimately be recommended as a model.

[31] See also J.O. Latigo, 'Tradition-Based Practices in the Acholi Region' in L. Huyse and M. Salter (eds), *Traditional Justice and Reconciliation after Violent Conflict* (2008) 113 *et seq.*

[32] PRI, *Eight Years On…* (2010) 63 *et seq.*

[33] See B. Ingelaere, 'The Gacaca Courts in Rwanda' in L. Huyse and M. Salter (eds), *Traditional Justice and Reconciliation after Violent Conflict* (2008) 48 *et seq*, 52.

[34] On traditional Gacaca, see ch 2, section I above; on the mechanisms practised in Sierra Leone, Uganda, and Burundi, see J.A.D. Alie, 'Reconciliation and Traditional Justice' in L. Huyse and M. Salter (eds), *Traditional Justice and Reconciliation after Violent Conflict* (2008) 144; T. Murithi, 'African Approaches to Building Peace and Social Solidarity' 6 *African Journal on Conflict Resolution* (2006) no 2, 14; A. Naniwe-Kaburahe, 'The Institution of Bashingantahe in Burundi' in L. Huyse and M. Salter (eds), *Traditional Justice and Reconciliation after Violent Conflict* (2008) 167 *et seq.*

[35] See also PRI, *Access to Justice in Sub-Saharan Africa* (2000) 2 *et seq.*

Appendix

The Gacaca Law (Organic Law No 16/2004 of 19 June 2004 as modified by Organic Laws No 28/2006 of 27 June 2006, No 10/2007 of 1 March 2007, and No 13/2008 of 19 May 2008)

The following coordinated version of the Gacaca Law as of May 2008 has been put together by the author. It is based on Organic Law No 16/2004, and includes the amendments of 2006, 2007, and 2008.[1] All amendments are reprinted in italics. Since the version prior to the 2008 amendment was applied in the majority of the Gacaca trials, the following version includes both the provisions prior and subsequent to the 2008 amendment. Regarding some provisions, the 2008 amendment merely rephrases the former provision in slightly different language. In these cases, it is obsolete to reprint both. Instead, only the 2008 version is provided. In my study, the version reprinted here is quoted as the 'Gacaca Law'. If the version of the law as reprinted here includes two alternative provisions, the one referred to is indicated, unless the statement refers to both versions of the provision. I have not corrected any errors in the law text. In the most obvious cases, I inserted corrections in square brackets or footnotes.

Organic Law No 16/2004 [of 19 June 2004] establishing the organisation, competence and functioning of Gacaca Courts charged with prosecuting and trying the perpetrators of the crime of genocide and other crimes against humanity, committed between October 1, 1990 and December 31, 1994

As modified by

Organic Law No 28/2006 of 27 June 2006,

Organic Law No 10/2007 of 1 March 2007, and

Organic Law No 13/2008 of 19 May 2008

We, Kagame Paul,
President of the Republic;
The Parliament has adopted and we sanction, promulgate the following Organic Law and order it to be published in the Official Gazette of the Republic of Rwanda.
The Parliament:
The Chamber of Deputies, in its Cession of June 17, 2004;
The Senate, in its session of June 10, 2004;

[1] Given the Constitution of the Republic of Rwanda of 04 June 2003, as amended to date, especially in its Articles 9–1 and 2, 61, 62, 88, 90, 93, 108, 118–7, 152 and 201;

[2] Revisited the organic law no 40/2000 of January 26, 2001, setting up Gacaca courts and organizing prosecutions for offences constituting the crime of genocide or crimes against humanity, committed between October 1, 1990 and December 31, 1994, as modified and completed to-date;

1 In the official English versions as published in the Official Gazette of the Republic of Rwanda no special of 19 June 2004, no special of 12 July 2006, no 5 of 1 March 2007, and no 11 of 1 June 2008.

[3] Revisited the organic law no 08/96 of 30th August 1996 on the organization of prosecutions for offences constituting the crime of genocide or crimes against humanity committed since October 1, 1990;

[4] Revisited the decree-law no 09/80 of July 7, 1980 establishing the Code of judicial organization and competence confirmed by the law no 01/82 of January 26, 1982, as modified and completed to date;

[5] Revisited the decree-law no 21/77 of August 18, 1977 instituting the penal code as modified and completed to date;

[6] Revisited the law of February 23, 1963 on the Code of criminal procedure, as modified and completed to date;

[7] Considering the crimes of genocide and the crimes against humanity committed in Rwanda from October 1, 1990 to December 31, 1994;

[8] Considering that such crimes were publicly committed in the eyes of the population, which thus must recount the facts, disclose the truth and participate in prosecuting and trying the alleged perpetrators;

[9] Considering that testifying on what happened is the obligation of every Rwandan patriotic citizen and that nobody is allowed to refrain from such an obligation whatever reasons it may be;

[10] Considering that the committed acts are both constituting offences provided for and punished by the Penal Code, and crimes of genocide or crimes against humanity;

[11] Considering that the crime of genocide and crimes against humanity are provided for by the International Convention of December 9, 1948, relating to repression and punishment of the crime of genocide.

[12] Considering the convention of November 26, 1968 on imprescriptibility of war crimes and crimes against humanity;

[13] Considering that Rwanda ratified those Conventions with the decree-law no 8/75 of February 12, 1975 ratifying different International Covenants on human rights, disarmament and preventing and suppressing actions that may result into conflicts among peoples and countries and published them in the Official Gazette of the Republic of Rwanda, without, however, providing for special sanctions for these crimes until the time when they were committed;

[14] Considering, consequently, that prosecutions must be based on the penal code of Rwanda;

[15] Considering the necessity to eradicate for ever the culture of impunity in order to achieve justice and reconciliation in Rwanda, and thus to adopt provisions enabling rapid prosecutions and trials of perpetrators and accomplices of genocide, not only with the aim of providing punishment, but also reconstituting the Rwandan Society that had been destroyed by bad leaders who incited the population into exterminating part of the Society;

[16] Considering the necessity for the Rwandan Society to find by itself, solutions to the genocide problems and its consequences;

[17] Considering that it is important to provide for penalties allowing convicted persons to amend themselves and to favour their reintegration into the Rwandan Society without jeopardizing the people's normal life;

Adopts:

TITLE I: OFFENCES UNDER THE APPLICABILITY OF THIS ORGANIC LAW

Article 1

This organic law establishes organization, competence and functioning of Gacaca courts charged with prosecuting and trying the perpetrators of the crime of genocide and crimes against humanity, committed between October 1, 1990 and December 31, 1994, or other crimes provided for in the penal code of Rwanda, but according to the declarations from the Public prosecution or testimonies against the defendant, as well as the defendant's confessions in relation to criminal acts carried out with the intention of committing genocide or crimes against humanity.[2]

Article 2

The persons or their accomplices prosecuted for their participation in criminal acts that put them in categories 2 and 3, as defined by article 51 of this organic law, are answerable to Gacaca Jurisdictions referred to in Title II of this organic law. Gacaca courts apply the provisions of this organic law.

Persons who, by the virtue of acts committed, rank in the first category, as defined in Article 51 of this organic law, are tried before to ordinary courts which apply the common law content and procedure rules subject to exceptions provided for by this organic law.

As regards the subject of the action, only provisions of this organic law prevail.

Persons referred to in the preceding paragraphs, are tried before the courts defined in those paragraphs, even if their co-defendants are prosecuted by courts different from theirs. In that case, their co-defendants can only be summoned to testify in that trial.

Article 2 [as modified by article 1 Organic Law No 13/2008]

Any person or an accomplice prosecuted for an act that puts him or her in the first category, paragraph 3, 4 and 5, the second and third category as provided in article 9 of this law [article 51], shall be tried by Gacaca Courts referred to in Title II of this law. Gacaca courts shall apply the provisions of this law.

Any person prosecuted for an act that puts him or her in the first category, paragraph 1 and 2 as provided in article 9 of this law [article 51] shall be tried by ordinary or military courts applying Ordinary Rules of Procedure but subject to exceptions provided by this Organic Law.

This Organic Law shall apply to all acts provided herein.

Persons referred to in the proceeding paragraphs shall be tried by courts named therein and although a co-accused is prosecuted by a different court, he or she may be summoned to testify in a specific trial.

[2] *Sic.* The French version is clearer: 'La présente loi organique porte sur l'organisation, la compétence et le fonctionnement des Juridictions Gacaca chargées des poursuites et du jugement des infractions constitutives du crime de génocide et d'autres crimes contre l'humanité commis entre le 1er octobre 1990 et le 31 décembre 1994, ou des infractions prévues par le code pénal qui, selon les accusations du Ministère Public ou les témoignages à charge aussi bien que les aveux du prévenu, ont été commis dans l'intention de faire le génocide ou d'autres crimes contre l'humanité.'

TITLE II: SETTING UP, ORGANISATION AND COMPETENCE FOR GACACA COURTS AND RELATIONSHIP WITH OTHER INSTITUTIONS

CHAPTER ONE: SETTING UP AND ORGANISING GACACA COURTS

SECTION I: SETTING UP AND JURISDICTION

Article 3 [as modified by article 2 Organic Law No 13/2008]

It is hereby established a Gacaca Cell Court, Gacaca Sector Court and an Appeal Court.

These courts shall hear cases of crimes of genocide or other crimes against humanity committed between October 1, 1990 and December 31, 1994, in such a manner as provided for by Organic Law No 16/2004 of 19/6/2004 establishing the organisation, competence and functioning of Gacaca Courts charged with prosecuting and trying the perpetrators of the crime of genocide and other crimes against humanity, committed between October 1, 1990 and December 31, 1994 as amended to date.

Article 4 [as modified by article 2 Organic Law No 28/2006]

The jurisdiction of Gacaca Court of the Cell and that of the Sector are the former Cell and the former Sector respectively while that of Appeal is the former Sector as such structures were provided for by the law before the Organic law No 29/2005 of 31/12/2005 determining administrative entities of the Republic of Rwanda was published in the Official Gazette.

The list of Gacaca Courts is indicated on appendix of this Organic Law [No 28/2006].

SECTION II: ORGANS OF GACACA COURTS

Sub-section 1: General Provisions

Article 5

The Gacaca Court of the Cell is made up of a General Assembly, a Seat for the Gacaca Court and a Coordination Committee.

The Gacaca Court of the Sector, as well as the Gacaca Court of Appeal are made up with a Sector General Assembly, a Seat for the Gacaca Court and a Coordination Committee.

The competent instance which has the powers to appoint the Seat members or the competent one to appoint members of the Coordination Committee, is also competent for their replacement.

Sub-section 2: The General Assembly

Article 6 [as modified by article 3 Organic Law No 13/2008]

The general assembly of the Gacaca Cell Court shall be composed of all the residents of the jurisdiction of that Court aged eighteen (18) years and above.

When it appears that the number of residents of that jurisdiction aged eighteen (18) years and above is less than Two hundred (200), that jurisdiction shall be merged with another Gacaca Cell Court within the same jurisdiction of the Gacaca Sector Court to make a Gacaca Cell Court. The same shall apply when it appears that the number of persons with integrity as defined in article 8 of Organic Law no 16/2004 of 19/6/2004 establishing the organisation, competence and functioning of Gacaca Courts charged with prosecuting and trying the perpetrators of the crime of genocide and other crimes against humanity, committed between October 1, 1990 and December 31, 1994, as amended to date is not reached. The merged Gacaca Courts of the Cells shall proceed to re-elect persons of integrity.

When merged Gacaca Cell courts fail to raise the required number of persons of integrity, and there are no other Gacaca cell courts in the jurisdiction of the Sector Gacaca court, the Gacaca Cell courts shall be merged with the Gacaca Cell courts falling in the jurisdiction of the neighboring Sector Gacaca court. The Sector Gacaca court where the merged courts formerly belonged shall also be merged with the Sector Gacaca court where the merged Gacaca cell courts belonged.

The decision to merge a Gacaca Cell Court with the jurisdiction of another shall be taken by the National Service in charge of the follow up, supervision and coordination of the activities of Gacaca Courts on its own initiative or upon request by the Mayor of a District informing the Governor of the Province or the Mayor of Kigali City.

Article 7

The General Assembly for the Sector is composed of the members of the following organs:

1° The Seats for the Gacaca Court of the Cells constituting that sector;

2° The Seat for the Gacaca Court of the Sector;

3° The Seat for the Gacaca Court of Appeal.

Sub-section 3: The Seat for the Gacaca Court

Article 8 [as modified by article one Organic Law No 10/2007]

Each Bench of the Gacaca Court is made up of seven (7) persons of integrity and two (2) substitutes.

A Gacaca Court may have more than one Bench where necessary.

The new Bench shall elect from its members an executive committee and shall be given cases to be tried.

The National Service of Gacaca Courts draws up the modalities for the establishment of the Benches of Gacaca Courts and their collaboration modalities.

Article 9

Before exercising his or her duties, every member of the Seat for the Gacaca Court shall take the following oath:

"I .... solemnly swear to the Nation that I shall:

1° diligently fulfill the responsibilities entrusted to me;

2° remain loyal to the Republic of Rwanda;

3° observe the Constitution and the other laws;

4° work for the consolidation of national unity;

5° conscientiously fulfill my duties of representing the Rwandan people without any discrimination whatsoever;

6° never use the powers conferred on me for personal ends;

7° promote respect for the freedom and fundamental rights of human beings and safeguard the interests of the Rwandan people.

Should I fail to honour this oath, may I face the rigours of the law: So help me God."

Article 10

A member of the Seat for the Gacaca Court cannot judge or decide on a case in which he or she is a party or is prosecuted:

1° his or her spouse;

2° his or her parent, grandfather and grandmother, relatives, children and grandchildren or those of his or her spouse;

3° his or her uncles, aunts and maternal or paternal cousins;

4° the person with whom it was already existing serious enmity;

5° the person with whom he or she has deep friendship relations;

6° the person for whom he or she is a guardian;

7° any other relation considered incompatible with the honest person's independence.

In one of these hypotheses, the member of the Seat concerned shall decline to act in the case. Failure to do so, any person who knows about the existence of one of these causes informs, before the plea as to the content, the Seat which decides all matters ceasing.

However, the concerned person so objected to is admitted to testify for or against the prosecution.

Sub-section 4: The Coordination Committee

Article 11

Members of the Seat for a Gacaca Court elect among themselves, with a simple majority, the Coordination Committee made up with a President, a first Vice-President, a second Vice-President and two secretaries, all of them must know how to read and write Kinyarwanda.

The members of the Coordination Committee are elected for a one (1) year mandate which may be renewed.

The secretaries of Gacaca Courts shall be responsible for report making and assume the functions of secretaries for Gacaca Courts

Article 12

The Coordination Committee shall carry out the following functions:

1° to convene, preside over meetings and coordinate activities of the Seat for the Gacaca Court;

2° to register complaints, testimonies and evidences given by the population;

3° to receive files for the accused answerable to Gacaca Court;

4° to register appeals filed against judgments passed by Gacaca Courts;

5° to forward to the Gacaca Courts of Appeal, files of judgments appealed against;

6° to register decisions made by organs of the Gacaca Court;

7° to collaborate with other institutions in implementing decisions made by the Gacaca Court.

SECTION III: MEMBERS OF THE ORGANS FOR GACACA COURTS

Article 13 [as modified by article 4 Organic Law No 13/2008]

The General Assembly of a Gacaca Cell Court shall elect from itself seven (7) persons of integrity that will constitute the bench and two (2) deputies.

The General Assembly of a Gacaca Sector Court shall elect, from itself seven (7) persons of integrity and two deputies for each required bench of Gacaca Court of Appeal and

seven (7) persons of integrity and (two) deputies for each bench required in the Gacaca Sector Court.

Subject to provisions of article 102 of Organic Law No16/2004 of 19/6/2004 establishing the organisation, competence and functioning of Gacaca Courts charged with prosecuting and trying the perpetrators of the crime of genocide and other crimes against humanity, committed between October 1, 1990 and December 31, 1994, as amended to date, general elections of persons of integrity for Gacaca Courts shall be organized and conducted by the National Electoral Commission.

A Presidential Order shall determine the necessary guidelines for electing members of the organs of Gacaca Courts.

Article 14 [as modified by article 3 Organic Law No 10/2007]

Members of the benches of Gacaca Courts are Rwandans of integrity elected by the General Assemblies of their Cells of residence.

A person of integrity is any Rwandan meeting the following conditions:

1° not to have participated in genocide;

2° to be free from the spirit of sectarianism;

3° not to have been definitively sentenced to a penalty of at least six (6) months of imprisonment;

4° to be of high morals and conduct;

5° to be truthful;

6° to be honest;

7° to be characterised by a spirit of speech sharing;

8° to be free from genocide ideology

Ideology of genocide consists in behaviour, a way of speaking, written documents and any other actions meant to wipe out human beings on the basis of their ethnic group, origin, nationality, region, colour of skin, physical traits, sex, language, religion or political opinions.

Any person of integrity who is at least twenty-one (21) years old and meeting all the conditions required by this organic law, can be elected a member of an organ of a Gacaca Court without any discrimination whatsoever, such as that based on sex, origin, religion, opinion or social position.

Article 15 [as modified by article 4 Organic Law No 28/2006]

Can not be elected member of the seat for a Gacaca Court:

1° the person exercising a political activity;

2° a Government official;

3° the soldier or the policeman who is still in active service;

4° the career magistrate;

5° the member of the leadership of a political organization

This ineligibility, however, is waived when the person's resignation from his or her position is accepted.

Leaders referred to in the second point, first paragraph of this article, are the Governor of the Province, Members of the Executive Committee of the City of Kigali, that of the District and those members of the political and administrative committee at the Cell level.

Cannot elect or be elected as a person of integrity, anybody who appears on the list of genocide suspects. However, those who committed offences against property only can elect.

Article 16 [as modified by article 4 Organic Law No 10/2007]

Any person elected as a member of the organs for Gacaca Courts shall be replaced for one of the following reasons:

1° to be absent from the meeting sessions of the organs of Gacaca Courts for three (3) consecutive times without giving any convincing reasons;

2° to be definitively convicted of a crime punishable by a sentence of at least six (6) months of imprisonment;

3° to prompt sectarianism

4° to exercise one of the activities provided for in article 15 of Organic Law nº 16/2004 of 19/6/2004 establishing the organisation, competence and functioning of Gacaca Courts charged with prosecuting and trying the perpetrators of the crime of genocide and other crimes against humanity, committed between October 1, 1990 and December 31, 1994 or occupying a position that is likely to impede participation in the sessions of the organs of Gacaca Courts;

5° to have a disease likely to prevent him or her from participating in the activities of the organs of Gacaca Courts;

6° to do any act incompatible with the quality of a person of integrity;

7° resignation for personal reasons;

8° to be prompted by genocide ideology;

9° death.

The decision to dismiss a member of the organs of Gacaca Courts who has been absent from their activities for three (3) consecutive times without convincing reasons, has instigated sectarianism or has done an act incompatible with the quality of a person of integrity, shall be made in writing, by the members of the Bench of the Gacaca Court, after consultations with the General Assembly of his or her Cell of residence. The member so dismissed shall be subject to a public caution before the General Assembly and can no longer be elected as a person of integrity.

Other reasons for the replacement referred to in this article, are ascertained by the same organ of the Gacaca Court.

Article 16 [as modified by article 5 Organic Law No 13/2008]

An elected member of any organ of Gacaca Courts shall be replaced due to any of the following reasons:

1° absence from the Gacaca organ meetings for three (3) consecutive times without giving convincing reasons;

2° definitive conviction for an offence that carries a term of imprisonment of at least six(6) months;

3° promoting sectarianism;

4° revealing details of camera proceedings;

5° engaging in any of the activities provided for in article 15 of Organic Law nº 16/2004 of 19/6/2004 establishing the organisation, competence and functioning of Gacaca Courts charged with prosecuting and trying the perpetrators of the crime of genocide and other crimes against humanity, committed between October 1, 1990 and December 31, 1994 as amended to date or engaging in an activity that is likely to impede participation in the activities of Gacaca Court organs;

6° infection of a disease that is likely to prevent him or her to follow up activities of Gacaca Court organs;

7° doing any act that is incompatible with qualities of a person with integrity;

8° voluntary resigning;

9° being characterised by the genocide ideology;

10° death.

A decision to dismiss a member of the organs of Gacaca Court who has been absent from his or her activities for three (3) consecutive times without convincing reasons, promoting sectarianism, revealing details of camera proceedings or has done an act incompatible with the qualities of a person of integrity, shall be made in writing by members of the Gacaca Court Bench after consultation with the General Assembly of the Cell. A dismissed member shall be subject to a public caution before the General Assembly and shall no longer be suitable to be elected as a person of integrity.

Other reasons in this article that lead to replacement of a member of Gacaca court organs shall be confirmed by the same organ of the Gacaca Court.

Any dismissed member of the bench of a Gacaca Court for revealing details of camera proceedings shall be prosecuted for that offence by the same court and shall be liable to a term of imprisonment ranging from one (1) to three (3) years.

Prosecution of a former member of the bench of a Gacaca Court for the offence of revealing details of camera proceedings shall be heard in a separate case.

SECTION IV: FUNCTIONING OF THE ORGANS OF GACACA COURTS

Article 17

The General Assembly for the Gacaca Court of the Cell holds an ordinary meeting once a week and an evaluation meeting once every three months and an extraordinary meeting anytime deemed necessary.

It is convened and presided over by the President of the Coordination Committee, on his own initiative or on the request of at least one third (1/3) of the members of the Seat for the Gacaca Court.

When the President has a legitimate reason or refuses to convene the General Assembly, the latter is convened by one of his or her deputies.

Article 18

The General Assembly of the Gacaca Court of the Cell only meets legitimately if at least one hundred members are present.

Article 19

The General Assembly of the Sector shall meet once every three months in its ordinary sessions, and any time in its extraordinary session if need be.

It is convened and presided over by the President of the GACACA Court of Appeal, on its own initiative or on the request of one fourth (1/4) of its members. The President of the Gacaca Court of the Sector becomes the Vice-President.

When the President and the Vice-President have legitimate reasons or refuse to convene the General Assembly, the latter is convened by the elder person of integrity on the request of one fourth (1/4) of its members. The present persons of integrity choose, among themselves, the President.

Article 20

The General Assembly of the Sector meets legitimately if at least two thirds (2/3) of its members are present.

Article 21

Hearings for Gacaca Courts are public, except when there is a hearing in camera decided by the Gacaca Court, or on the request of any interested person and decided in a pronounced judgement for reasons of public order or good morals.

The decisions and deliberations of judges are made in secret.

Article 22

In the Gacaca Court of the Cell, the day and time for meetings are fixed by the General Assembly. In other Gacaca Courts, the day and time are determined by the Seat members of the Court and communicated to the population.

Article 23 [as modified by article 5 Organic Law No 10/2007]

The Bench of the Gacaca Court meets legitimately if at least five (5) of its members are present.

When the quorum is not reached due to the absence of some members, the meeting is postponed.

When the quorum is not reached due to an absolute unavailability of the members for various reasons, it is completed by substitutes.

If the quorum is not reached, following objection or competence disclaimer from some of the Bench members, it is completed by their substitutes until the last decision or the closure of hearings.

When all Bench members are objected to or disclaim competence, the assistance of persons of integrity from the nearest Gacaca Court having the same competence is sought until the decision is taken or the closure of hearings. This cannot withhold those persons of integrity from elsewhere to carry on their duties in their usual Court.

The objected Bench, disclaimed Bench or any other person interested in the case, shall immediately inform the National Service in charge of following up, supervising and coordinating the activities of Gacaca Courts to decide on the Gacaca Court from which the persons of integrity can be borrowed.

Article 24

The Seat for a Gacaca Court shall decide by consensus, and failing this, it decides with the absolute majority of its members.

If simple majority is not reached, it is proceeded to a new vote; each member of the Seat for the Gacaca Court having, however, to choose between the two positions which previously obtained more votes.

Article 25

Judgments must be motivated. They are signed or marked with a fingerprint by all members of the Court who have seated in the proceedings and ruled on them.

Article 26

Whenever need be, Gacaca Courts seek assistance from legal experts appointed by the National service in-charge of the follow up, supervision and coordination the activities of Gacaca Courts.

Article 27

The Coordination Committee of the Gacaca Court meets as often as necessary, convened by its President, on his or her initiative or on request of at least two (2) of its members.

When the President has a legitimate motive for not summoning the Coordination Committee, the latter is summoned by one of his deputies.

Article 28

To sit legitimately, the Coordination Committee shall bring together at least three (3) of its members.

Article 29

Every Rwandan citizen has the duty to participate in the Gacaca courts activities.

Any person who omits or refuses to testify on what he or she has seen or on what he or she knows, as well as the one who makes a slanderous denunciation, shall be prosecuted by the Gacaca Court which makes the statement of it. He or she incurs a prison sentence from three (3) months to six (6) months. In case of repeat offence, the defendant may incur a prison sentence from six months (6) to one (1) year.

Is considered as refusing[3] to testify on what he or she has seen or known, any person who apparently knew something on a given matter denounced by others in his or her presence, without expressing his or her own opinion.

Is considered as refusing to testify:

1° Anyone who, once summoned to testify before the Court after knowing that he or she is holder of a testimony, refuses to declare by avoiding to speak or deliberately evading the question put to him or her;

2° Anyone who, once summoned by the Court and does not appear deliberately without reasons, avoiding to be questioned in as much as the summons is clearly notified to him or her.

Is considered as a perjurer,[4] anyone who gives a testimony ascertaining that he or she is telling only the truth and holds evidences for that, takes an oath and signs it; but later on it appears to be false and done on purpose.

The perjury is prosecuted during the very hearing of the matter in which the prosecuted person has given the testimony, if it is discovered that the person did it or on purpose.

Article 30

Anyone who exercises pressures, attempts to exercise pressures or threatens the witnesses or the Seat members of the Gacaca Court shall incur a prison sentence from three (3) months to one (1) year. In case of repeat offence, the defendant risks a prison penalty from six (6) months to two (2) years.

Is regarded as an act of exercising pressures on a Court, anything aiming at coercing the Seat into doing against its will, translated into actions, words or a behaviour threatening the Seat, and clearly meaning that if the latter fails to comply with, some of its members or the entire Seat may face dangerous consequences. However, when the pressure is performed, provisions of the penal code of criminal procedure are applied by ordinary courts.

Is considered as an attempt to exercise pressures on a Court, any behaviour translated into words or acts, showing that there has been an attempt to coerce a Court into taking a decision in a way or another.

[3] This paragraph is meant to refer to 'omitting' rather than 'refusing' to testify as mentioned in art 29(2), see the French version of the law.

[4] This paragraph refers to making 'a slanderous denunciation' as mentioned in art 29(2), see also the French version of the law, which uses the term 'dénonciation mensongère' in both paragraphs.

Is regarded as an act of threat on the Court or witnesses, words and actions threatening the witnesses or the Seat members of a Gacaca Court, aiming at winning acceptance for his own wish at all costs.

Are considered as [attempts of][5] threatening the Court or the witnesses, words or actions clearly meant to threaten the witnesses or the Seat members for a Gacaca Court, with the intention of winning acceptance for his or her wish.

Article 31 [as modified by article 6 Organic Law No 10/2007]

Cases tried pursuant to Article 29 of Organic Law nº 16/2004 of 19/6/2004 establishing the organisation, competence and functioning of Gacaca Courts charged with prosecuting and trying the perpetrators of the crime of genocide and other crimes against humanity, committed between October 1, 1990 and December 31, 1994 may be opposed and appealed against in accordance with the procedure provided for by this Organic Law.

Nevertheless, cases tried by the Gacaca Court of Appeal at the first resort, are appealed against in the nearest Gacaca Court of Appeal or in another bench of the Gacaca Court of Appeal that tried the case if it is available.

Article 32

The Seat for the Gacaca Court taking cognisance of offences stated in articles 29 and 30, decides all matters ceasing and retires to deliberate on whether it is an offence to be prosecuted according to these articles. When the prosecution of the offence is confirmed, the Seat announces the day of the hearing, notifies it to the defendant, and records it in the notebook of activities before carrying on the Court's activities.

When an offence is committed outside the Court, the plaintiff can file his or her complaint in a written form or during the General Assembly. When he or she declares before the General Assembly, the case is registered and put on the agenda for the next meeting.

In case it is notified to the President, he/she hands it to the secretary who records it in the notebook of activities, mentioning the plaintiff, motive, date of submission and the date of reception from the President. After recording, the President informs the General Assembly, and they decide on the date of examining the complaint.

On the hearing day, the President checks if the required number of persons of integrity, the accused and witnesses are present; their identities are registered, and after, reminds the provisions of the law, states the accusation and gives the floor to the defendant for presenting his or her defence and witnesses.

After their declarations, the President gives the floor to the witnesses for prosecution and any other interested person who wants to say something in the General Assembly, asks the accused to react to it, afterwards the Seat members retire for deliberations. The judgement is recorded in the notebook of activities and bears the signatures of all Seat members.

When the Seat takes an imprisonment decision, it fills out an arrest warrant which is forwarded to the nearest security organ or the representative of the National Service in charge of the follow up Gacaca Courts' activities for handing it over to the organs charged with arresting and detaining.

Detention pending trial is forbidden for the prosecuted persons whose offences are stated in articles 29 and 30 of this organic law, apart from persons referred to in article 30 when they are prosecuted by the public prosecution.

[5] See the French version.

SECTION V: THE DUTIES OF GACACA COURTS

Sub-section 1: The duties for the organs of the Gacaca Court of the Cell

Article 33

The General Assembly of the Gacaca Court of the Cell exercises the following attributions:

1° Electing Seat members of the Gacaca Court of the Cell and their deputies;

2° Attending the activities of the Gacaca Court of the cell for the non-members of the seat and take the floor only upon request;

3° Assisting the seat of Gacaca Court in the establishment of a list of persons:

a) who reside in the cell;
b) who resided in the cell before the genocide, locations they kept shifting to and routes they took;
c) killed in their Cell of residence;
d) killed outside their cell of residence;
e) killed in the cell while they were not residing in it;
f) victimized and their damaged property;
g) alleged authors of the offences referred to in this organic law.

4° Presenting evidences or testimonies on all persons suspected of having committed the crime of genocide and on others who took part;

5° Examining and adopting activity report established by the Gacaca Court.

All residents of the Cell shall tell the facts of events which took place, especially in their home villages and give evidence, denounce the authors and identify the victims.

Article 34

The Seat for the Gacaca Court of the Cell exercises the following attributions:

1° With the participation of the General Assembly, to make up a list of persons:

a. who reside in the cell;
b. who were residing in the Cell before the genocide, locations where they kept shifting to and routes they took;
c. killed in their Cell of residence;
d. killed outside their Cell of residence;
e. killed in the cell while they were not residing in it;
f. victimized and their damaged property;
g. who took part in the offences referred to in this organic law.

2° to receive confessions, guilt plea, repentance and apologies from the persons who participated in genocide;

3° to bring together the files forwarded by the Public Prosecution;

4° to receive evidences and testimonies and other information concerning how genocide was planned and put into execution;

5° to investigate testimonies;

6° to categorize the accused as per the provisions of this organic law;

7° to put on trial and judge cases for the accused whose crimes classify them in the third category;

8° to give a ruling on objection to Seat members for the Gacaca Court of the Cell;

9° to forward to the Gacaca Court of the Sector, the files of the defendants classified in the second category;

10° to forward to the Public Prosecution, the files for the defendants classified in the first category;

11° to elect members of the Coordination Committee.

A victim referred to in point 1°–f is anybody killed,[6] hunted to be killed but survived, suffered acts of torture against his or her sexual parts, suffered rape, injured or victim of any other form of harassment, plundered, and whose house and property were destroyed because of his or her ethnic background or opinion against the genocide ideology.

Sub-section 2: The duties for the Gacaca Court of the Sector and the Gacaca Court of Appeal

Article 35

The general Assembly for the Sector has the following attributions:

1° to supervise the functioning of all Gacaca Courts in the Sector, without meddling in their ways of conducting proceedings;

2° to replace persons of integrity for the Gacaca Court of the Sector and the Gacaca Court of Appeal;

3° to receive and solve problems of the functioning of Gacaca Courts, not related to proceedings;

4° to report to the National Service in charge of the following up, supervision and coordination of the activities of Gacaca Courts, and provide advice to it.

Article 36

The Seat for the Gacaca Court of the Sector exercises the following remit:

1° making investigations, if necessary, on testimonies given;

2° receiving confessions, guilt plea, repentance and apologies from genocide perpetrators;

3° taking decisions relating to objections to the Seat members of the Gacaca Court;

4° putting on trial and ruling on cases falling in its competence according to this organic law, after making sure that the accused forwarded to it, have been categorized in conformity with the alleged offences, and those found in the first category are forwarded to the Public Prosecution;

5° examining appeals against judgments passed by Gacaca Court of the Cell;

6° electing members of the Coordination Committee.

[6] The Kinyarwanda and French versions do not refer to those killed themselves, but to only to those whose next of kin were killed ('umuntu wese wiciwe', 'dont les siens ont été tués').

Article 37

The Seat for the Gacaca Court of Appeal carries out the following attributions:

1° making investigations, if necessary, on testimonies given;

2° taking decisions relating to objections to the Seat members of the Gacaca Court;

3° putting on trial and ruling on cases falling in its competence according to this organic law, after making sure that the accused forwarded to it have been categorized in conformity with their offences, and those found in the first category, are forwarded to the Public Prosecution;

4° examining appeals against judgements passed by the Gacaca Court of the Sector;

5° electing members of the Coordination Committee.

Article 38

As regards offences relating to rape or acts of torture against sexual parts, the victim chooses among the Seat members for the Gacaca Court of the Cell, one or more to whom she submits her complaint or does it in writing. In case of mistrust in the Seat members, she submits it to the organs of investigations or the Public Prosecutor.

In case of death or incapacity of the victim, the complaint shall be secretly lodged by any interested party in the manner provided for by the paragraph one of this article.

The person of integrity entrusted with such a complaint, forwards it secretly to the Public Prosecution for further investigations.

It is prohibited to publicly confess such an offence. No body is permitted to publicly sue another party. All formalities of the proceedings of that offence shall be conducted in camera.

Article 38 [as modified by article 6 Organic Law No 13/2008]

A victim of the offence of rape or sexual torture may submit her or his complaint to the Sector Gacaca Court where the offence was committed from, the judicial police or the public prosecution.

In case the victim to any other above offences is dead or is incapacitated to lodge such a complaint, a concerned party may secretly lodge such a complaint in a manner provided in proceeding paragraph.

It is prohibited to publicly confess commission of any of the above crimes. No person shall be permitted to initiate proceedings in respect to any of the above offences against another in public. All formal proceedings in respect to the above offences shall be held in camera.

Delegates of the National Service in charge of the follow up, supervision and coordination of the activities of Gacaca Courts, security officers, and Trauma Counsellors may follow up a matter being tried in camera.

CHAPTER TWO: THE COMPETENCE OF GACACA COURTS

Article 39

Gacaca Courts have competences similar to those of ordinary courts, to try the accused persons, on the basis of testimonies against or for, and other evidences that may be provided.

They may in particular:

1° Summon any person to appear in a trial;

2° Order and carry out a search of or to the defendant's.[7] This search must, however, respect the defendant's private property and basic human rights;

3° Take temporary protective measures against the property of those accused of genocide crimes;

4° Pronounce sentences and order the convicted person to compensate;

5° Order the withdrawal of the distrait for the acquitted person's property;

6° Prosecute and punish trouble makers in the court;

7° Summon, if necessary, the Public Prosecution to give explanatory information on files it has investigated on;

8° Issue summons to the alleged authors of offences and order detention or release on parole, if necessary.

Article 40

The National Service in charge of the follow up, supervision and coordination of the activities of Gacaca Courts, determines, on its own initiative or on the request of the Seat for the Gacaca Court concerned, or any person suffering encroachment, by means of regulations, the ways to rule on disputes relating to competences of Gacaca Courts and follows up its implementation.

SECTION I: RATIONAE MATERIAE

Sub-section 1: The Gacaca Court of the Cell

Article 41 [as modified by article 7 Organic Law No 10/2007]

The Gacaca Court of Cell only deals, at the first and last resort, with offences relating to property. It also deals with the objection against the sentence it has pronounced in the absence of the parties.

Gacaca Court of Cell classifies into categories accused persons suspected of having committed offences provided for in articles one and 51 of Organic Law n°16/2004 of 19/6/2004 establishing the organisation, competence and functioning of Gacaca courts charged with prosecuting and trying the perpetrators of the crime of genocide and other crimes against humanity, committed between October 1, 1990 and December 31, 1994, as modified and complemented to date.

Sub-section 2: The Gacaca Court of the Sector

Article 42 [as modified by article 8 Organic Law No 10/2007]

The Gacaca Court of Sector deals at first resort, with defendants whose offences classify them into the second category and opposition made against sentences pronounced in the absence of the parties.

It also deals with the appeal lodged against judgements pronounced for offences provided for in articles 29 and 30 of Organic Law no16/2004 of 19/6/2004 establishing the organisation, competence and functioning of Gacaca courts charged with prosecuting and trying the perpetrators of the crime of genocide and other crimes against humanity, committed between October 1, 1990 and December 31, 1994 and other decisions taken by the Gacaca Court of Cell.

[7] *Sic*. This is supposed to mean 'Order and carry out a search of the defendant', see the French version.

Article 42 [as modified by article 7 Organic Law No 13/2008]

The Gacaca Sector Courts shall hear at the first level cases of persons who committed offences that put them in the first category, point 3, 4 and 5 and in the second category as stipulated in article 9 of this law [article 51] together with reviewing[8] *of cases that were determined in absence of an accused.*

It shall also determine appeals emanating from offences in article 29 and 30 of Organic Law No16/2004 of 19/6/2004 establishing the organisation, competence and functioning of Gacaca Courts charged with prosecuting and trying the perpetrators of the crime of genocide and other crimes against humanity, committed between October 1, 1990 and December 31, 1994 as amended to date and other decisions taken by the Gacaca Court of the Cell.

Sub-section 3: The Gacaca Court of Appeal

Article 43 [as modified by article 9 Organic Law No 10/2007]

The Gacaca Court of Appeal deals with appeal lodged against sentences pronounced at first resort by the Gacaca Court of the Sector.

In addition, it deals with objection lodged against sentences pronounced in the absence of the parties.

SECTION TWO: RATIONAE LOCI

Article 44 [as modified by article 10 Organic Law No 10/2007]

The Gacaca Court of the area where an offence was committed is the one that is competent to hear it.

Persons who committed offences in different places are tried before competent Courts in accordance with provisions stated in the first paragraph of this article.

However, if the author of the crime cannot be prosecuted by the Gacaca court of where the crime was committed or when it was committed beyond the borders of Rwanda, the Gacaca Court of the area of his/her residence or domicile may prosecute him/her.

Article 45

When it appears in the file to communicate to the Gacaca Court in conformity with article 47 of this organic law, that the defendant has committed offences in different places, the Public Prosecution forwards it to each Gacaca Court of the Cell of where crimes were committed.

CHAPTER THREE: RELATIONSHIP BETWEEN GACACA COURTS AND OTHER INSTITUTIONS

SECTION I: RELATIONSHIP BETWEEN THE PUBLIC PROSECUTION AND GACACA COURTS

Article 46

The organs of the Public Prosecution shall proceed to their mission of receiving denunciations and complaints, and investigating on offences referred to in this organic law.

[8] This provision refers to the means of appeal of opposition (arts 86 *et seq*), not review; see the French version.

However, before beginning such investigation, they will have to make sure that the Gacaca Court has not tried or has not begun to examine these cases so as to avoid unnecessary task.

The files investigated by the Public Prosecution in conformity with the first paragraph of this article, are forwarded to the competent Gacaca Court of the Cell.

Article 47

The files investigated by the Public prosecution, but which were not yet forwarded to competent Courts by March 15, [2001] shall be forwarded to the Gacaca Court of the area where each crime was committed for the categorization of defendants.

The Public prosecution carry on communicating to Gacaca Courts of the Cell or to the Court called to recognisance of the case, evidences collected against prosecuted persons in the files it has investigated.

When the Gacaca Court of the Cell which has made the categorization, has already forwarded the file to the competent Court to hear the case before it receives the prosecution file, the concerned Public Prosecution forwards the evidences collected to the Gacaca Court of the Cell and its copy to the competent Gacaca Court which has competence to hear it.

In case it is clear that in the file that the accused committed the offences of rape or sex related crimes, the prosecution shall not refer the file to the Gacaca Court of the Cell.

Article 47 [as modified by article 8 Organic Law No 13/2008]

The organs of the prosecution department shall continue liaising and facilitating Gacaca Courts with any evidence got in the course of investigations about accused persons.

Article 48

The Prosecutor General of the Republic supervises the organs of the Public Prosecution in proceedings referred to in this organic law.

SECTION II: RELATIONSHIP BETWEEN ADMINISTRATIVE ORGANS AND GACACA COURTS

Article 49

Leaders of administrative organs in which Gacaca Court function shall provide them with premises in which they shall perform their duties, as well as sensitize the population for their active participation. They exercise a steady monitoring of the functioning of Gacaca Courts and provide them with necessary materials, in collaboration with the National Service in charge of follow up, supervision and coordination of the activities of Gacaca Courts.

SECTION III: RELATIONSHIP BETWEEN THE GACACA COURTS AND THE NATIONAL SERVICE CHARGED WITH THE FOLLOW UP, SUPERVISION AND COORDINATION OF ACTIVITIES OF GACACA COURTS

Article 50

The National Service in charge of follow up, supervision and coordination of the activities of Gacaca Courts, follows up, supervises and coordinates Gacaca Courts' activities in the country.

It also issues rules and regulations relating to the smooth running of Gacaca Courts, as well as the conduct of persons of integrity, without prejudice to the Gacaca Courts' ways of trying.

TITLE III: PROSECUTION OF OFFENCES AND PROCEEDINGS

CHAPTER ONE: PROSECUTED PERSONS

Article 51 [as modified by article 11 Organic Law No 10/2007]

Following acts of participation in offences referred to in article one of Organic Law n°16/2004 of 19/6/2004 establishing the organisation, competence and functioning of Gacaca courts charged with prosecuting and trying the perpetrators of the crime of genocide and other crimes against humanity, committed between October 1, 1990 and December 31, 1994, the accused may be classified in one of the following categories:

First Category:

1° The person whose criminal acts or criminal participation place among planners, organisers, incitators, supervisors and ringleaders of the crime of genocide or crimes against humanity, together with his or her accomplices;

2° the person who, at that time, was in the organs of leadership, at national, prefecture, sub-prefecture and commune levels, leaders of political parties, members of the high command of the army and gendarmerie, of communal police, leaders of religious denominations, or illegal militia groups and who committed those offences or encouraged other people to commit them, together with his or her accomplices;

3° the person who committed acts of rape or sexual torture, together with his or her accomplices;

4° The Prosecutor General of the Republic shall publish, at least twice a year, the list of persons classified in the first category, forwarded to him or her by Gacaca Courts of the Cell.

Second Category:

1° the well known murderer who distinguished himself or herself in the area where he or she lived or wherever he or she passed, because of the zeal which characterized him or her in the killings or excessive wickedness with which they were carried out, together with his or her accomplices;

2° the person who committed acts of torture against others, even though they did not result into death, together with his or her accomplices;

3° the person who committed dehumanizing acts on the dead body, together with his or her accomplices.

4° the person whose criminal acts or criminal participation place among the killers or authors of serious attacks against others, causing death, together with his or her accomplices;

5° the person who injured or committed other acts of serious attacks, with intention to kill them, but who did not attain his or her objective, together with his or her accomplices;

6° the person who committed or participated in criminal acts against persons, without any intention of killing them, together with his or her accomplices.

Third Category:

The person who only committed offences against property. However, if the author of the offence and the victim have agreed on an amicable settlement on their own initiative, or before the public authority or witnesses, before this organic law came into force, he or she cannot be prosecuted.

Article 51 [as modified by article 9 Organic Law No 13/2008]

Commission of offences in article 1 of Organic Law No16/2004 of 19/6/2004 establishing the organisation, competence and functioning of Gacaca Courts charged with prosecuting and trying the perpetrators of the crime of genocide and other crimes against humanity, committed between October 1, 1990 and December 31, 1994 as amended to date, an accused may be put in one of the following categories:

First Category:

1° any person who committed or was an accomplice in the commission of an offence that puts him or her in the category of planners or organisers of the genocide or crimes against humanity.

2° any person who was at a national leadership level and that of the prefecture level: public administration, political parties, army, gendarmerie, religious denominations or in militia group, and committed crimes of genocide or crimes against humanity or encouraged others to participate in such crimes, together with his or her accomplice;

3° any person who committed or was an accomplice in the commission of an offence that puts him or her among the category of people who incited, supervised and ringleaders of the genocide or crimes against humanity;

4° any person who was at the leadership level at the Sub-Prefecture and Commune: public administration, political parties, army, gendarmerie, communal police, religious denominations or in militia, who committed any crimes of genocide or other crimes against humanity or encouraged others to commit similar offences, together with his or her accomplice;

5° any person who committed the offence of rape or sexual torture, together with his or her accomplice.

The Prosecutor General of the Republic shall publish at least twice a year, a list of offenders in the first category forwarded by the Gacaca Cell Courts.

Second category:

1° a notorious murderer who distinguished himself or herself in his or her location or wherever he or she passed due to the zeal and cruelty employed, together with his or her accomplice;

2° any person who tortured another even though such torture did not result into death, together with his or her accomplice;

3° any person who committed a dehumanising act on a dead body, together with his or her accomplice;

4° any person who committed or is an accomplice in the commission of an offence that puts him or her on the list of people who killed or attacked others resulting into death, together with his or her accomplice;

5° *any person who injured or attacked another with the intention to kill but such intention was not fulfilled, together with his or her accomplice;*

6° *any person who committed or aided another to commit an offence against another without intention to kill, together with his or her accomplice.*

Third category:

A person who only committed an offence related to property. However, when the offender and the victim come to a settlement by themselves, settle the matter before the authorities or before the witnesses before commencement of this law, the offender shall not be prosecuted.

Article 52

The person in the position of authority at the level of the Sector and Cell, at the time of genocide, are classified in the category corresponding to offences they have committed, but their positions of leadership exposes them to the most severe penalty within the same category.

Article 53

For the implementation of this organic law, the accomplice is the person who has, by any means, provided assistance to commit offences with persons referred to in article 51 of this organic law.

The fact that any of the acts aimed at by this organic law has been committed by a subordinate, does not free his or her superior from his or her criminal responsibility if he or she knew or could have known that his or her subordinate was getting ready to commit this act or had done it, and that the superior has not taken necessary and reasonable measures to punish the authors or prevent that the mentioned act be not committed when he or she had means.

CHAPTER TWO: PROCEDURE OF CONFESSIONS, GUILT PLEA, REPENTANCE AND APOLOGIES

SECTION I: ACCEPTANCE OF CONFESSIONS, GUILT PLEA, REPENTANCE AND APOLOGIES AND CONDITIONS REQUIRED

Article 54

Any person who has committed offences aimed at in article one of this organic law, has right to have recourse to the procedure of confessions, guilt plea, repentance and apologies.

Apologies shall be made publicly to the victims in case they are still alive and to the Rwandan Society.

To be accepted as confessions, guilt plea, repentance and apologies, the defendant must:

1° give a detailed description of the confessed offence, how he or she carried it out and where, when he or she committed it, witnesses to the facts, persons victimized and where he or she threw their dead bodies and damage caused;

2° reveal the co-authors, accomplices and any other information useful to the exercise of the public action;

3° apologise for the offences that he or she has committed.

Article 55 [repealed by article 10 Organic Law No 13/2008]

Genocide perpetrators coming under the first category who have had recourse to the procedure of confessions, guilt plea, repentance and apologies for their offences before their names appear on the list drawn up by Gacaca Court of the Cell, shall enjoy commutation of penalties in the way provided for by this organic law.

Article 56

Shall enjoy commutation of penalties in the way provided for by this organic law, persons in the 2nd category who:

1° confesses, pleads guilty, repents, apologises before the Gacaca Court of the Cell draws up a list of authors of genocide;

2° already appearing on this list, have had recourse to the procedure of confessions, guilt plea, repentence and apologies after publication of the list of authors of genocide.

Article 56 [as modified by article 11 Organic Law No 13/2008]

A punishment for an offender in the first and second category may be commuted in accordance with this law and this includes:

1° any person who confessed, pleaded guilty, repented and asked for forgiveness before the Gacaca Cell Court finalises to prepare the list of offenders that had a hand in the genocide;

2° any person refereed to above who confessed, pleaded guilty, repented and asked for forgiveness after the list was prepared.

Article 57

If it is found out subsequently offences that a person has not confessed, he or she is prosecuted, at any time, for these offences and shall be classified in the category in which the committed offences place him or her, and is punishable by the maximum penalty provided for this category.

SECTION II: PROCEDURE OF CONFESSIONS, GUILT PLEA, REPENTANCE AND APOLOGIES

Article 58 [as modified by article 12 Organic Law No 13/2008]

A confession, guilty plea, repentance and forgiveness shall be done before a dully constituted bench, a judicial police officer or a public prosecutor investigating the case in accordance with article 46 of Organic Law No16/2004 of 19/6/2004 establishing the organisation, competence and functioning of Gacaca Courts charged with prosecuting and trying the perpetrators of the crime of genocide and other crimes against humanity, committed between October 1, 1990 and December 31, 1994 as amended to date.

The Bench, the Judicial Police Officer or the Public Prosecutor in charge of investigating the case shall inform the accused of his or her rights and benefits that emanate from a confession, guilty plea, repentance and request for forgiveness.

However, if a person confesses for the first time before an appellate court or when the case is being reviewed, the offender shall not enjoy commutation of punishment because of a delayed confession.

Sub-section 1: Procedure of confessions, guilt plea, repentance and apologies before the officer of the criminal investigation or before the officer of the public prosecution

Article 59

For files which are not yet forwarded to the Gacaca Courts of the Cells, the criminal investigation Department or the public prosecution receives the confessions, guilt plea, repentance and apologies. The conclusions from confessions, guilt plea, repentance and apologies shall be received and transcribed by an Officer of the criminal investigation or by the Public Prosecutor. If confessions are forwarded in writing, the Officer of the criminal investigation or the Public Prosecution asks the petitioner to endorse it.

The petitioner signs or marks with a fingerprint the minute containing the confessions, guilt plea, repentance and apologies and confirms what has been approved, as well as the minute containing confessions, if there is any, before the Officer for the criminal investigation or the Public Prosecutor who also endorses them.

Article 59 [as modified by article 13 Organic Law No 13/2008]

Judicial Police or the Public Prosecution shall receive confessions, guilty pleas, repentance and requests for forgiveness for the accused persons submitted to them. What is stated in the confession, guilty plea, repentance and request for forgiveness shall be recorded down by a judicial police officer or by a public prosecutor. If the submission is written, the judicial police officer or the public prosecutor shall request the petitioner to endorse it.

A petitioner shall sign or mark with a finger print the minute containing his or her confession, guilty plea, repentance and request for forgiveness or confirm what has been admitted as well as signing or mark with a finger print the minute containing the confession before a judicial police officer or a public prosecutor who shall also endorse it.

Article 60

If the Public Prosecutor finds that the confessions, guilt plea, repentance and apologies are in conformity with the required conditions, he or she concludes the file by establishing a note of investigation containing the petitioner's declarations and forwards it to the competent Gacaca Court of the Cell.

In case he or she finds that the confessions, guilt plea, repentance and apologies do not meet conditions required, or that the investigation has revealed that the petitioner's confessions, guilt plea, repentance and apologies are false, he or she states in an explanatory note the elements missing, concludes the file, and forwards it to the competent Gacaca Court of the Cell.

The Gacaca Court of the Cell, after checking if the confessions, guilt plea, repentance and apologies done before the Officer for the criminal investigation or the Public Prosecutor are complete, accepts or rejects them.

Article 60 [as modified by article 14 Organic Law No 13/2008]

If a Public Prosecutor finds that a confession, guilty plea, repentance and request for forgiveness is in conformity with the required conditions, the public prosecutor shall prepare a minute containing what the accused stated, conclude the file and submit the case file to a competent court.

If a Public Prosecutor finds that a confession, guilty plea, repentance and request for forgiveness does not meet the required conditions, or that the investigations show that the petitioner who confessed, pleaded guilty, repented and asked for forgiveness did not tell the truth, the public prosecutor shall prepare an explanatory note stating the missing elements, conclude the file and submit the case file to a competent court.

Article 61

The minutes containing confessions, guilt plea, repentance and apologies established by the Public Prosecutor[,] the officer for the criminal investigation or in conformity with articles 59 and 60 of this organic law, [are] forwarded to the Gacaca Court of the Cell of where the offence was committed, and read publicly, in case petitioner has reason beyond control preventing him or her to appear and apologise in public.

Article 61 [as modified by article 15 Organic Law No 13/2008]

A minute containing a confession, guilty plea, repentance and request for forgiveness prepared by a public prosecutor or a judicial police officer in accordance with article 13 and 14 of this law [articles 59, 60], shall be submitted to a competent court and shall be read in public if for reasons beyond control, the petitioner is not able to attend and ask for forgiveness in public.

Sub-section 2: Procedure of confessions, guilt plea, repentance and apologies before Gacaca Courts

Article 62 [as modified by article 16 Organic Law No 13/2008]

Any person who committed the offence of genocide and other crimes against humanity committed between October 1, 1990 and December 31, 1994, may confess, plead guilty, repent and ask for forgiveness before a dully constituted competent bench.

Without prejudice to the second paragraph of article 54 of Organic Law no 16/2004, of 19/6/2004 establishing the organisation, competence and functioning of Gacaca Courts charged with prosecuting and trying the perpetrators of the crime of genocide and other crimes against humanity, committed between October 1, 1990 and December 31, 1994 as amended to date, an offender may upon request confess, plead guilty, repent and ask for forgiveness orally or in written form putting his or her signature or fingerprint.

Article 63

The confessions, guilt plea, repentance and apologies are subject to the minute established by the secretary of the Gacaca Court and signed or marked with a fingerprint by the defendant and members of the Court Seat.

The Seat for the Gacaca Court checks if the confessions, guilt plea, repentance and apologies fulfils conditions required and if the petitioner's declarations are true.

CHAPTER THREE: HEARING AND JUDGEMENT

SECTION I: HEARING AND JUDGEMENT BEFORE GACACA COURTS OF THE SECTOR AND GACACA COURTS OF APPEAL

Article 64

In case of confirmed confessions, guilt plea, repentance and apologies, the hearing proceeds as follows:

1° the President of the session calls the case and invites defendants to the bar:

2° each defendant establishes his or her identity;

3° the President of the session requests the plaintiffs identity;

4° the Court secretary makes known to the defendant every charge against him or her, and reads the minute of the defendant's confessions;

5° the President of the session asks each defendant to comment on accusations;

6° any interested person takes the floor to testify in favour or against the defendant; [the defendant] responds to questions put to him or her. Every person taking the floor to testify on which he or she knows or witnessed, takes oath to tell the truth by raising his or her right arm, saying: "I take God as my witness to tell the truth";

7° the plaintiff describes all the offences suffered and how they were committed, if he or she has knowledge of them;

8° if the defendant is present, responds to the plaintiff's declarations;

9° the Seat for the Gacaca Court establishes a list of the victims and offences each of them suffered, the defendant is given floor to respond;

10° the Court secretary reads the statement of hearing, the Court checks the conformity of its content with the declarations and, if need be, the statement of hearing is corrected;

11° the Seat asks the plaintiff and the defendant if they have additional information;

12° the parties to the trial and all the others who took floor during the hearing, together with members of the Seat put their signatures or fingerprints on the statement hearing containing the defendant's confessions;

13° the hearing is declared closed, unless the Seat deems it necessary to postpone it so as to check certain issues.

Article 65

For files which do not contain confessions, guilt plea repentance and apologies or when the Gacaca Court has rejected them, the hearing proceeds as follows:

1° the President of the session calls the case and invites defendants to the bar;

2° each defendant establishes his or her identity;

3° the President asks the plaintiff his or her identity;

4° the secretary of the court makes known to the defendant every charge against him or her;

5° the President of the Gacaca Court reads out to the defendants, articles 54, 55 and 57 of this organic law so that they understand the confession, guilt plea, repentance and apologies procedure, and asks them if they want to use it. The interested persons in confessing, guilt pleading, repenting and apologizing, are asked to do it there and then, the hearing proceeds in the order provided for, for those who have confessed, pleaded guilty, repented and apologized.

For those who do not want to confess, plead guilty, repent and apologise, the hearing proceeds in the following way:

a) the President of the session gives the summary of the nature of the case and reads the provided evidences establishing the defendant's guilt;

b) the President of the session asks each defendant to give his or her defence;

c) the Court hears witnesses for or against prosecuted persons, if need be, hears evidences from the Public Prosecution if it is summoned to the trial. Every person taking the floor to testify on what he or she knows or witnessed swears to tell the truth by raising the right hand up and saying: "I take God as my witness to tell the truth."

d) the defendant gives his or her defence;
e) any interested person, takes the floor and the defendant answers to questions put to him or her;
f) the Seat of the Gacaca Court establishes a list of the victims and offences that each of them suffered; the defendant is given floor to respond;
g) the secretary of the Court reads the statement of hearing; the Court checks the conformity of its content with the declarations and, if need be, the statement of hearing is corrected;
h) the Seat asks the plaintiff and the defendant if they have additional information;
i) the parties to the trial and all the others who took floor during the hearing, together with the members of the Seat, put their signatures or fingerprints on the statement of hearing;
j) the hearing is declared closed, unless the Seat deems it necessary to postpone it so as to check certain issues.

Article 66

For files of defendants with neither known address nor residence in Rwanda referred to in article 98 of this organic law, the hearing shall proceed as follows:

1° the President of the session calls the case and invites the defendants to the bar.

2° if he or she finds that they are present, the hearing proceeds in conformity with article 65 of this organic law. In case some are present and others are absent, those who are present shall be judged in accordance with the provisions of article 65 of this organic law.

In reference to the absentees as well as those who did not appear, the hearing shall proceed in the following manner:

a. the President of the session asks the plaintiff's identity;
b. the secretary of the court makes known to the defendant every charge against him or her;
c. the President of the session gives the summary of the nature of the case, reads out provided evidences establishing the defendant's guilt;
d. the Court hears witnesses and, if necessary, hears the Public prosecution's evidences when it is summoned to the trial;
e. any interested person takes the floor on request;
f. the plaintiff describes all offences suffered and how they were omitted;
g. the Seat of the Gacaca Court establishes a list of the victims and offences suffered by each one of them;
h. the secretary of the Court reads the statement of hearing; the Seat checks the conformity of its content with the declarations and, if need be, the statement of hearing is corrected;
i. the Seat of the Gacaca Court asks the plaintiff if he or she has anything to add to the hearing;
j. the parties to the trial and members of the Seat put their signatures or fingerprints on the statement of hearing;

k. the hearing is declared closed, unless the Seat deems it necessary to postpone it so as to check certain issues.

As regards pronouncement, notification, appeal and objection to the judgements passed within such circumstances, provisions for judgements by default apply.

Article 67

Any judgement passed by the Gacaca Court of the Sector or the Gacaca Court of appeal mentions the following;

1° the Court that has passed it;

2° the names of Seat members who gave rulings;

3° the identity of the parties to the trial;

4° charges against the defendant;

5° the facts presented by the parties;

6° the motives of judgement;

7° the offence of which the defendant is found guilty;

8° the penalties pronounced;

9° the identity of the victims and the inventory of suffered offences;

10° the presence or absence of the parties;

11° if the hearings and the pronouncement of judgements were made public;

12° venue and date for judgement;

13° the provisions of this organic law which have been applied;

14° the legal period for appeal.

SECTION II: HEARING AND JUDGEMENT BEFORE THE GACACA COURT OF THE CELL

Article 68

For files relating to the offences against property, the hearing proceeds as follows:

1° the President of the session states the household concerned with the case;

2° the President of the session recalls the household's property damaged and known, on basis of the list of victims and damaged property;

3° the President of the session gives the floor to any person who has anything to add to the information on the list;

4° the seat for the Gacaca Court adopts the inventory of damaged property;

5° the President of the session reads the names of the defendants having damaged the household property, basing on the list of defendants;

6° each defendant presents his or her identity;

7° the President of the session requests the representative of the suffered household or any person interested to give his or her identity;

8° the secretary of the Court states each of the damaged property and their authors;

9° the President of the session asks each defendant to react to the accusations and present his or her defence;

10° the President of the session asks the household representative or any person who so wishes to react to the defendants' declarations;

11° the Seat for the Gacaca Court adopts the list of the victims, damaged property and the authors, each defendant is given floor to react;

12° the Seat of the Court explains to the convicted defendants, modalities for granting the compensation provided for by this organic law, by asking each defendant to decide on his or her means and the period of payment, in case of conviction;

13° the secretary of the Court reads the statement of hearing; the Seat checks the conformity of its content with the declarations and, if need be, the statement of hearing is corrected;

14° the Seat asks the plaintiff and the defendant whether they have anything to add to the hearing;

15° the parties to the trial and the Seat members put their signatures or fingerprints on the statement of hearing;

16° the hearing is declared closed, unless the Seat deems it necessary to postpone it so as to check certain issues.

Article 69

The judgement for offences against property passed by the Gacaca Court of the Cell shall mention the following:

1° the Court that has passed it;

2° the names of the Seat members who gave rulings;

3° the identity of the parties to the trial;

4° the damaged property requiring reparation;

5° the facts presented by the parties;

6° the motives of judgement;

7° the damaged property which must be repaired and the defendants responsible;

8° the identity of the victims and the inventory of their damaged property;

9° the modalities and the period for reparation;

10° the presence or absence of the parties;

11° if the hearings and the pronouncement of judgement were made public;

12° venue and date for judgement;

13° the provisions of this organic law which have been applied.

Article 70

Once the hearings are closed, or when deemed necessary to take any decision, the Seat of the Gacaca Court retires for deliberations and takes decision on the same day the following day.

The judgement or the decision taken are pronounced publicly in the meeting or in the next hearing, before starting that meeting or hearing.

SECTION III: MAINTAINANCE OF LAW AND ORDER DURING THE HEARINGS

Article 71

The hearing shall be carried out in calmness. Any person who takes the floor, must be characterized by politeness in speech and behaviour before the persons of integrity, parties, witnesses and the audience at large.

The President of the session can interrupt any person not conforming to the speech taking modality without bawling or rushing him or her in a way or another.

If necessary, the President of session can give a warning to the troublemakers in the Court, eject or put him or her in detention for a period not exceeding forty eight (48) hours, according to the gravity of the offence. When the committed offence is a criminal offence, the Seat forwards the case to the security organs, for prosecution basing on the ordinary laws.

CHAPTER FOUR: PENALTIES

Article 72 [as modified by article 17 Organic Law No 13/2008]

Offender in the first category:

1° who refused to confess, plead guilty, repent and ask for forgiveness or whose confession, guilty plea, repentance or request for forgiveness is rejected shall be liable to life imprisonment with special provisions;

2° who confessed, pleaded guilty, repented and asked for forgiveness after being put on the list of offenders shall be liable to a term of imprisonment ranging from twentyfive (25) to thirty (30) years of imprisonment;

3° who confessed, pleaded guilty, repented and asked for forgiveness and such confession, guilty plea, repentance and request for forgiveness is acceptable before being put on the list of offenders shall be liable to a term of imprisonment ranging from twenty (20) to twenty-four (24) years of imprisonment.

Article 73 [as modified by article 14 Organic Law No 10/2007]

Defendants falling within the second category referred to in the first, second and third paragraph of article 11 of this organic law [article 51], who:

1° refused to confess, plead guilty, repent and apologise, or whose confessions, guilt plea, repentance and apologies have been rejected, incur a prison sentence of thirty (30) years or life imprisonment

2° confessed, pleaded guilty, repented and apologised after being included on the list of the accused and whose confession, guilt plea, repentance and apologises have been accepted , incur a prison sentence ranging from twentyfive (25) to twenty-nine (29) years, but:

a) they serve a third (1/3) of the sentence in custody;

b) a sixth (1/6) of the sentence is suspended;

c) half (1/2) of the sentence is commuted into community service.

3° confessed, pleaded guilty, repented and apologised before being included on the list of the accused, incur a prison sentence ranging from twenty (20) to twenty-four (24) years, but:

a) they serve a sixth (1/6) of the sentence in custody;

b) a third (1/3) of the sentence is suspended;

c) half (1/2) of the sentence is commuted into community service.

Defendants falling within the second (2nd) category referred to in the fourth (4th) and fifth (5th) paragraph of article 11 of this organic law [article 51], who:

1° refused to confess, plead guilty, repent and apologise, or whose confessions, guilt plea, repentance and apologies have been rejected, incur a prison sentence ranging from fifteen (15) to nineteen (19) years;

2° confessed, pleaded guilty, repented and apologised after being included on the list of the accused and whose confession, guilt plea, repentance and apologies have been accepted, incur a prison sentence ranging from twelve (12) to fourteen (14) years, but:

a) they serve a third (1/3) of the sentence in custody;

b) a sixth (1/6) of the sentence is suspended;

c) half (1/2) of the sentence is commuted into community service;

3° confessed, pleaded guilty, repented and apologised before being included on the list of the accused and whose confessions, guilt plea, repentance and apologies have been accepted, incur a prison sentence ranging from eight (8) to eleven (11) years, but:

a) they serve a sixth (1/6) of the sentence in custody;

b) a third (1/3) of the sentence is suspended;

c) half (1/2) of the sentence is commuted into community service

Defendants falling within the second category referred to in the sixth (6th) paragraph, who:

1° refused to confess, plead guilty, repent and apologise, or whose confessions, guilt plea, repentance and apologies have been rejected, incur a prison sentence ranging from five (5) to seven (7) years, but:

a) they serve a third (1/3) of the sentence in custody;

b) a sixth (1/6) of the sentence is suspended;

c) half (1/2) of the sentence is commuted into community service;

2° confessed, pleaded guilty, repented and apologised after being included on the list of the accused and whose confession, guilt plea, repentance and apologies have been accepted, incur a prison sentence ranging from three (3) to four (4) years, but:

a) they serve a third (1/3) of the sentence in custody;

b) a sixth (1/6) of the sentence is suspended;

c) half of the sentence is commuted into community service;

3° confessed, pleaded guilty, repented and apologised before being included on the list of the accused and whose confessions, guilt plea, repentance and apologies have been accepted, incur a prison sentence ranging from one (1) to two (2) years, but;

a) a sixth (1/6) of the sentence in custody;

b) a (1/3) of the sentence is suspended;

c) half (1/2) of the sentence is commuted into community service.

Article 74

Should a person who is serving community services sentence commit another crime, the period he or she has already served becomes void and he or she shall serve the remaining prison sentence in custody as well as be prosecuted for the new crime he or she committed.

Article 74 [as modified by article 18 Organic Law No 13/2008]

If a person is serving community service sentence or is on a suspended sentence and is convicted of another crime, the period the offender had served on community service or on suspended sentence, shall become void and the offender shall serve the remaining sentence in prison and shall also serve the punishment for the new committed crime.

However, when a person is not found guilty of the new offence, he/she shall be released to serve the remaining period of community service sentence or suspended sentence taking into consideration the time spent in prison.

Article 75

Defendants who committed offences relating to property, are only sentenced to the civil reparation for what they have damaged.

Article 76 [as modified by article 15 Organic Law No 10/2007]

Persons convicted of the crime of genocide or crimes against humanity are liable to deprivation of their civil rights in the following manner:

1° persons falling within the 1st and 2nd category are liable to deprivation of the right:

a) to be elected;

b) to become leaders, to serve in the armed forces, to serve in the National Police and other security organs, to be a teacher, a medical staff, magistrates, public prosecutors and judicial counsels;

2° persons in the first category are liable to permanent deprivation of rights prescribed in item 1o of this article.

3° persons in the second category, items 1o, 2o and 3o who refused to confess or whose confessions have been rejected, are liable to permanent deprivation of rights prescribed in item 1o of this article.

4° persons in the second category items 1o, 2o and 3o whose confessions have been accepted and those in items 4o, 5o and 6o are deprived of those rights only for the duration of the sentence given by the competent Court.

5° The names of the persons falling within the first and the second category, convicted of the crime of genocide, together with a short description of their identities and the crimes they committed, shall be posted in the history section of the genocide memorials. Those names shall also be posted at the offices of their Sectors, registered in their 'criminal record' and published on the Internet.

Article 77 [as modified by article 19 Organic Law No 13/2008]

When there is a material combination of offences each of which classifies the offender in the same category, the maximum sentence provided in that specific category shall apply.

However, an offender who committed different offences placing him or her in the second category, point 6°, shall be liable to the maximum penalty of the same category, point 6°.

Article 78 [as modified by article 20 Organic Law No 13/2008]

Persons convicted of the crime of genocide or other crimes against humanity who at the time of commission of the offence were fourteen (14) years but less than eighteen (18) years of age are punished as follows:

Offender[s] in the first category:

1° who refused to confess, plead guilty, repent and ask for forgiveness, or whose confession, guilty plea, repentance and request for forgiveness were rejected shall be liable to a term of imprisonment ranging from ten (10) to twenty (20) years;

2° who confessed, pleaded guilty, repented and asked for forgiveness in accordance with article 14 of this Organic Law [article 60] after preparing a list of offenders who participated in the genocide and whose confession, guilty plea, repentance and request for forgiveness were accepted, shall be liable to a term of imprisonment ranging from eight (8) to nine (9) years;

3° who confessed, pleaded guilty, repented and requested for forgiveness in accordance with Article 60 of this Organic Law,[9] *before preparation of the list of offenders who participated in the genocide and whose confession, guilty plea, repentance and request for forgiveness were accepted, shall be liable to a term of imprisonment ranging from six (6) years and six (6) months to seven (7) years and six (6) months.*

Offender[s] falling in the second category referred to in points 1°, 2° and the 3° of article 9 of this Organic Law [article 51]:

1° who refused to confess, plead guilty, repent and ask for forgiveness or whose confession, guilty plea, repentance and request for forgiveness were rejected, shall be liable to a term of imprisonment ranging from ten (10) to fifteen (15) years;

2° who confessed, pleaded guilty, repented and asked for forgiveness after being put on the list of offenders shall be liable to a term of imprisonment ranging from six (6) years and six (6) months to seven (7) years and six (6) months, but shall:

a) serve a third (1/3) of the sentence in custody;

b) have a sixth (1/6) of the sentence suspended;

c) have half (1/2) of the sentence commuted into community service;

3° who confessed, pleaded guilty, repented and asked for forgiveness before being included on the list of offenders shall be liable to a term of imprisonment ranging from six (6) to seven (7) years, but shall:

a) serve a sixth (1/6) of the sentence in custody;

b) have a third (1/3) of the sentence suspended;

c) have half (1/2) of the sentence commuted into community service.

Offender[s] falling in the second category referred to in point 4° and 5° of article 9 of this Organic Law [article 51]:

1° who refused to confess, plead guilty, repent and ask for forgiveness, or whose confession, guilty plea, repentance and request for forgiveness were rejected, shall be liable to a term

[9] This is meant to refer to art 60 Organic Law No 16/2004, as amended by art 14 Organic Law No 13/2008.

of imprisonment ranging from four (4) years and six (6) months to five (5) years and six (6) months;

2° who confessed, pleaded guilty, repented and asked for forgiveness after being included on the list of offenders shall be liable to a term of imprisonment ranging from four (4) to five (5) years, but shall:

a) serve a third (1/3) of the sentence in custody;

b) have a sixth (1/6) of the sentence suspended;

c) have half (1/2) of the sentence commuted into community service;

3° who confessed, pleaded guilty, repented and asked for forgiveness before being included on the list of offenders and whose confession, guilty plea, repentance and request for forgiveness were accepted, shall be liable to a term of imprisonment ranging from two (2) years and six (6) months to three (3) years and six (6) months, but shall:

a) serve a sixth (1/6) of the sentence in custody;

b) have a third (1/3) of the sentence suspended;

c) have half (1/2) of the sentence commuted into community service;

Offender[s] falling in the second category point 6° of article 9 of this Organic Law [article 51]:

1° who refused to confess, plead guilty, repent and ask for forgiveness or whose confession, guilty plea, repentance and request for forgiveness were rejected, shall be liable to a term of imprisonment ranging from two (2) years and six (6) months to three (3) years and six (6) months but shall:

a) serve a third (1/3) of the sentence in custody;

b) have a sixth (1/6) of the sentence suspended;

c) have half (1/2) of the sentence commuted into community service.

2° who confessed, pleaded guilty, repented and asked for forgiveness after being included on the list for offenders shall be liable to a term of imprisonment ranging from one (1) year and six (6) months to two (2) years and six (6) months, but shall:

a) serve a third (1/3) of the sentence in custody;

b) have a sixth (1/6) of the sentence suspended;

c) have half (1/2) of the sentence commuted into community service;

3° who confessed, pleaded guilty, repented and asked for forgiveness before being included on the list of the offenders shall be liable to a term of imprisonment ranging from six (6) months to one (1) year and six (6) months, but shall:

a) serve a sixth (1/6) of the sentence in custody;

b) have a third (1/3) of the sentence suspended;

c) have half (1/2) of the sentence commuted into community service.

Article 79

Persons who were less than fourteen (14) years old, at the time of the charges against them, cannot be prosecuted, but they can be placed in special solidarity camps.

A Prime Minister's decree determines the modalities for conducting such solidarity camps.

Article 80 [as modified by article 17 Organic Law No 10/2007]

In case of default by the convicted person to properly carry out community service, the concerned person is taken back to prison to serve the remaining sentence in custody.

In that case, the Community Service Committee in the area where the convicted person is carrying out community service shall prepare an ad hoc report and submit it to the Gacaca Court of the Sector where community service is perlodged which will fill in the form to return the defaulting person to prison.

In case this is not possible, that report shall be submitted to the Gacaca Court that tried the person serving his or her community service.

A Presidential Order shall establish and determine modalities for carrying out community service.

Article 80 [as modified by article 21 Organic Law No 13/2008]

A person sentenced to both a custodial sentence and to serve community service shall first serve community service and if it is proved that the work was exemplary executed, then, the custodial sentence shall be commuted into community service.

However, when it is not possible to immediately start community service, time spent while waiting shall be taken into account when considering the period for a suspended sentence. This provision shall apply to persons sentenced by Gacaca Courts before coming into force of this Organic Law [No 13/2008].

When a person is sentenced to carry out community service or is on a suspended sentence ceases to perform to his or her expectation, the offender shall be taken to serve the remaining custodial sentence imposed by court.

When an offender has to be taken to prison to serve a term of imprisonment on account of bad behaviour, the committee for community service of the place where the offender was doing his or activities from, shall prepare a report about his or her conduct and submit it to the Gacaca court which tried the offender in the last instance or the Gacaca court of the same jurisdiction where community service is done or to the court of the Lower Instance Court if the Gacaca courts completed their activities for purposes of confirming the imprisonment.

When an offender has to be taken to prison to serve a term of imprisonment on account of the bad behaviour while serving a suspended sentence, the National Police shall prepare a report on his or her conduct and submit the same to the Prosecution Service which refers to it requesting the Gacaca Court which tried the concerned person in the last resort or the Gacaca Court of the place where he or she resides but with the same jurisdiction as the Gacaca Court which tried him or her in the last resort, or to the Lower Instance Court, if Gacaca Courts have completed their activities, which orders imprisonment.

A Presidential Order shall define and determine modalities for carrying out community service as an alternative penalty to imprisonment.

Article 81 [as modified by article 18 Organic Law No 10/2007]

While determining penalties, the sentence less than that provided for in the law can not be applied under the pretext of mitigating circumstances. However, in case such mitigating circumstances exist, the minimal sentence provided for shall be applied.

The person convicted of the crime of genocide who commenced serving the sentence, shall not be released on bail.

Article 81 [as modified by article 22 Organic Law No 13/2008]

While determining penalties, no sentence shall be passed that is lower than the minimum or higher than the maximum sentence provided for a particular offence under the pretext of mitigating factors. However, when mitigating factors do exist, a minimum or maximum sentence shall be passed provided for that offence.

CHAPTER FIVE: SUMMONS OF DEFENDANTS AND NOTIFICATION OF JUDGEMENTS

Article 82

The summons are issued by the secretary of the Gacaca Court, through the grassroots organs of where the defendant resides or to the authority of where he or she is detained.

The summoned person who refuses to appear is brought by means of the forces of law and order.

Article 83

At the closing of the hearing, the parties to the trial and the persons present in the hearing are informed of the day and the hour for the judgement pronouncement.

Article 84

When the judgement is pronounced, parties present in the trial affix their signatures or their fingerprints in the register of the pronounced judgement. If they are not satisfied with the Court rulings, the parties declare their intention to appeal and it is registered.

Judgement passed by default, as well as that pronounced in the defendant's absence, is legally notified by a written notification of judgement, which the secretary of the Court forwards to the defendant through the Coordinator of the Sector of where he/she resides or to the authority of where he/she is detained.

The judgement passed against a person who has neither known address nor residence in Rwanda, is notified in the same way as he or she was subpoenaed as it is prescribed by article 99 of this organic law.

CHAPTER SIX: MEANS OF APPEAL

Article 85

The means of appeal recognized by this organic law are the following: Opposition, Appeal and Review of judgement.

SECTION I: OBJECTION[10]

Article 86

The judgements passed by default under the provisions of this organic law, opposition may be made against.

The objection is brought before the Court which has passed the judgement at the first level. The petitioner registers it to the secretary of the Gacaca Court.

The opposition is only admissible if the defaulting party pleads a serious and legitimate reason which impeded him or her from appearing in the trial concerned. The Court shall assess the ground of admissibility, admit or reject it.

[10] In arts 41, 43, 66, and 86, 'objection' is used as a synonym for 'opposition'.

Article 87

The opposition period is fifteen (15) calendar days, starting from the day of the notification of judgement passed by default.

Article 88

The party making opposition who does not appear cannot petition for another opposition.

SECTION II: APPEAL

Article 89

Judgements relating to offences against property passed by the Gacaca Court of the Cell cannot be subject to appeal, but other cases are subject to appeal before the Gacaca Court of the Sector which gives a ruling in the last resort.

Judgments passed by the Gacaca Court of the Sector at first instance, are appealed against before the Gacaca Court of appeal which gives a ruling in the last resort.

Article 90 [as modified by article 19 Organic Law No 10/2007]

The defendant, plaintiff or any other interested person may appeal against a judgment passed by a Gacaca Court, in the interest of justice.

Article 91

The time of lodging an appeal is fifteen (15) calendar days, starting from the day the judgement is pronounced if it was passed by default, or starting from the day following the notification of judgement passed by default against which he or she did not make an opposition.[11] The case is judged in the same way as before.

Article 92

If the Gacaca Court to which an appeal is referred, finds that the appellant has been classified in an inaccurate category, it classifies him or her in the category corresponding to offences of which he or she is accused and tries him or her at first and last resort.

However, when it finds that he or she is classified into the first category, the Gacaca Court forwards the file to the Public Prosecution.

Article 92 [as modified by article 23 Organic Law No 13/2008]

When it appears to the last appellate Gacaca court handling the matter that an appellant was wrongly categorised, the same court shall put the appellant in the right category and try him or her as a first and last instance court.

However, when court finds that an appellant is in the first category point 1o and 2o, it shall submit his or her case file to the Public Prosecution.

SECTION III: REVIEW OF JUDGEMENT

Article 93 [as modified by article 20 Organic Law No 10/2007]

A judgement can be subject to review when:

1° a person was acquitted in a judgement passed in the last resort by an ordinary court, but is thereafter found guilty by a Gacaca Court;

[11] The English wording of this provision is incorrect. The first alternative is supposed to refer to judgments passed *in the presence* of the parties (see the French version: 'prononcé contradictoire du jugement').

2° a person was convicted in a judgement passed in the last resort by an ordinary court, but is thereafter found innocent by a Gacaca Court;

3° a judgement was passed in the last resort by a Gacaca Court, and later on there are new evidence proving contrary to what the initial judgment of that Gacaca Court was grounded;

4° a person was given a sentence that is contrary to legal provisions of the charges against him or her.

Persons entitled to lodge a review of the judgement are the defendant, the plaintiff or any other person acting in the interest of justice.

The Gacaca Court of Appeal is the only competent court to review judgements passed in the last resort.

Article 93 [as modified by article 24 Organic Law No 13/2008]

A case determined by a Gacaca court may be reviewed if:

1° it was determined at a last appellate[12] level of a Gacaca Court and later new evidence contradicting what was based on is discovered;

2° an accused was given a sentence that is inconsistent with the law.

An accused, victim or any person in the interest of justice may request for review of a case.

The Gacaca appeal court is the only competent court to review a case that was fully determined by another Gacaca court.

A case determined at a last appellate level by an ordinary or military court may also be reviewed by the same court.

CHAPTER SEVEN: COMPENSATION FOR DAMAGED PROPERTY AND OTHER FORMS

Article 94

Cases relating to damaged property shall be brought before the Gacaca Court of the Cell or other courts before which the defendants appear. However, such judgements shall not be appealed against.

Article 95

The reparation proceeds as follows:

1° Restitution of the property looted whenever possible;

2° Repayment of the ransacked property or carrying out the work worth the property to be repaired.

The Court rules on the methods and period of payment to be respected by each indebted person.

In case of default by the indebted person to honour his or her commitments, the execution of judgement is carried out under the forces of law and order.

[12] Contrary to what the wording suggests, review is not limited to appeals judgments. It was not intended to amend the provision to that effect. See the French version, which refers to 'jugement coulé en force' in the old as well as the new version.

Article 96

Other forms of compensation the victims receive shall be determined by a particular law.

TITLE IV: MISCELLANEOUS, TRANSITIONAL AND FINAL PROVISIONS

Article 97

The public action and penalties related to offences constituting the crime of genocide or crimes against humanity are imprescriptibly.

Article 97 [as modified by article 25 Organic Law No 13/2008]

Prosecution and punishment for the crimes related to genocide or crimes against humanity shall not be time-barred.

Crimes of genocide and other crimes against humanity identified after winding up and closure of Gacaca courts shall be prosecuted and tried by ordinary and military courts applying the Ordinary Rules of Procedure but without prejudice to application of special provisions provided for by Organic Law no16/2004 of 19/6/2004 establishing the organisation, competence and functioning of Gacaca Courts charged with prosecuting and trying the perpetrators of the crime of genocide and other crimes against humanity, committed between October 1, 1990 and December 31, 1994 as amended to date.

Subject to the matter being tried, provisions of Organic Law No16/2004 of 19/6/2004 establishing the organisation, competence and functioning of Gacaca Courts charged with prosecuting and trying the perpetrators of the crime of genocide and other crimes against humanity, committed between October 1, 1990 and December 31, 1994 as amended to date shall only apply.

Article 98

Courts dealing with cases of genocide and other crimes against humanity provided for by this organic law, can put to trial persons who have neither had address nor residence in Rwanda or who are outside Rwanda, if there are complementary evidences or serious guilt clues, whether they have previously been or not been crossexamined.

Article 99 [as modified by article 5 Organic Law No 28/2006]

If the defendant has neither known address nor residence in Rwanda, the summons' period is one month. The Secretary of the Gacaca Court or the Court Registar in person or with assistance from other organs displays a copy of the summons on the premises of the court which must try the case and on the offices of Districts, Provinces and of the City of Kigali.

The copy of the summons can only be displayed in public places intended for that purpose.

Trials for the persons so summoned, are brought before Gacaca Courts, in accordance with article 66 of the Organic Law no 16/2004 of 19/06/2004 establishing the organisation, competence and functioning of Gacaca courts charged with prosecuting and trying the perpetrators of the crime of genocide and other crimes against humanity, committed between October 1, 1990 and December 31, 1994, whereas before the Ordinary Courts, they follow the procedure provided for cases of defendants put to trial by default.

Article 100

The cases already forwarded to the courts before the publication of this organic law in the Official Gazette of the Republic of Rwanda, shall remain handled by the same courts.

Provisions provided for by the ordinary laws shall apply thereto, without prejudice to special provisions of this organic law. As for the subject of the action, those courts shall apply provisions of this organic law.

However, if it appears that the person prosecuted in that manner, is charged with codefendants who are in the same category, by the Gacaca Court, provisions of article 2 of this organic law shall apply.

Article 100 [as modified by article 26 Organic Law No 13/2008]

Genocide-related cases that are within the jurisdiction of Gacaca Courts which had been referred to ordinary and military courts for prosecution before publication of this Organic Law [No 13/2008] in the official gazette of the Republic of Rwanda shall be tried by Gacaca courts in the following manner:

1° cases before the Higher Instance and Military courts where no decision has been taken on a last appellate level, shall be tried in the first instance by the Sector Gacaca courts where the offence was committed;

2° Appeal cases before the High Court of the Republic and the Military High Court where no decision on a last appellate level has been taken, shall be tried by the Gacaca appeal court where the offence was committed;

Cases determined by the High court and Military court and time within which to lodge an appeal has not yet expired, shall be appealed and tried in the Gacaca appeal court where the offence was committed.

3° Cases before the Supreme Court and no final decision has been taken, shall be tried in the last instance by the Gacaca appeal Court where the offence was committed.

Cases heard by the High Court of Republic and the Military High Court and time within which to lodge an appeal has not yet expired, shall be tried and appealed against in the Gacaca appeal court where the offence was committed.

Cases referred to in point 3° of this Article shall not be subject to review.

Article 101

The National Service in charge of the follow up, supervision and coordination of the activities of Gacaca Courts shall establish rules and regulations on the way the organs of Gacaca Courts formerly set up by Organic Law no 40/2000 of January 26, 2001 organizing the prosecutions for offences constituting the crime of genocide and crimes against humanity, committed between October 1, 1990 and December 31, 1994, as modified and completed to date, are replaced by those set up by this organic law.

Article 102

Elections to replace a person of integrity who cannot continue with his or her duties, due to any reason, are conducted by the Coordination Committee of the Court which hosts those elections.

However, when there are persons of integrity of the list of deputies, they assume their duties following the order of the list, without any other restriction.

Article 103 [as modified by article 6 Organic Law No 28/2006]

Persons of integrity elected before the publication of this organic law [No 28/2006] continue their activities in Gacaca Courts as they appear on the appendix of this Organic Law [No 28/2006].

Article 104

Persons convicted by Gacaca Courts in conformity with articles 32 and 37 of the Organic Law no 40/200[0] of January 26, 2001 organising prosecutions for offences constituting the crime of genocide and crimes against humanity, committed between October 1, 1990 and December 31, 1994, as modified and completed to date, serve their sentences in accordance with the provisions of this organic law. Those who have already served at least six (6) months of imprisonment shall be released immediately after the publication of this organic law in the Official Gazette of the Republic of Rwanda.

Article 105

Organic law no 08/96 of August 30, 1996 organizing proceedings for offences constituting the crime of genocide and crimes against humanity committed from October 1, 1990 and organic law no 40/2000 of January 26, 2001 setting up Gacaca Courts and organizing prosecutions of offences constituting the crime of genocide and crimes against humanity, committed between October 1, 1990 and December 31, 1994, as modified and completed to-date, and all previous legal provisions contrary to this organic law, are hereby abrogated.

Article 106

This Organic Law comes into force on the date of its publication in the Official Gazette of the Republic Rwanda.

Kigali, on 19/6/2004
(signatures)

Glossary

(ach—Acholi, fr—French, kr—Kirundi, krw—Kinyarwanda, ksh—Kiswahili)

Abunzi	mediation committee (krw)
agacaca	grass, lawn (krw)
akazu	'little house'; circle of courtiers at the court of the king; core of the Hutu Power movement (krw)
Banyarwanda	'ethnic' Rwandan (krw, plural; singular: Munyarwanda)
Bashingantahe	mediator (kr, plural; singular: Mushingantahe)
cachot	dungeon, communal lock-up (fr)
ceceka	silence, keeping quiet (krw)
gacaca nkristu	Christian Gacaca (krw)
génocidaire	perpetrator of crimes during the genocide, suspect of such crimes (fr)
Ibuka	'remember', Rwandan victim organization (krw)
imidugudu	villages, lowest administrative entity (krw, plural; singular: umudugudu)
ingando	solidarity camp (krw)
inkiko gacaca	Gacaca courts, term for the modern Gacaca (krw, plural; singular: urukiko gacaca)
Interahamwe	'those who fight together', notorious militia backed by the government during the genocide (krw)
inyangamugayo	person of integrity, Gacaca judge, mediator (krw, singular, plural)
Kangura	'wake others up', magazine that fuelled ethnic hatred during between 1990 and 1994 (krw)
mato oput	'drinking a bitter drink from oput roots', restorative mechanism in Northern Uganda (ach)
minerval	secondary school fees (fr)
mwami	king (krw)
Nyumbakumi	group of 10 households, former lowest administrative entity in Rwanda (ksh)
nyumbakumi	leader of a group of 10 households (ksh)
rescapé	survivor of the genocide (fr)
tigiste	person serving community service (fr)
ubushingantahe	traditional mechanism for conflict resolution in Burundi (kr)

List of References

All websites were last visited in June 2011.

Books and Articles

Akehurst, M., 'Custom as a Source of International Law', 47 *British Yearbook of International Law* (1974/75), 1–53

Akhavan, P., 'Beyond Impunity: Can International Criminal Justice Prevent Future Atrocities?' 95 *American Journal of International Law* (2001), 7–31

Akilimali, A., 'Le TPIR comme un élément du retour à la réconciliation nationale, au rétablissement et au maintien de la paix: échecs et compromis', *Revue juridique du Rwanda* (2006) no 1, 164–89

Alie, J.A.D., 'Reconciliation and Traditional Justice: Tradition-Based Practices of the Kpaa Mende in Sierra Leone', in Huyse, L. and Salter, M. (eds), *Traditional Justice and Reconciliation after Violent Conflict: Learning from African Experiences* (Stockholm: IDEA, 2008), 123–46

Allen, T., 'The International Criminal Court and the Invention of Traditional Justice in Northern Uganda', 107 *Politique Africaine* (2007), 147–66

Alliot, M., 'Les résistance traditionnelles au droit moderne dans les Etats d'Afrique francophones et à Madagascar', in Poirier, J. (ed), *Etudes de droit africain et de droit malgache* (Paris: Editions Cujas, 1965), 235–56

Allott, A.N., 'African Law', in Derrett, J.D.M. (ed), *An Introduction to Legal Systems* (London: Sweet & Maxwell, 1968), 131–56

Alvarez, J.E., 'Crimes of States/Crimes of Hate: Lessons from Rwanda', 24 *Yale Journal of International Law* (1999), 365–483

Ambos, K., 'The Legal Framework of Transitional Justice: A Systematic Study with a Special Focus on the Role of the ICC', in Ambos, K., Large, J. and Wierda, M. (eds), *Building a Future on Peace and Justice: Studies on Transitional Justice, Peace and Development* (Berlin: Springer, 2009), 19–103

—— *Internationales Strafrecht: Strafanwendungsrecht – Völkerstrafrecht – Europäisches Strafrecht*, 2nd edn (München: C.H. Beck, 2008)

—— Malarino, E. and Elsner, G. (eds), *Jurisprudencia latinoamericana sobre derecho penal internacional* (Berlin: Konrad-Adenauer-Stiftung, 2008)

Amstutz, M.R., 'Is Reconciliation Possible after Genocide?: The Case of Rwanda', 48 *Journal of Church and State* (2006), 541–65

André, C., 'Terre rwandaise, accès, politique et réformes foncières', in Reyntjens, F. and Marysse, S. (eds), *L'Afrique des Grands Lacs: Annuaire 1997/1998* (Paris: L'Harmattan, 1998), 141–73

Antkowiak, T.M., 'Truth as Right and Remedy in International Human Rights Experience', 23 *Michigan Journal of International Law* (2002), 977–1013

Arendt, H., *Eichmann in Jerusalem: A Report on the Banality of Evil* (London: Faber and Faber, 1963)

Assmann, A., *Der lange Schatten der Vergangenheit: Erinnerungskultur und Geschichtspolitik* (München: C.H. Beck, 2006)

Baines, E.K., 'The Haunting of Alice: Local Approaches to Justice and Reconciliation in Northern Uganda', 1 *International Journal of Transitional Justice* (2007), 91–114

Baker, B., '"He Must Buy What He Stole and Then We Forgive": Restorative Justice in Rwanda and Sierra Leone', *Acta Juridica* (2007), 171–92

Barkan, E., *The Guilt of Nations: Restitution and Negotiating Historical Injustices* (Baltimore: John Hopkins University Press, 2000)

Bassiouni, M.C., *Introduction to International Criminal Law* (Ardsley: Transnational Publishers, 2003)

—— and Wise, E.M., *Aut dedere aut judicare: The Duty to Extradite or Prosecute in International Law* (Dordrecht: Martinus Nijhoff, 1995)

Bayer, H.-W., 'Der Ausschluß der Staatshaftung', in Mosler, H. (ed), *Haftung des Staates für rechtswidriges Verhalten seiner Organe: Länderberichte und Rechtsvergleichung* (Köln: Heymanns, 1967), 768–75

Behrendt, U.P., *Die Verfolgung des Völkermordes in Ruanda durch internationale und nationale Gerichte* (Berlin: Berliner Wissenschafts-Verlag, 2005)

——'The Prosecution of the Rwandan Genocide', in Werle, G. (ed), *Justice in Transition—Prosecution and Amnesty in South Africa and Germany* (Berlin: Berliner Wissenschafts-Verlag, 2006), 227–37

Boraine, A. and Levy, J. (eds), *The Healing of a Nation?* (Rondebosch/Cape Town: Justice in Transition, 1995)

Borland, R.M., 'The Gacaca Tribunals and Rwanda after Genocide: Effective Restorative Community Justice or Further Abuse of Human Rights?', 8 *Swords and Ploughshares: A Journal of International Affairs* (2003)

Braeckman, C., *L'enjeu congolais: L'Afrique centrale après Mobutu* (Paris: Fayard, 1999)

Brathwaite, J., *Crime, Shame and Reintegration* (Cambridge: Cambridge University Press, 1989)

—— 'Principles of Restorative Justice', in von Hirsch, A., Roberts, J., Bottoms, A.E., Roach, K. and Schiff, M. (eds), *Restorative Justice and Criminal Justice: Competing or Reconcilable Paradigms?* (Oxford: Hart Publishing, 2003), 1–20

—— 'Restorative Justice and De-Professionalization', 13 *The Good Society* (2004) no 1, 28–31

Brooks, R.E., 'The New Imperialism: Violence, Norms, and the "Rule of Law"', 101 *Michigan Law Review* (2002/03), 2275–340

Brounéus, K., 'Truth-Telling as Talking Cure? Insecurity and Retraumatization in the Rwandan Gacaca Courts', 39 *Security Dialogue* (2008), 55–76

Brownlie, I., *Principles of Public International Law*, 7th edn (Oxford: Oxford University Press, 2008)

Bubenzer, O., *Post-TRC Prosecutions in South Africa: Accountability for Political Crimes after the Truth and Reconciliation Commission's Amnesty Process* (Leiden: Martinus Nijhoff, 2009)

Buckley-Zistel, S., '"The Truth Heals"? Gacaca Jurisdictions and the Consolidation of Peace in Rwanda', 80 *Friedenswarte* (2005), 113–29

—— 'Remembering to Forget: Chosen Amnesia as a Strategy for Local Coexistence in Post-Genocide Rwanda', 76 *Africa: The Journal of the International African Institute* (2006), 131–50

—— 'Frieden entwickeln? Eine kritische Analyse der Strategien der Internaitonal Gebergemeinschaft zur Friedenskonsolidierung in Ruanda', 25 *Sicherheit und Frieden* (2007), 77–81

—— 'We Are Pretending Peace: Local Memory and the Absence of Social Transformation and Reconciliation in Rwanda', in Clark, P. and Kaufman, Z.D. (eds), *After Genocide: Transitional Justice, Post-Conflict Reconstruction and Reconciliation in Rwanda and Beyond* (London: Hurst & Co., 2008), 125–43

Bundesminister der Finanzen and Schwartz, W. (eds), *Die Wiedergutmachung nationalsozialistischen Unrechts durch die Bundesrepublik Deutschland*, vol III (München: C.H. Beck, 1985)

Burgess, P., 'A New Approach to Restorative Justice—East Timor's Community Reconciliation Processes', in Roht-Arriaza, N. and Mariezcurrena, J. (eds), *Transitional Justice in the Twenty-First Century: Beyond Truth versus Justice* (Cambridge: Cambridge University Press, 2006), 176–205

Burghardt, B., *Die Vorgesetztenverantwortlichkeit im völkerrechtlichen Straftatsystem: Eine Untersuchung zur Rechtsprechung der internationalen Strafgerichthöfe für das ehemalige Jugoslawien und Ruanda* (Berlin: Berliner Wissenschafts-Verlag, 2008)

Burnet, J.E., 'The Injustice of Local Justice: Truth, Reconciliation, and Revenge in Rwanda', 3 *Genocide Studies and Prevention* (2008), 173–93

Busingye, J., *Reality and Challenges of Legal and Judicial Reconstruction in Rwanda* (Presentation given at a seminar hosted by the Center for International Legal Cooperation, The Hague, 7 December 2006), available at <http://www.cilc.nl/Post_Conflict_Situations.pdf>

Capellà i Roig, M., 'Jurisdicciones *gacaca*: Una solución local al genocidio ruandés', 56 *Revista Española de Derecho Internacional* (2004), 765–76

Cassel, D., 'The Expanding Scope and Impact of Reparations Awarded by the Inter-American Court of Human Rights', in De Feyter, K., Parmentier, S., Bossuyt, M. and Lemmens, P. (eds), *Out of the Ashes: Reparation for Victims of Gross and Systematic Human Rights Violations* (Antwerpen: Intersentia, 2005), 191–223

Cassese, A. 'Crimes against Humanity', in Cassese, A., Gaeta, P. and Jones, J.R.W.D. (eds), *The Rome Statute of the International Criminal Court: A Commentary*, vol I (Oxford: Oxford University Press, 2002), 353–78

—— *International Criminal Law*, 2nd edn (Oxford: Oxford University Press, 2008)

Chakravarty, A., 'Gacaca Courts in Rwanda: Explaining Divisions within the Human Rights Community', 1 *Yale Journal of International Affairs* (2005/06) no 2, 132–45

Chalk, F., 'Hate Radio in Rwanda', in Adelman, H. and Suhrke, A. (eds), *The Path of Genocide: The Rwanda Crisis from Uganda to Zaire* (New Brunswick: Transaction Publishers, 1999), 93–107

Chrétien, J.-P., 'Hutu et Tutsi au Rwanda et au Burundi', in Amselle, J.-L. and M'Bokolo, E. (eds), *Au cœur de l'ethnie: ethnie, tribalsme et état en Afrique* (Paris: Editions La Découverte, 1985), 129–65

—— '"Presse libre" et propagande raciste au Rwanda: Kangura et "les 10 commandements du Hutu"', 42 *Politique Africaine* (1992), 109–20

—— *Rwanda: Les médias du génocide* (Paris: Karthala, 1995)

Christie, N., 'Conflicts as Property', 17 *British Journal of Criminology* (1977), 1–15

Clapham, A., *Human Rights Obligations of Non-State Actors* (Oxford: Oxford University Press, 2006)

Clark, P., 'Hybridity, Holism, and "Traditional" Justice: The Case of the *Gacaca* Courts in Post-Genocide Rwanda', 39 *The Georgetown Washington International Law Review* (2007), 765–837

—— 'The Rules (and Politics) of Engagement: The *Gacaca* Courts and Post-Genocide Justice, Healing and Reconciliation in Rwanda', in Clark, P. and Kaufman, Z.D. (eds), *After Genocide: Transitional Justice, Post-Conflict Reconstruction and Reconciliation in Rwanda and Beyond* (London: Hurst & Co., 2008), 297–319

—— *The Gacaca Courts, Post-Genocide Justice and Reconciliation in Rwanda: Justice Without Lawyers* (Cambridge: Cambridge University Press, 2010)

Cohen, S., *States of Denial: Knowing about Atrocities and Suffering* (Cambridge: Polity Press, 2001)

Colvin, C.J., 'Overview of the Reparations Program in South Africa', in de Greiff, P. (ed), *The Handbook of Reparations* (Oxford: Oxford University Press, 2006), 176–214

Corey, A. and Joireman, S.F., 'Retributive Justice: The *Gacaca* Courts in Rwanda', 103 *African Affairs* (2004), 73–89

Cousineau, M., 'L'établissement de l'Etat de droit au Rwanda: un but irréalisable', 28 *Ottawa Law Review* (1997), 171–90

Cryer, R., Friman, H., Robinson, D. and Wilmshurst, E., *An Introduction to International Criminal Law and Procedure* (Cambridge: Cambridge University Press, 2007)

Daly, E., 'Transformative Justice: Charting a Path to Reconciliation', 12 *International Legal Perspective* (2001/02), 73–183

—— 'Between Punitive and Reconstructive Justice: The Gacaca Courts in Rwanda', 34 *New York University Journal of International Law & Politics* (2002), 355–96

Damgaard, C., *Individual Criminal Responsibility for Core International Crimes: Selected Pertinent Issues* (Berlin: Springer, 2008)

d'Argent, P., *Les réparations de guerre en droit international public: la responsabilité internationale des Etats à l'épreuve de la guerre* (Bruxelles/Paris: Bruylant/L.G.D.J., 2002)

Day, M., 'Alternative Dispute Resolution and Customary Law: Resolving Property Disputes in Post-Conflict Nations, a Case Study of Rwanda', 16 *Georgetown Immigration Law Journal* (2001/02), 235–56

De Beer, D., *Loi rwandaise du 30 août 1996 sur l'organisation des poursuites des infractions constitutives du crime de génocide ou de crimes contre l'humanité: Commentaire et jurisprudence*, 2nd edn (Kigali: Alter Egaux Editions, 1999)

de Greiff, P., 'Justice and Reparations', in de Greiff, P. (ed), *The Handbook of Reparations* (Oxford: Oxford University Press, 2006), 451–77

Delmas-Marty, M., 'Le crime contre l'humanité, les droits de l'homme, et l'irréductible humain', *Revue de science criminelle et de droit pénal comparé* (1994), 477–90

Des Forges, A., *Leave None to Tell the Story: Genocide in Rwanda* (New York: Human Rights Watch, 1999)

—— and Longman, T., 'Legal Responses to Genocide in Rwanda', in Stover, E. and Weinstein, H.M. (eds), *My Neighbor, My Enemy: Justice and Community in the Aftermath of Mass Atrocity* (Cambridge: Cambridge University Press, 2004), 49–68

Deslaurier, C., 'Le "bushingantahe" peut-il réconcilier le Burundi?', 92 *Politique Africaine* (2003), 76–96

Desrosiers, M.-E., 'Quand justice et réconciliation ne font qu'un: Les juridictions Gacaca au Rwanda', in Conoir, Y. and Verna, G. (eds), *Faire la paix: Concepts et pratiques de la consolidation de la paix* (Saint-Nicolas: Les Presse de l'Université Laval, 2005), 115–37

Dexter, T. and Ntahombaye, P., *The Role of Informal Justice Systems in Fostering the Rule of Law in Post-Conflict Situations: The Case of Burundi* (Geneva: Centre for Humanitarian Dialogue, 2005), available at <http://www.hdcentre.org/files/Burundi%20report.pdf>

Digneffe, F. and Fierens, J. (eds), *Justice et gacaca: L'expérience rwandaise et le génocide* (Namur: Presses universitaires de Namur, 2003)

Dlamini, C.R.M., 'The Effects of Customs, Religions and Traditions on the Right to a Fair Trial in Africa', 33 *The Comparative and International Law Journal of Southern Africa* (2000), 318–32

Douglas, L., *The Memory of Judgment: Making Law and History in the Trials of the Holocaust* (New Haven: Yale University Press, 2001)

Drumbl, M.A., 'Rule of Law amid Lawlessness: Counseling the Accused in Rwanda's Domestic Genocide Trials', 29 *Columbia Human Rights Law Review* (1998), 545–639

—— 'Punishment, Postgenocide: From Guilt to Shame to *Civis* in Rwanda', 75 *New York University Law Review* (2000), 1221–326

—— 'Sclerosis: Retributive Justice and the Rwandan Genocide', 2 *Punishment & Society* (2000), 287–308

—— 'The (Al)lure of the Genocide Trial: Justice, Reconciliation, and Reconstruction in Rwanda', in Barnhizer, D. (ed), *Effective Strategies for Protecting Human Rights: Economic Sanctions, Use of National Courts and International Fora and Coercive Power* (Aldershot: Ashgate, 2001), 217–34

—— 'Law and Atrocity: Settling Accounts in Rwanda', 31 *Ohio Northern University Law Review* (2005), 41–74

—— *Atrocity, Punishment, and International Law* (Cambridge: Cambridge University Press, 2007)

Du Bois-Pedain, A., *Transitional Amnesty in South Africa* (Cambridge: Cambridge University Press, 2007)

Elias, T.O., *The Nature of African Customary Law* (Manchester: Manchester University Press, 1956)

Ellicott, K. (ed), *Countries of the World and Their Leaders: Yearbook 2007*, vol 2 (Detroit: Thomson Gale, 2006)

Eltringham, N., *Accounting for Horror: Post-Genocide Debates in Rwanda* (London: Pluto Press, 2004)

Eörsi, G., 'Private and Governmental Liability for the Torts of Employees and Organs', in Tunc, A. (ed), *International Encyclopedia of Comparative Law*, vol XI (Torts), Part 1 (Tübingen: Mohr, 1983), chapter 4

Eser, A., 'Individual Criminal Responsibility', in Cassese, A., Gaeta, P. and Jones, J.R.W.D. (eds), *The Rome Statute of the International Criminal Court: A Commentary*, vol I (Oxford: Oxford University Press, 2002), 767–948

Feliciati, C.C., 'Restorative Justice for the Girl-Child in Post-Conflict Rwanda', 7 *International Women's Studies* (2006) no 4, 14–35

Fernandez, L., 'Reparation for Human Rights Violations Committed by the *Apartheid* Regime in South Africa', in Randelzhofer, A. and Tomuschat, C. (eds), *State Responsibility and the Individual: Reparation in Instances of Grave Violations of Human Rights* (The Hague: Martinus Nijhoff, 1999), 173–87

—— 'Post-TRC Prosecutions in South Africa', in Werle, G. (ed), *Justice in Transition—Prosecution and Amnesty in South Africa and Germany* (Berlin: Berliner Wissenschafts-Verlag, 2006), 65–81

Ferstman, C.J., 'Domestic Trials for Genocide and Crimes against Humanity: The Example of Rwanda', 9 *African Journal of International and Comparative Law* (1997), 857–77

Fierens, J., '*Gacaca* Courts: Between Fantasy and Reality', 3 *Journal of International Criminal Justice* (2005), 896–919

Fink, J.B., 'Deontological Retributivism and the Legal Practice of International Jurisprudence: The Case of the International Criminal Tribunal for Rwanda', 49 *Journal of African Law* (2005), 101–31

Fletcher, G.P., *The Grammar of Criminal Law: American, Comparative, and International*, vol 1: Foundations (Oxford: Oxford University Press, 2007)

—— *Tort Liability for Human Rights Abuses* (Oxford: Hart Publishing, 2008)

Fomété, J.-P., 'Countdown to 2010: A Critical Overview of the Completion Strategy of the International Criminal Tribunal for Rwanda (ICTR)', in Decaux, E., Dieng, A. and Sow, M. (eds), *From Human Rights to International Criminal Law: Studies in Honour of an African Jurist, the Late Judge Laïty Kama* (Leiden: Martinus Nijhoff, 2007), 345–400

Friese, S., *Politik der gesellschaftlichen Versöhnung: Eine theologisch-ethische Untersuchung am Beispiel der Gacaca-Gerichte in Ruanda* (Stuttgart: Kohlhammer, 2010)

Frowein, J.A. and Peukert, W., *EMRK-Kommentar*, 2nd edn (Kehl: N.P. Engel, 1996)

Gabisirege, S. and Babalola, S., *Perceptions About the Gacaca Law in Rwanda: Evidence from a Multi-Method Study* (Baltimore: John Hopkins University, Center for Communication Programs, 2001), available at <http://www.jhuccp.org/node/1095>

Gahima, G., 'Alternatives to Prosecution: The Case of Rwanda', in Hughes, E., Schabas, W.A. and Thakur, R. (eds), *Atrocities and International Accountability: Beyond Transitional Justice* (Tokyo: United National University Press, 2007), 159–81

Gakwaya, J., *Les moyens d'adéquation de la peine en droit rwandais* (Butare: Université Nationale du Rwanda, 1993)

—— *Les sanctions pénales en droit rwandais: Contribution à la recherche de leur efficacité* (Butare: Université Nationale du Rwanda, 1993)

—— 'Utilisation erronée de l'institution du Gacaca dans la recherche d'une solution au génocide rwandais', 4 *Revue de Droit Africain: doctrine et jurisprudence* (2000), 226–41

Gaparayi, I.T., 'Justice and Social Reconstruction in the Aftermath of Genocide in Rwanda: An Evaluation of the Possible Role of the Gacaca Tribunals', 1 *African Human Rights Law Journal* (2001), 78–106

Gasibirege, S., 'L'élection des juges inyangamugayo: rupture ou continuité?', in Ntaganda, E. (ed), *De la paix à la justice: les enjeux de la réconciliation nationale, Cahiers du Centre de Gestion des Conflits no 6* (Butare: Editions de l'Université Nationale du Rwanda, 2002), 93–127

Gattini, A., 'Breach of the Obligation to Prevent and Reparation Thereof in the ICJ's Genocide Judgment', 18 *European Journal of International Law* (2007), 695–713

—— 'Evidentiary Issues in the ICJ's *Genocide* Judgment', 5 *Journal of International Criminal Justice* (2007), 889–904

Ghandhi, P.R., *The Human Rights Committee and the Right to Individual Communication: Law and Practice* (Aldershot: Ashgate, 1998)

Goldstein Bolocan, M., 'Rwandan Gacaca: An Experiment in Transitional Justice', *Journal of Dispute Resolution* (2004), 355–400

González Cueva, E., 'The Peruvian Truth and Reconciliation Commission and the Challenge of Impunity', in Roht-Arriaza, N. and Mariezcurrena, J. (eds), *Transitional Justice in the Twenty-First Century: Beyond Truth versus Justice* (Cambridge: Cambridge University Press, 2006), 70–93

Gourevitch, P., *We Wish to Inform You That Tomorrow We Will Be Killed With Our Families* (New York: Picador, 1998)

Groninger, K., Bakansanga, A., Mukansoro, E., Kumpf, B. and Rieder, H., *Gacaca and Trauma: Psychosocial Guidance for Trauma Victims in Rwanda* (Kigali: Ibuka et al., 2007), available at <http://www.opsiconsult.com/publications.php>

Guerrero Orozco, J. and Goetz, M., 'Reparations for Victims in Colombia: Colombia's Law on Justice and Peace', in Ferstman, C., Goetz, M. and Stephens, A. (eds), *Reparations for Victims of Genocide, War Crimes and Crimes Against Humanity: Systems in Place and Systems in the Making* (Leiden: Martinus Nijhoff, 2009), 435–58

Haan, V., 'The Development of the Concept of Joint Criminal Enterprise at the International Criminal Tribunal for the Former Yugoslavia', 5 *International Criminal Law Review* (2005), 167–201

Hafner, D.L. and King, E.B.L., 'Beyond Traditional Notions of Transitional Justice: How Trials, Truth Commissions, and Other Tools for Accountability Can and Should Work Together', 30 *Boston College International and Comparative Law Review* (2007), 91–109

Hamber, B., 'Reparations as Symbol: Narratives of Resistance, Reticence, and Possibility in South Africa', in Miller, J. and Kumar, R. (eds), *Reparations: Interdisciplinary Inquiries* (Oxford: Oxford University Press, 2007), 252–79

Hamdorf, K., *Beteiligungsmodelle im Strafrecht: Ein Vergleich von Teilnahme- und Einheitstätersystemen in Skandinavien, Österreich und Deutschland* (Freiburg im Breisgau: Edition Iuscrim, 2002)

Hankel, G., '"Wir möchten, dass ihr uns verzeiht". Die Anfänge der Gacaca-Justiz in Ruanda', in Paech, N. (ed), *Völkerrecht statt Machtpolitik, Beiträge für Gerhard Stuby* (Hamburg: VSA-Verlag, 2004), 358–71

—— 'Justice in Transition—The Case of Rwanda', in Werle, G. (ed), *Justice in Transition—Prosecution and Amnesty in South Africa and Germany* (Berlin: Berliner Wissenschafts-Verlag, 2006), 175–83

—— 'An der Realität vorbei: Ruanda, dreizehn Jahre nach dem Völkermord', 43 *Der Überblick: Zeitschrift für ökumenische Begegnung und internationale Zusammenarbeit* (2007) nos 1/2, 78–87

—— 'Verordnete Versöhnung: Warum die Gacaca-Justiz in Ruanda gescheitert ist', 65 *Internationale Politik* (2007) no 1, 43–7

Harpster, E., 'Rwanda and the Problem of Peace', 2 *The American Undergraduate Journal of Politics & Government* (2002) no 1, 48–60

Harrell, P.E., *Rwanda's Gamble: Gacaca and a New Model of Transitional Justice* (New York: Writers Club Press, 2003)

Hayner, P.B., 'Fifteen Truth Commission—1974 to 1994: A Comparative Study', 16 *Human Rights Quarterly* (1994), 597–655

—— *Unspeakable Truths: Confronting State Terror and Atrocity* (New York: Routledge, 2001)

Hofmann, R., 'Victims of Violations of International Humanitarian Law: Do They Have an Individual Right to Reparation against States under International Law?', in Dupuy, P.-M., Fassbender, B., Shaw, M.N. and Sommermann, K.P. (eds), *Common Values in International Law: Essays to the Honour of Christian Tomuschat* (Kehl: N.P. Engel, 2006), 341–59

Honeyman, C., *Gacaca Jurisdictions: Transitional Justice in Rwanda: Observations from June 10–August 8, 2002* (Cambridge: Harvard University, 2002), available at <http://www.convenor.com/madison/PDF_Gacaca_Report.pdf>

—— Hudani, S., Tiruneh, A., Hierta, J., Chirayath, L., Iliff, A. and Meierhenrich, J., 'Establishing Collective Norms: Potentials for Participatory Justice in Rwanda', 10 *Peace and Conflict: Journal of Peace Psychology* (2004), 1–24

Huyse, L., 'Introduction: Tradition-Based Approaches in Peacemaking, Transitional Justice and Reconciliation Policies', in Huyse, L. and Salter, M. (eds), *Traditional Justice and Reconciliation after Violent Conflict: Learning from African Experiences* (Stockholm: IDEA, 2008), 1–22

Ingelaere, B., 'The Gacaca Courts in Rwanda', in Huyse, L. and Salter, M. (eds), *Traditional Justice and Reconciliation after Violent Conflict: Learning from African Experiences* (Stockholm: IDEA, 2008), 25–59

—— '"Does the Truth Pass Across the Fire Without Burning?" Locating the Short Circuit in Rwanda's Gacaca Courts', 47 *Journal of Modern African Studies* (2009), 507–28

Ironside, P., 'Rwandan *Gacaca*: Seeking Alternative Means to Justice, Peace and Reconciliation', 15 *New York International Law Review* (2002) no 2, 31–60

Jenkins, C., 'Taking Apology Seriously', in du Plessis, M. and Peté, S. (eds), *Repairing the Past? International Perspectives on Reparations for Gross Human Rights Abuses* (Antwerpen: Intersentia, 2007), 53–81

Jescheck, H.-H., 'The General Principles of International Criminal Law Set out in Nuremberg, as Mirrored in the ICC Statute', 2 *Journal of International Criminal Justice* (2004), 38–55

Jones, N.A., *The Courts of Genocide: Politics and the Rule of Law in Rwanda and Arusha* (Oxford: Routledge, 2010)

Kagame, A., *Un abrégé de l'histoire du Rwanda de 1853 à 1972*, vol 2 (Butare: Editions Universitaire du Rwanda, 1975)

Kamatali, J.M., 'The Challenge of Linking International Criminal Justice and National Reconciliation: The Case of the ICTR', 16 *Leiden Journal of International Law* (2003), 112–33

Karekezi, U.A., 'Juridictions Gacaca: Lutte contre l'impunité et promotion de la réconciliation nationale', in Ntaganda, E. (ed), *Les juridictions Gacaca et les processus de réconciliation nationale, Cahiers du Centre de Gestion des Conflits no 3* (Butare: Editions de l'Université Nationale du Rwanda, 2001), 9–96

—— Nshimiyimana, A. and Mutamba, B., 'Localizing Justice: Gacaca Courts in Post-Genocide Rwanda', in Stover, E. and Weinstein, H.M. (eds), *My Neighbor, My Enemy: Justice and Community in the Aftermath of Mass Atrocity* (Cambridge: Cambridge University Press, 2004), 69–84

Kienapfel, D., *Der Einheitstäter im Strafrecht* (Frankfurt am Main: Klostermann, 1971)

Kirkby, C., 'Rwanda's *Gacaca* Courts: A Preliminary Critique', 50 *Journal of African Law* (2006), 94–117

Kirs, E., 'Introduction and Critical Remarks Regarding the *Gacaca* System in Rwanda', 5 *Miskolc Journal of International Law* (2008) no 1, 50–6

Kitereza, A., *Mr. Myombekere and His Wife Bugonoka, Their Son Ntulanalwo and Daughter Bulihwali: The Story of an Ancient African Community* (Dar es Salaam: Mkuki na Nyota Publishers, 2002)

Klein, E., 'Individual Reparation Claims under the International Covenant on Civil and Political Rights: The Practice of the Human Rights Committee', in Randelzhofer, A. and Tomuschat, C. (eds), *State Responsibility and the Individual: Reparation in Instances of Grave Violations of Human Rights* (The Hague: Martinus Nijhoff, 1999), 27–41

Kritz, N.J., 'Coming to Terms with Atrocities: A Review of Accountability Mechanisms for Mass Violations of Human Rights', 59 *Law and Contemporary Problems* (1996) no 4, 127–52

—— 'Progress and Humility: The Ongoing Search for Post-Conflict Justice', in Bassiouni, M.C. (ed), *Post-Conflict Justice* (Ardsley: Transnational Publishers, 2002), 55–87

Kroker, P., 'Auf gutem Weg: Die Verfahren vor dem Rote-Khmer-Tribunal in Kambodscha', 122 *Zeitschrift für die gesamte Strafrechtswissenschaft* (2010), 685–705

—— 'Transitional Justice Policy in Practice: Victim Participation in the *Khmer Rouge* Tribunal', 53 *German Yearbook of International Law* (2011), 753–92

LaFave, W.R., *Criminal Law*, 4th edn (St Paul: Thomson West, 2003)

Latigo, J.O., 'Northern Uganda: Tradition-Based Practices in the Acholi Region', in Huyse, L. and Salter, M. (eds), *Traditional Justice and Reconciliation after Violent Conflict: Learning from African Experiences* (Stockholm: IDEA, 2008), 85–120

Laufhütte, H.W., Rissing-van Saan, R. and Tiedemann, K. (eds), *Leipziger Kommentar StGB*, vol 1, 12th edn (Berlin: De Gruyter Recht, 2006)

Lehmann-Richter, A., *Auf der Suche nach den Grenzen der Wiedergutmachung: Die Rechtsprechung zur Entschädigung für Opfer der nationalsozialistischen Verfolgung* (Berlin: Berliner Wissenschafts-Verlag, 2007)

Lemarchand, R., *Rwanda and Burundi* (London: Pall Mall Press, 1970)

—— 'Rwanda: The Rationality of Genocide', 23 *Issue: A Journal of Opinion* (1995) no 2, 8–11

—— and Martin, D., *Selective Genocide in Burundi*, London: Minority Rights Group, 1974

Le Mon, C.J., 'Rwanda's Troubled Gacaca Courts', 14 *Human Rights Brief* (2007) Issue 2, 16–20

Lin, O., 'Demythologizing Restorative Justice: South Africa's Truth and Reconciliation Commission and Rwanda's Gacaca Courts in Context', 12 *ILSA Journal of International and Comparative Law* (2005/06), 41–85

Lira, E., 'The Reparations Policy for Human Rights Violations in Chile', in de Greiff, P. (ed), *The Handbook of Reparations* (Oxford: Oxford University Press, 2006), 55–101

Lohse, V., 'Bashingantahe—Traditionelle Gerichte in Burundi mit unterbrochener Tradition', 36 *Verfassung und Recht in Übersee* (2003), 590–609

Lollini, A., 'L'istituzione delle giurisdizioni *Gacaca*: giustizia post-genocidio e processo costituente in Ruanda', *Diritto pubblico comparato ed europeo* (2004), 1513–41

Longman, T., 'The Complex Reasons for Rwanda's Engagement in Congo', in Clark, J.F. (ed), *The African Stakes of the Congo War* (New York: Palgrave Macmillan, 2002), 129–44

—— 'Justice at the Grassroots? Gacaca Trials in Rwanda', in Roht-Arriaza, N. and Mariezcurrena, J. (eds), *Transitional Justice in the Twenty-First Century: Beyond Truth versus Justice* (Cambridge: Cambridge University Press, 2006), 206–28

Lutz, E., Transitional Justice: Lessons Learned and the Road Ahead, in Roht-Arriaza, N. and Mariezcurrena, J. (eds), *Transitional Justice in the Twenty-First Century: Beyond Truth versus Justice* (Cambridge: Cambridge University Press, 2006), 325–41

Lykes, M.B. and Mersky, M., 'Reparations and Mental Health: Psychological Interventions towards Healing, Human Agency, and Rethreading Social Realities', in de Greiff, P. (ed), *The Handbook of Reparations* (Oxford: Oxford University Press, 2006), 589–622

McEvoy, K., 'Letting Go of Legalism: Developing a 'Thicker' Version of Transitional Justice', in McEvoy, K. and McGregor, L. (eds), *Transitional Justice from Below: Grassroots Activism and the Struggle for Change* (Oxford: Hart Publishing, 2008), 15–45

McGregor, H., 'Personal Injury and Death', in Tunc, A. (ed), *International Encyclopedia of Comparative Law*, vol XI (Torts), Part 2 (Tübingen: Mohr, 1986), chapter 9

Magnarella, P.J., 'The Background and Causes of the Genocide in Rwanda', 3 *Journal of International Criminal Justice* (2005), 801–22

Magsam, D., 'Coming to Terms with Genocide in Rwanda: The Role of International and National Justice', in Kaleck, W. (ed), *International Prosecution of Human Rights Crimes* (Berlin: Springer, 2007), 159–65

Makoroka, S., 'La justice de droit écrit: lutte contre l'impunité au Burundi et dans la région des Grands Lacs', in de Lespinay, C. and Mworoka, E. (eds), *Construire l'Etat de droit: Le Burundi et la région des grands Lacs* (Paris: L'Harmattan, 2000), 95–120

Malamud-Goti, J.E. and Grosman, L.S., 'Reparations and Civil Litigation: Compensation for Human Rights Violations in Transitional Democracies', in de Greiff, P. (ed), *The Handbook of Reparations* (Oxford: Oxford University Press, 2006), 539–59

Mamdani, M., *When Victims Become Killers: Colonialism, Nativism, and the Genocide in Rwanda* (Princeton: Princeton University Press, 2001)

—— 'African States, Citizenship and War: A Case-Study', 78 *International Affairs* (2002), 493–506

Manacorda, S., 'Culpability', in Cassese, A. (ed), *The Oxford Companion to International Criminal Justice* (Oxford: Oxford University Press, 2009), 288–9

Megwalu, A. and Loizides, N., 'Dilemmas of Justice and Reconciliation: Rwandans and the Gacaca Courts', 18 *African Journal of International and Comparative Law* (2010), 1–23

Melvern, L., *A People Betrayed: The Role of the West in Rwanda's Genocide* (London: Zed Books, 2000)

Méndez, J.E., 'The Right to Truth', in Joyner, C.C. (ed), *Reining in Impunity for International Crimes and Serious Violations of Fundamental Human Rights: Proceedings of the Siracusa Conference 17–21 September 1998*, (Ramonville St-Agne: Erès, 1998), 255–78

—— and Mariezcurrena, J., 'Accountability for Past Human Rights Violations: Contributions of the Inter-American Organs of Protection', 26 *Social Justice* (1999) no 4, 84–106

Meron, T., *Human Rights and Humanitarian Norms as Customary Law* (Oxford: Clarendon Press, 1989)

Meyerstein, A., 'Between Law and Culture: Rwanda's *Gacaca* and Postcolonial Legality', 32 *Law & Social Inquiry* (2007), 467–508

Mgbako, C., '*Ingando* Solidarity Camps: Reconciliation and Political Indoctrination in Post-Genocide Rwanda', 18 *Harvard Human Rights Journal* (2005), 201–24

Mibenge, C., 'Enforcing International Humanitarian Law at the National Level: The *Gacaca* Jurisdictions of Rwanda', in McCormack, T.L.H. (ed), *Yearbook of International Humanitarian Law*, vol 7, 2004 (The Hague: TMC Asser Press, 2006), 410–24

Minow, M., *Between Vengeance and Forgiveness: Facing History After Genocide and Mass Violence* (Boston: Beacon Press, 1998)

Molenaar, A., *Gacaca: Grassroots Justice after Genocide. The Key to Reconciliation in Rwanda?* (Leiden: African Studies Centre, 2005)

Morrill, C.F., 'Reconciliation and the *Gacaca*: The Perceptions and Peace-Building Potential of Rwandan Youth Detainees', 6 *The Online Journal of Peace and Conflict Resolution* (2004), Issue 1, 1–66, available at <http://www.trinstitute.org/ojpcr/6_1morrill1.pdf>

Morris, M.H., 'The Trials of Concurrent Jurisdiction: The Case of Rwanda', 7 *Duke Journal of Comparative & International Law* (1997), 349–74

Morris, V. and Scharf, M.P., *The International Criminal Tribunal for Rwanda*, vol 1 (Irvington-on-Hudson: Transnational Publishers, 1998)

Mucyo, J., '*Gacaca* Courts and Genocide', in Villa-Vicencio, C. and Savage, T. (eds), *Rwanda and South Africa in Dialogue: Addressing the Legacies of Genocide and a Crime Against Humanity* (Cape Town: Institute for Justice and Reconciliation, 2001), 49–54

Mujuzi, J.D., 'Steps Taken in Rwanda's Efforts to Qualify for the Transfer of Accused from the ICTR', 8 *Journal of International Criminal Justice* (2010), 237–48

Münkler, H., *Die neuen Kriege* (Reinbek bei Hamburg: Rowohlt, 2002)

Murerwa, S., Veldman, M. and Lankhorst, M., 'An Insight into *Abunzi* Justice', in *Kaléidoscope…, Bulletin no 31* (Bruxelles, RCN Justice & Démocracie, 2010), 9–11

Murithi, T., 'African Approaches to Building Peace and Social Solidarity', 6 *African Journal on Conflict Resolution* (2006) no 2, 9–33

Nagy, R., 'Traditional Justice and Legal Pluralism in Transitional Context: The Case of Rwanda's Gacaca Courts', in Quinn, J.R. (ed), *Reconciliation(s): Transitional Justice in Postconflict Societies* (Montreal: McGill-Queen's University Press, 2009), 86–115

Naniwe-Kaburahe, A., 'The Institution of Bashingantahe in Burundi', in Huyse, L. and Salter, M. (eds), *Traditional Justice and Reconciliation after Violent Conflict: Learning from African Experiences* (Stockholm: IDEA, 2008), 149–79

Nantulya, P.E., 'The Gacaca System in Rwanda', *Conflict Trends* (2001) no 4, 51–5

Naqvi, Y., 'The Right to the Truth in International Law: Fact or Fiction?', 88 *International Review of the Red Cross* (2006), 245–73

Ndikumana, L. and Emizet, K.F., 'The Economics of Civil War: The Case of the Democratic Republic of Congo', in Collier, P. and Sambanis, N. (eds), *Understanding Civil War*, vol 1 (Washington DC: The World Bank, 2005), 63–87

Newbury, C., *The Cohesion of Oppression: Clientship and Ethnicity in Rwanda 1860–1960* (New York: Columbia University Press, 1988)

Noor Muhammad, H.N.A., 'Due Process of Law for Persons Accused of Crime', in Henkin, L. (ed), *The International Bill of Rights: The Covenant on Civil and Political Rights* (New York: Columbia University Press, 1981), 138–65

Nowak, M., *CCPR Commentary*, 2nd edn (Kehl: N.P. Engel, 2005)

—— and McArthur, E., *The United Nations Convention against Torture: A Commentary* (Oxford: Oxford University Press, 2008)

Nsengiyumva, A.O., 'L'impact de la récente réforme juridique et judiciaire sur le fonctionnement quotidien de la justice au Rwanda', in *Justices & Transitions II, Bulletin no 16* (Bruxelles, RCN Justice & Démocracie, 2006), 11–13

Ntampaka, C., 'Le gacaca: une juridiction pénale populaire', in de Lespinay, C. and Mworoka, E. (eds), *Construire l'Etat de droit: Le Burundi et la région des grands Lacs* (Paris: L'Harmattan, 2000), 219–36

—— 'Le gacaca rwandais, une justice répressive participative', 6 *Actualité du droit international humanitaire* (2001), 211–25

—— 'Le retour à la tradition dans le jugement du génocide rwandais: le gacaca, justice participative', 48 *Bulletin des Séances Académie royale des Sciences d'Outre-mer* (2002), 419–55

Nzakunda, J., 'Les circonstances atténuantes et les causes légales de réduction des peines en droit rwandais', *Revue juridique du Rwanda* (2005) no 2, 15–60

Nzongola-Ntalaja, G., *The Congo from Leopold to Kabila: A People's History* (London: Zed Books, 2002)

Oomen, B., 'Donor-Driven Justice and its Discontents: The Case of Rwanda', 36 *Development and Change* (2005), 887–910

—— 'Rwanda's *Gacaca*: Objectives, Merits and Their Relation to Supranational Criminal Law', in Haveman, R. and Olusanya, O. (eds), *Sentencing and Sanctioning in Supranational Criminal Law* (Antwerpen: Intersentia, 2006), 161–84

—— 'Justice Mechanisms and the Question of Legitimacy: The Example of Rwanda's Multi-Layered Justice Mechanisms', in Ambos, K., Large, J. and Wierda, M. (eds), *Building a Future on Peace and Justice: Studies on Transitional Justice, Peace and Development* (Berlin: Springer, 2009), 175–202

Orentlicher, D.F., 'Settling Accounts: The Duty to Prosecute Human Rights Violations of a Prior Regime', 100 *Yale Law Journal* (1991), 2537–615

—— '"Settling Accounts" Revisited: Reconciling Global Norms with Local Agency', 1 *International Journal of Transitional Justice* (2007), 10–22

Osiel, M.J., 'Why Prosecute? Critics of Punishment for Mass Atrocity', 22 *Human Rights Quarterly* (2000), 118–47

Othmani, A., 'La reconstruction du système criminel de justice dans les situations post-conflictuelles' (Summary by Sébastien Annys), 43 *Revue de Droit Militaire et de Droit de la Guerre* (2004) nos 1–2, 145–7

Packer, G., 'Justice on a Hill: Genocide Trials in Rwanda', 49 *Dissent* (2002) no 2, 59–72

Paolillo, F.H., 'On Unfulfilled Duties: The Obligation to Make Reparation in Cases of Violation of Human Rights', in Götz, V., Selmer, P. and Wolfrum, R. (eds), *Liber Amicorum Günther Jaenicke – Zum 85. Geburtstag* (Berlin: Springer, 1998), 291–311

Paul, A.T., 'Das Unmögliche richten: Schuld, Strafe und Moral in Ruanda', 34 *Leviathan* (2006), 30–60

Peskin, V., *International Justice in Rwanda and the Balkans: Virtual Trials and the Struggle for State Cooperation* (Cambridge: Cambridge University Press, 2008)

Peté, S. and du Plessis, M., 'Reparations for Gross Violations of Human Rights in Context', in du Plessis, M. and Peté, S. (eds), *Repairing the Past? International Perspectives on Reparations for Gross Human Rights Abuses* (Antwerpen: Intersentia, 2007), 3–28

Plumat, I., 'Les juridictions *gacaca*: façonner des solutions adaptées à une réalité unique', in *Bulletin: Numéro Spécial Coutume* (Bruxelles: RCN Justice et Démocratie, 2004), 6–7

Pottier, J., *Re-Imagining Rwanda: Conflict, Survival and Disinformation in the Late Twentieth Century* (Cambridge: Cambridge University Press, 2002)

Prunier, G., *The Rwanda Crisis 1959–1994: History of a Genocide* (London: Hurst & Co., 1995)

—— *The Rwanda Crisis: History of a Genocide* [2nd edn] (London: Hurst & Co., 1997)

—— 'Opération Turquoise: A Humanitarian Escape from a Political Dead End', in Adelman, H. and Suhrke, A. (eds), *The Path of Genocide: The Rwanda Crisis from Uganda to Zaire* (New Brunswick: Transaction Publishers, 1999), 281–305

—— *Africa's World War: Congo, the Rwandan Genocide, and the Making of a Continental Catastrophe* (Oxford: Oxford University Press, 2009)

Quinn, J.R., 'Social Reconstruction in Uganda: The Role of Customary Mechanisms in Transitional Justice', 8 *Human Rights Review* (2007), 389–407

Raper, J., 'The Gacaca Experiment: Rwanda's Restorative Dispute Resolution Response to the 1994 Genocide', 5 *Pepperdine Dispute Resolution Law Journal* (2005), 1–56

Reed, W.C., 'Exile, Reform, and the Rise of the Rwandan Patriotic Front', 34 *The Journal of Modern African Studies* (1996), 479–501

Rempfer, D., *Die Graswurzelgerichtsbarkeit gacaca: der ruandische Weg zur Aufarbeitung innerstaatlicher Gewalt* (Saarbrücken: VdM Verlag Dr Müller, 2008)

Rettig, M., 'Gacaca: Truth, Justice, and Reconciliation in Postconflict Rwanda?', 51 *African Studies Review* (2008) no 3, 25–50

Reyntjens, F., *Pouvoir et droit au Rwanda: Droit public et évolution politique, 1916–1973* (Tervuren: Musée royal de l'Afrique centrale, 1985)

—— 'Le *gacaca* ou la justice du gazon au Rwanda', 40 *Politique Africaine* (1990), 31–41

—— 'Rwanda, Ten Years On: From Genocide to Dictatorship', 103 *African Affairs* (2004), 177–210

Richters, A., Dekker, C. and de Jonge, K., 'Reconciliation in the Aftermath of Violent Conflict in Rwanda', 3 *Intervention* (2005), 203–21

Robinson, D., 'Serving the Interest of Justice: Amnesties, Truth Commission and the International Criminal Court', 14 *European Journal of International Law* (2003), 481–505

Roche, D., *Accountability in Restorative Justice* (Oxford: Oxford University Press, 2003)

Roht-Arriaza, N., 'State Responsibility to Investigate and Prosecute Grave Human Rights Violations in International Law', 78 *California Law Review* (1990), 449–513

—— 'Reparations in the Aftermath of Repression and Mass Violence', in Stover, E. and Weinstein, H.M. (eds), *My Neighbor, My Enemy: Justice and Community in the Aftermath of Mass Atrocity* (Cambridge: Cambridge University Press, 2004), 121–39

—— 'The New Landscape of Transitional Justice', in Roht-Arriaza, N. and Mariezcurrena, J. (eds), *Transitional Justice in the Twenty-First Century: Beyond Truth versus Justice* (Cambridge: Cambridge University Press, 2006), 1–16

—— Prosecuting Heads of State in Latin America, in Lutz, E.L. and Reiger, C. (eds), *Prosecuting Heads of State* (Cambridge: Cambridge University Press, 2009), 46–76

Rombouts, H., *Victim Organisations and the Politics of Reparation: A Case Study on Rwanda* (Antwerpen: Intersentia, 2004)

—— 'Women and Reparations in Rwanda: A Long Path to Travel', in Rubio-Marín, R. (ed), *What Happened to the Women?: Gender and Reparations for Human Rights Violations* (New York: Social Science Research Council, 2006), 194–245

—— Sardaro, P. and Vandeginste, S., 'The Right to Reparation for Victims of Gross and Systematic Violations of Human Rights', in De Feyter, K., Parmentier, S., Bossuyt, M. and Lemmens, P. (eds), *Out of the Ashes: Reparation for Victims of Gross and Systematic Human Rights Violations* (Antwerpen: Intersentia, 2005), 345–503

—— and Vandeginste, S., 'Reparation for Victims in Rwanda: Caught Between Theory and Practice', in De Feyter, K.,Parmentier, S., Bossuyt, M. and Lemmens, P. (eds), *Out of the Ashes: Reparation for Victims of Gross and Systematic Human Rights Violations* (Antwerpen: Intersentia, 2005), 309–41

Ronzitti, N., 'Access to Justice and Compensation for Violations of the Law of War', 16 *Collected Courses of the Academy of European Law* (2007) Book 4, 95–134

Safferling, C.J.M., *Towards an International Criminal Procedure* (Oxford: Oxford University Press, 2001)

Salacuse, J.W., *An Introduction to Law in French-Speaking Africa*, vol 1: Africa South of the Sahara (Charlottesville: The Michie Company Law Publishers, 1969)

Sarkin, J., 'The Necessity and Challenges of Establishing a Truth and Reconciliation Commission in Rwanda', 21 *Human Rights Quarterly* (1999), 767–823

—— 'Promoting Justice, Truth and Reconciliation in Transitional Societies: Evaluating Rwanda's Approach in the New Millennium of Using Community Based Gacaca Tribunals to Deal with the Past', 2 *International Law Forum* (2000), 112–21

—— 'The Tension Between Justice and Reconciliation in Rwanda: Politics, Human Rights, Due Process and the Role of the Gacaca Courts in Dealing with the Genocide', 45 *Journal of African Law* (2001), 143–72

—— 'Reparations for Gross Human Rights Violations in Africa—The Great Lakes', in du Plessis, M. and Peté, S. (eds), *Repairing the Past? International Perspectives on Reparations for Gross Human Rights Abuses* (Antwerpen: Intersentia, 2007), 197–228

Schabas, W.A., 'Justice, Democracy, and Impunity in Post-Genocide Rwanda: Searching for Solutions to Impossible Problems', 7 *Criminal Law Forum* (1996), 523–60

—— 'The Rwanda Case: Sometimes it's Impossible', in Bassiouni, M.C. (ed), *Post-Conflict Justice* (Ardsley: Transnational Publishers, 2002), 499–522

—— 'Genocide Trials and *Gacaca* Courts', 3 *Journal of International Criminal Justice* (2005), 879–95

—— *The UN International Criminal Tribunals: The Former Yugoslavia, Rwanda and Sierra Leone* (Cambridge: Cambridge University Press, 2006)

—— 'Post-Genocide Justice in Rwanda: A Spectrum of Options', in Clark, P. and Kaufman, Z.D. (eds), *After Genocide: Transitional Justice, Post-Conflict Reconstruction and Reconciliation in Rwanda and Beyond* (London: Hurst & Co., 2008), 207–27

—— and Imbleau, M., *Introduction to Rwandan Law* (Cowansville: Ed. Yvon Blais, 1997)

Schilling, S., *Gegen das Vergessen: Justiz, Wahrheitsfindung und Versöhnung nach dem Genozid in Rwanda durch Mechanismen transitionaler Justiz: Gacaca Gerichte* (Bern: Peter Lang, 2005)

Schwarzenberger, G., *International Law*, vol 1, 3rd edn (London: Stevens and Sons, 1957)

Schwerin, K., 'German Compensation for Victims of Nazi Persecution', 67 *Northwestern University Law Review* (1972), 479–527

Seegers, M., *Das Individualrecht auf Wiedergutmachung: Theorie, Struktur und Erscheinungsformen der völkerrechtlichen Staatenverantwortlichkeit gegenüber dem Individuum* (Münster: Lit Verlag, 2005)

Segev, T., *The Seventh Million: The Israelis and the Holocaust* (New York: Hill and Wang, 1991)

Shelton, D., 'Private Violence, Public Wrongs, and the Responsibility of States', 13 *Fordham International Law Journal* (1989/90), 1–34

—— *Remedies in International Human Rights Law*, 2nd edn (Oxford: Oxford University Press, 2005)

—— 'The Right to Reparations for Acts of Torture: What Right, What Remedies?', 17 *Torture* (2007), 96–116

Simma, B., 'International Human Rights and General International Law: A Comparative Analysis', 4 *Collected Courses of the Academy of European Law* (1993) Book 2, 153–236

—— and Alston, P., 'The Sources of Human Rights Law: Custom, Jus Cogens, and General Principles', 12 *Australian Year Book of International Law* (1988/89), 82–108

Simpson, G., 'Men and Abstract Entities: Individual Responsibility and Collective Guilt in International Criminal Law', in Nollkaemper, A. and van der Wilt, H. (eds), *System Criminality in International Law* (Cambridge: Cambridge University Press, 2009), 69–100

Sinsebyimfura, V., 'Le Fonds d'Assistance aux Rescapés du Génocide (FARG), Presentation given at a seminar hosted by the Rwandan Ministry of Justice and ASF, Kigali, 7 to 9 June 2000', reprinted in *Séminaire sur la réparation pour les victimes du génocide et des crimes contre l'humanité commis au Rwanda entre le 1er octobre 1990 et le 31 décembre 1994* (Kigali: ASF/Minijust, 2000), 28

Slye, R.C., 'The Legitimacy of Amnesty under International Law and General Principles of Anglo-American Law: Is a Legitimate Amnesty Possible?', 43 *Virginia Journal of International Law* (2002/03), 173–247

Sosnov, M., 'The Adjudication of Genocide: Gacaca and the Road to Reconciliation in Rwanda', 36 *Denver Journal of International Law and Policy* (2008), 125–53

Staub, E., 'Justice, Healing, and Reconciliation: How the Peoples' Courts in Rwanda Can Promote Them', 10 *Peace and Conflict: Journal of Peace Psychology* (2004), 25–32

Stoll, H., 'Consequences of Liability: Remedies', in Tunc, A. (ed), *International Encyclopedia of Comparative Law*, vol XI (Torts), Part 2 (Tübingen: Mohr, 1986), chapter 8

Strain, J. and Keyes, E., 'Accountability in the Aftermath of Rwanda's Genocide', in Stromseth, J.E. (ed), *Accountability for Atrocities: National and International Responses* (Ardsley: Transnational Publishers, 2003), 87–133

Strang, H. and Brathwaite, J. (eds), *Restorative Justice: Philosophy to Practice* (Aldershot: Ashgate, 2000)

Tappert, W., 'Die Wiedergutmachung von Staatsunrecht im 20. Jahrhundert', 70 *Friedenswarte* (1995), 211–49

Taylor, J.B., *Right to Counsel and Privilege against Self-Incrimination: Rights and Liberties under the Law* (Santa Barbara: ABC Clio, 2004)

Teitel, R.G., 'Transitional Jurisprudence: The Role of Law in Political Transformation', 106 *Yale Law Journal* (1997), 2009–80

—— *Transitional Justice* (Oxford: Oxford University Press, 2000)

—— 'Transitional Justice Genealogy', 16 *Harvard Human Rights Journal* (2003), 69–94

—— 'Transitional Rule of Law', in Czarnota, A., Krygier, M. and Sadurski, W. (eds), *Rethinking the Rule of Law after Communism* (Budapest: Central European University Press, 2005), 279–94

Thalmann, V., 'Rwandan Genocide Cases', in Cassese, A. (ed), *The Oxford Companion to International Criminal Justice* (Oxford: Oxford University Press, 2009), 498–505

Thelle, E.H., 'The Gacaca Jurisdictions: A Solution to the Challenge of the Rwandan Judicial Settlement?', 13 *Human Rights in Development* (2001), 73–107

Thomson, S. and Nagy, R., 'Law, Power and Justice: What Legalism Fails to Address in the Functioning of Rwanda's *Gacaca* Courts', 5 *International Journal of Transitional Justice* (2011), 11–30

Tiba, F.K., 'The *Mengistu* Genocide Trial in Ethiopia', 5 *Journal of International Criminal Justice* (2007), 513–28

Tiemessen, A.E., 'After Arusha: Gacaca Justice in Post-Genocide Rwanda', 8 *African Studies Quarterly* (2004), 57–76

Tomuschat, C., 'Individual Reparation Claims in Instances of Grave Human Rights Violations: The Position under General International Law', in Randelzhofer, A. and Tomuschat, C. (eds), *State Responsibility and the Individual: Reparation in Instances of Grave Violations of Human Rights* (The Hague: Martinus Nijhoff, 1999), 1–25

—— 'Just Satisfaction under Article 50 of the European Convention on Human Rights', in Mahoney, P., Matcher, F., Petzold, H. and Wildhaber, L. (eds), *Protecting Human Rights: The European Perspective, Studies in Memory of Rolv Ryssdal* (Köln: Heymanns, 2000), 1409–30

—— 'The Duty to Prosecute International Crimes Committed by Individuals', in Cremer, H.-J., Giegerich, T., Richter, D. and Zimmermann, A. (eds), *Tradition und Weltoffenheit des Rechts: Festschrift für Helmut Steinberger* (Berlin: Springer, 2002), 315–49

—— 'Reparation for Victims of Grave Human Rights Violations', 10 *Tulane Journal of International and Comparative Law* (2002), 157–84

—— *Human Rights: Between Realism and Idealism* (Oxford: Oxford University Press, 2003)

—— 'Ein umfassendes Wiedergutmachungsprogramm für Opfer schwerer Menschenrechtsverletzungen', 80 *Friedenswarte* (2005), 160–7

—— 'La protection internationale des victimes', 18 *Revue universelle des droits de l'homme* (2006), 1–11

—— 'Reparation in Cases of Genocide', 5 *Journal of International Criminal Justice* (2007), 905–12

—— 'Reparation in Favour of Individual Victims of Gross Violations of Human Rights and International Humanitarian Law', in Kohen, M.G. (ed), *Promoting Justice, Human Rights and Conflict Resolution through International Law: Liber Amicorum Lucius Caflisch* (Leiden: Martinus Nijhoff, 2007), 569–90

Traßl, M., *Die Wiedergutmachung von Menschenrechtsverletzungen im Völkerrecht* (Berlin: Duncker & Humblot, 1994)

Trechsel, S., 'Why Must Trials Be Fair?', 31 *Israel Law Review* (1997), 94–119

—— *Human Rights in Criminal Proceedings* (Oxford: Oxford University Press, 2005)

Tulkens, F. and van de Kerchove, M., *Introduction au droit pénal: Aspect juridiques et criminologiques*, 2nd edn (Bruxelles: Kluwer Editions Juridiques Belgique, 1993)

Tully, L.D., 'Human Rights Compliance and the Gacaca Jurisdictions in Rwanda', 26 *Boston College International and Comparative Law Review* (2002), 385–414

Tutu, D., *No Future without Forgiveness* (New York: Doubleday, 1999)

Uvin, P., 'Difficult Choices in the New Post-Conflict Agenda: The International Community in Rwanda after the Genocide', 22 *Third World Quarterly* (2001), 177–89

—— 'The *Gacaca* Tribunals in Rwanda', in Bloomfield, D., Barnes, T. and Huyse, L. (eds), *Reconciliation after Violent Conflict: A Handbook* (Stockholm: IDEA, 2003), 116–29

—— and Mironko, C., 'Western and Local Approaches to Justice in Rwanda', 9 *Global Governance* (2003), 219–31

Vandeginste, S., 'Poursuite des présumés responsables du génocide et des massacres politiques devant les juridictions rwandaises', in Marysse, S. and Reyntjens, F. (eds), *L'Afrique des Grands Lacs: Annuaire 1996/1997* (Paris: L'Harmattan, 1997), 93–122

—— 'L'approche "vérité et réconciliation" du génocide et des crimes contre l'humanité au Rwanda', in Reyntjens, F. and Marysse, S. (eds), *L'Afrique des Grands Lacs: Annuaire 1997/1998* (Paris: L'Harmattan, 1998), 97–140

—— 'Réparation pour les victimes de génocide, de crimes contre l'humanité et de crimes de guerre au Rwanda', in Marysse, S. and Reyntjens, F. (eds), *L'Afrique des Grands Lacs: Annuaire 2000/2001* (Paris: L'Harmattan, 2001), 95–121

—— 'Rwanda: Dealing with Genocide and Crimes against Humanity in the Context of Armed Conflict and Failed Political Transition', in Biggar, N. (ed), *Burying the Past: Making Peace and Doing Justice after Civil Conflict* (Washington DC: Georgetown University Press, 2001), 251–86

—— 'Victims of Genocide, Crimes against Humanity, and War Crimes in Rwanda: The Legal and Institutional Framework of Their Right to Reparation', in Torpey, J. (ed), *Politics and the Past: On Repairing Historical Injustices* (Lanham: Rowman & Littlefield, 2003), 249–74

Van den Wyngaert, C., *Strafrecht, Strafprocesrecht & Internationaal Strafrecht* (Anwerpen: Maklu, 2006)

Vanderlinden, J., *Les systèmes juridiques africains* (Paris: Presses Universitaires de France, 1983)

van Dyke, J.M., 'The Fundamental Human Right to Prosecution and Compensation', in White, J.D. and Marsella, A.J. (eds), *Fear of Persecution: Global Human Rights, International Law, and Human Well-Being* (Lanham: Lexington Books, 2007), 189–221

van Houtte, J., 'Litiges et besoin juridiques au Rwanda: une enquête préliminaire', 5 *Revue juridique du Rwanda* (1981), 188–203

van Leeuwen, M., 'Rwanda's Imidugudu Programme and Earlier Experiences with Villagisation and Resettlement in East Africa', 39 *Journal of Modern African Studies* (2001), 623–44

Vansina, J., *Le Rwanda ancien: Le royaume nyiginya* (Paris: Karthala, 2001)

Waldorf, L., 'Mass Justice for Mass Atrocities: Rethinking Local Justice as Transitional Justice', 79 *Temple Law Review* (2006), 1–87

—— 'Rwanda's Failing Experiment in Restorative Justice', in Sullivan, D. and Tifft, L. (eds), *Handbook of Restorative Justice* (London: Routledge, 2006), 422–34

—— 'Censorship and Propaganda in Post-Genocide Rwanda', in Thompson, A. (ed), *The Media and the Rwanda Genocide* (London: Pluto Press, 2007), 404–16

—— 'Goats & Graves: Reparations in Rwanda's Community Courts', in Ferstman, C., Goetz, M. and Stephens, A. (eds), *Reparations for Victims of Genocide, War Crimes and Crimes Against Humanity: Systems in Place and Systems in the Making* (Leiden: Martinus Nijhoff, 2009), 515–39

—— 'A Justice "Trickle-Down": Rwanda's First Postgenocide President on Trial', in Lutz, E.L. and Reiger, C. (eds), *Prosecuting Heads of State* (Cambridge: Cambridge University Press, 2009), 151–75

—— 'Remnants and Remains: Narratives of Suffering in Post-Genocide Rwanda's *Gacaca* Courts', in Wilson, R.A. and Brown, R.D. (eds), *Humanitarianism and Suffering: The Mobilization of Empathy* (Cambridge: Cambridge University Press, 2009), 285–305

Walleyn, L., 'Justice as an Instrument of Conflict Prevention: "Avocats Sans Frontières" in Rwanda', 43 *Revue de Droit Militaire et de Droit de la Guerre* (2004) nos 1–2, 127–33

Weikl, K., *Gacaca im Spiegel der Menschenrechte: Rwandas schwieriger Weg zur Wahrheit* (Saarbrücken: VdM Verlag Dr Müller, 2010)

Wells, S.L., 'Gender, Sexual Violence and Prospects for Justice at the Gacaca Courts in Rwanda', 14 *Southern Californian Review of Law and Women's Studies* (2004/05), 167–96

Werchick, L., Prospects for Justice in Rwanda's Citizen Tribunals, 8 *Human Rights Brief* (2001) Issue 3, 15–17

Werle, G., 'Individual Criminal Responsibility in Article 25 ICC Statute', 5 *Journal of International Criminal Justice* (2007), 953–75

—— *Principles of International Criminal Law*, 2nd edn (The Hague: TMC Asser Press, 2009)

—— and Bornkamm, P., 'Transitional Justice—Der juristische Rahmen', in Weller, C. (ed), *Transitional Justice und Zivile Konfliktbearbeitung* (Marburg: Zentrum für Konfliktforschung, Philipps-Universität Marburg, 2008), 78–98, available at <http://www.philso.uni-augsburg.de/lehrstuehle/politik/politik1/forschung/pdf/Projektbericht_TJ_ZKB.pdf>

—— and Vormbaum, M., 'After the Fall of the Berlin Wall: Transitional Justice in Germany', in a collection published by United Nations University Press, forthcoming 2012

Widner, J., 'Courts and Democracy in Postconflict Transitions: A Social Scientist's Perspective on the African Case', 95 *American Journal of International Law* (2001), 64–75

Wierzynska, A., 'Consolidating Democracy Through Transitional Justice: Rwanda's Gacaca Courts' 97 *New York University Law Review* (2004), 1934–69

Wojkowska, E., *Doing Justice: How Informal Justice Systems Can Contribute* (Oslo: UNDP/ Oslo Governance Centre, 2006)

Zartman, I.W., 'Introduction: African Traditional Conflict "Medicine"', in Zartman, I.W. (ed), *Traditional Cures for Modern Conflict: African Conflict 'Medicine'* (Boulder: Lynne Rienner, 2000)

Zimmermann, A., Tomuschat, C., Oellers-Frahm, K., Tams, C. and Thienel, T. (eds), *The Statute of the International Court of Justice: A Commentary* (Oxford: Oxford University Press, 2006)

Print and Online Journalism

BBC (available at <news.bbc.co.uk>), 'Nicolas Sarkozy Admits Rwanda Genocide "Mistakes"', 25 February 2010

—— 'Kagame Rival Arrested in Rwanda', 21 April 2010

Cobban, H., 'The Legacies of Collective Violence: The Rwandan Genocide and the Limits of Law', 27 *Boston Review* (2002) no 2

Hirondelle News Agency (available at <hirondellenews.org>), 'General Opening of the Semi-Traditional Tribunals', 3 January 2007

—— 'Rwanda Liberates over 9192 Prisoners', 19 February 2007

—— 'A Rwandan Militant for Human Rights Sentenced to 19 Years Imprisonment', 28 May 2007

—— 'Verdict Saturday in the Appeal of a Famous Human Rights Activist', 9 August 2007

—— 'Sentence Confirmed in Appeal for a Human Rights Militant', 20 August 2007

—— 'A Gacaca Judge Affirms to Have Been Bribed by a Member of Parliament', 31 August 2007

—— 'Assassination of a Gacaca Court President', 18 October 2007

—— 'Seven Gacaca Judges of a Same Court Arrested in Southern Rwanda', 7 December 2007

—— 'Gacaca Judge Caught Bribing a Witness', 21 January 2008

—— 'Gacaca Courts Will Start Trying Rape Cases Next Month', 25 June 2008

—— 'Ibuka Report: 167 Genocide Survivors Murdered since 1995', 15 July 2008

—— 'Trial of Rwandan Army Officers Accused of Murdering Bishops in 1994 Begins', 20 August 2008

—— '17 under Investigation for Alleged Embezzlement of Funds', 8 January 2009

—— 'Gacaca Courts: 1.4 Million Cases Handled in Past Two Years', 6 February 2009

—— 'Eight Gacaca Judges Arrested over Corruption Allegations', 11 September 2009

—— 'Corrupt Gacaca Judge Caught Red-Handed', 18 November 2009

—— 'Final Brief on Gacaca Trials Expected End of September', 17 August 2010

—— 'Official Closure of Gacaca Courts Set for December, Says Justice Minister', 23 May 2011

Integrated Regional Information Network (IRIN) (available at <irinnews.org>), 'Parliament Approves Gacaca Tribunals', 16 February 2000

—— '90 Percent of Electorate Vote for Traditional Judges', 5 October 2001

—— 'Government Re-Arrests 787 Genocide Suspects', 14 May 2003

—— 'More Genocide Suspects Rearrested', 11 June 2003
—— '4,500 Prisoners Released', 23 March 2004
—— 'Investigations Begin for Gacaca Genocide Trials', 18 January 2005
—— 'Release of Thousands of Prisoners Begins', 1 August 2005
—— 'UN Tribunal Investigates 12 on Its Payroll', 29 June 2006
Le Monde, 'Trois mille Tutsis réfugiés au Congo-Léopoldville lanceraient une "attaque-suicide" contre le Ruanda', 6 February 1964
Libération, 'Ruzibiza, le témoin rwandais de Bruguière se rétracte', 14 November 2008
Roth, K. and Des Forges, A., 'Justice or Therapy?', 27 *Boston Review* (2002) nos 3–4
The East African (available at <http://www.theeastafrican.co.ke>), 'French Judges Lift Arrest Warrants against Rwandan Military Officials', 20 December 2010
The New Times (available at <http://www.newtimes.co.rw>), 'Government Sacks FARG Leaders', 15 January 2009
—— 'Government Appointees Have to Start Accepting Responsibility', 17 January 2009
—— 'Gumisiriza Wins Appeal', 26 February 2009
—— 'Genocide Survivors in Kanombe Up in Arms over Gacaca Ruling', 29 May 2009
—— 'Over 38, 000 in Jail over Genocide', 23 October 2009
—— 'IBUKA Officials Jailed over Survivors' Fund', 24 April 2010
—— 'Genocide Archives Launched', 11 December 2010

Reports and Manuals

Government Agencies (Rwandan, unless otherwise indicated)

Department of Gacaca Jurisdictions, Manuel explicatif sur la Loi organique portant création des juridictions Gacaca (Kigali: 2001)
—— Les juridictions Gacaca comme solution alternative au règlement du contentieux du génocide (Kigali: October 2003), available at <http://www.grandslacs.net/doc/3870.pdf>
National Service of Gacaca Courts, Programme de la collecte d'informations dans les Juridictions Gacaca (Kigali: November 2004) (translation from Kinyarwanda by Penal Reform International)
—— Number of Survivors of Genocide (Kigali: 2006), available at <http://www.inkiko-gacaca.gov.rw/En/EnIntroduction.htm>
—— Report on Data Collection (Kigali: 2006), available at <http://www.inkiko-gacaca.gov.rw/En/EnIntroduction.htm>
—— Summary of Persons Prosecuted for Having Committed Genocide (Kigali: 2006), available at <http://www.inkiko-gacaca.gov.rw/En/EnIntroduction.htm>
—— Byuma François Xavier's Case (Kigali: 12 June 2007), available at <http://www.inkiko-gacaca.gov.rw/En/EnIntroduction.htm>
National Unity and Reconciliation Commission (NURC), Nation-Wide Grassroots Consultations Report: Unity and Reconciliation Initiatives in Rwanda (Kigali: 2000), available at <http://www.grandslacs.net/doc/2814.pdf>
—— Report on the Evaluation of National Unity and Reconciliation (Kigali: June 2002), available at <http://www.grandslacs.net/doc/2805.pdf>

Royaume de Belgique and Royaume des Pays-Bas, Rapport de formulation: Projet d'Appui au Renforcement de l'Etat de Droit et de la Justice au Rwanda (December 2005)

Non-Governmental Organizations

African Rights, Gacaca Justice: A Shared Responsibility (Kigali: January 2003)

Amnesty International (available at <http://www.amnesty.org/en/library>), Reports of Killings and Abductions by the Rwandese Patriotic Army, April–August 1994, 14 October 1994, AI Index AFR 47/016/1994

—— Unfair Trials: Justice Denied, 8 April 1997, AI Index AFR 47/008/1997

—— The Troubled Course of Justice, 25 April 2000, AI Index AFR47/10/00

—— Gacaca: A Question of Justice, 17 December 2002, AI Index AFR 47/007/2002

—— The Enduring Legacy of the Genocide and War, 5 April 2004, AI Index AFR 47/008/2004

—— Human Rights Organization Forced to Closed Down, 10 January 2005, AI Index AFR 47/001/2005

—— Report 2010: The State of the World's Human Rights (London: Amnesty International, 2010)

—— Safer to Stay Silent: The Chilling Effect of Rwanda's Laws on 'Genocide Ideology' and 'Sectarianism' (London: Amnesty International, 2010)

—— UN-Cambodia Court: Excessive Secrecy, Exclusion and Fears of Inappropriate Interference, 8 June 2011, AI Index ASA 23/004/2011

Avocats Sans Frontières (ASF), Justice pour tous au Rwanda: Rapport semestriel, janvier–juin (2000)

—— Projet "Soutien au recueil des aveux": Rapport narratif d'activités d'octobre 2002 au 13 mars 2003 (2003)

—— Vade-Mecum: Le crime de génocide et les crimes contre l'humanité devant les juridictions ordinaires du Rwanda (Kigali/Bruxelles: Avocats Sans Frontières, 2004)

—— Monitoring des juridictions Gacaca, phase de jugement: Rapport analytique no 1: mars–septembre 2005 (Bruxelles: 2005), available at <http://www.asf.be/fr/publications>

—— Monitoring des juridictions Gacaca, phase de jugement: Rapport analytique no 2: octobre 2005–septembre 2006 (Bruxelles: 2006), available at <http://www.asf.be/fr/publications>

—— Monitoring des juridictions Gacaca, phase de jugement: Rapport analytique no 3: octobre 2006–avril 2007 (Bruxelles: 2007), available at <http://www.asf.be/fr/publications>

—— Rapport annuel 2008 (Bruxelles: 2008), available at <http://www.asf.be/fr/publications>

—— Monitoring des juridictions Gacaca, phase de jugement: Rapport analytique no 4: mai–décembre 2007 (Bruxelles: 2009), available at <http://www.asf.be/fr/publications>

—— Monitoring des juridictions Gacaca, phase de jugement: Rapport analytique no 5: janvier 2008–mars 2010 (Bruxelles: 2010), available at <http://www.asf.be/fr/publications>

Beyond Juba, Tradition in Transition: Drawing on the Old for Developing a New Jurisprudence for Dealing with Uganda's Legacy of Violence (Kampala: Makerere

University et al., 2009), available at <http://www.beyondjuba.org/working_papers/BJP.WP1.pdf>

Committee to Protect Journalists, Rwanda Shuts Critical Papers in Run-Up to Presidential Vote, 13 April 2010, available at <http://www.cpj.org/africa/rwanda>

Front Line, Rwanda: Disappearances, Arrests, Threats, Intimidation and Co-Option of Human Rights Defenders 2001–2004 (Dublin: Front Line, 2005), available at <http://www.frontlinedefenders.org/reports/54>

Human Rights Watch (HRW), Playing the 'Communal Card': Communal Violence and Human Rights (New York: Human Rights Watch, 1995)

—— World Report 2002: Events of 2001 (New York: Human Rights Watch, 2002)

—— Struggling to Survive: Barriers to Justice for Rape Victims in Rwanda (September 2004), available at <http://www.hrw.org/en/publications>

—— Killings in Eastern Rwanda (January 2007), available at <http://www.hrw.org/en/publications>

—— Gacaca Trial Condemns Activist to Prison, 30 May 2007, available at <http://www.hrw.org/en/publications>

—— Justice Compromised: The Legacy of Rwanda's Community-Based Gacaca Courts (New York: Human Rights Watch, 2011), available at <http://www.hrw.org/en/publications>

Institut de Recherche et de Dialogue pour la Paix (IRDP), Cahier No 2 (Kigali: December 2007)

Institute for Security Studies (ISS), The Gacaca Process: Eradicating the Culture of Impunity in Rwanda? (Pretoria: August 2005), available at <http://www.issafrica.org/uploads/050805RWANDA.PDF>

International Crisis Group (ICG) (available at <http://www.crisisgroup.org/en/regions/africa/central-africa.aspx>), International Criminal Tribunal for Rwanda: Justice Delayed, Africa Report no 30 (Nairobi: 7 June 2001)

—— Tribunal pénal international pour le Rwanda: le compte à rebours, Africa Report no 50 (Nairobi: 1 August 2002)

—— Rwanda at the End of the Transition: A Necessary Political Liberalisation, Africa Report no 53 (Nairobi: 13 November 2002)

—— Tribunal pénal international pour le Rwanda: pragmatisme de rigueur, Africa Report no 69 (Nairobi: 26 September 2003)

—— Congo: Une stratégie globale pour désarmer les FDLR, Africa Report no 151 (Nairobi: 9 July 2009)

International Federation for Human Rights (FIDH) and World Organisation against Torture (OMCT), Observatory for the Protection of Human Rights Defenders: Human Rights Defenders on the Front Line: Annual Report 2004 (Paris/Geneva: FIDH/OMCT, 2005)

Ligue Rwandaise pour la Promotion et la Défense des Droits de l'Homme (LIPRODHOR), Rescapés et droits humains: problèmes actuels des rescapés huit ans après le genocide (Kigali: 2002)

—— Situation des droits de la personne au Rwanda en 2002, Rapport annuel de la LIPRODHOR (Kigali: June 2003)

—— Situation des droits de la personne en 2003–2004 (Kigali: 2004), available at <http://www.liprodhor.org.rw/rapports.html>

—— *Problématique des informations et témoignages devant les juridictions gacaca* (Kigali: LIPRODHOR, 2006)

—— *Situation des droits de la personne en 2005* (Kigali: December 2006), available at <http://www.liprodhor.org.rw/rapports.html>

—— *Situation des droits de la personne au Rwanda: Rapport 2006* (Kigali: September 2007), available at <http://www.liprodhor.org.rw/rapports.html>

—— *Rapport de monitoring des prisons au Rwanda—Période: 1er trimestre 2008* (Kigali: Mars 2008), available at <http://www.liprodhor.org.rw/rapports.html>

—— *Byuma François-Xavier condamné à 17 ans de prison*, 16 March 2009, available at <http://www.liprodhor.org/2009/03/juridictions-gacacarevision-byuma-francois-xavier-condamne-a-17-ans-de-prison>

Penal Reform International (PRI) (available at <http://www.penalreform.org>), *Access to Justice in Sub-Saharan Africa: The Role of Traditional and Informal Justice Systems* (London: Astron Printers, 2001)

—— *PRI Research on Gacaca Report, Report I: Gacaca Jurisdictions and its Preparations: July–December 2001* (January 2002)

—— *PRI Research on Gacaca Report, Report III: April–June 2002* (July 2002)

—— *Annual Report 2002* (London: 2003)

—— *PRI Research on Gacaca Report, Report IV: The Guilty Plea Procedure, Cornerstone of the Rwandan Justice System* (January 2003)

—— *Research on the Gacaca, Report V* (September 2003)

—— *Research Report on the Gacaca, Report VI: From Camp to Hill, the Reintegration of Released Prisoners* (May 2004)

—— *Integrated Report on Gacaca Research and Monitoring, Report VII: Pilot Phase, January 2002–December 2004* (December 2005)

—— *Monitoring and Research Report on the Gacaca: Information-Gathering during the National Phase (Report VIII)* (June 2006)

—— *Monitoring and Research Report on the Gacaca: Community Service (TIG): Areas of reflection (Report IX)* (March 2007)

—— *Monitoring and Research Report on the Gacaca: Trials of Offences against Property Committed during the Genocide: A Conflict Between the Theory of Reparation and the Social and Economic Reality in Rwanda (Report X)* (July 2007)

—— *Monitoring and Research Report on the Gacaca: Testimonies and Evidence in the Gacaca Courts (Report XI)* (August 2008)

—— *Monitoring and Research Report on the Gacaca: The Settlement of Property Offence Cases Committed during the Genocide: Update on the Execution of Agreements and Restoration Condemnations (Report XII)* (August 2009)

—— *The Contribution of Gacaca Jurisdictions to Resolving Cases Arising from the Genocide: Contributions, Limitations, and Expectations of the Post-Gacaca Phase (Final Report)* (2010)

—— *Eight Years On... A Record of Gacaca Monitoring in Rwanda* (2010)

Projet d'Appui de la Société Civile au Processus Gacaca au Rwanda (PAPG), *Rapport d'activités: 1er semestre 2004* (Kigali: September 2004)

—— *Rapport d'activités: mai–juin 2006* (Kigali: November 2006)

—— *Rapport d'activités: juillet–août–septembre* (Kigali: January 2007)

Redress and African Rights (available at <http://www.redress.org/smartweb/reports/reports>), Extraditing Genocide Suspects From Europe to Rwanda: Issues and Challenges, Report of a Conference Organised by REDRESS and African Rights at the Belgian Parliament 1 July 2008 (London/Kigali: September 2008)

—— Survivors and Post-Genocide Justice in Rwanda: Their Experiences, Perspectives and Hopes (London/Kigali: November 2008)

Réseau des Citoyens Justice & Démocratie (RCN) (available at <www.rcn-ong.be>), Rapport d'activités 2003 (Bruxelles: June 2004)

—— La justice de proximité au Burundi: Réalités et perspectives (Bujumbura: December 2006)

Strategies 2000, Rwanda Decentralization Assessment, Submitted to the Ministry of Local Government and Social Affairs and USAID/Rwanda (July 2002)

Truth Commissions

El Salvador

Report of the Commission on the Truth for El Salvador: From Madness to Hope, annex to UN Doc S/25500 of 1 April 1993

Guatemala

Report of the Commission for Historical Clarification: Guatemala Memory of Silence: Tz'inil Na'tab'al: Conclusions and Recommendations (Guatemala: CEH, 1999)

Liberia

Final Report of the Truth and Reconciliation Commission of Liberia, vol I: Findings and Determinations (2009), available at <trcofliberia.org/reports/final-report>

Rwanda

Rapport de la Commission internationale d'enquête sur les violations des droits de l'homme au Rwanda depuis le 1er Octobre 1990 (Paris et al: FIDH et al. 1993)

Sierra Leone

Report of the Sierra Leone Truth and Reconciliation Commission: Witness to Truth, vol 2 (Freetown: TRC, 2004)

Report of the Sierra Leone Truth and Reconciliation Commission: Witness to Truth, vol 3B (Freetown: TRC, 2004)

South Africa

Truth and Reconciliation Commission of South Africa Report, vol 1 (Basingstoke: Macmillan, 1999)

Truth and Reconciliation Commission of South Africa Report, vol 6 (Cape Town: Juta, 2003)

Other

International Committee of the Red Cross (ICRC), Rwanda: Annual Report 1998 (Geneva, 1 June 1999)

Recommendations of the Conference Held in Kigali from November 1st to November 5th, 1995 on: 'Genocide, Impunity and Accountability: Dialogue for a National and International Response' (Kigali, December 1995)

Report of the Investigation into the Causes and Circumstances of and Responsibility for the Attack of 6 April 1994 against the Falcon 50 Rwandan Presidential Aeroplane, Registration Number 9XR-NN (Kigali, January 2010), available at <http://www.mutsinzireport.com>

International Organizations: Resolutions, Reports, and Other Instruments

African Union

African Commission on Human and Peoples' Rights Resolution 4(XI)92 of March 1992

United Nations

Commission on Human Rights

Report of the Working Group on Enforced or Involuntary Disappearances, UN Doc E/CN.4/1435 of 26 January 1981

Resolution 1989/13 of the Sub-Commission on Prevention of Discrimination and Protection of Minorities, UN Doc E/CN.4/Sub.2/1989/13 of 31 August 1989

Study concerning the right to restitution, compensation and rehabilitation for victims of gross violations of human rights and fundamental freedoms, UN Doc E/CN.4/Sub.2/1993/8 of 2 July 1993

Revised set of basic principles and guidelines on the right to reparation for victims of gross violations of human rights and humanitarian law, UN Doc E/CN.4/Sub.2/1996/17 of 24 May 1996

Question of the impunity of perpetrators of human rights violations, UN Doc E/CN.4/Sub.2/1997/20 of 26 June 1997

Report on the Situation of Human Rights in Rwanda, Submitted by the Special Representative, Mr. Michel Moussalli, pursuant to resolution 1998/69, 8 February 1999, UN Doc E/CN.4/1999/33

Basic principles and guidelines on the right to a remedy and reparation for victims of violations of international human rights and humanitarian law, annex to UN Doc E/CN.4/2000/62 of 18 January 2000

Report on the Situation of Human Rights in Rwanda, Submitted by the Special Representative, Mr. Michel Moussalli, pursuant to resolution 1999/20, 25 February 2000, UN Doc E/CN.4/2000/41

Updated set of principles for the protection and promotion of human rights through action to combat impunity, UN Doc E/CN.4/2005/102/Add.1 of 8 February 2005

Committee against Torture

Conclusions and Recommendations of the Committee against Torture: Indonesia, 22 November 2001, UN Doc CAT/C/XXVII/Concl.3

Conclusions and Recommendations of the Committee against Torture: Zambia, 23 November 2001, UN Doc CAT/C/XXVII/Concl.4

General Assembly

Resolution 2840 (XXVI) of 18 December 1971

Resolution 3074 (XXVIII) of 3 December 1973

Resolution on the Protection of Human Rights in Chile 34/179 of 17 December 1979

Resolution on the Protection of Human Rights in Chile 35/188 of 15 December 1980

Declaration of Basic Principles of Justice for Victims of Crime and Abuse of Power, annex to UN General Assembly Resolution 40/34 of 29 November 1985

Basic Principles and Guidelines on the Right to a Remedy and Reparation for Victims of Gross Violations of International Human Rights Law and Serious Violations of International Humanitarian Law, annex to UN General Assembly Resolution 60/147 of 16 December 2005

Human Rights Committee

General Comment 20/44 of 3 April 1992

General Comment 13/21 of 13 April 1984

Summary Record of the First Part (Public) of the 1611th Meeting, UN Doc CCPR/C/SR.1611 of 4 August 1997

General Comment 31/80 of 29 March 2004

International Law Commission

Preliminary Report on State Responsibility by Mr. Gaetano Arangio-Ruiz, Special Rapporteur, *Yearbook of the International Law Commission* (1988) II-1, 6 *et seq*

Draft Code of Crimes against the Peace and Security of Mankind, *Yearbook of the International Law Commission* (1996) II-2, 17 *et seq*

Report of the International Law Commission, 53rd session, *Yearbook of the International Law Commission* (2001) II-2, 1 *et seq*

Office of the High Commissioner for Human Rights (OHCHR)

Gacaca: Le droit coutumier au Rwanda: Rapport final de la première phase d'enquête sur le terrain (Kigali: 31 January 1996)

Gacaca: Le droit coutumier au Rwanda: Rapport final de la deuxième phase d'enquête sur le terrain (Kigali: 30 June 1996)

Democratic Republic of the Congo, 1993–2003: Report of the Mapping Exercise Documenting the Most Serious Violations of Human Rights and International Humanitarian Law Committed Within the Territory of the Democratic Republic of the Congo Between March

1993 and June 2003 (August 2010), available at <http://www.ohchr.org/EN/Countries/AfricaRegion/Pages/RDCProjetMapping.aspx>

Secretary General

The rule of law and transitional justice in conflict and post-conflict societies, UN Doc S/2004/616 of 23 August 2004

Security Council

Resolution 872 (1993) of 5 October 1993
Resolution 912 (1994) of 21 April 1994
Resolution 929 (1994) of 22 June 1994
Resolution 955 (1994) of 8 November 1994
Resolution 1166 (1998) of 13 May 1998
Resolution 1503 (2003) of 28 August 2003

UN Development Programme (UNDP)

Turning Vision 2020 to Reality: From Recovery to Sustainable Human Development, National Human Development Report (Rwanda: 2007), available at <hdr.undp.org/en/reports/nationalreports/africa/rwanda/rwanda_2007_en.pdf>

Annual Report 2007: Rwanda (Kigali: UNDP, 2008), available at <http://www.undp.org.rw/publication.html>

Other

Standard Minimum Rules for the Treatment of Prisoners, adopted by the First UN Congress on the Prevention of Crime and the Treatment of Offenders held at Geneva in 1955, and approved by Economic and Social Council resolutions 663 C (XXIV) of 31 July 1957 and 2076(LXII) of 13 May 1977, in *United Nations High Commissioner for Human Rights*, Human Rights: A Compilation of International Instruments, vol I, New York: United Nations, 2002, also available at <http://www2.ohchr.org/english/law/treatmentprisoners.htm>

Index

The manufacturer's authorised representative in the EU for product safety is Oxford University Press España S.A. of El Parque Empresarial San Fernando de Henares, Avenida de Castilla, 2 - 28830 Madrid (www.oup.es/en or product.safety@oup.com). OUP España S.A. also acts as importer into Spain of products made by the manufacturer.
Printed and bound by CPI Group (UK) Ltd, Croydon, CR0 4YY
14/09/2026
02216307-0009